More Than a Touch of Jeanious

The inside story on Wrangler UK advertising and promotions activity between 1975 and 1991

Robin Dilley

© Copyright Robin Dilley 2023
All rights reserved.
ISBN: 9798356381126

Introduction

People write books for a whole host of reasons. Primarily, they feel that they have a story to tell which they believe will be of interest to a wider audience. Many people have been acknowledged as the source of the quotation "everyone has a book inside of them." Jodie Picoult, bestselling American author, with over 24 novels to her name, has used this phrase but tellingly added, "but it doesn't do any good until you pry (sic) it out."

This sentiment resonates with me. I had always intended to write a book about my time at Wrangler after I left the company early in 1991. My work as a marketing consultant took off and such thoughts were put on a back burner.

I did write a book that was published. It was to celebrate the 100th Anniversary of a client company. They had presented me with all the background information and very little research was required on my part. To paraphrase Mark Twain, "all I had to do was cross out the wrong words."

I had numerous opportunities to relate anecdotal stories, from my time at Wrangler, during the hundreds of presentations I made over many years. This kept them fresh in my mind.

In about 2016, when already in my early 70's, my partner Ann suggested that I should make the effort to start the book writing process – "before you lose the capacity to remember."

Clearing out the attic provided a rich amount of material. Luckily, I have always been something of a hoarder. It took over a year to sort out all my Wrangler source material into something resembling an outline story.

Searching the internet provided additional material in the form of books and articles written by people covering the history of fashion. Many contained passing references to jeans advertising through the seventies and eighties.

I was often quoted, often erroneously, but most of the published information had been obtained through third parties, primarily advertising agencies, many years after the events took place.

Sadly, the internet searches also revealed that many colleagues, who had been involved in the Wrangler brand development process, were no longer with us. Others had scant knowledge of events that had taken place up to 44 years before. Several were able to corroborate my own recollections or provide a stimulus that evoked a lost memory.

An extremely creative period, in the brand development of jeans and jeans related clothing, was in danger of becoming a small paragraph in the history of fashion during the latter part of the 20th century. In fact, the work of Wrangler, Levi's, and other jeans companies was instrumental in creating the branded fashion market that we take for granted today.

This stimulated me into action. I was determined to set the record straight!

At an early draft stage, I contacted Len Weinreich. As Creative Director at advertising agency Wasey Campbell Ewald in the late 1970's, Len and his team had provided the springboard for developing an ongoing identity for the Wrangler brand.

His thoughts on my project were extremely important to me. He could not have been more positive. "Glad you've written a book about Wrangler……it doesn't deserve to be forgotten," he wrote to me.

Although it has taken well over six years to write, to plough through numerous edits and to publish, I hope that I have done justice to the work of the many talented individuals who worked for the company, advertising, sales promotions, design and public relations agencies and photographers, during my time as custodian of the Wrangler brand.

Writing a book is not for the faint hearted. As Winton Churchill so succinctly put it, "Writing a book is an adventure. To begin with it is a toy and an amusement. Then it becomes a mistress, then it becomes a master, then it becomes a tyrant. The last phase is just as you are about to be reconciled to your servitude, you kill the monster and fling him to the public."

My first job was with a small advertising agency in Leeds. The agency founder believed that communications should be all about presenting the truth. "Do that and your sincerity will shine through," he constantly reminded me. It resonated then and still does today – even in an era dominated by fake news!

After reading this book, I hope that you will agree that the truth can be far more interesting than fiction!

Acknowledgements

I have been advised by many friends, who were aware of my attempt to put pen to paper, that my efforts would be greatly enhanced by the inclusion of illustrations of some of the work produced during my tenure at Wrangler.

My loft at home produced a rich vein of possibilities when I uncovered a treasure trove of point-of-sale material and sales promotional items and photographs.

Unfortunately, obtaining permission to include this work would have required spending an inordinate amount of time tracking down the owners of copyright and seeking their permission to publish. Life is too short and many of the people concerned are, sadly, no longer with us.

So, readers, you will have to rely on my descriptive powers to give you an idea of the creativity involved.

Thankfully, my stash of material also included reports and articles that I had written and magazines containing articles written about the jeans market, which included comments made by myself and representatives of other jeans brands.

The internet also uncovered more information and quotations by competitors and advertising agency personnel that I have been able to draw on and have helped greatly to jog my memory.

My son Marc collected postcards. Those I sent home during my travels were kept by him. Reading them has helped me to place exact dates to specific events and given me an insight to my state of mind during stressful times.

I would like to acknowledge the expertise of all my colleagues at Wrangler particularly former Managing Director, Richard Webzell. His attitude to business and insistence in maintaining the mantra that the customer is always right, helped to shape my business dealings both during and after my time with the company.

It was my privilege to work with some of the brightest creative minds, great strategic thinkers, and excellent suppliers. The skills of all these people were undoubtably crucial to our ability to produce a great body of award winning and extremely effective work.

Most of all I am grateful to my family. My late wife Glenys was my rock through the whole of this period and kept things together during my long absences from home. My children, Marc and Becky spent their formative years with an absentee father but still managed to become mature adults of whom I am extremely proud.

I would also like to thank Ann, my current partner. It was she who encourage me to put pen to paper (or more precisely, fingers to the keyboard). She also proofread my various drafts and made helpful comments and suggestions along the route to this final version.

Last, but not least, credit must be given to my friend and former business partner, Leon LeBlanc. It was he who led me through the technical minefield of self-publishing and reformatted the final draft before publication.

Foreword

The mid 1970s marked the period when jeans began their transition from an iconic garment, worn by young, anti-establishment rebel rousers, to a 'must have' leisure accessory for a fashion-conscious mass market.

Throughout the 1950's and 1960's film stars such as Marlon Brando and James Dean had helped to promote a basic, hardwearing work-wear product and propel it to cult garment status.

In Europe, jeans had been introduced by sailors returning from trips to the United States. As friends and family requested additional garments for themselves, a limited import market developed around the major ports.

Those who could get their hands on a pair of Levi's or Wrangler jeans found themselves elevated to a position of fashion leaders. Those who were not, were prepared to pay almost any price to join the new fashion revolution.

The major American manufacturers of the most sought-after brands, quickly realised that what they saw as basic, work-wear commodity products, would command a premium fashion price in Europe.

In the late 1960's and early 1970's wholly owned sales subsidiaries were set up in the major European markets. These were quickly followed by manufacturing facilities in Belgium, Malta, and the United Kingdom.

In April 1975, I joined Blue Bell Apparel Limited. The company had been set up by the North Carolina based owners of the Wrangler jeans brand. Initially, they had situated their UK operation in the London area, like their main market rival Levi Strauss, but had quickly moved out of the Capital, making Nottingham their base.

Company folklore insisted that the board in Greensborough, North Carolina had acquired a map of the UK and stuck a pin into the centre of England. The pin was very close to the city of Nottingham, well known to them because of its Robin Hood connections, and this became their unanimous choice.

Whilst this might be a nice story, the reality was more connected to cost-effectiveness and the ease of distribution throughout the whole of the UK!

At the time that I arrived on the scene, the UK jeans market was still growing faster than the capacity of the major American brands to supply.

Blue Bell was operating a coupon rationing system. This ensured an even countrywide distribution of Wrangler jeans through the independent retailers who had been first to recognise the potential of the jeans concept.

The market was dominated by the classic American originals. Levi's was very much number one followed by Wrangler and Lee. Brutus was carving out a niche as a fashion alternative and British made brands such as Lee Cooper and Falmer had small brand shares.

Apart from shirt producers like Double Two, UK menswear brands had relied more on word of mouth than national advertising to increase their market share.

The mould was to be broken by the North American invaders!

By 1975, Levi's had already used national television with great effect!

My job was to develop a communications strategy, designed to claw back some of the Levi's brand share lead, by increasing awareness and sales of the Wrangler brand.

The increased competition that developed between Levi's and Wrangler, from the mid 1970's to the end of the 1980's, was widely referred to in the media as "The Jeans War."

Many articles and several books have included references to the advertising campaigns waged by both Levi's and Wrangler during this period. They tend to rely on third party evaluations and comments made by advertising agency executives who may (or may not) have been, party to the strategic and tactical decisions made at the time.

Other marketing activity such as strategic planning, market research, public relations, sales and product promotion, product merchandising and "mould-breaking" image photography, played a huge role in establishing Wrangler as a major brand of jeans and jeans related products.

These areas of the marketing mix have tended to be overshadowed by the more glamourous and visible top line advertising. They were also largely planned and developed by the Wrangler in-house marketing team. As a result, their value has been generally under reported by commentators.

I was responsible for the marketing planning and communications output of the Wrangler brand during the whole of the period from 1975 to 1991. This has given me a unique insight of a time during which jeans progress from an American work wear garment to fashion icon and, eventually, a staple commodity in nearly every wardrobe in the land.

No blood was spilt during the so called "Jeans War." It stimulated the creative output of all the participants and produced some great advertising, and equally ground-breaking marketing support activity.

The following narrative not only documents the development of some key elements of the marketing output generated by Wrangler and its major competitor, but also provides a commentary on the ever-changing social history of the time and explains how political upheaval impacted on some of the decisions made.

PART ONE
PLANNING FOR GROWTH

Chapter One

Learning the Wrangler Way

My first introduction to the Wrangler way of doing things came during the interview process.

I had been invited to the company headquarters in the North Nottinghamshire mining village of Calverton. Because I had not been advised otherwise, I assumed that I would arrive at the allotted time and after the interview would be free to fulfil the rest of my diary commitments for the day.

How wrong this assumption proved to be!

On arrival, I was informed that the interview would last the rest of the day and that part of the process would involve working alongside all the other competing final interviewees.

This could have been a daunting prospect, but I resolved to concentrate all my energies on projecting my suitability for the job rather than worrying about the competition.

The day started with a series of psychometric tests lasting three hours. These had clearly been designed to push to the maximum our ability to reason and cope well under prolonged pressure.

Today, these tests are commonplace but in the 1970's they were an eye-opening experience.

While the test results were being scrutinised by the company psychologist, flown in especially from the States for the purpose, we had lunch in the company canteen followed by a tour of the warehousing facility.

After a short break, the afternoon started with a one-to-one interrogation by the psychologist. His objective was to determine our aptitude for verbal reasoning during which our responses to the written test were challenged.

The day concluded with each of the short-listed candidates being quizzed, at some length, by the company Managing Director, Richard Webzell and the six other members of the Senior Management Team.

A few days later, I received a telephone call from Richard Webzell offering me the job. All the hard work during the extended interview period had obviously paid off.

On Monday 7 April 1975, I arrived at the Wrangler offices in Calverton for my first day of work. I was informed that I would undertake a formal induction process and then would work with my predecessor, Tony Hogan, during a short handover period.

I reported directly to Richard Webzell and would be working, as part of the Senior Management Team, with five other key Managers.

Richard (Dick) Webzell was a complex character. He had been employed by Jack Hill, an American who had set up the UK trading operation, as sales agent for the South of England. When Jack left, Dick became Managing Director.

He recognised that the fast growth of the company would be conditional on its ability to gain wide distribution through independent clothing retailers, and quickly established an experienced sales team to ensure this was achieved.

The early seventies had proved to be a difficult time for a lot of companies. Dick's sales agent background had instilled in him an appreciation that, "a sale is only a sale when the products are delivered and paid for."

At that time, the clothing market was very volatile. The decision was made to create a proactive credit control function.

During my induction tour of the departments, it was apparent how closely the sales and credit functions worked together. No orders were dispatched until a credit check had taken place to the satisfaction of all concerned.

The warehouse was state-of-the-art and far superior the any logistics system I had ever seen before.

It must be remembered, in the mid-seventies, computerisation was in its infancy. Yet, at Calverton, a complex IBM computer system, controlled order input and goods output. The warehouse itself was fully automated and engineered to maximise capacity and ease of goods picking and dispatch. All products were randomly stored and sited by situational and product barcodes.

It was a truly impressive operation!

Product development is a key department for any organisation seeking to develop an increased market share in the ever-fickle fashion market. This function at Wrangler was managed by Kevin Black and a small team of product developers.

Kevin had worked for many years in the retail fashion industry as chief buyer for a major departmental store group. He was fully aware of the needs of the retail customer but also understood that a successful buyer needs to anticipate what the style and colour trends will be many months in the future.

He and the merchandise team worked closely with the manufacturers to determine the fabrics and colour pallets that were predicted to make an impact on the fashion trend setters and followers.

With his team, he made frequent trips to fashion hotspots around the world such as Italy and America. Rodeo Drive in Los Angeles was particularly important. It was calculated that fashion and colour trends there, were six to twelve months ahead of the casual fashion markets of Europe.

The product developers had identified a growing market for tops to be worn with denim jeans. These included not only denim jackets and shirts, already closely associated with the Wrangler brand, but also American collegiate wear such as sweatshirts, tee-shirts, and casual jackets.

In the future, these would prove to be an integral part of the Wrangler product offering.

Following my induction to the operational departments, I was ushered in to see Dick Webzell himself. It was the first time I had been in the office since my interview. I was naturally apprehensive.

Dick welcomed me to the company and his working philosophy was explained.

Blue Bell Apparel was a fast-growing company. It was my job to ensure that sales growth of the product was maintained, and Wrangler brand awareness was increased.

Furthermore, there were rules that had to be adhered to. I would have relatively free rein to develop my ideas, but company policy decreed that any expenditure over $25 would require the counter signature of my immediate superior, Dick Webzell himself. Clearly, I was going to have a very close relationship with the top man.

Dick was one of the old school of managers. Wrangler might be selling Jeans and casualwear, but any representative of the organisation was expected to show respect to suppliers and customers by presenting themselves in the best possible light. Suits and ties were very much the order of the day for male staff and formal 'business' attire for females.

Although this approach may seem old fashioned today, the logic was sound. The key market was 16-34-year-olds. Most of the top management and salesforce were at the top end of this scale and, although most felt they looked good in the Wrangler product, few of them really showed it off to best effect.

Then there were the Blue Bell Apparel values. The giving and acceptance of gifts from customers and suppliers, except for obvious corporate giveaways like pens and key rings, was not allowed.

Fraternisation with customers and suppliers, beyond that required to do the job was not encouraged. Of relevance to my role was an unwritten requirement to ensure that I never abused my position by compromising myself with models and artists that I might hire.

The underlying message was perfectly clear!

Blue Bell Apparel was a non-union operation. The management applied an "Open-Door Policy." If any member of staff had a grievance, they were encouraged to take it up with their line manager. if they were not satisfied with the outcome, they could then take their problem all the way to Dick Webzell himself.

All staff were paid above the market rate and had industry leading conditions of employment. As Dick explained "a happy and contented workforce is a productive workforce."

Managers were expected to work hard but, as I would find out later, they were also allowed to play hard.

Members of staff could be members of the union of their choice, but the company would only negotiate with them as individuals. This created an interesting situation a year or so later when the TGWU tried to recruit some of the workforce.

Once the formal part of the induction process was completed, I was re-introduced to Tony Hogan the man I was replacing. I would be working with him for a couple of weeks to ensure a smooth handover.

I had met Tony previously during my initial interview and, after I had been appointed, had been invited by him to attend a meeting of the communications heads of all the wholly owned subsidiaries of the Blue Bell International Division.

This meeting took place in London some weeks before I officially joined the company. I attended with the blessing of my employer, the Menswear Division of the CWS Ltd, for whom I had worked for nearly seven years.

As a result, I had the opportunity to understand how the culture of the company translated across borders and how the Wrangler brand, and its future development, was perceived by my future colleagues in other European countries.

The Wrangler advertising account was handled by the London office of Doyle Dane Bernbach (DDB), an agency with an excellent track record for pan European brand development. During the meeting, it became clear that the Wrangler brand was at different stages of development in different countries. As a result, there were difficulties in producing a consistent imagery for all markets that would have the required impact.

The London office of Burke Inc., one of the foremost international research operators, presented the findings of a Wrangler Brand Positioning and Modelling exercise that had been carried out in all the major European markets. It defined the key attributes of the ideal jeans brand in each market and modelled all the key brands on two axes (Good Value to Poor Value and Fashionable to Unfashionable).

This meaty tome was to prove invaluable to me as I looked for ways of differentiating the Wrangler brand in the UK and Ireland.

Socialising afterwards, I learned some important criteria for ensuring the smooth navigation of the minefield of international meeting expenses. All attendees were on company expenses, but intense rivalry existed between meeting participants to minimise their personal contribution.

Tony Hogan had informed me that UK representatives had honed this down to a fine art and that I would be expected to maintain the honour of the country in this respect.

We were both from Yorkshire, so I assured him that I had inherited the trait of being careful with money. This is something that all children born in the county have drilled into them from birth. Never-the-less, I was keen to discover any useful tips he might be able to pass on. After all, my international marketing experience had, until now, been limited.

The Wrangler UK rules for minimise the cost of international expenditure were: -

Never sit in the front of a taxi (the bill is always presented to the person in this seat)

Follow the protocol of first to the bar and first away. People arriving at the bar will always give you their order thinking that you will generously take the bill. The bill will be proffered to the last person standing at the bar who, to satisfy the honour of the company, will pay. This should never, in any circumstances be you.

Never sit in the corner seat in a restaurant. When the bill arrives the rest of the table will be able to disappear leaving the person trapped in the corner to pay.

Always have a plan B should you find yourself in any of the bill payer situations.

With a few notable exceptions, these rules were to stand me in good stead throughout the whole of my time with the company.

Although we both had a previously held Advertising Managers jobs with menswear companies in the Leeds area, Tony and I had totally different introductions into the industry.

He had been to Art College and then worked for carpet manufacturer and a well-known branded shirt company. As an accomplished artist, he favoured a creative approach and tended to be design orientated. The large designer's drawing board that dominated my new office was testament to his approach.

I, on the other hand, came from a family of master tailors starting with my great grandfather. Instead of following the family tailoring tradition, I became an adman.

In the late 1950s and early 1960s the Leeds advertising scene was dominated by many well-known clothing manufacturers such as Burtons, Hepworth's, John Collier, and Weaver to Wearer.

These manufacturers were not keen on the London breed of admen who they regarded with suspicion. They preferred to spend their hard earned 'brass' locally with people who knew the business rather than travel to the bright lights of London and pay more for less.

I was taught the mechanics of the trade. This involved not only understanding what needed to be communicated and to whom, but also how to develop an advertising idea into an effective message in any chosen media. I became more of an ideas man who relied on "creative types" to translate my ideas on to paper.

During my first weeks at Blue Bell, I was commuting daily by car from my home in Yorkshire, a round trip of around 160 miles. It quickly became clear that this was impractical. Before he left the company, Tony had suggested that I should always have my passport at the ready as I might be required to travel anywhere in Europe at a moment's notice.

Clearly, living at home during the week was not feasible and I took a room in the Admiral Rodney public house in the minster town of Southwell. This arrangement lasted for four months before I was able to purchase a house in the town and my family finally moved down to join me.

Living way from home could have been a lonely experience but my fellow members of the Wrangler management team. They rallied round inviting me out to play darts in the local hostelries and to have meals at their homes. It was clear that they were a close-knit team who had readily welcomed me as a member.

Representatives of the wider international team were frequent visitors to Calverton and, being the only member of the team with evenings to spare during the week, I took on the unofficial role of 'entertainments officer'.

On one occasion, I took out one of the computer 'wiz kids' from America for a game of darts in a nearby country pub. We ended up playing a couple of the locals. My colleague was impressed at their mathematical dexterity in the way they were instantly able to determine the total required to finish the game.

This was something his excellent American college education had not prepared him to do.

He was somewhat less impressed when I told him that their skill at darts meant they could readily subtract the scores to come up with a total required but were less able to add the numbers together beyond the exact score of 501 required to complete the game.

On another occasion, I was asked to join four of our in-house auditors, from the Wrangler Head Office in Brussels, for dinner in a nearby pub restaurant.

Thinking that they would pay the bill, I made the fatal mistake of taking the corner seat.

During the meal, everything was extremely cordial but when the bill arrived, they quickly melted away leaving me facing a hefty payment. I saw them huddled in a group and congratulating themselves on their ability to play the right card in the Wrangler international expenses game.

To extract myself, I quickly came up with my plan B.

Calling over the waitress, I announced in a loud voice, that I would wash up and my colleagues would dry. The whole restaurant waited to see what would happen, and after a few moments, one of the auditors returned and paid the bill. I congratulated myself on my ability to play the expenses game and win.

In 1975, Wrangler Jeans for the European markets were being manufactured in plants in Belgium, Malta, and Falkirk in Scotland.

It was important for me to understand the manufacturing process and to determine what differentiated the Wrangler product from those of the many other brands competing for an increasing slice of the market in the UK and Ireland.

A visit to the plant in Falkirk was organised.

My previous employer, the CWS Menswear division, operated thirteen factories throughout the UK and I was no stranger to the manufacturing processes in the clothing industry.

The Blue Bell factory was in another league!

In 1975, it employed close to 800 employees in a state-of-the-art complex. Although the manufacturing process relied heavily on the skills of the workforce, wherever possible, functions were automated and utilised the very latest machinery. Blue Bell was continuously investing in research and development. A special facility had been set up at the company headquarters, in Greensboro, North Carolina. This ensured that the production line capacity, in all its plants, was maximised without compromising the quality of the finished garments.

Although I was a company employee, the plant engineers were reluctant to show me too much of what they described as "Blue Bell Technology."

There was a training line where new machinists honed their skills for many weeks before they were allowed onto the production line.

Each machinist was responsible for one element of the manufacturing process. There were several checks made along the way to ensure that quality standards were maintained. At the end of the line was a huge sign with the words "Remember, the next inspector is the customer."

Despite its size, the factory was a happy one and every single member of the workforce was proud of the work that they produced. All employees had a name badge, first names only, and the factory General Manager was a regular visitor to the shop floor. He made a point of chatting to individuals about their families and lives away from work. Of course, it was impossible for him to know everyone but careful briefing from line managers made it appear that he did.

This approach, and the same Open-Door Policy employed in Calverton, meant that the whole factory worked together as a team to maximise efficiency and improve output.

The production of the Wrangler product was heavily engineered. It became clear to me, following conversations and meetings with colleagues from the USA and our

European Head Office in Brussels, that most of the key managers had started their career paths as engineers. Porter B Thompson, to whom Dick Webzell reported directly, was the President of the European operation. He had an accountancy background.

The collective attitude, to what was called marketing strategy, was simple. "We produce ex thousand units a week of first-class product. YOU GUYS GO OUT AND SELL IT!"

This brings me neatly to the Wrangler Sales operation.

In 1975, Wrangler had Area Sales Managers who were responsible for the sales regions of the south of England, the Midlands, the North of England/Northern Ireland, and Scotland.

Each sales region was divided into sales areas each with their own sales representative or, in some cases a sales agent, around thirty people in total.

In the Republic of Ireland there was a sales operation of three sales representatives reporting directly to the General Manager, who worked out of an office with a limited warehouse facility, just off the Naas Road in Dublin.

The UK Sales Managers and the General Manager in Ireland, all reported directly to Dick Webzell.

The Area Sales Managers had regular meetings with the Management Team in Calverton and their own sales teams. These were used to facilitate the dissemination of information on which product lines were selling well and those that were not. The sales information was collated weekly to ensure that the production line in the Blue Bell factories could adjust the production mix and minimise the stockholding of slow-moving lines.

Wrangler attended the two main trade shows, MAB held in September in Harrogate and IMBEX held in London in February. As the sell into the trade was approximately six months ahead of the products appearance in the retail outlets, the MAB show promoted products for sale the following Spring season. The IMBEX show promoted products for sale the following Autumn.

Blue Bell Limited had leased a flat/office in the West End of London just behind Harley Street and close to the buying offices of many of the key accounts and jean shop chains. It also had a small office/showroom, three bedrooms, a kitchenette, and a garage.

As I would be spending a lot of time in London, this facility was to prove very beneficial.

My first field meeting with any of the sales managers was with Mark Lovatt, South of England Area Sales Manager. He suggested that we visit one of the main retail jeans chains, Jean Jeanie, to give me a feel for how the Wrangler brand was perceived against the major competitors.

As we were leaving their offices, Mark spotted his opposite number from Levi's. He was just about to introduce me, when I move forward and greeted him like a long-lost friend. Mark was taken aback until Peter Abbiss, the man from Levi's, explained that we were old school friends and former members of the West Park Old Boys Rugby Union Club.

I had not seen him for eight or so years and had no idea that he worked for the competition.

Small world!

Shortly after this encounter, Dick Webzell organised a two-day sales conference at the Burrough Court Conference Centre near Melton Mowbray in Leicestershire.

The conference took place over the weekend starting on the Saturday morning and finishing on the Sunday evening. It presented a perfect opportunity for me to meet all the Wrangler salesforce in one place and to judge for myself how they presented themselves both as individuals, and as a team.

Whilst the daytime sessions involved members of the Calverton Head office team, who were present to update the salesforce on a whole series of issues, the Saturday evening session was very much a salesforce only affair moderated by Dick. The rest of the management team was excluded. It was clear that the sales function held a privileged position within the organisation.

At 9.30pm, when this session was over, the drinks flowed. it was evident to me that the mantra of the company was "work hard, play hard."

Around the offices in Calverton, Dublin and the factory in Falkirk were framed Blue Bell Mission Statements. These documents made clear that the company was the sum of its workforce and that, by working hard for the common good, the organisation would achieve its goal of being the largest provider of jeans and jeans related clothing In the UK and Ireland.

My initial assessment was that this was indeed the case and that the focused approach, building on the product and workforce strengths, would help increase product distribution and market share.

Ironically, the first major project that I was given was nothing at all to do with jeans or jeans related tops.

The company had decided that, as part of the "jeans related clothing" offer, we should market Wrangler Boots.

In the USA the boots were manufactured for Blue Bell Inc. by the iconic American manufacturers, Lucchese Boots. This company had its origins in Palermo in Sicily where the father of the founders was a shoemaker. In 1882, brothers Salvatore and Joseph emigrated to the USA. The following year, they set up shop as bootmakers at Fort Sam Houston.

By the 1970's their Lucchese branded cowboy boots were THE product to be seen wearing. As such, they were highly prized by everyone, from cowboys to film stars and politicians.

In the UK, we already sold Wrangler cowboy hats and a limited range of Wrangler belts. It was felt that a small range of Wrangler boots would be a logical extension.

None of the senior management or salesforce had any experience in the footwear market. Similarly, none of our key retailers were footwear specialists. Despite this, it was agreed to go ahead with the project. It was felt that Blue Bell Apparel had nothing to lose.

A "live test" would give us some idea of demand, give us a better understanding of any logistical problems, and determine how we might extend into "jeans related footwear," in the future.

I examined the product in detail and read up everything that was available about the production techniques. Apparently, each boot was made up of around 147 individual pieces stitched together to manufacture a finished product of the highest possible quality.

The production technique was too complicated to explain but the label on the product had a picture of an old timer careful crafting a boot in his hand. The wording read "Inside they're 100 years old." This clear reference to the Lucchese heritage was something that could be built on.

I then looked for a promotional hook that could be used in publicity.

In the 60's, "These Boots are made for Walking," a song written by Lee Hazelwood and sung by Nancy Sinatra, had reached number one in the UK charts. "Perhaps this might be adapted as a soundtrack for use in a possible radio or television advertisement?" I thought to myself.

A call to Lee Hazelwood's music agent in London scuppered that idea. He wanted too much money for the rights.

A supplier of mine in Leeds was a silk screen printer. A customer of his had acquired a collection of original advertising mirrors, each over 100 years old. They had worked together to reproduce volume quantities. These were being successfully marketed to the wholesale trade in the United States of America.

The silk screen process was used to print the design from behind and to seal in the mirrored image. This was the same method used in the production of the original mirrors. The wooden frames were also treated and aged and so that they also had the same look and feel of the real thing.

It was clear that a Wrangler boot mirror was "the unique something" that would say everything we wanted to say about the new product.

One of my old rugby playing colleagues in Leeds had just set up his own design agency and, for small fee, produced the initial design and finished artwork.

The Wrangler Boot mirror was produced in 1975 with a limited print run of 500. From memory, each mirror cost around £8 to manufacture. About half the quantity went to America and 125 were distributed to retailers who bought the product in the UK. The balance taken up by my marketing colleagues in Germany, Holland and Scandinavian.

Today copies of the mirror resurface from time to time on sites such as eBay. The last one I saw, was sold for about £70.

The Wrangler boots sold well, even though distribution had been limited to a small number of retail outlets. The experience was to prove invaluable when the time was right to extend the Wrangler brand franchise into footwear.

There is a "sting in the tail" of this story.

Sometime in late 1975 or early 1976, the head of marketing for Blue Bell in Scandinavia was sitting drinking in a bar in Stockholm in Sweden.

After a while, he was joined by an American wearing jeans and casual shirt and denim jacket. They struck up a conversation over a drink. My colleague explained he worked for an American company and was promoting Wrangler jeans across Scandinavia.

The American explained he was in the music business and that he was a big fan of the Wrangler product.

Over a few more drinks, they were on first name terms and real drinking buddies. The conversations turned to what projects they were currently working on.

The American was none other than Lee Hazelwood. The very person who had written the song "These boots are made for Walking." He had also produced the number one single featuring Nancy Sinatra.

Lee had left the Hollywood scene behind and was now living in semi-seclusion in Sweden.

My colleague said that he was developing a television commercial to launch Wrangler Boots in Scandinavia. He outlined the script and explained that the voice over would be in English and the commercial would probably be used in other European markets.

He was looking to cast a gravelly voiced American artist to give his commercial real authenticity. Without hesitation, his new-found buddy agreed to take on the job himself. Some small consideration was agreed in the bar, probably to do with the supply of Wrangler merchandise.

So that was how Lee Hazelwood became integral to the advertising campaign for Wrangler Boots in Scandinavia and the UK!

Chapter Two

Marketing plan! What marketing plan?

At my previous employer, the CWS Menswear Group, the product was somewhat dated but there was a clear marketing plan. As a result, the product managers were fully aware what their targets were and what was needed, in terms of product development and market share increases, to achieve them.

With Blue Bell Apparel, it was a somewhat different situation.

Brand awareness and demand for Wrangler jeans was high but production was struggling to keep up with that demand.

Blue Bell was a manufacturing giant and the engineers at the factories in Europe were confident that they would be able to boost production to the levels required.

For the sales orientated subsidiaries this presented a problem. Obviously, a shortage of supply had resulted in an increased demand. It would have been easy to apply a first come first served policy to jeans sales.

In the UK, the company realised that good distribution was the key to future growth. This could only be achieved by evenly allocating the product across all sales regions and through a defined number of distribution outlets. In this way, all the salesforce could be given meaningful targets for growth that would reflect future sales potential across the whole of the UK.

To achieve this, an ingenious system had been devised.

Each salesperson was allocated a quantity of 'ration stamps' equal to the number of jeans available across their sales area. It was left to the individual salesperson to use their allocation wisely so that the brand could enjoy product visibility on the high street.

Dick Webzell was convinced that the independent retailers were key to achieving the high profile required. He had worked closely with the Area Sales Managers to identify the key retailers in each sales area that the sales representatives needed to develop a relationship with. "Look after them now and they will reward you with their loyalty in the future," he contended.

The Wrangler range had always included a limited range of western style tops such as the distinctive Wrangler denim jackets and shirts.

In 1974, a range of American collegiate sweatshirts, tee-shirts and hooded sweatshirts had also been introduced. They were manufactured in the USA, by Champion Sportswear and were clearly branded with the Wrangler logo on the front.

A product manager had been employed to extend the tops range to include casual jackets and other associated garments. All were designed to complement the range of denim and cord jeans.

Eight weeks into the job, I was called into Dick Webzell's office. The purpose of the meeting was to discuss how my induction was going and to talk about my suggestions for moving the brand forward.

During the meeting, he asked me to produce a five-year advertising plan. I asked for a copy of the five-year marketing plan to enable me to ensure that the communications were geared to achieving the targets set.

"What marketing plan?" he replied.

My heart sank!

Surely, I thought to myself, a company as seemingly sophisticated as Blue Bell, was not operating in a 'seat of pants' manner?

After further discussion, it became clear that Blue Bell Inc. in North Carolina required Blue Bell Apparel Limited to send back a detailed financial report each month. This included accurate sales figures, against sales targets and profit and loss account information on all product lines.

In addition, some data existed on market share and brand awareness levels. The Burke research document, presented at the international meeting that I had attended before joining the company, gave a lot of detailed information on brand perceptions and positioning.

All the information, required to put together a marketing plan, was already in the hands of the company. It simply needed to be brought together, assessed, and a blueprint created that could be used to develop a comprehensive marketing plan for future growth.

It looked as though I had just extended the scope of my job!

Over the next weeks, I immersed myself in the task. Working with my colleagues in the Senior Management Team and the Area Sales Managers, I brought together all the information required to produce an analysis of the strengths, weaknesses, opportunities, and threats of Blue Bell the company and the Wrangler branded products.

The brand name Wrangler was well regarded. Wrangler branded merchandise was seen to be of good quality and hardwearing. As a genuine American brand, it was perceived as enjoying all the attributes required of a major market player.

Levi's was clearly the jeans brand leader and its "Leader of the Pack" TV commercial, directed by Alan Parker, had clearly helped to secure its number one position. It was regarded as THE jeans brand to be seen in.

Brutus had tried to usurp their dominance with its "Jeans On" commercial. The jingle became a number one hit for David Dundas. This occurred nearly a decade before Levi's were to make such associations an art form.

Unfortunately for them, Brutus was perceived as a fashion brand. It was not an American original and its quality was not as good as the major brands.

Wrangler had an excellent reputation with menswear retail trade. Whilst there were jeans supply problems, buyers appreciated that the company was being honest with them and felt that the stamp allocation system was fair to all.

This was helped by the Blue Bell internal sales and credit operations. Each sales representative had their own internal sales coordinator. As a result, every customer had a named contact at Head Office who was tasked with resolving any queries about delivery of product orders.

Credit control was especially important!

A lot of people had jumped on to the jeans retail bandwagon. Many were underfunded and poorly managed. The Blue Bell mantra was clear. "A sale is only a sale when the product is delivered and paid for."

To ensure that adequate controls were in place, the credit control department, managed by Tony Fleet, worked closely with the retail trade, Wrangler Head Office sales coordinators, the salesforce, and major competitors. In this way, the company used its advance knowledge of any retailer who might be in financial difficulties, to control product distribution and minimise potential financial risk.

This openness encouraged retail buyers to work with Tony, and their named credit coordinator, to sort out any short-term cashflow problems.

All in all, the result of my company and product audit was very encouraging.

The Wrangler brand commanded a price premium and Blue Bell the company enjoyed an excellent reputation amongst major independent retailers.

Early brand share analysis indicated that Wrangler was a distant number two to Levi's but ahead of all the other leading brands such as Lee, Lee Cooper, and Brutus.

The growing range of Wrangler tops had been well received by the market, especially the denim western jacket. This had achieved something of a cult status and was perceived by the fashion leaders as a "must have classic."

The Blue Bell product manager for the tops range had included a highly visible Wrangler logo on the front of every garment. In the 1970's, this type of overt product branding was almost unheard of in the UK menswear market.

Initial research confirmed that the consumers regarded the presence of the logo as "a badge of quality and fashion awareness." This was justification of the premium price they were being asked to pay.

Not every retail buyer was convinced!

I remember vividly a conversation I had with a buyer at a leading chain of jeans wear retailers.

He was hesitating about placing an order for Wrangler Tee-shirts. Whilst accepting that the quality of the fabric and manufacturing was superior to anything else available at the time, the price premium appeared to be a barrier. "I can retail cotton tee-shirts from my current source for the same price as the wholesale price that you charge" he explained.

"But can you buy a Wrangler tee-shirt at that price?" I countered. He had to agree that he could not. A trial order was placed. The product flew out of his shop, and he became an early adopter of the whole of the Wrangler tops range.

Conversations, with the Area Sales Managers, revealed that they had put in place a sales strategy for selling in tops. This operated alongside the rationing policy that Blue Bell had introduced to ensure fair distribution of Wrangler jeans.

Leading retailers were prepared to buy the heavily branded tops range to help reinforce their position on the high street as a leading supplier of the Wrangler brand. This, at the time when high demand was outstripping the available production capacity for Wrangler jeans.

I now focused my attention on the communication strategy that I had inherited.

My empire consisted of a part time secretary, who I shared with Kevin Black the Merchandise Manager, and a dedicated member of the warehouse team who was responsible for the distribution of point-of-sale material.

The Wrangler salesforce carried a stock of the latest Wrangler decals, giveaways and posters and sent in requests via a point-of-sale order form. These were processed and then despatched from the warehouse.

The company had acquired a Volkswagen Beetle that had been factory customised internally with Wrangler denim seat coverings and externally in with 'W' stitching and Wrangler logos. The close working relationship that our agency DDB enjoyed with VW (Peter Pleasance was Account Director for both VW and Wrangler) had made this possible.

I was given to believe that at the time only two or three had been produced. Down the line, Volkswagen was hoping to market them commercially.

In addition, my department was also the proud owner of an old London Routemaster double decker bus. A lot of time and expense had gone into a facelift that included replacing the iconic red exterior into a moving, blue and yellow billboard for Wrangler. The upstairs seats had been removed and replaced with tables and chairs. With the benefit of hindsight, a less drastic renovation might have been equally effective and, in the long term, would have provided a greater return on investment.

Both vehicles were available to the retail trade, a week at a time, for promotional purposes. They were very much in demand during the summer carnival period and for new shop openings.

Amongst the other sales promotional items available were Wrangler branded illuminated shop signs. The signs were a charge item. The price included individual customisation with the retailer's shop name and application for planning permission. This process was a very time-consuming operation. Doing this in-house ensured that Blue Bell maintained control over distribution and that the signs were only available to, and only used by, bone fide Wrangler stockists.

Cooperative press advertising was much beloved by the retail trade in the 1970's. This enabled Wrangler stockists to communicate the message to their customers, that they were suppliers of the brand. Several 20cm double column press advertisements were available featuring Wrangler jeans, shirts, jackets, and sweatshirts. Participating retailers added their details in the space allocated at the bottom of the advertisement. Bluebell then contributed 50% of the cost of the advertising space.

The system was "loosely'" controlled through the Area Sales Managers. When I carried out an examination of the take up, it was clear that it was the smaller stockists who were claiming a disproportionate percentage of the funds available.

A public relations budget was mainly utilised to maintain awareness of the brand through the retail trade magazines, to support the brands presence at the two major trade exhibitions and publicise new range additions such as collegiate sweatshirts.

Some of the budget was also used to part sponsor the International Festival of Country Music that had been held at Wembley Arena just before I arrived at Blue Bell.

Blue Bell Inc. had signed a limited sponsorship deal with Jackie Stewart who was at the time the current F1 Motor Racing World Champion. As far as I could tell, for the UK market this involved approval to use a poster that featured Jackie's name, face, racing car and the Wrangler logo, as a point of sale item.

When I joined the company, DDB, our advertising agency, had developed a national 48 sheet poster campaign that featured Wrangler Jeans and tops. Although this was to be the first truly national advertising campaign for the Wrangler brand, it would need to be closely monitored to see whether the objectives of increasing brand awareness and market share had been achieved.

This was key to the development of future advertising strategy given that two of the brands major competitors, Levi's, and Brutus, were using television as their main advertising media.

In 1975, brand share figures were not very reliable. They appeared to have been based on the assumption that sales of jeans in the UK market equated to around 1 jean unit per capita head of population. This calculation equated to total sales of around 50 million units. In other words, every 1% of claimed market share equated to 500,000 units sold.

On this basis, I estimated that Levi's was jeans brand leader with about 9% share, followed by Wrangler at 7% and Brutus 3%.

Of course, not every company used the same basis to calculate the share that they quoted to authoritative research organisations such as Mintel. Many of the smaller brands, with no access to real data, tended to "over-egg" the figures that they quoted. Whatever the basis that was used, it was clear to me that the top three brands only accounted for about 20% of the total market. The other 80% was made up of a myriad of smaller brands, own brands and unbranded, commodity suppliers.

The Blue Bell factories were under producing but were gearing up to increase output by as much as 50%/60% before the end of the decade. This provided an opportunity to increase Wrangler brand share significantly, year on year, at the expense of the 80% of the market not held by the top three brands.

In theory, Wrangler had the ability to reach at least brand share parity with Levi's, or even overtake them, without the need for a head-to-head confrontation.

After only a couple of months in post, it had become apparent that the company was growing quickly. Recruiting new staff, in all areas, was a major priority. Unfortunately, devising and placement of recruitment advertising was assumed to be the responsibility of the Advertising Department.

Not only was I spending time with my fellow managers determining staff requirements, writing recruitment advertisements and placing them in the appropriate media, I was also collating the responses and providing a sort of low-key Human Resources service.

Clearly, it was important that I develop a clear focus to increase the visibility and awareness of the Wrangler brand. This would assist the salesforce to increase brand penetration and brand share.

A Human Resources Manager was recruited!

Mass media advertising was integral to achievement of our planned growth. Whilst it might not be possible to match the TV spend of the major competitors in the short term, an opportunity did exist to dominate brand awareness at the point of purchase.

At CWS, I had a team of two "window dressing consultants" who worked with their retail colleagues to create excitement in the shop windows and where the products were displayed instore. This had worked very well. I felt that such a role could be extended to ensure that the Wrangler brand presence, using the excellent point of sales tools already available, would enable the brand to punch well above its weight.

I coined the job title Field Promotion Representative (FPR) for the new roles. Their mandate was to identify, with the help of their sales colleagues, the key independent Wrangler stockists, in every major town. They would then set up a calendar of regular visits aimed at merchandising the Wrangler product both in the shop windows and at the point of purchase.

Initially, we employed four individuals to look after the South, the Midlands, the North of England, and Scotland/ Northern Ireland.

It was always my intention to extend the FPR role to cover promotional activities outside the shop environment in places frequented by the prime market groups. This included night clubs, sports venues, carnivals, and other special events.

The mixture of skills required were totally new to the clothing market and more associated with the 'Fast Moving Consumer Goods' (FMCG) area. It was clear that it was unlikely any one individual would be skilled in all aspects of the job. A conscious decision was made to recruit people who were keen to expand their sales promotional knowledge, to take on new challenges and to learn new marketing skills.

The first intake included a trained window dresser, an in-store merchandiser, a sales promotion assistant, and an ex-professional footballer. They were encouraged to work together as a team and exchange skill sets to improve their knowledge in those areas of the job where they had little experience.

At that time, many retailers did not have the resources to employ a professional to undertake the role and were only too happy to allow the Wrangler FPR's into their shops. As a result, we not only maximised exposure of the brand, but also developed special relationships with all the retailers we worked with.

It was two years before Levi's introduced their own team of sales promotional professionals. By this time, the Wrangler FPR's were well established and had widened the scope of their activities in the way that I had originally envisaged.

Chapter Three

Protecting the Wrangler brand name

Blue Bell Inc had determined that the Wrangler brand was a key component of its product portfolio. The organisation had taken out Trademark protection across the world not only for the brand name but also for the way it was used in marketing, both on the products and in the media.

The company had also patented the "W" stitching that appeared on the back pockets of jeans and on the front pockets of "western style" shirts and jackets. Protection was also obtained covering the relative positioning of branding labels used, in conjunction with the "W" stitching, on all Wrangler products.

To maintain this protection, it was necessary to be consistent in the way that the brand was presented. This involved the typeface and colour combinations used. Legal representatives also recommended that whenever the name Wrangler was used in body copy, it should be followed by the ™ symbol.

Whilst these legal precautions had been taken, unscrupulous manufacturers would still try to find a way to jump on the back of the awareness that we had spent a lot of time, effort, and money to develop. Phrases like "Wrangler type jacket" were used to "pass off" inferior products as the genuine article.

It was made clear to me, at the onset, I should not only ensure that my use of the Wrangler name complied with the legalities of Trademark protection but also that attempts at "passing off" by others should severely dealt with.

Trade Mark Owners Association

Before I joined Blue Bell, I had similar responsibilities at the CWS Menswear Group. As a result, I had a good working relationship with the Trade Mark Owners Association. It had been set up in 1886 to help companies register and protect their trademarks and to search the viability of any new brand or sub brand names before registration took place.

Although the name has changed to Nucleous IP, it continues to provide a high-quality service in brand an intellectual property protection.

Throughout the 1970's and 1980's Blue Bell used their valuable services to protect the Wrangler brand properties and the numerous "sub brand names" that we developed during this time.

Herbert Smith Solicitors

Registering brand and sub brands can be a blunt instrument unless the threat to act against transgressors is followed through. Worldwide, Blue Bell subsidiaries were instructed to adopt a "no tolerance" approach and to use the threat and/or option of legal action immediately we became aware that our brand name protection was being abused.

Herbert Smith was recognised as the world's leading advocates in brand and intellectual property protection. Their London office worked closely with Dick Webzell and me. Evidence we provided was frequently used in litigation that they undertook on our behalf.

Whilst there were some actions that required them to use the full weight of trademark protection legislation, most were against attempts at "passing off" fakes, or similarly branded items, as Wrangler originals.

The more "famous" the brand became in the UK, the greater the number of interventions Herbert Smith was making on our behalf.

We now had another method by which to judge the success of our promotional marketing efforts!

Developing a new Wrangler Brand Manual

The typeface selected for the Wrangler brand name was unique with a lower case "g" with an extended "tail." The distance from the bottom of the "g" to the top of the capital "W," known as the "x height," was far more than in most conventional type faces. This was a double-edged sword. On the one hand it added to the brands uniqueness. On the other, it limited the overall size width that could be obtained when the brand name was used in isolation, on such items as advertising sites around sports grounds.

At the end of the 1970's such promotional activity was on the rise and the size had been standardised. The only way to maximise the visibility of the Wrangler name in such circumstances, was to use capital letters, but this was not a viable option.

It was agreed to shorten the length of the "g" to normal proportions and to issue a manual to standardise its use across Europe and the rest of the International Division.

At the time, American Robert McConnell (Bob) was President of Blue Bell International working out of the Head Office in Brussels. He handed full responsibility for the task to another American, Rafael Labrador (Raf), who was Vice President – Marketing.

Raf was known to be a stickler for detail, We all felt that the project was in a very safe pair of hands.

Months later, the task was completed and all the senior marketing staff across the International Division were summoned to a meeting in Brussels for the grand unveiling. Dick and I represented the UK and Ireland.

Bob McConnell was a somewhat a mercurial character. He had a reputation for "calling a spade a spade" and for the speed of his decision making. After welcoming everyone to the meeting and expressing his support for the re-branding process that we would all be undertaking, he called on Raf to unveil his masterpiece.

Raf was the opposite of Bob, he was extremely thorough in his approach and was always keen to "dot all the I's and cross all the t's." A full slide presentation (PowerPoint was a mere pipe dream then) was the order of the day.

After 30 minutes, it was clear that Bob was losing interest. When Raf finished his formal presentation Bob's mind was clearly elsewhere. With a flourish, Raf produced his "pièce de resistance," a beautifully bound, patiently crafted, forty-odd paged, brand manual.

"Can you let me have a look at that, Raf," Bob demanded. Leafing through it, he was clearly troubled. "Raf, I asked for a manual, not a bible," he exclaimed, casually tossing Raf's pride and joy back to him. Unfortunately, it fell out of the intended recipient's hands, hit the floor losing several of its perfectly bound pages.

Raf was undeterred, he was clear in his mind that his work of art would be of practical use to everybody connected with the rebranding process.

In the end, the views of both Bob and Raf were vindicated. When the final versions were circulated about 4 weeks later, the meticulously crafted sheets were part of a loose-leaf binder. Over the next decade some sheets were removed, and additional sheets added. The "loose leaf bible" became an invaluable tool and reference point.

PART TWO

A CONSISTENT BRAND STRATEGY INTERPRETED BY DIFFERENT ADEVERTISING AGENCIES

Chapter Four

Working with Advertising Agencies

Paul Jobling, in his book "Advertising Menswear Masculinity & Fashion in the British Media Since 1945," has attributed quotes to me under the section on jeans advertising.

I admit to not having read the whole book. The sections that I have been able to review on the Internet have been clearly written from the perspective of the advertising agencies involved rather than the client companies themselves.

Indeed, the paragraph on the key challenges facing the advertising agencies, in what was a demographically diverse market, I am quoted as saying, as part of an interview in 1980, that it was necessary "to pitch the image of the innovatory group, without alienating other target markets."

Unfortunately, the quote has been attributed to me as Robin Dilley of Collett Dickenson Pearce. At the time, I was Head of Advertising at Wrangler Jeans.

CDP was my advertising agency.

In that capacity, I was explaining to the interviewer the communication problems that we as a client had identified, and which we were asking our advertising agency to solve. I am also quoted as identifying the 'innovatory group' as 13-20 years. I can only assume this was a typographical error, in the source article, because this age segment never was a part of the strategic targeting process.

In 1979, we had identified 16-24-year-olds as a key market sector. They bought more jeans (up to 3 pairs per capita) and were especially difficult to target because, to a 16-year-old, a 24-year-old was regarded as positively geriatric. Within this segment, the fashion leaders were to be found. They were 'early adopters' of new fashion trends. Not all fashion trends were taken up by the volume buying group of 'fashion followers.' Those that were became volume sellers.

Both Wrangler and Levi's aimed their product development at the volume market.

Later in his book, in the Chapter headed "More than just a number – A new style of Advertising for the 1990's," Paul asserts, "But by and large, Wrangler had struggled to find a consistent identity in, and for its publicity, changing advertising agents no less than six times between 1973 and 1990."

As I was the person in charge of the Wrangler brand advertising from 1975 to 1991, I can refute the idea that there was any confusion of the part of the company in respect of the direction the brand was seeking to take.

The main objective of our total marketing spending (media advertising was only a part, albeit the most visible part of our marketing mix), was to maintain the appeal of the Wrangler product mix against the prime target groups, increase positive brand awareness, improve brand perception and maintain/increase market share in the jeans and related clothing sectors.

This did not change throughout the period in question!

The fashion market is very different to fast moving consumer goods (fmcg) markets. Consumers of fashion products are fickle. Until the leading jeans manufacturing companies started to promote their products using mainstream media advertising, they were not very brand conscious. Fashion companies tended to bring out new product ranges every six weeks. As a result, were never able to crack the volume market.

Wrangler, as a leading clothing brand, brought out only two complete ranges a year and yet our warehouse in Calverton was distributing a total of close to 2000 stock keeping units (sku's).

We were very much in the volume sales market!

Just as subtle changes to the fashion styles took place in this period i.e., flares in the 70's, straight jeans, and stone washed jeans in the 80's, so our advertising agencies were faced with the need to be at the forefront of advertising style and execution.

The key to success was to maintain a consistency in the marketing message. In the case of Wrangler, we wished to be perceived as manufacturers of quality, fashionable products, projecting the brand using techniques and imagery that would help to maintain its relevance to the key consumers.

We were looking for our advertising agencies to fully interpret our brief and to produce creative work that would not only increase positive perceptions of our brand but, more importantly, would motivate our target market to buy more of our products.

A close examination of the brands output between 1975 and 1991 indicates that by and large these objectives were met.

To achieve this, we did change agencies several times along the way!

During my time as custodian of the Wrangler brand, I never actually fired an advertising agency nor was Blue Bell ever fired by an agency - despite subsequent stories to the contrary!

Often outside factors were responsible for such a move, but we always maintained good relationships and the "divorces" were always amicable.

It must be remembered that during the 1970's and 1980's, having a jeans account in their 'stable' was a feather in the cap of an advertising agency wishing to display their true creative credentials. Because of this, business development directors in most of the leading agencies of the day would regularly call me, unsolicited, to try to convince me that my existing agency was not performing as well as their agency would if I were to appoint them to the account.

Stories were always appearing in the media that claimed that Wrangler was "looking around" when we were doing nothing of the kind. I always suspected that leaking such a story was a tactic employed by agency chiefs to unsettle the incumbent advertising agency. It also gave them a reason to call me again to try and encourage me to place them on my non-existent pitch list.

Whatever the reason, I was extremely popular in advertising agency circles at that time!

Working on an account like Wrangler could apparently boost the individual's CV considerably. Such was the high-profile nature of the advertising output of the major suppliers of jeans.

Over the years, I have read articles and advertising agency literature naming people who claimed to have worked on the Wrangler advertising account at one time or another. Some indeed may have done so in a minor capacity, but many had never been on my radar.

I have also read stories, mainly from creative people who did work on the account, making somewhat exaggerated claims about the success of creative output for which they were responsible. Some bore little resemblance to the extensive post advertising market research that we, as the client, had instigated at the time.

Looking back, I am happy, that throughout my time at Blue Bell, the Wrangler advertising brief was consistent and much of the creative output was memorable, impactful, and contributed greatly to the growth of the company.

In 1975, when I first joined the company, the aim was to make Wrangler the UK's number one brand in the jeans and jeans related clothing markets.

It was Wrangler who introduced the collegiate sweatshirt and T-shirt to the UK market in 1974. The brand also launched the hooded sweatshirt and made denim jackets, bomber jackets and casual jackets 'must have' accessories for jeans made in denim and corduroy.

Wrangler also produced, and launched, a successful range of chinos.

I think it is true to say, it was the merchandising team at Blue Bell Apparel who had the fashion vision that helped the marketing team create, for the first time, a branded casualwear market in which Wrangler became the key player.

During the 1970's and 1980's there was only one denim jacket that enjoyed credibility with the fashion leaders. It was the one that was branded Wrangler!

In today's retro market, original 70's Wrangler jeans and jackets are much sought after and command premium prices. If only I had set aside some Wrangler merchandise, then, for a rainy day!

The Wrangler jeans related clothing products were manufactured to the same exacting standards that the company applied to jeans manufactured in its own factories.

For the company, and its employees, 'quality' was more than just a word. It became a mantra for the machinist who manufactured the products and those involved in the quality control process. It applied also to the suppliers of yarns and fabrics and findings such as buttons, rivets, and zips.

But more importantly, it was reinforced by the guarantees that Blue Bell gave to the retailers who sold the product and the consumers who bought Wrangler garments through their outlets.

Wrangler jeans were originally manufactured from 14¾oz, left hand twill indigo denim (no more twisted seams) with care and attention lavished on the quality of the stitching and the strength of the pockets.

If the slightest imperfection was found in a finished pair of jeans, they were consigned to the "seconds" pile. "Seconds" from Wrangler became a lucrative market for the retail trade because these were infinitely superior to imported "first quality products," supplied by some of the other jeans companies.

We produced a poster that emphasised the manufacturing benefits such was our confidence in the added value benefits that we offered both the retailer and his customers.

Until well into the late 1970's, if a zip broke on a pair of Wrangler jeans within twelve months of purchase, Blue Bell guaranteed to replace the whole product. Eventually, when a spate of returns of jeans with broken zips reached epidemic proportions, an independent testing organisation was called in to investigate. Tests identified that some consumers were deliberately damaging the zip, close to the end of the guarantee period, to claim a free new pair.

Only then did Blue Bell alter its returns policy!

The guarantee was changed with the company offering to replace any faulty broken zip with a new one. Almost overnight, the number of jeans returned because of a broken zip reduced to almost zero!

Even today, the words 'fashion' and 'quality' appear to be diametrically opposed.

However, the Burke research we had undertaken in 1974, revealed that the Wrangler brand had an excellent quality rating and a good perception as a fashion brand.

It was clear, that Blue Bell had a unique opportunity to position products branded Wrangler as "quality garments for the fashion-conscious core market."

I had always been conscious of the importance of a consistent approach to the advertising message. I also understood that to be effective, any piece of communication needed to be seen, to be read, to be understood and to be acted upon.

When I started my advertising career, I joined a small advertising agency in Leeds as a trainee. Called Heslock Advertising Limited, it used the slogan, "Truth in Advertising," to promote itself.

I had joined the agency straight from school at a time when TV Advertising was in its infancy and the populace at large were much less media savvy. Nevertheless, I found the slogan at odds with my perception of what advertising was all about. I proffered my opinion to the Managing Director, who had set up and still owned the business. He sat me down and offered me some invaluable advice. "Only take on a client who can prove to you that the product they wish you to promote is able to live up to the expectations and the promise that they wish you to make on its behalf."

Initially, I thought this was just another piece of advertising agency waffle. To clarify his thoughts, he followed up with a piece of advice that has stood me in good stead throughout my career.

"Robin," he explained, "anyone can sell anything once, but a customer will only repeat purchase if the claims made pre-sale are substantiated after the sale, when the customer has been satisfied that what they have purchased has met, or ideally exceeded, their expectations. What is more, if the supplier, salespeople, and advertising agency have total belief in the product they are trying to sell, they become true advocates and their enthusiasm and belief, in what they are saying, will successfully shine through."

He concluded with the words, "That Is what I mean by truth in advertising!"

In the case of the Wrangler product, I was happy with quality, customer support and fashion content. What's more, I was also satisfied that all the staff at Blue Bell provided the best support in the industry, and were market leaders in product design, development, and production.

Research told us that the retail trade also believed this to be true.

The limited consumer research the company had carried out, prior to my joining them, showed that customers of the brand were very positive in their product quality and fashion perceptions. Even non-purchasers were aware that Wrangler was a major brand of jeans and had positive perceptions about it.

The senior marketing team consisted of Dick Webzell, Kevin Black, who was responsible for all product development and quality control, and me. All three of us worked closely together and had input in the direction that the company would take in respect of sales and profit targets, product ranges, product range development, marketing planning and communications targeting and implementation.

Each of us respected input that the others might be able to contribute to our individual areas of expertise. We worked on the principle of mutual trust, understanding and awareness that the final decision, on any aspect of the marketing mix, rested with the member of the team with ultimate line management responsibility for the area under discussion.

This approach resulted in some fierce discussion but, surprisingly little conflict!

With the agreement of the other members of the team, it was decided our advertising agency, DDB, would be briefed to produce a campaign for 1976 that would emphasise that Wrangler "was more than just a jeans brand."

The Wrangler brand was a guarantee of quality and fashionability that Blue Bell applied with confidence to all its jeans and jeans related clothing ranges.

This approach would clearly differentiate Wrangler from all our competitors.

Chapter Five

Doyle Dane Bernbach – 1974 to 1976

Originally, Blue Bell Inc. had assumed that it would be possible to apply a common communications strategy across the whole of Europe, much as they did in the domestic market in the United States. For this reason, they appointed first, J Walter Thompson and then Doyle Dane Bernbach to develop a pan European strategy and communications campaign.

This had proved difficult, not only because of the number of different European languages involved, but also culture clashes and concept problems in the different countries. This was particularly true within the key markets of the UK, Germany, France, Benelux, and Italy.

It was also hoped the advertising that was performing so well for the brand in America, would readily translate to all international markets.

What the marketing management in the USA had failed to realise was that, in America, jeans were perceived very much as work wear garments. The Wrangler image, forged by its name and association with rodeo cowboys was, rightly, reinforcing that stereotype.

In Europe, jeans were perceived somewhat differently. The product was a "must have" garment of the young and rebellious epitomised in movie and stage performances of anti-establishment stars such as James Dean, Marlon Brando and the rock and roll stars of the 50's and 60's. It was the fashion badge of the young and was far removed from the cowboy image that Wrangler was hoping to portray across all markets.

The American association of the brand was a positive for the markets in the UK, Germany, Scandinavia, and Benelux. In Italy, the basic American jeans were not as popular as the 'home grown' high fashion styles. Whilst in France, anything American was seen in an extremely negative light.

In 1976, the Levi's account was with McCann Ericson. They had developed almost a franchise for advertising to the young target group through their work with Coca Cola, Martini and, of course Levi's.

The lifestyle advertising pioneered by McCann's, during this period, featured beautiful people, clearly enjoying themselves. It translated across international borders. There was a downside. It was becoming a generic style of communication to the young. Consumers were finding it increasingly difficult to identify the advertising output of one lifestyle brand from another.

The account team at DDB understood the problems that they faced and had tried hard to meet the expectations of the key markets. Wrangler Account Director, Peter Pleasance was also Account Director on the VW account. As a result, he had acquired a vast experience in pan-European advertising campaigns. Account Manager, Robin Hunter-Coddington, was fluent in about six European languages and was also number two to Peter on the VW account.

DDB had a reputation for cutting edge advertising and was home to several creatives who were to make their mark in the future, working on the advertising for a rival brand of jeans, at another advertising agency.

After lengthy discussions, I was confident that they not only understood the brief but had the creative talent to produce the goods.

At that time, the advertising budget for Wrangler was calculated as a percentage of projected turnover. In 1975, it was not sufficient for the brand to utilise television advertising of the kind being pioneered by its major rivals Levi's and Brutus. This made the job of establishing a coherent, more fashionable image much more difficult.

My initial research, on the outdoor poster campaign that I had inherited, showed that Wrangler was holding its own in respect of Levi's and was ahead of Brutus in brand awareness.

When it came to fashionability, the brands advertising on television, were viewed in a much more positive light. If it could be afforded, television was the place to be for our advertising campaign in 1976!

Talks with the agency, and my business planning colleagues at Blue Bell Apparel, established that we were looking to increase unit sales by something of the order of 15%. This goal was a distinct possibility because we now had production capacity to achieve the additional volume sales required.

We wanted the agency to create a television and cinema campaign, within our budget, that was visible, creative, and effective in stimulating demand.

On the face of it, the Wrangler proposition was relatively straightforward. "Blue Bell Apparel produce a range of jeans and jeans related products under the Wrangler brand that are superior, in both quality and design, to those marketed by our competitors."

The challenge for the agency was to represent this proposition, creatively in a way that would appeal to the core 16-24-year-old market. At the same time, the execution should avoid falling into the generic advertising trap, employed by other brands seeking to appeal to these elusive consumers.

Easier said than done!

DDB determined to hit the problem head on. The Wrangler proposition was based on the premise "Wrangler – We make more than just blue jeans." The storyboard outlined the basic premise but was light on detail as to how the creative differentiation would be achieved. Peter Pleasance explained that the execution would avoid all the usual clichés. It would feature real people enjoying life as real people do. The Wrangler product would be the star and an element of humour would be injected as a key part of the execution.

He didn't quite say "trust us," but he came very close!

I came to admire Peter as a superb salesman of an idea. DDB had employed the best production company, the best talent, and the best director.

Could anything possibly go wrong!

This was only my second involvement in TV commercial production and my first as 'the main client.' It is probably true to say that I was a little naïve and for the first and only time, allowed myself to be entirely led by the experts in whom I had placed complete trust.

On the face of it, there was nothing wrong with completed commercial. The product looked good. The Wrangler branding was clearly visible. The background music had a good beat. Fast cutting allowed a lot of Wrangler products to be included. The Wrangler logo and payoff line was highly visible at the end.

Unfortunately, my abiding image was of an overweight 40 something, wearing a tight-fitting Wrangler sweatshirt over a very large beer belly. Fine while he held his belly in, but the director had instructed him to let it go. The belly acquired a life of its own.

Amusing, I suppose, but not really the abiding image I was expecting!

Anyway, the commercial was aired. in the cinema and on television. Nobody was critical but, at the same time, it did not receive critical acclaim.

It did a job, but it had not set the world on fire!

The post advertising research was a little disappointing. Although brand awareness and brand perception of Wrangler had increased, top of mind awareness of the advertising content was relatively low. Clearly there was still some work to be done!

Whilst the Wrangler advertising might not have excited our target consumers, it had caused a frenzy amongst business development directors in rival advertising agencies to DDB. Apparently, Wrangler was looking around for a new advertising agency.

It was news to me!

We had decided to follow our jeans and jeans related clothing advertisement with a short television campaign in support of Wrangler Boots. A commercial had been made for the Blue Bell subsidiary in Scandinavia.

Briefly the plot was as follows, "Three horsemen are riding down a street typical of the set of any American cowboy movie. All that is visible of them are their jeans clad legs and Wrangler cowboy boots. They draw up outside the corral and two of the horseman dismount and tie up their steeds. The two dismounted riders then smack the rump of the third horse causing it to take off down the street leaving the third rider suspended in mid-air with his boots clearly displayed. A dog barks and the 'hanging rider' rubs one boot behind the other."

The laconic voice of Lee Hazelwood provided the narrative.

The commercial script was presented to the Advertising Standards Authority who gave it full clearance to be aired across the UK.

DDB made some slight changes to end the frame replacing the original Swedish with English titles spending around £3500 on this, and the production of copies for the TV companies with whom space had been booked.

When the final version was presented to the ASA it was banned for being "too violent." Apparently, they considered a mock hanging unsuitable for the British television screens.

I protested to DDB. "It is clear to anyone watching, that the so-called hanging scene is a joke," I argued. "We should appeal the decision, and if the ASA still uphold it, we should bill them for the production cost incurred," I continued.

I never knew whether negotiations ever got that far, but the ASA partly relented, "providing the advertisement is aired after 10pm."

Our PR people used the ban, and part ban stories, to ensure that the commercial was far more visible than it might otherwise have been.

I had decided to continue to work with DDB on the creative direction for 1977. The Wrangler team liked the people, and they liked us. We were working with the 'A Team' of one of the best advertising agencies in the world. They understood our brand objectives and we agreed that they were right for moving the brand forward in a positive way.

The DDB creative team came up with an interesting concept that they were keen to explore. This involved two American football teams playing a game in a large stadium in front of a big crowd.

One team, the Wrangler Team, would be dressed in denim jeans and, above the waist, with the normal American Football attire. Their tops and helmets were planned to be heavily Wrangler branded using the distinctive logo and blue and yellow brand colours. The other team would be conventionally dressed.

During the game, the rival team would suffer extensive damage to their kit whilst the Wrangler Team would retain their pristine look and totally dominate their opponents.'

Peter Pleasance was in full super sell mode. "Just think of the impact that this advertisement will make," he enthused. "It will reinforce the Wrangler American pedigree without the cowboy connotations," he continued. "We will be able to demonstrate the quality of the Wrangler branded product but in a totally different way." Finishing with a flourish, he boomed "It will totally blow away the competition!"

Neither Dick Webzell nor I was impressed. An awkward silence reigned.

Finally, I broke the deadlock. "I can understand where you are coming from," I proffered, "We are not entirely convinced that you will be able to pull off such a big production within the budget we have available. For the commercial to work, we will need access to a stadium, a large crowd and two teams of players and all the specialised kit personalised for the Wrangler Team," I suggested.

"We thought you might say that." Peter responded. "We have a plan. Our creative directors and production people will go out to the USA and source everything. We are convinced we can pull it off."

"How much will all that cost?" I asked.

"Only £10,000," replied Peter.

"Only £10,000!" Dick and I chorused with incredulity. At that time £10,000 was an awful lot of money to commit on an idea that we were not 100% sold on and which the agency might not be able to deliver.

Today it is relatively easy, with digital technology, to deliver the effects that DDB would have to reproduce to give the advertisement the authenticity required. In 1976, digital technology was not an option that was available.

I was honest with Peter. I told him that we had been approached by other agencies and would probably have to talk to one or two in case we were unable to proceed with DDB's recommendations.

We agreed to go along with the agencies suggestion to move forward with the recce.

"What happens about the £10,000 if you find you are unable to deliver?" I queried.

"You have my word that DDB will take the hit in those circumstances," Peter assured us.

Five weeks or so later we returned to DDB and were ushered into the board room for the big presentation.

The walls were surrounded by big blow-ups of the proposed stadium in Los Angeles. Bright blue helmets and American football shirts branded with the Wrangler logo were arranged on a table. Things certainly looked promising.

Peter started his presentation. He enthusiastically explained how it had been difficult to source a venue because the American Football season was almost over but there was a match taking place in Los Angeles within an appropriate time frame.

During the scheduled breaks in the game, the ground, the players, and the crowd shots for the commercial would take place. The close-up contact shots would then be organised in a more controlled environment.

"There are just one or two problems," Peter advised. "The match is a college final in the Watts district of Los Angeles. Our presence might not be welcomed, and it may prove impossible to organise the required insurance."

To this day, I am still not certain whether this was the real reason why DDB backed off. It could have been a face-saving excuse for their inability to deliver the promise of the idea they had created.

But clearly, we had come to the parting of the ways and needed to move on.

Chapter Six

Wasey Campbell Ewald – 1977 to 1979

One of the advertising agencies who had contacted me at the end of 1976 was Wasey Campbell Ewald.

When I began to feel uneasy about the direction that the DDB creative work was going, I contacted them to arrange an exploratory meeting.

At the time, Wasey's was the number two UK agency in the American owned Interpublic Group. Its senior management team comprised the formidable triumvirate of Colin Goodson, Chairman, Hugh Burkitt, Managing Director and Len Weinreich, Vice Chairman and Executive Creative Director.

We had briefly talked a few months before. It was clear to me then, that they understood our market and were keen to work with us. The only potential problem was that the number one Interpublic agency in London at that time was McCann Ericson. They handled the Levi's account. "Not a problem," Colin Goodson had assured me. "We are in direct competition with them and are keen to show the world that we can be produce much more creative and effective advertising for our clients."

Dick Webzell came with me to the initial meeting. The collapse of our creative talks with DDB meant that time was not on our side. We either had to go back to the drawing board with DDB or find a new partner.

We were not expecting a creative presentation from Wasey's but that is exactly what we got!

In the Wasey's boardroom we met the whole management team. Reiterating my conversations with them a few months earlier, they told us that they understood where we were in the market, knew where we wanted to be but, more importantly, were confident they knew what needed to be done to get us there.

Len Weinreich stepped up and pointed to the Wrangler logo projected onto a screen. "The core objective of our advertising concept will be to make the Wrangler brand famous and to make the products to which it is applied synonymous with the very best in quality and fashionability."

He had already gained our full attention!

"To achieve this, we have come up with an idea that will not only break the mould of advertising in the jeans sector, but it will also capture the imagination of 16-24-year-olds. Furthermore, it will do it in a way that will not alienate the rest of the potential market," he continued.

I waited for a storyboard to emerge that would reveal the BIG idea. It was not forthcoming!

Instead, with a flourish, Len produced a script and proceeded to describe each of the main characters in the proposed commercial. He then acted out the lines he had written for each of them.

The main one was a parody of the archetypal American adman complete with bow tie and 'stand out', tasteless jacket and slacks. He was pitching the "big idea" to his client, a shadowy figure, Mr. Wrangler, who was seated behind a big desk. The story went something like this, "Mr. Wrangler," says the adman, "we want to tell the world about your products." He motions to his two acolytes who leap onto the boardroom table and break into an excruciating song and dance routine whilst moving towards Mr. Wrangler.

Mr. Wrangler puts his head in his hands and before responding quizzically, "Rickenbacker, why don't you just say I make great clothes?"

Rickenbacker displays his disappointment, but only for a few seconds. His face then breaks into a smile before he responds. "Great idea!" He then turns to his secretary and commands, "Get that down."

The Wrangler logo that Len had projected on the front of the screen was now replaced with a logo and slogan that read, "Wrangler, (logo) the very best - because Mr. Wrangler says so!"

I should admit, at this stage, that there was no thunderous applause from either of us. Having said that, when Len had finished the script, I think we both realised that the idea "had legs."

Mr. Wrangler came across as someone who believed in his product and wanted to promote it in a believable way. He had put Rickenbacker down, when the bad idea had been presented to him, but did so in a kindly and patient way. Mr. Wrangler was the good guy. Rickenbacker would become the comical foil who would make him, and the claims he made about his products, believable to everyone who saw the commercials.

We were sold by the concept and agreed that Wasey's should work up the idea to the next stage.

Clearly, we had our new campaign we would now have to tell DDB that we had a new agency. Dick Webzell and I carried out that task before the move to Wasey's was confirmed.

A lunch appointment was arranged with Peter Pleasance. Over a nice meal and a glass or two of wine we explained our decision.

Peter was not at all surprised. Not only was he aware that we were moving the account to Wasey's, but he also knew the outline of the Mr. Wrangler campaign.

It was difficult to keep a secret in the close-knit London advertising scene!

When DDB had been appointed, we had opened a trade account for them so that all the agency staff could place monthly orders for Wrangler products at wholesale prices. Peter asked if the facility would still be available. We were happy to confirm that it would.

Our parting of the ways was very amicable.

Just as we were about to leave the restaurant, Peter pulled an envelope from his jacket pocket. "The only matter to resolve is the cost of the exploratory trip to the States that we agreed upon. I have the invoice here," he explained, waving the envelope theatrically in the air and pulling out an invoice for £10,000. "We were unable to deliver our part of the bargain," Peter continued. "So, there is only one course of action that we can take about the outstanding amount."

He then proceeded to tear the invoice into small pieces dropping them into the ashtray on the table. Having done this, he then set fire to the contents.

The embers of that flame signalled to start of a new era for the Wrangler brand!

The success and longevity of the "Mr. Wrangler" campaign idea would rest on the shoulders of the two main characters. Casting them correctly was the key to everything. Wasey's had decided it was important that each of the key characters in the commercials should be from North America and not British actors talking with an American accent.

Len Weinreich and his creative team comprising Nick Shackleton, Barry Daborn and Martin Hodges, had narrowed the shortlist down to four. Each of them would be competing for the two main parts.

The final choice was inspired!

Matt Zimmerman was handed the role of "Rickenbacker." He was born in Canada and educated in Detroit. He had come to the UK in 1959 to study drama at the London Academy of Music and Dramatic Arts. At the time he was cast, he had performed in films and on the stage but was best known for voicing Alan Tracy in Thunderbirds.

Don Fellows, who was cast as "Mr. Wrangler," was born in Salt Lake City and raised in Madison, Wisconsin. He served in the United States Merchant Marines during World War Two and was a graduate of the University of Wisconsin and a member of the Actors Studio. After appearing on the stage and in films in the USA, he moved to London in 1973 to further his stage career.

Their partnership, in the production of a series of Wrangler television commercials, was to last for 3 years.

Encouraged by the advertising agency, we had tied both key characters into long term, fixed fee contracts to last for four years. This was a big risk on our part. It would prove costly if the campaign was not successful!

The "Mr. Wrangler" advertising concept, developed by Wasey's, was transferable to a whole range of other media. Like any good idea, it worked equally well on posters, on radio and at the point of purchase.

In year one, the agency developed five television commercials. From memory these were shot by Peter Webb and produced by Jackie Bateman. Alongside these, the creative team produced several four sheet poster concepts for use in bus shelters. In conjunction with the agencies Sales Promotion Director, Tim Arnold, a range of point-of-sale material was produced to merchandise the advertising in retail outlets.

As well as posters and stickers the agency developed several badges carrying messages such as, "Bigger Rickenbacker," "Mr. Wrangler said to wear this," "Mr. Wrangler likes Me" and "Good Grief, Rckenbacker." These were introduced as in store give-aways.

The latter slogan was used in the first batch of commercials to express the frustration felt by Mr. Wrangler when Rickenbacker was presenting some of his most extreme ideas.

Before long the badges were being swapped by young people attempting to collect the whole set.

The expression, "Good Grief Rickenbacker," was adopted as a put down in the classroom and in the workplace.

Whilst I was doing some recent research, I typed into the search engine on my computer the words "Good Grief Rickenbacker." To my astonishment it brought up a discussion that had taken place in 2008 on a Questions and Answers site. It was responding to the question "Good Grief Rickenbacker, what does it refer to? And why do we say it?"

One person thought it might have some connection with the American World War 1 flying ace Eddie Rickenbacker. Someone else thought it might be something to do with the Rickenbacker guitar that rock icons such as John Lennon used.

A respondent remembered the phrase from a film something like, but not necessarily, Police Academy. They went on to say that phrase was said in response to a subordinate, Rickenbacker, saying something really stupid (sic) and the superior rolling his eyes and saying the words "Good Grief Rickenbacker." (The Mr. Wrangler/Rickenbacker scenario)

Another correctly identified it as an expression used in a television advertisement for a jeans brand in the 1970's. For Wrangler jeans, they thought.

Too many years had expired, since the last thread in the discussion, for me to respond and explain the why's and wherefore's. The truth is often stranger than the fiction.

The phrase "Good Grief" was in relatively common usage in the UK at the time. It was regarded as a mild expletive that would not offend anyone who heard it. Certainly, its appearance in the Mr. Wrangler commercials had nothing to do with the Snoopy dog cartoons as some people thought at the time.

Similarly, when deciding a name for the hapless advertising executive, neither Eddie Rickenbacker nor the Rickenbacker guitar figured as the inspiration. After all, both were icons of success, not failure!

In fact, a short list of names was drawn up.

I was led to believe that the name "Spielvogel" was also a contender. It was allegedly withdrawn when the creatives at Wasey's realised that a Carl Spielvogel was on the executive committee and board of directors of their parent company, the Interpublic Group.

This sounds like a good story but unlikely to be true!

The reality was far more mundane. Rickenbacker had more of a ring to it than any of the other contenders on the list. When Matt Zimmerman was selected for the role, it seemed to fit his persona perfectly.

The phrase "Good Grief Rickenbacker" caught the imagination of the public and became something of a catchphrase for the whole Wrangler campaign.

The main message of the advertising was extended by the success of the Blue Bell team of Field Promotion Representatives. They did a fantastic job of merchandising the advertising message at the point of sale. The FPR's were also able to extend the scope of their own job function by organising, in conjunction with key retailers, "Mr.

Wrangler and Rickenbacker" promotion evenings in nightclubs around the country. During these events they handed out promotional tee-shirts and badges.

Because of the campaign, sales of Wrangler products rose dramatically with the Blue Bell Apparel sales force able to sell in more stock on the back of our promised advertising and promotional activity.

Advertising awareness research during the campaign showed how successfully Wasey's had been in targeting the core consumers.

The campaign had a polarising effect. Older people, used to a more generic style of jeans advertising, were either unsure or downright hostile towards what they had seen. However, the key target market really loved the new approach. Their awareness and perception of the Wrangler advertising and products improved. The Wrangler market share grew!

Some key retailers seemed to like the results of the advertising but needed reassurance about the content. The operatives in the Wrangler jeans factory in Falkirk had brought up the question of the advertising in several of their internal staff meetings. They sought assurances that it was positioning 'THEIR' product in a positive light.

After conversations with the agency, it was decided that we would face the criticisms head on.

A Mr. Wrangler and Rickenbacker cartoon style trade advertisement was produced. In tongue in cheek style, it showed a retailer with a cartoon bubble with the words "I hate it, I hate it…" and another of a young customer whose bubble contained the words "I love it, I love it."

The advertisement also contained a graphic showing the post advertising survey results. This illustrated just how successful the campaign had proved to be.

Retailers were urged to cash in on its success by buying in more products for the next sell in season.

I made a trip to Falkirk to present the initial five commercials to the assembled 800 strong workforce at the Wrangler factory. They were shown how the results of the advertising had been measured and how positively it had been received by the jeans buying public.

Its success would require all the employees in the factory to produce even more of their top-quality products in the future. They seemed to appreciate the gesture and the fact that they had now been given ammunition to counter any adverse comments they might receive from their own circle of friends.

The success of the campaign became apparent when the Blue Bell salesforce began to encourage retailers to refer to them as "Mr. Wrangler," and began to use the credibility of the character in the commercial as part of their sell-in technique.

The campaign was now referred to "our advertising" whereas when the commercials were first aired it was referred to as "Robin Dilley's advertising".

I am positive, that in the early days of the campaign, I was being called "Rickenbacker" behind my back. A lot of my colleagues associated the bumbling adman in the commercials with me, because I was the person who had agreed that the commercials should be made and shown in the first place.

I was quick to point out that I was really "Mr. Wrangler" and that the advertising was "the very best because Mr. Wrangler (me) said it would be." And so, thankfully, it proved to be!

Certainly, I had been careful to ensure that the first five commercials were heavily branded. In my experience creatives, within some advertising agencies, believed the clients brand got in the way of the presentation of their creative ideas.

Not so with Len Weinreich and the Wrangler account team led by Philip Batchelor!

They used my insistence, that the Wrangler logo at the end of the commercials should be as big as possible, as a sort of insider's joke. For the last three commercials of the first series, the end of each commercial was changed slightly. The Wrangler logo and the line "the very best - because Mr. Wrangler says so!" appeared on the screen, as before. Mr. Wrangler's voice was then heard saying the words, "Bigger Rickenbacker" and the logo size was increased in size to fill the screen. This piece of humour, at my expense, reinforced the advertising message.

Our Public Relations agency was quick to use the success of the advertising to increase the Wrangler presence in the trade and fashion media.

In the 1970's, fashion PRs believed that fashion editors were reluctant to travel further than South Moulton Street, in London, to look at a fashion range, particularly a range produced by a jeans company! It appeared to be universally accepted, if you wanted your product to be seen, you had to take the ranges to them, leave the products they selected in their offices and accept that you might never see them again.

Even then, there was no guarantee that they would be featured in the magazine or newspaper!

Using the authority that the Mr. Wrangler advertising had imbued in the Wrangler brand, and the interest that it this created in the Wrangler product ranges, editors and their assistants were making requests to come to our showroom and see for themselves what all the fuss was about.

In addition, the agency set up interviews for "Rickenbacker" (Matt Zimmerman) to appear on radio shows and TV programmes such as Crackerjack.

As promised at the original presentation, the Wrangler advertising, the Wrangler brand and, more importantly, the Wrangler product was becoming "famous."

In year two of the campaign Wasey's produced another four commercials using the successful "Rickenbacker" and "Mr. Wrangler" format.

Matt Zimmerman had been cast in the musical "Annie" which had been launched at the Victoria Theatre in London in 1978. He played the part of Bert Healey, a DJ, whose persona was not a million miles from that of "Rickenbacker." In the programme for the show, reference was made to the many stage, films, and television shows that Matt had appeared in. My attention was drawn to the final paragraph which indicated that he was "well known as Rickenbacker in the TV commercials for Wrangler Jeans."

In an interview years later, Matt refers to this time and is quoted as saying, "….as a result of that campaign, Wrangler had a wonderful success. So, did I. It paid for my first house."

We had already held discussions with Wasey's about how the "Mr. Wrangler" campaign might be extended into other media. Radio was the obvious contender. In the late 1970's, the medium was in its infancy in the UK but had been adopted by our core 16-24 year old customers. It enabled creative executions that were impossible to achieve through the visual media.

We all felt that the "Mr. Wrangler" and "Rickenbacker" characters were sufficiently well established for us to indulge our creative fantasies. The agency had come up with several ideas and two had been produced.

The first involved the quality of Wrangler zips.

The commercial opened to the noise of traffic and Rickenbacker opens with words something like this, "Mr. Wrangler, we have clothed the Empire State building in denim and, to demonstrate the strength and quality of your jeans, we have engineered a giant zip on the end of which we have attached a 40-ton weight. At my command, the weight will be released. The zip will open as the weight plummets towards the ground."

He shouts out the command, "Release the weight." On the soundtrack can be heard the noise of the giant zip opening.

Cut to Mr. Wrangler, "Rickenbacker, isn't that your automobile over there?"

Cut back to Rickenbacker, "Stop the weight." The soundtrack is filled with the sound of Rickenbacker's car being crushed by the weight followed by the adman sobbing.

An exasperated Mr. Wrangler utters the words, "Good Grief Rickenbacker!"

This is followed by the words "Wrangler, the very best - because Mr. Wrangler says so."

In a similar vein, Rickenbacker tells Mr. Wrangler that he has brought him to see his name carved out of the Rockies in letters many metres tall. The adman asks for the helicopters, hovering overhead, to lift off the coverings a reveal his masterpiece. There is a slight pause before Mr. Wrangler speaks, "Rickenbacker, there is only one 'n' in Wrangler."

During this time, I was approached by the producers of the film "Grease" who invited me to attend a special preview showing of the movie. They wanted to solicit some form of Wrangler involvement as a sponsor.

Clearly, both the film and its soundtrack offered endless possibilities for association with the brand. I signed a deal that allowed us to utilise the "Grease" logo on specially produced point of sale material. Also included in the package, we secured limited use of some of the key songs on the backing track that would eventually form the basis of the best-selling album.

To tie in with the film, we added a couple of further radio commercials. In one, Mr. Wrangler meets Rickenbacker. Rickenbacker explains that he has brought him to Athens to celebrate his connection with Greece. "Rickenbacker, it's not Greece the country, it's Grease the movie," exclaims Mr. Wrangler.

The radio campaign ran in the autumn of 1978. It proved very popular, and tapes were produced containing some of songs from the movie "Grease" interspersed with the Wrangler radio commercials. These became much sought after promotional giveaways.

The "Empire State Zip" and the "Wrangler in the Rockies" concepts were developed as posters to be used in retail stores. In this way, we merchandised the radio campaign successfully at the point of sale.

Advertising awareness research, carried out at the end of 1978, indicated that top of mind awareness, of the whole Mr. Wrangler TV and radio campaigns and its content, was very high. Both Wasey's and I were amazed when the research also revealed that many of the respondents believed that they had seen the "Zip" and "Rockies" radio advertisements on television.

I was even more pleased when an article in Campaign, the major trade magazine for the advertising industry, appeared on 8 December 1978. Under the headline, "Why Jeans Manufacturers are enjoying record sales," it was revealed that the market share for Levi's was now 14%, followed by Wrangler 12% and Brutus 7%. These figures slightly underestimated the Wrangler market share, according to our own figures, but did confirm that Wrangler was fast closing the gap on the market leader.

Our marketing was clearly working!

The sell in for the 1979 spring ranges had taken place in September 1978. Blue Bell achieved record sales for both the Wrangler jeans and jeans related tops ranges. As a reward for their efforts, Dick Webzell had announced that, subject to similar results from the autumn trade shows, the 1979 sales conference would be held offshore for the first time.

It was with some optimism that I planned for the International Men's and Boy's wear Exhibition to be held at Olympia, in London, on the 18-22 February 1978. Prior to the show we had previewed the ranges to key retailers in London, Manchester, and Glasgow. Feedback and orders placed at all three venues were extremely encouraging.

Our stand had been designed to accommodate every member of the Blue Bell salesforce each with their own clearly defined selling area. At the entrance to the stand was a large sign welcoming all potential buyers with the words "Mr Wrangler said to give you a big welcome."

Highlights of the first morning included a visit from Jilly Johnson, a famous glamour model of the day. She arrived wearing one of our "Wrangler Wralph" dog costumes. It was not revealed that she was inside it until a crowd of photographers gathered for a pre-arranged photoshoot. Whilst they were very interested in a visit to our exhibition stand by a former page three girl, our retail customers seemed more interested in another, far more flamboyant character who 'bounced' on to the stand when Jilly had left.

Matt Zimmerman or should I say "Rickenbacker" had arrived!

Forgotten were the early criticism of the "Mr. Wrangler" commercials. At the end of two years, the campaign had captured the imagination of trade and consumers alike. Everyone wanted to talk to him, have their photographs taken with him and have him provide an autograph either as himself, or as the "Rickenbacker" character he played in the commercials.

Matt and I explained what "Rickenbacker" would be up to in the next campaign that would be starting soon. The interest that this generated enabled our salesforce to secure extra orders.

When I took him for a tour round the exhibition the reaction was the same. People on the stands of our major competitors were coming over to shake his hand. Visitors to the exhibition were requesting his autograph. Even the customers and staff on the Levi's stand were pointing and calling out his name. Despite my trying to dissuade him, he leapt onto the stand of our major competitor to bathe in the adulation.

Thankfully, the Levi's management saw the funny side of the incident!

The first day of the exhibition was when the large independent retailers came to look before they bought. It was also the day that 'A-list' celebrities came to see the latest ranges and extoll the virtues of manufacturers whose products they were being paid to endorse.

And yet, these brand ambassadors were all been overshadowed by a character from a Wrangler television commercial!

I should have been very happy that the gamble we had taken two years before appeared to be providing payback in such a spectacular fashion. Yes, I was basking in my own moment of glory, but the seeds of doubt were beginning to be sown in my mind.

The "Mr. Wrangler" campaign was launched as a sort of anti-establishment response to the generic advertising that had been a feature of advertising for jeans in the early to middle 1970's. It was aimed at a specific target market, 16-24-year-olds, who appreciated its humour and understood and bought into its message. The fact that their parents did not fully comprehend the advertising was a positive reinforcement that Wrangler was the brand to buy, because "Mr. Wrangler" understood their needs and knew what made them tick.

Looking back now, that Sunday afternoon in September 1978 probably marked the beginning of the end for "Rickenbacker" and the advertising he had helped to make famous.

Wasey's produced another four commercials featuring "Mr. Wrangler" and "Rickenbacker." These ran during the late Spring and Summer of 1979 but, increasingly, I had the feeling that the creative momentum was being lost and that, as a result, the campaign was losing its appeal amongst the key target market.

Commercials originally aimed at, and loved by 16-24-year-olds, had been derided by older consumers. After three years, the detractors had now got the message. The Mr Wrangler/Rickenbacker scenario was being widely quoted in the 'serious' media.

In the 28 June 1979 edition of the Guardian, an article written by Jane McLoughlin (now an author of several novels) appeared under the headline "The Wrangler way of life."

This was not a fashion or marketing piece but a serious business interview featuring Edwin Morris, Chairman of Blue Bell Inc. who was in Europe visiting new manufacturing plants in Ireland and Spain.

The writer introduces him not as the leader of a company with a turnover $872,036,000 but as the fictious benevolent, shadowy character in the Wasey's advertising commercials.

"Mr Wrangler is really the sort of grandfatherly gentleman whose kindly creased smile invites a flood of letters from wives and mothers sharing little confidences about their washing problems, how little Johnnie is growing so fast, and how worrying their husbands' weight problems ae becoming," Jane writes in the opening paragraph. "And Mr Wrangler listens to them, one and all – and applies what he learns from them to his expertise in making jeans."

The article continues in this vein, "He (Mr Morris) is in Britain under an alias, of course – though his staff admit they always think of him as Mr Wrangler, so he is not really in disguise."

The references to the advertising campaign continue. "So it was the nice Mr Morris who allowed Rickenbacker his say at the interview; even encouraged him from time to time with "don't you think so, Dick? Most of the time, when Mr Morris is on the other side of the Atlantic in Greensboro, North Carolina, Rickenbacker becomes a sleek top executive in his own right – Dick Webzell, UK managing director, no less –

but when Mr Wrangler is over here, Mr Webzell admits he thinks of himself in the Rickenbacker role."

The extensive article was excellent, and reference was made, towards the end, to the dangers of the product moving from cult fashion to a commodity item and contains an early assertion, much repeated by fashion journalists.

As Jane McLoughlin puts it, "Jeans have destroyed the concept of class, low or high, poor or rich, everyone wears jeans after all. But doesn't that hold a hidden threat to the future. Surely sometime, some place, a reaction may swell and the denim dream will be over."

Mr Wrangler (Edwin Morris) seeks to reassure her that the scenario is some time in the future. The Wrangler brand, he explains, has many exciting plans for growth and the article concludes on a positive note.

"Now there are 90 manufacturing plants in America, and eight countries throughout the world. The pioneering spirit of marketing is extending the empire on which the sun of success will not soon set. That's for certain: Mr Wrangler says so."

Another factor was also coming into play as the Blue Bell product development team began the process of producing their new ranges for Spring 1980.

Jeans had, up till then, been garments that were fashionable because of their unique position as a badge of the rebellious. The product appealed to the teenagers of the 50's because they had started a trend. At the end of the 70's, jeans were also a 'must have' casual accessory of their children.

The product had its own life cycle. Each year a new pair was bought in their raw dark denim state and used as a best pair. With frequent washing, the indigo dye bled out to produce a lighter pair for less formal occasions.

Nearly every jeans wearer had a pair that was close to the end of the cycle. The bottoms were frayed, the colour had faded and there were holes in the knees. This favourite pair was worn about the house but never outside. When they were finally consigned to the 'jeans graveyard,' a new pair was bought, and the other existing jeans moved down the fashion pecking order.

All this was about to change!

How to care for a pair of jeans was one of the key messages that Wrangler had used to enable customers to get the best out of the product.

Tips included:

Do Not Bleach.

Always wash inside out for even colour loss.

Do not use in proximity to acid i.e., Car batteries.

The merchandising team were about to launch a new concept – stonewashed Jeans.

The process involved rigorous washing using pumice stone, water, and bleach to create a worn, washed out look not dissimilar to a pair of jeans at the end of their lifecycle.

Whilst wear tests had shown that this new look was well received by the fashion innovators, its introduction presented a risk for a quality brand like Wrangler, and a potential erosion of some of the brand values that we had fought so hard to build.

The jeans market was entering a new phase where fashion styling was to become a key factor of product and brand development. A lot of Wrangler customers had old 'bleached out' jeans in their wardrobes that now had the 'right look' in the marketplace.

The Blue Bell team had anticipated that this might happen and had consigned the 70's flare jeans to the fashion wilderness and replaced them with new, straight leg styles.

To be at the cutting edge of jeans fashion, a new wardrobe had to be bought!

Up to this moment, Blue Bell had employed strict quality controls on the colour and tensile strength of the denim fabric that the company sourced. Any colour or quality variation in a cloth length meant that jeans made from that fabric could only be sold as seconds.

We had heard stories that some larger retailers were already buying up large quantities of Wrangler seconds and stonewashing these themselves to sell at a premium.

Our quality control people carried out their own tests and found garments previously classified as seconds could, when stonewashed, meet all the Blue Bell quality criteria. Additional tests were carried out with our designated laundries to ensure that all Wrangler branded, stonewashed garments provided a consistent quality of output that fell within the strict tolerances our engineers and merchandise teams had laid down.

We could rightly claim that Wrangler stonewashed jeans "were the very best – because Mr. Wrangler said so.".

I had long conversations with Wasey's about the direction that the Wrangler advertising should take in 1980. It was our belief that the "Mr. Wrangler" advertising campaign had successfully achieved its objectives and that, like the Wrangler product, it was time for a change of direction.

In an article published in September 1982 in Midlands Magazine, I was quoted as saying, "In the menswear trade you develop a gut sense about what the consumer is going to want in six months' time. It's the same way with the advertising; you develop a similar gut feeling that it's time to move on."

This gut feeling was not shared by account team at Wasey's. They still felt that the campaign still had 'legs.'

Suddenly, I was receiving calls again from business development directors of rival agencies telling me that "they had heard that we were looking around and could their agency be considered for a pitch?"

Then it was the turn of the advertising and marketing trade press who wanted me to comment on stories "that Wasey's were in danger of losing the Wrangler account." No matter how much I refuted the rumours, they continued apace and the relationship with Wasey's became strained.

We had enjoyed an excellent creative period with the agency. Their advertising output had played a pivotal role in moving the Wrangler brand forward. Only weeks before, independent research data showed that we had overtaken Levi's and we were now number one jeans brand in the UK and Ireland.

Having said that, we could not agree on a creative strategy to move the brand into a new decade and increasingly changing market conditions.

Decisive action needed to be taken!

At this stage, I concluded that the only positive way forward was to do what the industry in general was telling me I was already doing, to talk to one or two other agencies. Because of the strength of our relationship, Wasey's were made aware of our intentions. A shortlist of three, including Wasey's, was drawn up.

During the process, I recalled a series of conversations I had in 1976 with an agency called Collett Dickenson Pearce (CDP). They were putting together a poster campaign for their client Pretty Polly. One of their creative teams had come up with an idea featuring a wonderful pair of legs adorned in Pretty Polly tights. The headline ran: - "When was the last time a man said you had a great pair of jeans."

Their proposition was that, with our permission, they would change the end of the headline to read "……. a great pair of Wrangler jeans."

They had argued that such a change would be advantageous to both brands and would give Wrangler even greater national exposure.

This was a view that I did not share. The poster ran with the original headline. It is now regarded as one of the all-time great outdoor advertisements.

I suspected at the time that the contact had been made with a view to getting me into CDP to discuss the Wrangler account and that the Pretty Polly proposed headline change was simply a way of making the initial contact.

CDP were THE creative 'hot shop' of the 60's and 70's. Although their star was said to be waning, they still had some of best creative minds in the advertising world on their books.

I called my original contact and made an appointment to go in and talk to them.

Over the following months, it was determined that two of the agencies on the short list would be asked to pitch.

The first agency, not named here to spare their blushes, had gone to great expense of hiring the actress, Sandra Dickinson, to play out the scenario of the commercial they felt would help the Wrangler brand move forward.

At that time, American born Sandra was well known for her portrayals of dumb blondes with her unique high-pitched voice. In the proposed commercial, she played "Rickenbacker's" secretary in a spin-off of the "Mr. Wrangler" commercials.

The agency in question had fallen at the first hurdle!

Dick Webzell and I expected that CDP would pull out all the creative stops to secure the Wrangler account. We were somewhat surprised when John Hewson, the Media Director stepped forward to lead their presentation.

John explained that superb creative work would be completely worthless if the core market did not see it. He went on to say that the agency had concentrated their efforts to ensure they had the means of reaching the 16-34-years old key consumers through targeted media buying.

"For years we have been told that trying to reach such a precise market is impossible," he explained. "We have worked with the television companies and are convinced that we have found a formula that will enable us to buy into this market effectively, within the advertising budget that we think you will make available to us," John continued. "Your competitors will not be using the same creative, targeted approach to media buying and we are convinced that our advertising, when we have developed it, will be more visible and more effective than theirs."

I was left with a stark choice. We could either continue the existing "Mr. Wrangler" advertising concept with Wasey's, change agencies and buy into the alternative "Mr. Wrangler" scenario or move to CDP based on a more precisely targeted and cost-effective media buying approach, with the promise of a memorable advertising concept to follow.

In the end, I recommended that we take the riskier "something new" approach being offered by CDP. To his credit Dick Webzell accepted my recommendation and we reluctantly advised Wasey's that we would be leaving for pastures new.

As I explained, in a press interview in 1982, "I've worked on both sides of the advertising fence and I know that a successful agency is not simply a reputation – it's a group of people that you can sit down with in the certainty that they have faith in your product and an appreciation of your objectives. We had that in our time at Wasey's and my gut feel was telling me that we would be able to develop a similar relationship at CDP."

We parted with Wasey's on excellent terms.

The "Mr. Wrangler" campaign they developed "to make Wrangler famous" did not win any advertising awards. Despite that, I believe it was perhaps the most successful advertising ever produced in the jeans sector, at every objective level.

Chapter Seven

Collett Dickinson Pearce 1980-1986

At Wasey's, we had established a significantly improved level of positive brand awareness and become brand leader.

What we were asking CDP to do was to project a stronger brand image in which our core consumers could identify with their peer group – "young people in their own environment wearing Wrangler jeans and jeans related products."

Collett Dickinson Pearce had won the Wrangler account because of their media pitch and on the understanding that the agency, widely recognised as the most creative in London, would have no problem coming up with a great advertising idea.

After a few weeks, I got the feeling that the creative challenge was proving more difficult than they had anticipated. Whilst the creatives vanished into their 'darkened rooms' to seek inspiration for the creative content, I worked with the account team, led by Ian Schooler along with John Hewson, the Media Director of the agency, to agree the campaign objectives and budget.

Once the objectives were clearly laid down and understood, the first query from John Hewson was "how much have you got to spend?"

This was a question that I had been frequently asked before by agency media executives.

My response to John was, "You know what the campaign objectives are. You have a pretty good idea what the Wrangler spend with Wasey's was. You tell me what you feel we need to spend to meet the objectives for our new campaign." I assured him that if his media proposal came in above our budget, we would tell him. If it came in below, we would be very happy.

He got the picture!

A short time before, I had asked the media director of another large advertising agency how many times he had told a client that the budget that was being proposed, was more than required to achieve their objectives. "Never," was his honest reply.

The board of CDP were taking a close interest in how the campaign was progressing. Geoff Howard-Spink had assumed the role of "Alternative Account Director" for the Wrangler project. Chairman John Salmon and Managing Director John Spearman were keeping the pressure on the creatives and media planners to deliver the goods.

John Spearman was keen to show that he was a firm advocate for the Wrangler product. Always immaculately presented in expensive suits, shirts, and ties, he had taken to wearing a pair of Wrangler jeans, with immaculate creases, below the waist, whilst retaining his formal appearance above it.

Just as I was beginning to get a little nervous about the length of time that was being taken, I received a call from Ian Schoolar. He informed me that the creatives believed that they had come up with the big idea and that he would appreciate if I could call into the agency so that they could run it past me.

At the meeting, the idea for the new commercial was explained. Basically, the commercial concept, "Diary of a pair of Jeans," told the story of a week in the life of a pair of Wrangler jeans that are bought and worn by a typical laddish member of the target audience.

"Monday, the jeans are sitting on the shelf of the store. Tuesday, they are tried on by a young man who buys them on the spot. Wednesday, he wears them whilst playing football with his friends. Thursday, walking past the stage door of a nearby theatre, he is mistaken for a rock star by a group of teenage girls. Friday, he starts dating a girl he has just met. Saturday, he takes her for a ride in his car. Sunday, they are refused entry into an upmarket restaurant who have a no jeans policy. Unabashed they go off together to find somewhere else to eat."

The pay-off-line was "Wrangler, your real two-legged friend."

The CDP creative team of John Kelley and John O'Driscoll explained the story would be told using a soundtrack reminiscent of the delivery used by "Ian Drury and the Blockheads." It would be shot on video just like a pop promo.

They were convinced that the theme would resonate with the target market. Whilst maintaining the Wrangler quality theme, it told a story that young people would be able to relate to using a language that they would fully understand.

I quite liked the idea and asked the agency to develop a story board, do some limited qualitative research with young people, and select an appropriate production house and Director. At that stage, they would then make a full presentation to me, Dick Webzell and Kevin Black.

For some reason, the big presentation took place in a small room of the historic Saracen's Head Hotel in Southwell, a small minster town about 7 miles from the Blue Bell offices in Calverton. Geoff Howard-Spink took the role of lead presenter and, I think John Salmon was there to make the creative presentation. Such a high-powered representation simply illustrated how keen CDP was to sell their creative package.

Many in the London ad world were saying that their creative star was on the wane. Great work for Wrangler would be the perfect response!

As I recall, Geoff explained that they had received positive results from the limited research they had undertaken. They had an artist for the soundtrack and the best film production company in the country, Garretts, would oversee production on their behalf. A young up and coming Director, David Mallett, who had produced work for the likes of Queen and David Bowie, was their choice of Director.

The commercial would break new ground as it would be shot entirely on video to give it the authentic feel of a pop promo. John then presented the story board.

Neither Dick nor Kevin had really had much to do with the concept development. They were naturally keen to dot all the i's and cross all the t's. For them the product, and how it was presented, was far more important than the creative techniques employed in the commercials production.

John Salmon patiently attempted to quell their fears as we went through the storyboard frame by frame.

It was important, from a timing point of view that everything was signed off immediately so that we could meet production, post-production, and airtime dates.

As I had expected, Kevin and Dick had plenty of questions they needed answers to. I could see Geoff out of the corner of my eye. He was clearly getting agitated and priming himself to make an intervention. Suddenly, he leant forward a delivered a bombshell line. "Mr. Webzell, this is a commercial not a f****** documentary."

The Wrangler contingent went very quiet. I felt like putting my head in my hands, or, perhaps more fittingly, rushing out of the meeting to lie down in a darkened room.

Dick Webzell looked stunned! In all the time I worked with him, I had never heard him use even the mildest expletive, not even in a social situation.

I broke the ice by suggesting that Dick, Kevin, and I discuss any concerns privately before coming to a decision on the recommendation from the agency. To their credit, my colleagues agreed that if I felt that the CDP creative solution was the right way forward, then they would support that decision.

CDP were given the go-ahead to move into the production of the commercial, but Dick Webzell never really forgave Geoff Howard-Spink for the language he had used to make his point.

Several years later, when Geoff left CDP to set up Lowe Howard-Spink with Frank Lowe, the advertising weekly publication, Campaign, ran a story about him. The great and the good of the advertising world came forward and the article was full of gushing praise of Geoff from his peers and clients. In the middle of the piece, a paragraph stood out in bold type. The gist was something like this, "Dick Webzell, Managing Director of Wrangler Jeans said: - 'I never liked the way that he resorted to expletives when putting over his point of view."

The heated moment of those years before had clearly not been forgotten even though we had never discussed it between ourselves, or indeed during the many congenial meetings that we had with Geoff himself, in the intervening period.

Following the TV campaign, CDP recommended that a cinema campaign using the "Diary of a pair of jeans" commercial would help to reinforce the increased positive awareness amongst the important 16-34-year-olds.

There was a small technical issue.

The original campaign had been shot on video tape. This would have to be transferred to film before it could be used in cinemas. In the early 1980's this was not a straightforward as it would be today.

The only place that this could be done to achieve the required quality, was in a film laboratory in Los Angeles. The video was duly despatched, the technicians worked their magic. We were advised that the result was stunning.

Prior to the launch of the "Diary of a Pair Jeans" cinema campaign the agency was keen to organise a preview on a large cinema screen. Dick Webzell, Kevin Black, and I had a series of meetings in London over a two-day period towards the end of May 1980. It was agreed that we would meet up with CDP at the offices of Pearl and Dean, the cinema advertising distributors, and then move on from there to a viewing theatre. We naively assumed that this would not take long and planned to organise dinner afterwards.

The "top brass" at Pearl and Dean greeted us warmly and we were plied with drinks and canapes. It was then explained that our viewing theatre was The Empire Leicester Square. The occasion was a private, pre-release showing of "The Empire Strikes Back" movie. The Wrangler advertisement was featured amongst the reel of advertisements.

"Diary of a Pair Jeans" looked fantastic on the large screen and the movie was spectacular!

Unfortunately, we had been on the go since the early hours and had consumed a lot of alcohol and very little food. It was too late for dinner by the time the show had ended. We thanked our hosts for their hospitality, made our way to the Wrangler company flat and went straight to bed. During the night I became unwell. A lack of food and an excessive alcohol intake had taken its toll on my stomach. Next morning my colleagues suggested I miss out on the planned agenda of meetings and return home by train.

Although the cinema campaign preview was seared into my memory for all the wrong reasons, buying into the advertising reel of a major blockbuster movie proved to be a major coup.

Both the television advertising and follow up cinema campaign proved to be a great success and Wrangler increased its sales to reinforce its market share lead over Levi's.

At the beginning of 1981, CDP presented a second script featuring the same concept as that used in the first "Diary of a pair of jeans" advertisement. It was proposed that we used the same main characters, production company and Director.

The original concept had received high awareness and sales of Wrangler jeans had risen so we had no hesitation in signing off the new script. A slightly higher advertising budget was made available to ensure that visibility via television and cinema would remain high.

When I searched for the Wrangler "Diary of a pair of jeans" advertisement on the internet recently, it was this second commercial that I found.

Over the intervening years, the two scripts appear to have been blended in people's minds. The consumer chatrooms were still remembering the concept behind both these Wrangler advertisements, well over 30 years after they had appeared.

Fortunately, I was present at both shoots and can still remember virtually every aspect of both, probably because it was my head that was on the line!

The script of the second commercial, called "Then there was one" turned up in my own archive and went as follows: -

"Five pairs of Wrangler Jeans bursting out the door. One pair left his bike in bits and then there was four.

Four pairs of Wrangler jeans with a flat old battery. One pair pushed a bit too hard and then there was three.

Three pairs of Wrangler Jeans standing in a queue. One pair knew the manager and then there was two.

Two pairs of Wrangler jeans about to have some fun. Big brother said out of order and then there was one.

Now the moral of this story, if she deserts you in the end, as long as you have Wrangler you have a real two-legged friend.

Ere, I thought she went home!"

Many of the online enthusiasts of the advertisement remembered the main female character played by Donna Fielding. Donna was a member of a famous dance group called Hot Gossip. For a short period of time, she was in a relationship with David Essex.

During the shoot of the second commercial, Donna told us that after the release of "Diary of a pair of Jeans," she and David Essex were returning from a holiday and were coming through customs at Heathrow Airport in London.

A customs officer stopped them and said to Donna "I know you. You're the girl from the Wrangler Jeans advertisement." He seemed totally unaware that her travelling companion was a big, big star.

The story reinforced our own feelings that the advertising was really working! The "Diary of a pair of jeans" advertising was not only helping Wrangler to maintain its market share and sell more product, it was also much admired by the advertising industry.

The Republic of Ireland was part of my area of responsibility. Whilst it had its own stand-alone marketing budget, it was under my control and used the same advertising creative work as the United Kingdom. Media buying also was also under the control of the UK agency. This had worked well in the past because television coverage from both sides of the border was easy to pick up. As a result, the advertising pounds spent in Ireland had been very effective.

Awareness had been measured using a Gallup Poll, but no separate measurement had been taken in Ireland.

After the "Diary of a Pair of Jeans" advertisement had been aired, I decided to compare the results in Ireland with those north of the border. CDP had used their buying power in Ulster to target the prime 16-24-year-old consumers. The same strategy had not been employed in the Irish Republic.

Irish Marketing Surveys conducted an Omnibus survey very similar to Gallup across Ireland, north and south.

I commissioned a survey using the same questions that had been asked in England, Wales, and Scotland. The survey revealed that awareness of the Wrangler brand was very high. Interestingly, awareness of Wrangler advertising was much higher the Ulster TV area than in the Republic of Ireland.

I made the decision the hire a Dublin based agency to buy space in Ireland using the same media buying strategy as used by CDP in the UK.

After a short search, and based on recommendations from our media contacts, Young Advertising was appointed. The account Director on the Wrangler account was Donald Helme. A fellow Yorkshireman, he had spent many years on the Irish advertising scene and was well versed in both markets. CDP were happy to work with Young Advertising to extend the reach of the advertising they had created in London.

The new strategy was a great success. Omnibus research carried out in 1981, after the "Then there was one" advertisement had been aired, indicated that awareness of Wrangler advertising in Ireland was higher than any other brand, just as it was right across the UK.

Not only was the advertising highly visible, it was also very effective!

Despite being outspent by Levi's, we were vying with them for number one jeans brand. Wrangler was also one of the leading brands in the shirt, jacket, and knitwear markets.

During 1981 the campaign received several awards. These included a bronze arrow at the British Television Advertising Awards and a gold award at The Rank Cinema Advertising Awards. I have never been a great fan of award ceremonies. They tend to be self-congratulatory affairs where people over-indulge themselves in any number of ways. What's more they always tend to be in London and require a long trip and an overnight stay.

An invitation, from CDP, to attend the Rank Cinema Advertising Awards was extended to include my wife, Glenys. It was a 'black tie' dinner event that also included an overnight stay at the Royal Lancaster Hotel. The opportunity to obtain so many 'brownie points' was just too good to miss.

I accepted!

The evening did not start well. We travelled down from Nottinghamshire by car with the intention of arriving at the venue at around 7.00pm. On the outskirts of London, Glenys said she thought she had left her evening shoes behind. I pulled over and a quick search of the car boot revealed that this was indeed the case. "Where can I get a new pair of shoes at this time of night," Glenys exclaimed! Ever the Yorkshireman, I suggested that she could wear the casual shoes she had on. "No one will notice," I added.

This did not go down well!

Thinking on my feet, I came up with an inspired solution. We were not far from north London. A new 'out of town' shopping centre called Brent Cross had recently opened. I felt sure that if I could get there quickly it would still be open and that there would be a shoe shop with plenty of choice. It was open when we arrived. There was a shoe shop. A very expensive shoe shop stocked with very expensive pairs of shoes. Surprise, surprise, they had just what Glenys was looking for.

Driving on to the Royal Lancaster, we arrived with very little time to spare. Just enough time in fact to change before going down to the main conference room in which the event was taking place. All the great and the good of the advertising world were already at the pre-dinner cocktail party. We joined up with John Hewson who was one of the hosts on the CDP table.

The awards were being presented by Prince and Princess Michael of Kent. They were circulating around the room and were being introduced to various guests by one of the Directors from Rank Cinema Advertising. Eventually they made it to us. "Are you up for an award?" Prince Michael enquired. In the noisy atmosphere, I could not make out what he said. "Are you up for an award?" he repeated. "I don't think so," I replied.

We shook hands and they moved on.

When we were called to our table, we met the other guests of the agency. These included the Director of Advertising for the tobacco company Gallaher's and her partner, the Marketing Director of Cinzano and his partner, Glenys and I, John Hewson and our main host, John Richie representing the board of CDP.

Many years later John was to become more widely known as the father of film Director Guy Richie and, for a time, father-in-law of pop icon Madonna.

The evening was a great success. Fantastic food, great service and copious amounts of liquid refreshment was enhanced by plenty of lively conversation. Then came the real reason that we had all been gathered, the awards themselves.

During the evening, John Hewson had revealed that Wrangler had indeed been shortlisted for an award in the fashion category.

Gallaher's had been nominated, for one of their multi-award-winning commercials for Benson & Hedges cigarettes. Cinzano were also in the running for one of their classic advertisements featuring Leonard Rossiter and Joan Collins.

The presentations unfolded in alphabetical order. As a result, the Cigarette category would be followed by the Drinks category and then Fashion.

Before we knew it, the shortlisted candidates for the first award of interest to the people on our table were announced. "And the winner is…." the compere paused for effect, "Benson & Hedges." My tablemate went forward with John Richie and collected her award from Princess Michael of Kent.

Before we could finish celebrating this victory for our table, the shortlist for the Drinks category was announced. The compere followed the same practiced routine announcing, "And the winner is …… Cinzano." Two out of two for our table and yet more celebrations.

I was beginning to feel very nervous. If Wrangler failed to win, the evening could prove to be something of an anti-climax. The moment of truth dawned very quickly. I heard the compere announce the shortlist for the Fashion award. "And the winner is…." the compare seemed to pause for longer than any of the other awards, "Wrangler Jeans for 'Then there was one'."

The applause was deafening as I went forward with John Hewson to collect our award.

I remember that there was a loud burst of very dramatic music and Princess Michael responded by saying to me "What are we going to do to follow that?" Without thinking, I replied "What can we do in front of all these people?"

She looked puzzled. Then she laughed and presented me with the award.

Back at our table, my return was greeted with enthusiasm. Three out of three was the best possible outcome and a good excuse for John Ritchie to break open the champagne.

Whilst we were revelling in our success in London, events were unfolding at the headquarters of Blue Bell Inc. in Greensboro, North Carolina that would have a profound impact on the development of the Wrangler brand across all the international markets.

On the 9 June 1981, Blue Bell announced that Bass Brothers Enterprises, an oil rich Texas family company, had filed statements with the Federal authorities that would allow it to buy up to 50 per cent of Blue Bell's common stock. At that time, the Bass Brothers owned a 9 per cent stake in Blue Bell but they were legally obliged to register any interest in buying more with the Federal Trade Commission and the Justice Department.

In a telephone interview with journalist Sandra Salmans, Chief Executive of Blue Bell Inc., L Kimsey Mann observed that Bass had indicated that its purchases of Blue Bell stock was "…. for investment purposes only and I have no reason not to believe that." He cautioned that Bass may decide not to buy additional shares. However, Mr Mann acknowledged, "I am a little concerned." Quite just how concerned, and what impact it would make to the way the business operated, was several years into the future.

In the UK, and the rest of the European operation, it was a matter of "business as usual."

During 1981, several changes at CDP had an impact on the Wrangler account team at the agency. Ian Schoolar had been offered the role of Managing Director at, the Saatchi & Saatchi owned, Hall Advertising in Edinburgh. It was an opportunity too good for him to miss. As a Scot, he could return to his homeland whilst taking a leading role in what was arguably the best agency in Scotland.

His departure signalled the first major break in the account 'A Team' that had been instrumental in my decision to move the Wrangler account to CDP in the first place.

Geoff Howard-Spink realised the significance of the change so early into our relationship. He made a point of reassuring me that in his role as "Alternative Account Director" he would take personal responsibility for overseeing all activity on the Wrangler account until a new Account Director was appointed and had their feet firmly under the table.

Unfortunately, within months of the meeting Geoff had left CDP to set up a new agency, Lowe Howard-Spink, with Frank Lowe!

A new team of Mike Hemingway supported by Mike Turnbull, with John Spearman taking on the role of "Alternative Account Director," provided the continuity that was needed.

At the end of 1981 we started discussions with CDP about the creative approach to our advertising for 1982. Looking back on the Wrangler marketing strategy at the time. I was reminded that the jeans market was under some strain. If the 1970's had been the years of boom, I predicted that "the 1980's would probably go down as the years of consolidation."

It was clear that the successful brands at that time were beginning to show signs of suffering from what I coined at the time "The Benchmark Syndrome." This phenonium occurs when a brand or brands gather around themselves all the values associated with their market.

In the jeans market both Wrangler and Levi's were regarded as benchmark brands.

Other brands positioned themselves against us by promoting themselves as either, more or less expensive, better, or worse quality, more, or less fashionable. In a fast-moving market (the 1970's), this had worked in favour of Wrangler and Levi's and helped the brands to leadership of the sector.

It appeared to the Wrangler team, there was a danger that the brand would be perceived as "middle of the road." In a fashion market "middle of the road" can also be regarded as "off the fashion track." Unless action is taken to change such a perception, a brand can quickly lose its market share.

Economic factors were having an increasing impact on the purchasing decision process of the key 16-24-year-olds. This segment was not only important in the purchasing sense (they still represented 50% of the top price segment), it also contained the fashion innovators to which the rest of the market related.

If they moved their allegiances in another direction, the rest of the market could quickly follow!

Our choice of product to promote and the style of communication was going to be particularly important if Wrangler was going to maintain, and/or improve, its brand perception and market share.

Our main competitor, Levi's, was obviously of a similar mind.

Early in 1982, they moved their advertising account into a new start up agency called Bartle Bogle Hegarty (BBH). It was a clear signal that they were anxious to close the gap, that Wrangler had developed, following the highly successful advertising that CDP had created for us in 1980 and 1981.

In 1982, the right image, featuring the right product was going to be especially important, for both brands!

CDP was keen to continue their strategy of a single product approach putting the whole spend against Wrangler jeans and using creativity to maintain an advantage over the competition. We pointed out to the agency that Wrangler was not only a supplier of denim jeans.

Our merchandising team had been at the forefront of the market for "jeans related clothing." This included corduroy jeans, chino casual trousers, tee-shirts, knitwear, shirts, and casual jackets. In nearly every category, Wrangler was selling more products than many of the perceived leading brands.

We were convinced, that to our target market, the brand Wrangler meant more than just blue jeans!

As more and more jeans brands entered an ever more competitive market, it was our contention, that it would become more and more difficult for the major jeans brands to maintain their year-on-year growth volumes.

Using the strength of the overall product line would help Wrangler to maintain a competitive advantage and to grow our turnover. This was particularly relevant at a time when the volume jeans product was moving from a fashion to a commodity item.

As a result, we concluded that our 1982 advertising campaign should feature the whole product line. If CDP felt that this was an impossible task, they did not show it. They simply went away to find the creative solution. The job was handed to a new creative team at the agency comprising copywriter Mike Everett and Art Director Paul Smith.

Just how arduous a task they felt they had been given was never voiced to me at the time. During my research, I came across an online conversation that took place many years later. The discussion centred around the development of the creative idea for the new Wrangler commercial. During the discussion, Paul Smith had commented, "Idea? Since when has advertising needed an idea? In fact, nothing ever got past John Salmon without it having an earth wire down to an idea and as much as Brutus was simply about sexy jeans, this (my creative requirement for the next Wrangler campaign) was the worst brief ever, a range ad for Wrangler jeans."

Whatever their initial reservations they came up with a highly creative solution!

I remember the pitch as though it was yesterday. Unusually, the creative team were very involved. They presented a complicated storyboard with a lot of disparate images that did not really tell a story. It featured the payoff line, "What's going on, Wrangler that's what's going on."

To back up the storyboard, we were shown a very rough black and white video with fast cut imagery. It was very much in the style of the early pop promo's that were appearing everywhere at the time.

The creative team explained that the format allowed a lot of Wrangler products to be introduced. Its fast-cutting pace would break new ground in the world of TV advertising production. The simple idea that Wrangler branded products are "What's going on" and therefore, THE casual clothes for the trendy core consumers. Such a statement would be totally believable.

It was a difficult concept to buy into. CDP were not an agency that made things easy for their clients!

We wanted advertising that worked, and understood, that the range brief was something the agency had struggled with. We had trusted them to deliver the single product approach using the "Diary of a pair of jeans" and the "Then there was one" concepts. They had come up trumps. We would just have to trust them again.

Once more my head was on the line!

CDP had chosen Brooks Fulford Cramer Seresin as the production company for the new commercial, now named "Frozen Images." They were very much at the head of the game at that time. Kevin Godley and Lol Cream (one half of the pop group 10CC) had been chosen by them as Directors on the shoot.

There were a few uncertainties. Not all of them were fully highlighted to us at the time.

We were told that nearly all the quick cut techniques, illustrated on the storyboard, would break new ground, and require the use of untried techniques to pull them off. Furthermore, Kevin Godley and Lol Cream had never made a TV commercial on film, although they had dabbled in video. The rough-cut video, shown as part of the initial creative presentation, was one of their experimental efforts.

I cannot be 100% sure, but I think the words "Trust us," were actually uttered by the CDP presentation team.

Perhaps we had enjoyed a particularly good lunch before the presentation? Or maybe the Wrangler sales projections were looking very encouraging? Whatever the reason, the gamble seemed worth taking and approval was given.

Looking back, and with hindsight, I am convinced that the production team had no idea how they would pull off such a complicated feat within the budget we had agreed. The new advertisement would have to be spectacular to match the success of its predecessors!

By this time, I was a veteran of many commercial shoots. This was the first where I had really no idea how the finished result would look. Mark Andrews the television producer from CDP had explained that the shoot would be spread over six days.

The scenes featuring the Wrangler products were to be shot on two separate days, one in the studio and the other on location at the home of the Copthall Swimming Club in Barnet, in North London. The remaining four days had been set aside for other, non-product related action and post-production.

It was my job to ensure that, whatever else happened, the Wrangler merchandise would look its best. As a result, I agreed that I would only be attending the live action elements of the shoot.

The first day of shooting appeared chaotic. This was partly because there was so much going on. The pun is intentional! This was the first major piece of work that Godley and Crème had ever directed. They were anxious to keep everybody happy and listen to advice, on every aspect of the shoot, from other members of the production team.

Unlike many directors I had worked with, they appeared to understand that the Wrangler product was the real star of the show. They went out of their way to ensure everything looked pristine before the cameras rolled.

In another part of the studio, robotic dancers Barbie Wilde & Tik and Tok, who were all members of mime-music-dance group Shock, were practising several routines. They were assisted by a somewhat camp, Italian choreographer. I found out recently, that he was called Bruno Tonioli.

Many years later he was to find fame as one of the judges on "Strictly Come Dancing" and its equivalent in the USA. In his autobiography, Bruno explains that the Wrangler shoot was one of his first big breaks after arriving in the UK from Italy. Another of the many firsts on this shoot.

My own recollection of Bruno in action, was hilarious. The four models dressed in Wrangler clothes had to walk down a street talking and laughing amongst themselves.

No problem you would have thought!

Unfortunately, one of the male models found this extremely difficult. When he walked, he managed to move his left arm in time with his left leg and his right arm with his right leg. Try this at home. It is very difficult to do! After four abortive takes Kevin Godley exclaimed "Where the hell is that choreographer?" Or words to that effect!

Bruno came running. The problem was explained. Bruno attempted to remedy the situation. After several minutes, and many explosive Italian tantrums, the penny finally clicked with the model. The scene was finally completed to the satisfaction of everyone.

The remaining product and robotic dancing sequences went with barely a hitch. It appeared to me that only the Directors were aware how all the segments would finally fit together to tell a cohesive story.

Several days later, the action was transferred to Copthall.

At the bottom of the swimming pool was a large blown-up image of a face of one of the robotic dancers. This was taken from a sequence on the first day of the shoot. I had arrived at around 8.00am. The production crew had been working through the night to position the photographic blow-up in position at the bottom of the pool, at the foot of the high diving board.

The main shot involved two couples wearing outfits from the Wrangler casualwear range having a good time. One of the girls leaves the group and appears to dive into the pool and though the blown-up image.

The production company had provided a stunt double for the model. She was wearing the same outfit and would execute the dive from the top of the high diving board. Once the dive had been completed the real model would float on her back in the water.

To ensure the safety of all concerned, divers were on hand at the side of the pool. The production manager was in the water. He was following the directions of Godley and Creme who were also on the poolside.

We had provided a total of six complete outfits for the model and stunt double.

The first dive looked fine to me. Unfortunately, the Directors were unimpressed. They asked for it to be done again. The stunt double had to dry off, go through hair and makeup and change into another outfit before she could climb to the top of the high board again.

An hour later she was ready to go. The entry looked perfect but again Godley and Creme asked for the stunt to be done again. "What exactly am I doing wrong?" asked the stunt double. "You're not making a splash," exclaimed the Directors in unison.

The stunt double, who had been an international diving star, looked perplexed. "I wish that you had told me that before," she replied. "I have been trained to try and never make a splash," she continued. "Tell me how big a splash you want me to make, and I will do it, no problem!"

Another hour, more hair and makeup and a third outfit later, she again climbed to the top of the high board and executed a perfect dive with the requisite amount of splash.

"It's a take," exclaimed the Directors. Cue loud applause from all the production crew and a sigh of relief from me.

We only had two spare outfits left!

Six weeks later, I went to London to see the first cut. The finished commercial can still be found on You Tube. The complexity of its fast cutting and ground-breaking techniques is difficult to explain but basically the "Frozen Images" advertisement went as follows: -

"Mother and father figures are sitting on a settee. Mother is knitting.

The picture is torn in two. Cut to two couples walking down a street wearing Wrangler casual clothes and jeans. One of the girls is holding the torn picture in her hand.

Cut to same girl standing at a bus top with a line of robots dressed as men from the city (bowler hats and umbrellas)

The girl pushes the first one and the rest fall like ninepins.

The remaining one touches the girls Wrangler clad bottom with a robotic movement of his hand.

She pushes him over and he falls on his back.

Fast cut to a picture of the two young couples in Wrangler casual clothes.

One of the girls comes alive and dives through face of robot who was seen earlier falling on his back.

She is then seen swimming on her back as a robotic dancer breaks through her image.

Male and female robots dance across the stage. The scene is frozen, and part of the backdrop becomes a door through which the two Wrangler clad couples dance.

Fast cut back to the robotic couple. The male robot lets go of female robot who falls to the ground.

Cut to large Wrangler logo and the words, "That's What's Going on."

The two Wrangler clad couples are seen walking away."

Over the imagery, a soundtrack, specially composed and performed by Godley and Crème, repeats the message.

"What's going on? What's going on?

Wrangler that's what's going on.

I said Wrangler that's what's going on.

Wrangler that's what's going on!"

For the first time, I was fully aware of the strength of the execution, of what was a relatively simple concept. CDP, Godley and Creme and the production company, had come up with the goods!

Quite how close to the wire everyone had come during the production of the commercial was not clear to me until, during my research, I came upon an online conversation (9 May 2013) between Dave Dye (a well-known London Agency Creative Director) and Mark Andrews the Production Manager at CDP at the time the advertisement was created.

The "Frozen Images" commercial had been included by Dave Dye in a list of his favourite advertisements of all time. Mark Andrews had responded as follows:

"Thank you to Dave Dye for a great selection and in particular for choosing Wrangler. It was my first proper production at CDP (and who'd have thought that this was CDP's way to go?) with copywriter Mike Everett and Art Director Paul Smith.

It probably looks a bit 'so what' to today's younger creatives because of their total immersion in and acceptance of post-production as a normal way of life now, but in those days, it was an extraordinarily difficult technical challenge to pull off.

It was done with enormous photo blow-ups. The pool scene alone took a day and a night!

Indeed, it cost Brooks, Fulford, Cramer, Seresin, the production company, quite a lot more than they'd budgeted.

Quite frankly, no-one knew just how long it would take to shoot. Kevin Godley and Lol Creme were great to work with because although they weren't regular directors at the time, I came from a Music-Video background and understood why they needed to do things as they did.

A terrific client for trusting us."

In a way, I am grateful that the background problems never really surfaced at the time, and I had allowed CDP to develop the commercial on a "strictly need to know" basis.

Perhaps, if I had known all the facts, I may not have stuck my neck out quite so far!

Nevertheless, I am grateful, that precisely how far over the line I had gone, was still appreciated all those years later.

The "Frozen Images" commercial was well received by the sales force and helped them to increase distribution, not only of the Wrangler jeans lines, but also of the whole Wrangler range.

Similarly, the retail trade got behind the advertising concept. This enabled the Wrangler Field Promotion Representatives to secure valuable exposure, during the main campaign period, in store windows and at point of purchase.

More importantly, the new approach went down very well with the core market who not only bought more Wrangler jeans but were also encouraged to look at, and buy, other non-denim items from the Wrangler casualwear ranges.

Bartle Bogle Hegarty had thrown down a gauntlet with their first piece of creative work. It featured a national poster campaign for Levi's black jeans. The creative content showed one black sheep facing in the opposite direction from the rest of the herd of white sheep. The slogan proclaimed, "When the world zigs, zag."

Clearly, both brands were using cutting edge creativity to change the way they were perceived by the fashion innovators!

Post advertising research showed awareness of the Wrangler brand had increased across all markets, but particularly amongst the 16-24-years-old, prime target group. Top of mind awareness of the Wrangler advertising had increased to its highest level ever, dwarfing that of all our major competitors. An analysis of brand share data indicated that we were neck and neck with the brand leader Levi's in jeans sales. We were competing for brand leadership with major brands in other product areas such as casual shirts, casual trousers, knitwear, and jackets.

It was clear that despite their reservations about having been given "the worst brief ever, a range ad for Wrangler jeans," the CDP creative team of Mike Everett and Paul Smith had managed to produce an advertising concept that not only received acclaim from their peers in the advertising world, but also helped their client to achieve their sales objectives.

The 1982 awards season produced a further raft of awards for Wrangler advertising creativity for the "Then there was one" commercial which had run in 1981. These included a silver arrow at the British Television Advertising Awards, a silver lion at the Cannes Advertising Film Festival and a silver medal at the International Film & Television Festival of New York. The "Frozen Images" commercial had received a similar amount of acclaim from the key consumers and retail fashion world. It had also help Wrangler to achieve the required sales results!

As we started to plan our campaign for 1983, a piece of breaking news reached my desk. It was from the Blue Bell Head Office in the USA. Apparently, Bass Brothers Enterprises had continued to purchase Blue Bell's common stock. Their 9 per cent stake had grown considerably and the Blue Bell Board had become pre-occupied with "this crisis."

Two years before in June 1981, the Chairman of the Board had acknowledged, "I am a little concerned." By the middle of 1982, concern had turned to panic. The company had employed consultants to try and resolve how to stop the "share raiders."

A possible solution was a management buyout. This would require the board to re-examine the structure of its international operations and to reduce its expenditure.

The short-term outcome was that the marketing budget for the UK and Ireland was to be cut back. This was not the sort of news that I was expecting. The timing could not have been worse!

I had just completed a marketing analysis with the influential Henley Research Centre. This had identified the balance of spending power was changing and that "a number of factors" were threatening the short, and long-term attitudes to branded jeans.

The dynamic of the three key markets had changed, largely because of the economic situation.

This would have a marked impact on the key 16-24 market because 50% of the prime jeans market were either unemployed or in youth opportunities programmes. In addition, rates of pay in job creation schemes were low (£20-£25 per week) matching dole payments of (£25 per week). There was also an over-supply of young, inexperienced labour.

This was resulting in a widening of pay differentials that would increasingly affect the spending power of this important segment.

The rise of the over 25's would impact the market in the future. Despite zero population growth, Henley was predicting that age structures would shift. The trend through the 80's would be a continued rise of the 25-44 age segment, and these would grow significantly through the decade from 15 million in 1982 to 16.5 million by 1992.

Henley talked about a Two Nations Concept which would pitch one market segment against another.

Areas included: -

Employed	vs	Unemployed
White	vs	Black
Rural	vs	Urban
South (East)	vs	North (West)
Young Outlook	vs	Youth
Better off	vs	Less Well off
A B C1	vs	C2 D E

Henley also asserted that these economic factors had split the clothing market into two groups. One would provide added value and fashion forward products. The other would promote value for money through a less fashionable product mix. They were recommending a change in marketing direction and suggested a different message was required for different segments of the market. They believed that Wrangler needed to be spending more money, not less!

Our conversations with CDP were constructive. They understood the position we found ourselves in.

Levi's, through their new advertising agency, were "upping the ante." We were sure they would be aware what was happening with Blue Bell in the USA. This convinced us that they would increase their advertising spend and try to grow their market share in the UK.

To combat this, it was agreed that we would maintain a good presence on television using the tried and tested formula that specifically targeted the hard to reach 16-24-year-olds. This would be supplemented by a small (2month) outdoor campaign.

This could only be achieved by reducing production costs considerably!

The CDP creative team went away to consider the possibilities one of which involved "tweaking" the existing "Frozen Images" commercial. A few weeks later they came back to us with their recommendations.

Their in-house production team had done some video editing on the Godley and Creme commercial. The result was the creation of a commercial that maintained all the positive elements of the original whilst giving it a new freshness. The cost of carrying out the refinements, necessary for broadcast quality, was relatively small. As a result, the bulk of the smaller budget available could be spent airing the commercial at a level that the agency was confident would maintain the share of voice for Wrangler.

They also produced a 48-sheet poster comprising a montage of different images including Wrangler product shots, commercial stills, fashion accessories and a girl wearing a Wrangler jacket over a tutu. The Headline read "What's Going On?" the pay off-line featured a 'cut and pasted' Wrangler logo and the words "That's What's Going On."

At the beginning of 1982, Wrangler product merchandisers right across Europe were expressing concerns that, as fashion values were changing, the use of the Wrangler logo as a garment symbol was becoming increasingly less effective. This was especially so in the high fashion and the ladies wear markets.

They felt the Blue Bell needed to develop an "alternative brand symbol" that could add value to the product rather than simply branding it.

In the middle of that year, a European Task Force was made up of representatives from all the marketing divisions. I was given the unenviable task of chairing it. Coming up with a design brief that everyone could agree on was difficult. Choosing a designer to fulfil the brief was even more fraught.

Naturally, the Italians wanted an Italian, the Germans wanted a German and so on!

Eventually a shortlist was drawn up, and after sending out the brief and then carrying out extensive face-to-face interviews, two designers were chosen to move forward with design proposals. One was a corporate image designer from Germany and the other a clothing designer from the UK.

From the designs submitted, five were selected by the Task Force and these were consumer tested in every individual market.

Prior to the research, the Task Force had made a preferred selection from one of the alternatives developed by the UK designer, Thankfully, for all concerned, this selection was the one that the research confirmed was the best to carry forward.

Registration of the design was applied for throughout Europe, and, after some minor teething problems, this was achieved by the middle of 1983. This enabled the new symbol to be applied to the Spring 1984 ranges that were sold in at trade fairs across Europe from August 1983 onwards.

It was also included on a 48-sheet poster that ran in the UK for two months at the end of 1983.

The original version of the "Frozen Images" commercial had been entered for a significant number of advertising awards in 1983.

It came away with a raft of the most influential. These included the 1983 Kodak Craft Award and Gold arrow at The British Television Awards, the Honours Award for most effective use of Music from The Advertising Creative Circle, the Honours Award for the Freshest New Special Effects from The Advertising Creative Circle. The most prestigious, was a Silver Pencil award for Most Outstanding 60 Second Commercial at the Designers and Art Directors Association Awards in 1983 (No gold was awarded that year).

Post-advertising research of the re-edited 1983 version of "Frozen Images" indicated that, despite the budgetary constraints, advertising awareness had increased. Top of mind awareness of the Wrangler brand was also high amongst the core market.

It was also noted that the two major brands, Levi's and Wrangler, enjoyed the strongest images, highest awareness and highest preference to purchase levels of any other brands.

Despite this, it appeared that the market share of both brands appeared to be eroding – albeit slowly.

Something was clearly wrong!

In August 1983, I employed the Qualitative Research Company to carry out several group discussions around the UK. These confirmed the view within Blue Bell UK that buying attitudes were changing. Research also indicated that there was an apparent gap between perception of the Wrangler brand and the product.

It would have been easy for the UK marketing team at Wrangler to blame the advertising agency. After all, we felt we had good distribution through the trade and good penetration within the key market groups.

Up to this time, the market had been growing organically. Levi's and Wrangler had increased market share at the expense of all the other players.

The gloves were now off!

I had developed a close relationship with the market research department of ICI whilst with the CWS Menswear Group. This had continued when I moved to Blue Bell. When the department became a private company, Textile Marketing Studies, I worked closely with them to refine their panel data on the textile market. In 1980 they began measuring the jeans market providing us with regional sales breakdowns on a quarterly basis.

The data provided to us had been sophisticated over the years but was only able to evaluate the shares of the major brands of jeans over three key geographic regions of the UK. These were the North, Midlands, and the South.

If we were to increase sales penetration, it was necessary for us to be able to evaluate the penetration of jeans by outlet, and identify the Wrangler share of it, down to salesman area levels. In addition, we needed to ensure that we were aware of all Wrangler and non-Wrangler outlets and the share of Wrangler jeans within them.

If it was possible to provide all Wrangler sales personnel with this data, it might prove invaluable in the setting up of a sophisticated Sales Advancement Programme (SAP).

Unfortunately, no such data was available. We would have to develop it ourselves.

This involved lot of groundwork by the Wrangler sales administration team in Calverton. They had available to them a Retail Directory of clothing outlets by town across the UK and Yellow pages. A test of the Nottinghamshire area concluded that a combination of Retail Directory and Yellow pages only provided information on 2% more outlets than the Retail Directory alone!

We combined lists by representative area using the Retail Directory and each outlet was telephoned and asked whether they stocked men's, ladies, or children's jeans. For existing Wrangler stockists, we now had records that might help us to extend our product ranges, but the list of non-Wrangler stockists was still too large and needed to be refined into outlets of high and low potential.

At that time, I approached research company CACI, to enquire whether their recently developed "A Classification of Residential Neighbourhoods" (ACORN), might be able to provide the required data.

Working with them, we profiled jeans purchasers by each of the 38 ACORN types. The system was based on Local Expenditure Zones (LEZ) which were centred on the approximate catchment areas of 1101 shopping centres throughout the UK.

Because CACI had the ACORN profile types living within each of the LEZ zones, they were able to provide a BUYING POWER INDEX REPORT (BPI) showing each LEZ area in descending order of importance. By splitting each of the sales representative territories into their respective LEZ areas, we provided a LEZ report for each individual member of the Wrangler salesforce.

Following an agreement with another research company, SAMI, we obtained listings of the number of Men's, Ladies and Children's clothing outlets within the 1000 leading shopping centres and distribution outlets in the UK. Combining this with the ACORN BPI reports provided us with a list of actual outlets within each LEZ in descending order of index importance.

By cross referencing this information with that obtained through our own telephone survey, the Wrangler Area Sales Managers were able to feed out listings, to the representatives under their control, starting with all the clothing retailers in the areas of highest propensity to purchase jeans and jeans related clothing.

The first stage of SAP was implemented at the end of 1983 as part of the extension of the Spring 1984 selling season.

Today, the collection of such sophisticated sales development information is taken for granted. Back then, without high powered desktop computers and computer search engines, it was every bit as ground-breaking as the creative work that had been developed for us by our advertising agencies.

The Wrangler marketing team agreed that 1984 would be a pivotal year for the onward development of the Wrangler brand!

Discussions with the retail trade had advised us that their margins were under pressure, and they were increasingly reluctant to buy forward at the same levels they had done in the past. Additionally, some of the smaller brands were providing styles that were not only perceived as more fashionable but also gave the retailer far better sales margins than the core brands, Levi's and Wrangler, were able to do.

The objectives for the 1984 campaign were clear. The advertising needed to assist the sell-in to the trade. Retailers needed to be given a compelling argument to maintain their commitment to stock the Wrangler brand and to buy forward.

The campaign proposition needed to be equally compelling so that the promise of what was to come, could be used by the Wrangler salesforce to assist distribution to targeted growth outlets and augment the sell in.

The advertising needed to aggressively promote the brand to increased consumer sales to both men and women.

My message to the Wrangler team at CDP was that from now on we would be measuring the effectiveness of our advertising, not by the number of awards that had been won, but by the additional number of sales the campaign generated.

Our strategy was clear. In 1984, we needed to address our attention to both the trade and to target consumers. Our message to the trade would reinforce the benefits of stocking our product. With Wrangler, they were buying a quality garment made using the best materials available and supported by a heavy and effective advertising spend.

Up until 1982, the market for jeans had been growing every year and the products produced by the core brands had been perceived as volume fashion lines. Wrangler advertising had successfully projected our products in a highly creative and innovatory way.

With the market at best stalled, we felt that we should change the emphasis back to core merchandise and project our brand values in a way that consumers could relate to.

Since the mid 1970's, television had proved to be the most effective medium for achieving immediate large-scale awareness. It did have drawbacks. For instance, it was expensive for a campaign of meaningful proportions, to target the core 16-24 years old target market. They were light viewers, reaching them was becoming increasingly more difficult. Additionally, television production costs were going through the roof.

At the start of our relationship with CDP, they had recognised this fact. Their media buying tactics to reach 16-24-year-olds via television, had been instrumental in their securing the Wrangler account. For the first three years of our relationship this had worked in our favour. Unfortunately, larger, fast moving consumer goods companies started promoting products to the same target market.

Neither Wrangler nor Levi's could compete with their huge budgets. As a result, the medium of television was becoming more expensive and less effective for us.

Interestingly, in 1983 Wrangler had been the only jean company advertising nationally on the first commercial channel. Levi's, the only other company utilising the medium, had ploughed all its television budget into the relatively newly formed Channel 4.

There was also a requirement, on our part, to spread our advertising over a longer period than previously, and to have content flexibility in a rapidly changing market environment. This was a real challenge for our advertising agency, but they responded in a most positive manner.

To dominate the trade media, CDP recommended that most of the budget should be spent with the two major trade journals, Menswear and Drapers Record. Working with these publications, they devised a front-page wrap round. This format allowed Wrangler, to not only dominated the front and inside front covers of the magazines, but also to maximise the creative and visual potential available to the creative team at CDP.

The schedule was designed to give Wrangler regular exposure over the whole year.

Research had shown that Wrangler television and cinema advertising was regarded by the consumer as being unique and highly creative. The downside was that attitudes to the Wrangler product had changed very little.

CDP felt that the use of 48 sheet posters and double page spreads in "youth interest magazines" would enable the advertising content to be more product orientated.

The creative team came up with an 'advertising style' which retained the payoff line "Wrangler - That's What's Going On" from the highly successful "Frozen Images" television commercial.

The advertising agency recruited several focus groups comprised of 18-21- year- old men and women from the core jeans market. The participants were encouraged to express their opinions about advertising, contemporary music, and magazines before being shown a selection of 'outline' magazine advertising concepts for Wrangler jeans.

Older groups, comprising 20-25-year-old men and women, were encouraged to discuss their attitudes towards shopping for clothes and jeans. These groups were shown several advertising poster concepts for Wrangler jeans.

Resulting from the research, four of the magazine concepts were developed.

One of them featured a young man and young women on a dance floor. In a cartoon bubble coming from the woman's mouth is the word "Stretch?" The bubble from the man's mouth has the words "Yeah and they don't Kajagoogoo's."

Kajagoogoo was a famous pop group at the time. The young people understood the pop connection as well as the thinly veiled reference to an intimate part of the young man's anatomy.

On the other hand, their parents had little or no awareness of the pop group connotation but would be very clearly aware of the anatomical reference. They would express their outrage, to the delight of their children to whom the advertising was aimed.

As a result, CDP argued, the Wrangler advertisement would become even more relevant to its intended recipients!

The other three magazine advertisements were all created in a similar vein and with the similar expected outcomes.

Concepts for the three outdoor posters had also been well received by the participants in the older focus groups. It was decided to move forward with these and a further idea that had not been shown. The three initial creative ideas promoted different denim styles.

"Stonewashed," featured a strong image of a woman in a shower holding a sponge and wearing a great fitting pair of Wrangler stonewashed jeans.

"Bleached," featured several robotic looking male mannequins each wearing a bleached denim shirt and jeans and positioned in an Egyptian desert location. And yes, the agency did go all the way to Egypt for the shoot to "ensure the look was authentic."

This was done despite my protestations over the cost!

"Stretch," featured a surreal room in which every object was covered in stretch denim fabric. This included the walls, the telephone, and its stand – even the rubber plant! Through the open door was a tantalising view of a stretch denim clad women alongside her denim covered sports car.

Each individual image was powerful, but the campaign consistency was created by the positioning of style description, "STRETCH," "STONEWASHED" and "BLEACHED." These ran vertically from the top left of the design towards the bottom left.

The Wrangler logo, with the accompanying new Wrangler symbol and the line "THAT'S WHAT'S GOING ON," was positioned in the bottom right-hand corner of each poster.

The final poster projected fashion items from within the Wrangler range. The picture featured an exploding mirror that reflected a different Wrangler product image within each of the larger flying shards.

Today's advanced computer technology would make light work of producing such a concept. Back in 1983 it was much more difficult – and expensive!

Like the other posters, the descriptive wording "IMPROVE YOUR IMAGE" appeared vertically on the left of the poster but with the word "IMAGE" as a mirror image.

The media package was impressive. The largest concentration of 48 sheet posters were planned to appear in towns throughout England and Wales with a population of 100,000 plus. In Scotland, the posters would be placed in towns where Wrangler had a strong presence. In addition, line by line sites would appear in Wrangler areas of strength.

The campaign was scheduled to run every month from March to July 1984 and again in September on that year.

Over the same time scale four insertions in each of 17 Youth Interest and Music Press titles were booked. Publications included Blitz, Smash Hits, Record, I-D, Which Bike and Bike.

Each of the concepts that had been researched would be seen once in each publication.

CDP was confident that, what the campaign lost from the lack of impact afforded by television exposure, would be more than compensated for by targeted impact and longevity of the new outdoor and magazine campaign.

During their conversations with the 'pop magazines,' the CDP creative team had met a freelance fashion stylist called Ray Petrie. He was working with magazines such as The Face, I-D and Arena. These magazines were constantly looking for new models who would stand out from the crowd.

Ray had already earned a reputation for finding new and up-and-coming talent.

At Wrangler, we were undertaking a similar mission to bring new life to the PR and promotional photography for our Spring 1984 ranges. A meeting was organised. Ray was confident that he "could deliver the goods" and went away to find the new faces.

At the end of October 1983, he facilitated a Wrangler PR shoot that featured Nick, a new model that Ray was confident would one day become famous, and a young female model called Yasmin who I understood was about 18 years old at the time and on one of her first modelling assignments.

The shoot went well. The resultant pictures were everything that we wanted.

Looking back, with the benefit of hindsight, the shoot was somewhat historic. Yasmin was to become one of the top fashion models of the 1980's. She later married Simon Le Bon of pop group Duran Duran.

Ray Petrie went on to create the fashion House, Buffalo. He collaborated with some of the top photographers of the day to create a new style of hard hitting "streetwise" fashion imagery. Sadly, he died in 1989, at the age of only 41.

And Nick? Well, more about him later!

At the end of October 1983, the advertising campaign developed by CDP was presented to the Wrangler salesforce. It was very enthusiastically received. By the end of December, every salesman had copies of the magazine and posters advertisements together with a comprehensive media schedule. This enabled them to follow up with retailers, who had placed orders previously for the Spring 1984 ranges, to organise top up orders covering the Spring/Summer campaign period.

Wrangler Field Promotion Representatives were made aware of the point-of-sale material that was available. The package included posters made from all the press advertisement and proof miniatures of the four outdoor posters. The latter had been produced from the proofing plates and printed on high quality paper.

Upmarket jeans outlets, who had not previously utilised posters in their shops, were to be offered posters that had been specially encapsulated in plastic and then eyeletted in the top corners. As a result, they could be offered for display in the shop window or at point of sale.

A lot of effort was put into the creation of a totally integrated marketing programme where the top line advertising and the supporting bottom line sponsorship and sales promotional activities worked seamlessly together.

In Ireland, the same media advertising strategy was being developed.

Towards the end of 2015, I contacted Donald Helme who was the Wrangler Account Director at Young Advertising in 1983. He to remembered vividly my going into the agency in Dublin to present the creative work that CDP and produced for the 1984 campaign.

Apparently, I started my presentation with the words, "We are going to leap forward into the past." Communicating with him thirty-two years later, he claimed that this comment had stuck in his mind and "absolutely described what was being planned."

I admit that the actual context of my remarks had escaped me until Donald's comments reminded me of what I had said all those years before. Looking back, and with hindsight, I have concluded that I was referring to the fact that Wrangler marketing was going back to reinforcing the core values of the brand, as we had after I joined Blue Bell in 1975. Not only that, but we were also planning to use the same media mix we had used then, magazines and outdoor posters.

The leap forward, was undoubtedly the use of state-of-the-art product distribution and media targeting techniques, coupled with up-to-the-minute creative executions.

The ranges for Autumn 1984 were sold into the trade at the IMBEX show in London in February 1984, at the Futura Trade Fair in Ireland and at smaller shows at other venues across the UK.

Even before the new campaign had started, the Wrangler salesforce was able to remind the trade buyers that they would be supported by a heavy advertising presence in September, at the start of the Autumn selling period. This fact also helped to convince the retail trade to buy forward on the core jeans lines that were being promoted as part of our campaign.

At the end of April 1984, an analysis of the 'SAP' results was a mixture of good and bad news. The good news, our sales of denim jeans to existing customers had been good and forward orders were encouraging following two months of the advertising campaign. The bad news was that sales penetration of the non-Wrangler customers, targeted through the research programme, were not reaching the unit sales levels that had been set.

Conversations with the Area Sales Managers revealed that the salesforce had successfully opened accounts and taken orders from some of these new customers. However, they were finding it much more difficult to get them to order forward. Low margin expectations, in a difficult market, was a commonly used reason given for not doing this. Smaller brands were apparently working on much smaller sales lead times.

We decided to approach the problem head on.

An incentive package was produced. The promotion invited retailers to "Turn to the Wrangler Blue Denim Bonus and make more money from the sales of Wrangler jeans." The proposition was geared to sales of a limited number of core denim and stretch denim jean styles available in washed and stonewashed finishes.

It was a simple concept, "Buy more Wrangler jeans – make more margin."

The mechanics were also simple and easy to understand. With every order of 12 pairs of jeans the retailer would receive a voucher to the value of one additional pair.

Vouchers were accrued monthly and could be redeemed in blocks of 10. Consequently, the more jeans ordered, the more vouchers would be issued. Dependent on the quantities ordered, margin increases ranged from 18.5% to 22.2%

This offer was time limited and related to orders placed between 2 July and October 1984 for delivery prior to 31 December of that year. Participating retailers were reminded that the national advertising and point of sale support was available in July and September. The earlier they booked forward, the more jeans they would sell.

The promotion was well received by the Wrangler salesforce and enabled them to break down some of the barriers to forward booking that existed, particularly amongst new Wrangler stockists.

A major programme of sales promotional activity was devised aimed at the consumer to assist sales through selected retail outlets. These included a "Summer Savers" promotion that offered customers buying Wrangler merchandise to a value of £20, a voucher worth £5 off their next Wrangler purchase.

A "Wrangler Olympics" promotion was developed in conjunction with Olympic Holidays to capitalise on the publicity surrounding the Olympic Games in Los Angeles. The consumer element consisted of a voucher against every Wrangler purchase offering the recipients money off Olympic Holidays in Greece and entry into a prize draw to win a free holiday in Greece, a Wrangler outfit and pocket money.

In some of the larger retailers, we added a staff incentive element. In keeping with the Olympics theme, staff were encouraged "to climb a performance ladder" to achieve bronze, silver, and gold awards.

The children's market was not forgotten. We produced a branded and boxed Wrangler calculator. This was offered at nominal cost to supporting retailers. The instore consumer proposition was simple. "Buy Wrangler childrenswear merchandise to a value of £17 and receive a free calculator."

In the middle of 1984, CDP developed a plan for a short burst of advertising that comprised of three television commercials. These were intended to air from

September 1984 to complement the "What's going on?" outdoor poster campaign that had already been booked to support our on-going SAP activity.

Two of the scenarios involved studio-based set ups. The other was altogether more complicated. It recreated a key scene from the 1945 romantic drama "Brief Encounter," directed by David Lean and starring Celia Johnson (Laura) and Trevor Howard (Alec).

In the original film, Laura and Alec meet by chance, just before the outbreak of World War II. Whilst waiting for their trains, they are drawn to each other and fall in love. At the end of the first meeting, they agree to meet again at the same location. Laura leans out of her railway carriage window and says a reluctant goodbye to Alex, as her train pulls out of the station.

In the Wrangler version this set up was repeated.

It was recommended that the illusion of the pre-war period would be created by using of a railway carriage and steam engine of the time. The male lead would appear to be a soldier about to go to war. When the train pulled out of the station the camera would pan back to show that he is wearing a pair of Wrangler Jeans.

Will they or will they not meet again? The viewers questions would be partly answered by the payoff line "What's going on? Wrangler that's what's going on!"

I was anxious to keep the production costs to a minimum to maximise the available media spend.

"We have investigated the production logistics. We are proposing that the studio-based commercials will be filmed back-to-back at a studio in London." I was told. "The 'Brief Encounter' commercial will be filmed at York railway station. An engine and rolling stack will be hired from the adjacent Railway Museum. The production costs have been pared back and there are sufficient funds available to ensure that the 20 second cameos will be highly visible, when they are aired," The CDP production team assured me.

The go-ahead was given. Some weeks later, I met up with the agency account team, creatives, and production crew, on the concourse of York railway station. The platform we had been allocated was used regularly as a film venue and was closed to the public. When I arrived the rolling stock and cameras were already in place and the actors were going through rehearsals and camera checks.

Time was not on the Directors side. There would be only one opportunity to capture "our engine and the rolling stock," as the train left the platform.

In the event, everything went to plan and by mid-afternoon, the commercial was "in the can."

The following day, the studio-based commercials were being shot. CDP had arranged for first-class rail tickets to be booked from York to London, Kings Cross for me, and the agency personnel. The train arrived at the station. To our surprise the seats in the first-class compartments were either occupied or those remaining had been reserved. We did not know when the shoot would finish, consequently reserved seats had not been booked. After a lot of searching, we did find seats in the restaurant car where we were able to relax, refresh and unwind in relative comfort.

Next day the studio set ups were completed without incident.

The fully integrated marketing package, including the 'cameo' TV campaign, was unprecedented for the UK Fashion market. It sent a strong message to our major competitors that Wrangler really meant business!

The euphoric bubble surrounding our successful SAP activity was about to burst in spectacular fashion. Not because of any action we had taken, but because of a decision being made, 3000 miles away, at the headquarters of Blue Bell Inc. in Greensboro, North Carolina.

In an article in the Lakeland Ledger dated 7 October 1984, Scott McCartney, talks about the effect that the attentions of the Bass brothers Robert, Ed, Perry, and Sid had on the boards of listed companies such as Blue Bell Inc. He was quoted as saying, "Blue Bell Inc. the North Carolina maker of Wrangler jeans had bought out the Basses (share of the business) in a deal similar to the Texaco transaction. The 'family' (Bass brothers Robert, Ed, Perry & Sid) profit by $50 million."

This was the spur for the Board of Blue Bell Inc. after a long period of uncertainty, to take some decisive action!

A court hearing in Delaware on the 19 October 1984 paved the way for a leverage buyout of Blue Bell Inc. by 50 of the company's top executives. Of these, only two were non-Americans. One of those was Dick Webzell the Managing Director of Blue Bell in the UK.

On the 26 October 1984, a notification was sent out to Shareholders advising them that a special meeting was being held in Greensboro, on 16 November 1984, urging them to accept the offer that had been agreed at the previous hearing.

In a message to shareholders dated 28 November, it was confirmed that the buyout had been approved and the deal "was consummated" on 27 November.

As members of the UK management team, we had mixed emotions about the transaction.

On a positive note, we all owned Blue Bell shares that we had acquired, at a fixed price, as part of the company's bonus scheme. This meant, although we were required to surrender our share holdings, we would do so at a healthy profit. On the other hand, we no longer had any equity in the new company and, in the short, medium, and long term, seemingly very little security.

It was always in my mind that such a deal might happen!

Whilst the European Division that included the UK, had always made a good net contribution to the bottom line of the whole organisation, in a difficult trading climate, some of the European subsidiaries were struggling.

With only two non-Americans having equity in the new organisation, it seemed possible that the Board of the new company could decide to cut marketing costs even further. They might even sacrifice some of the main strugglers, to make the organisation attractive for a possible takeover in the future.

We did not have long to wait to find out!

Dick Webzell advised us that the UK, Ireland, and Scandinavian markets would continue to trade as wholly owned subsidiaries. They would be renamed the Northern European Division.

Discussions had begun to start the process of turning over some subsidiaries to Licensees, in other key markets. Alberto Calo, from the Brussels office, was taking charge of the operation and we were asked to provide him with as much support as he might need.

The advertising budget for the UK and Ireland would have to be cut back dramatically. This at a time, when our SAP efforts were beginning to bear fruit with both the retail and consumer markets.

The difficult decision was made to cut back the number of Field Promotion Representatives from six to three. Those remaining would have bigger areas to cover. This would restrict their support to retailers who provided the biggest return on investment.

The advertising budget had always weighted 80/20 in the favour of above the line activity.

In my planning for 1985, I was left with no alternative but to change the weighting to 50/50. This decision would make it difficult for CDP to continue to maintain our share of voice in the main line media. It would allow us to continue our support to the retail trade at the point of purchase, at the same level that we had established during the 1984 campaign.

An analysis of the activity we had generated in 1984 identified that the integrated activity had helped to increase distribution and unit sales. This meant that despite the change in strategy, or more likely, because of it, we had closed the gap on Levi's, despite their higher spend.

Just how worried they were, was not apparent to the Wrangler team at the time!

In a recent recollection of his work, John Hegarty of BBH, the Levi's advertising agency, was quoted as saying, "Believe it or not, after winning the Levi's account in 1982, we were in danger of losing the business in '84". He goes on to explain that Levi's were struggling to come up with a product solution "in a last-ditch attempt to revive sales."

Just what they came up with, and the BBH creative solution to sell the concept to the important 16-18-year-old market, would become apparent in the fullness of time.

At the end of 1984, all this was a long way down the line.

My briefing to CDP, advised them that in the short term it would be necessary for us to cut back on the advertising expenditure.

"We will need to make our advertising pound go further. Our creative ideas will have to be hard hitting to enable us to combat the Levi's backlash that I am sure will come." I explained. "At the same time, the ratio of production to media spend will need to be pared back to ensure that more money is available to air the creative work that you produce."

CDP had built their reputation on creative excellence with big brands. These accounts had been able to provide big budgets, for big productions that not only won awards, but also increased sales.

Wrangler was no longer a member of that club. At least in the short to medium term!

I was not certain whether they would be willing to maintain their relationship with us on the new terms. The CDP account management team assured me that they would. "We understand the situation and appreciate your honesty. The Wrangler account is important to us and we will work with you to maximise the budget that is now available," I was assured.

In the end, the same media mix that had proved successful in 1984 was developed, albeit at a slightly lower level of exposure. The 1985 creative work was a mixture of existing and new creative ideas.

Whilst the CDP management team understood the need for a more prudent approach, it was not the culture of the CDP creative department to let a reduced budget get in the way of "the pursuit of excellence."

In my early days in the advertising world, an agency gained its revenue from media expenditure alone. Working as a production manager, my role had been to ensure the production expenditure, that was quoted, and then charged at cost, was kept within agreed budgets without minimising creative output or watering down a good creative idea.

As a Yorkshireman, it was part of my culture to "be careful with my cash."

These attributes were very much to the fore during this difficult period. Inevitably, it caused a degree of friction between me and the agency as I struggled to rein the creatives in. I was developing something close to paranoia about their attitude to the Wrangler product and the Wrangler brand. It seemed to me at the time, that the creative idea was becoming more important than the projection of the product.

What we were looking for was creative ideas that were fashionably appealing enough to encourage our core market to go out and buy the Wrangler product.

The scale of possible further cutbacks placed on the Blue Bell operations in Europe were made even more apparent when, on 5 March 1985, the following announcement appeared in the American newspaper, Daily News Record. "Blue Bell Inc. has agreed in principle for three European companies to manufacture and market Wrangler brand apparel in Europe. The European companies are Bernard Tapie Group in France, Spain's, Tycesa (in Spain, Portugal, and Germany) and Italy's Fiorucci."

It added, "Under the agreement, all three firms will have the right to manufacture a number of different items, including basic denim jeans."

Today, the clothing industry is regarded as a close-knit business. In the 1980's it was perhaps even closer.

I had gone to school with the person running the Levi's sales organisation. I knew many of the other members of the Levi's marketing team. As a result, I realised that they would be fully aware of the agonies that the Blue Bell was going through and how the decisions made in the USA might affect our marketing plans in the UK.

The advertising world was similarly close knit.

BBH (the advertising agency for Levi's) would know about the creative problems and financial constraints that CDP was working under. By the same token, CDP would have been fully aware of the problems that BBH was experiencing in its relationship with their client.

I used to tell my marketing team, "If I sneeze in Calverton, within minutes I will get a call from my opposite number in Northampton (where Levi's had their HQ) enquiring if I had caught a cold."

My information was that our integrated campaign had them on the run. We had taken the core jeans high ground and a similar approach from Levi's would not help them to regain it.

They were also aware of the strain that the Blue Bell Management Buyout was putting on our ability to respond to any increase they might make to their advertising spend. What they needed was to put all their effort behind a product or concept that Wrangler, in the UK, would not be able to respond to.

Our trade intelligence was advising us that, during the latter part of 1985 Levi's, was taking soundings from key retailers about their attitudes to the 501 jeans style. We could not really believe that they might be considering making an "ill-fitting, button fly jean" the hero of their next campaign.

It had its' followers, particularly within the fashion-conscious gay community and represented the origins of the Levi's product line. It could be argued that it was the original jean.

Even Levi's needed to be convinced. As John Hegarty recently recalled, "It (Levi's) was launching the 501 in a last-ditch attempt to revive sales. Did we (BBH) have the ability to create a campaign that captured the imagination of 16 to 18-year-olds? It was a formidable task. Almost everything about the product didn't work. When researched, nobody liked the button fly. The cut of the jeans, its silhouette, was not fashionable and they were going to retail at more than £20. This was unheard of. The jeans buyer at Selfridges refused to stock them."

There was nothing coming out of our market intelligence, that was telling the Wrangler marketing team the trade was convinced 501 would become the saviour of the Levi's brand. Nor did anyone believe that it could make a major impact on sales volumes in a still static market. Never-the-less, we concluded that stranger things had happened and internally, and in conjunction with CDP, we started to look at how we might respond, with a campaign of our own that focused on a volume product that was a Wrangler exclusive.

501 was regarded as product concept that had been developed by Levi's to incorporate features built into its original denim products, made, and sold by them since the late 1800's. Wrangler was acknowledged as the original five pocket western jean. It had been specially designed in 1947 by Blue Bell Inc especially for rodeo cowboys. The style epitomised all the durability, fit, American origins and fashion attributes that the core jeans market was looking for.

We agreed this was the product that should be the star of our advertising.

During our talks with CDP, we stressed that it was important to promote the product's American ancestry without reverting to the somewhat clichéd and dated cowboy imagery. Research over many years had consistently indicated that this was a turn off for UK consumers.

CDP had heard that the 1986 campaign for Levi's would be very much television and cinema orientated. If Wrangler was to compete with them for share of voice, it would be necessary for us to be as highly visible as possible. We would need to use the same media.

The media mix was agreed, but the creative solution was to prove more difficult. With a much-reduced budget, and a need to retain a high visibility in an expensive medium, the advertising message would need to be hard-hitting and visually strong.

The creatives went into their darkened room to mull over the brief and to come up with a solution.

Four weeks later, I went to see what ideas they, and the CDP media people had developed.

To ensure that the commercial would be sufficiently visible, a 30 second commercial was envisaged. The campaign would start in the middle of April 1986 and run for four months.

The creative solution was "all American" in its approach.

A fervent, young, good looking American politician, dressed in a casual, short-sleeved, open necked shirt, is pictured at a microphone lined podium. The backdrop behind him is entirely filled by a huge American flag.

As he begins his speech, the camera zooms in towards him.

With more than a passing resemblance to the style of President Kennedy, he begins his oration. "I believe that the things that made America great should keep America great."

The camera pans in closer and closer as he continues, "Liberty, Equality, Freedom of choice."

At this point the camera is positioned to the side of the podium and the viewers can see that he is wearing a pair of fantastic fitting jeans as he says the words, "And Wrangler jeans!"

The camera closes in on the back pocket and the Wrangler patch. Up comes the Wrangler logo and the strapline.

It was another of those "trust us" moments!

The whole commercial rested on the ability of the key actor to hold the attention of the audience through to the final reveal, in the final five seconds of a 30 second commercial.

The CDP production team tried to reassure us that, because the commercial would be shot in one take, the continuity from the first frame to the final reveal would be seamless. They insisted that the message contained in the commercial was clear. It met the brief, and the proposition was strong and impactful.

The decision was made to go ahead with their recommendation.

We agreed on the main actor. He was appearing in a cult TV programme (his name escapes me!) and was regarded as something of a 'hunk' by the young teens market.

The product had been chosen, a pair of tight fitting, Wrangler western jeans. We had also selected a white, short-sleeved, 'Oxford shirt' from the Wrangler casualwear range. The product fitting had gone exceptionally well. The selected merchandise had been handed over to the production company.

I was really looking forward to the shoot. After all, what could possibly go wrong?

What appear to be simple shoots are often the most problematic.

Because the commercial was being shoot in one take, the camera set up and rehearsal revolved around production technicalities. This meant that members of the production crew had been standing in for "the talent" whilst the camera angles were sorted out.

When the actor arrived, it was my job to ensure that the Wrangler product look at its best. Imagine my surprise when I discovered that the agreed Wrangler shirt had been discarded for a non-Wrangler designer model.

"Why is he not wearing the Wrangler shirt?" I asked the wardrobe mistress. "The creatives (from CDP) asked me to use this one they had brought with them," she replied.

I called over the creatives. "Why have you made a decision to change the shirt?" I enquired. "We didn't like the cut of the Wrangler shirt, so we have changed it," they advised.

I reminded them that this was a Wrangler commercial. The product combination had been agreed before-hand.

I was adamant. "No Wrangler shirt, no shoot!"

Calls were made to the Account Director for the Wrangler account. Caught between renegade creatives and a now irate client, he tried to broker a compromise. I had made my point. Now I was prepared to offer a way forward. "If you take the Wrangler brand label from the pocket of the Wrangler shirt and sew it in position over the pocket of the "designer shirt," then I will be happy to proceed."

The wardrobe mistress did the business, and the shoot went ahead without further mishaps.

The pre-shoot trauma was put behind me and the rushes looked very promising.

Looking back now, that altercation probably signalled the beginning of the end of our relationship with CDP. After all, if the ideas men did not wholly believe in the Wrangler products they were working with, how could they be expected to produce the sort of hard hitting, product advertising we were looking for?

The "'I believe'" commercial was well received by the Wrangler sales force and the retail trade and the sell in for the spring/summer ranges had exceeded expectations.

In another studio, at around the same time, BBH were shooting a commercial for Levi's that would resonate across the whole market!

We had heard through the trade that the new Levi's advertisement would indeed be featuring the 501 jeans style. There was no huge confidence that the core market would rush out to purchase what even Levi's considered to be an "anti-fit" style with a button fly.

In addition, the proposed retail price that would also break the £20 barrier.

Our trade estimates indicated that total pre-advertising sell-in for 501's was in the region of 80,000 units. These were not numbers that would set the world alight!

As the end of the year approached, I heard that Levi's would be launching their new advertisement on Boxing Day 1985. It seemed a strange time to do so. In the back of my mind, I wondered if BBH had one eye on the 1986 advertising awards season.

For an advertisement to qualify, it had to be shown at least once in 1985!

On reflection however, I figured it was part of a strategy to market the advertising ahead of its real launch date. It would enable them to test the reaction of the core market to its message and encourage the retail trade to rethink their lack of willingness to stock the 501 jeans style in meaningful quantities.

The idea of awards might have also featured in the thinking!

I was distracted somewhat by news from Greensboro. Even though "the ink was still dry" on the Management Buy Out, the Blue Bell Board were already looking around for a potential buyer.

One way or another, 1986 was to prove to be memorable – for all the wrong reasons!

Despite protests from my family, I insisted that we watch the Levi's advertisement, on its TV debut, on Boxing Day 1985. I had been advised by one of my trade contacts when it would be appearing.

I thought it would be interesting to gauge the reaction of different sections of the market. My son was 15 and daughter 13 at the time. Neither my wife nor I were aware of the content of the advertisement we were going to see, but all the family was expecting an advertisement featuring Levi's.

Not exactly a perfect research sample but it covered all the bases. I figured my children would probably be biased in favour of Levi's. After all, Dad worked for Wrangler!

I had a great deal of respect for the BBH creatives John Hegarty and Barbara Noakes who had come up with the concepts. In Roger Lyons, they had chosen one of the best commercial directors in the business. There was no doubt in my mind, whatever was to come up on screen, it would be impactful and beautifully shot.

As a great fan of Marvin Gaye, the opening bars of his hit, "I heard it through the Grapevine," commanded my attention. "Not Marvin himself," I thought, "but a very good impersonation." The model who entered the launderette was also very familiar. It was Nick Kamen, a more mature, slimmed down version of the model who had featured in the Wrangler shoot, facilitated by Ray Petrie, at the end of October 1983.

Undressing in public and sticking clothes in a washing machine was not new. CDP had produced an advertisement for Hamlet using the same concept.

BBH's execution took the idea to a whole new level!

It was to make Levi's 501's, Nick Kamen and BBH famous. Subsequent hype around the commercial has created a myth, and blurred the reality surrounding its impact, that is still prevalent to this day.

On Boxing Day 1985, I was dealing with the here and now, not the future!

How had the advertising gone down with my own mini group – my own family?

My wife loved it, my son thought it was "alright," (high praise for a 15-year-old boy). My 13-year-old daughter was drooling over Nick Kamen and his revealed body. I'm not sure that she was aware, or cared, exactly which product from the Levi's range was being advertised.

For my part, it was clear that "Laundrette" was a great piece of advertising, but I was unsure exactly what Levi's was expecting it to achieve. If the aim was to set the brand apart, by projecting a product that had a very limited distribution, then they were treading on very dangerous ground.

The advertisement was too heavily branded 501 for it, in my mind, to achieve anything other than to create consumer demand for the 501 jeans product. As the brand had limited retail distribution, it would be interesting to see what they would do if, as I suspected, demand exceeded supply.

Early in 1986, it was announced that Wrangler jeans would change its denim supply from left hand to right hand twill. This brought the brand into line with all our competitors and, in one fell swoop, took away one of the key added value benefits that Wrangler jeans had always enjoyed.

The main reason behind the move resulted from the decision to close several of the wholly owned subsidiaries in Europe and move over to licensees. This reduced considerably the Blue Bell production volumes across Europe and had increased the fabric price accordingly.

It was felt that it was no longer viable for Wrangler to remain the only major manufacturer using left hand twill, despite all the marketing advantages it gave us!

My thoughts were pre-occupied with the here and now.

The Levi's "Laundrette" commercial was launched with much fanfare. As I had predicted, it helped to change the buying habits of its intended audience, 15-19-year-olds. Every young man saw himself as a budding Nick Kamen.

The "anti-fit" 501 jeans enabled them to feel confident wearing this product.

At that time, the "perfect" male model figure had a 32" waist and a 34" inside leg. Research had told us that many men would buy a pair of jeans with these measurements and squeeze their own, "less than perfect body," into them. With 501, fit was not a problem. Wearing them, young men felt that they were making a fashion statement about themselves. Wearing the same jeans as Nick Kamen made them feel "cool."

Unfortunately, because of the products limited distribution, potential customers were finding it difficult to locate the product.

This is where the Levi's PR machine stepped in!

At the time, I felt that the decisions at Levi's UK Head Office and a strategy devised and implemented by Peter Shilland PR, were never given full credit. Even now, it seems to me that BBH are still taking all the plaudits for what turned out to be a seminal moment in the promotion of jeans. For me, the real success of the campaign was driven by Levi's themselves and the work of their PR agency. Their joint efforts turned a potential disaster into a great success story, but their decisions could have badly misfired.

I knew Peter Shilland (Managing Director of the PR company that bore his name) from his time of Marketing Director of Levi's Northern Europe Division and then head of Levi's in-house PR operation. When he left Levi's to set up his own PR company, his old company became his very first client.

Peter knew the jeans market in the UK and Ireland. He knew the key retailers and had at his disposal as much market information as I was privy to at Wrangler. His PR recommendation was bold but not without risk. He made the lack of distribution a strength not a weakness.

The gist of his message to the trade and the media was roughly as follows, "The Laundrette advertisement has led to an unprecedented demand for Levi's 501's. Those retailers who stocked them have sold out and want more. Those who did not are clamouring for stock to meet the customer led demand. The Levi's factories are working hard to produce more 501's and the company is seeking additional stock from other markets."

This great story for the press received fantastic coverage. The more difficult the product was to find, the more the market wanted it!

The Marvin Gaye original recording of "I heard it through the Grapevine" was re-released with images from the commercial and the Levi's 501 logo clearly visible on the sleeve. This reignited the demand through its exposure in the record shops much frequented by the core jeans customers. The record itself entered the charts providing even more fantastic coverage for the Levi's 501's.

While all this was going on, at Wrangler we were looking forward to the launch of our own TV advertising campaign. The "I believe" commercial was scheduled to appear from 17 April 1986.

On the 5 April 1986, the 'La Belle' night club in West Berlin was bombed. Three people, including a US Serviceman, were killed and 229 people were injured. Intelligence implicated Libyan agents operating out of East Germany.

President Regan ordered an airstrike on Libya on the 14 April. This was despite protests from France, Spain and Italy who refused to let the American planes fly over their territory. 45 aircraft, many flying from US bases in the UK, dropped bombs and missiles on Libyan military targets including the residence of, the then Libyan leader, Col. Gaddafi. One American aircraft was shot down and there were an estimated 60 casualties on the ground. Gaddafi claimed that one of the dead was his recently adopted daughter, Hanna.

A diplomatic outcry ensued. The British media were particularly critical of the British Government for allowing the planes to fly from UK bases.

As the news broke, I received a telephone call from my account Director at CDP. "Robin, have you seen the news," he asked. I said I had. He continued, "We have been advised by the TV companies to withdraw the 'I Believe' commercial. It is felt to air a commercial, that so strongly supports American values, would be insensitive at a time when American actions in Libya are being so roundly criticised around the world."

"Have we a plan B?" I queried.

"We could run one of the old Wrangler television commercials. Our advice is to hold off until the fuss has died down and then air the commercial from the end of May to the end of June, with another burst later in the year," he replied.

I had no alternative but to agree with the course of action recommended. Unlike Levi's, I was unable to deploy the Wrangler PR team to turn any negative publicity into a positive.

Thankfully, the Wrangler retailers supported our decision even though they were geared to promote the product featured using the supporting advertising material provided.

Sometimes, situations can be turned to your advantage, as Levi's had been able to do. At other times, you must adopt a philosophical approach and just accept that there is nothing you can do.

This was one of those occasions!

Losing one of the key months for jeans sales was not good news, especially when the "success" of heavy Levi's advertising was the hot topic within the trade.

When the campaign eventually ran, it was well received and achieved the sales results expected. When it came to share of voice, for the first time for many years, our main rival had come out on top.

In July 1986, it was announced that Blue Bell Holdings, our parent company had been taken over by The VF Corporation the owner of the Lee jeans brand.

The merger was well received by the markets in the USA.

In an article by Eric Schmitt published in the American financial press on the 28 July 1986, much was made of the fact that, "The combination of Blue Bell, which makes Wrangler jeans, and VF, whose H.D. Lee division is the nation's third most popular brand of jeans, gives VF 25 percent of the jeans market, (approximately the same share it was estimated that Levi's held at that time)." It went on to say that both analysts and executives at both companies said the merger created a good strategic fit. "They clearly diversify our product line," Lawrence R Pugh, VF's chairman and chief executive was quoted as saying.

The money markets in the States were out of touch with what was happening in the world outside the US. Just how out of touch was epitomised by a quote from a

Jeffrey Edelman and influential US retail analyst at the time, "Jeans is a no-growth business that's losing its fashion dominance."

In less than a year that quote would come home to bite him!

The article quotes sources from both organisations saying that "Edward J Bauman, Blue Bell's chairman and chief executive met with Mr Pugh in early June 1986 to discuss a merger. The two men quickly agreed that the companies had complementary product lines and that a merger would help both concerns." Mr Pugh explained that the merger would be an excellent deal for shareholders adding "the merger would not force any layoffs through consolidation."

Back in Calverton, Dick Webzell called together the senior management team to explain exactly how the events in the USA would affect us. He was clearly of the opinion it would be "business as usual" and we would continue to develop plans for the coming year,1987, on that basis. "The top management of VF will be visiting Calverton in the not-too-distant future to meet us all in person and explain how the VF acquisition and forward planning exercise, currently being carried out, will cement the new relationship," he advised.

Within six months all would be clear!

Claims surrounding the success of the Levi's advertising campaign were somewhat exaggerated at the time. In the aftermath of the first burst of advertising, it was widely quoted that sales of 501's had risen by 8-fold because of the 1986 advertising campaign. As the original sales base for 501's was so small before the campaign, I can accept that figure.

Later claims about large rises in the Levi's total jeans market share do not really bear scrutiny.

There is no denying, however, the "Laundrette" commercial had sold more 501's than anyone (including the marketing team at Levi's) could possibly have expected. Probably, it could have provided the catalyst that turned around the fortunes of Levi's.

It certainly stimulated the whole jeans market. Retailers and the media were once more talking up jeans as the fashion item of the moment.

The only problem for Wrangler was how could we take advantage of it?

Because of the takeover, we were somewhat in limbo. What would the new company require of us? Wrangler was head-to-head with Lee (already a VF brand) in the UK, and most other international markets. Would this lead to a re-positioning for one or both brands?

These were questions that would need to be answered as soon as the dust had settled!

During the planning and marketing development cycle for 1987, we had to carry on with an air of normality. This meant analysing the Wrangler sales and advertising results against those of Levi's and then objectively planning the way forward. All this in a year that we expected at best, to be one where we would be "treading water" whilst Levi's would be "kicking on."

The decision was made to concentrate a larger percentage of our marketing budget to merchandising the Wrangler product at the point of purchase. The budget available for national advertising would still allow us to afford a visible advertising presence. However, we would not have the same level of spend that we had enjoyed previously.

Bearing this in mind, we started the advertising planning discussion for 1987 with our advertising agency.

It would be wrong to suggest that the relationship with CDP was not strained. The "I Believe" commercial had done a reasonable job. It was not the fault of the agency that world affairs had affected their initial campaign plans.

Wrangler had managed to hold our unit sales figures, but we had lost out massively to Levi's in respect of share of voice.

Against all the odds, Levi's 501 was THE jeans fashion leader on the block.

Trade talk indicated that the next campaign for Levi's would also feature 501. It was rumoured that it would be equally as impactful as "Laundrette."

There was no way that we would be able to match their projected spend! We needed a big creative idea. It would have to be single minded in its requirement to promote Wrangler jeans, at the same time clearly differentiating it against Levi's 501.

Being vastly outspent by Levi's in the past, had not stopped CDP from coming up trumps with a big creative, effective, and yet affordable advertising concept. Could they do it again? The agency had some real creative talent at its disposal. I was confident that they could!

At around this time I was approached by Tamara Ingram of Saatchi & Saatchi. Saatchi's were one of the few agencies with a high profile outside the advertising world. This was largely due to the work they had produced for the Conservative party that had been instrumental in getting Margaret Thatcher elected as Prime Minister in 1979.

They had expressed interest many times about our working together. I presumed that this was just another pitch for the Wrangler advertising account. When I met up with Tamara in the Saatchi HQ at Charlotte Street in London, she was at pains to distance herself from the agency's new business team.

It turned out that her father was John Michael Ingram. He had been one of the pioneers of projecting London as THE fashion capital of the world during the "swinging sixties." I knew of him as the founder of the fashion forecasting agency Design Intelligence.

At that time, Tamara was Account Director on the Unilever account and was putting together a radio campaign to launch Ariel low temperature washing powder. The creatives at the agency felt it would be great if one of the major brands of jeans could be persuaded to endorse the product in one of the advertisements.

Jimmy Young, one of the top radio personalities in the 1980's, would be the star of the campaign. The advertisements would be presented in the interview style that Jimmy Young used on his top-rated radio show. Incisive discussions with the great and the good, were interspersed with the very latest popular music hits.

I could see the benefit of involvement.

The campaign was scheduled to start after our 1986 campaign had finished. It would give the Wrangler brand good exposure at a time when share of voice had been eroded. The only problem was that Blue Bell Inc. had never previously allowed the Wrangler brand to be used as an endorsement for someone else's product.

I promised Tamara that I would get back to her after contact had been made with the technical engineers in Greensboro. Several days later, permission was given to go ahead, "provided that there was no direct endorsement of Ariel."

Tamara said this was OK, but then advised that they wanted me to be the Wrangler spokesman in the Jimmy Young interview. "That way you can ensure that the content meets the guidelines you have been given." She was very persuasive. I reluctantly agreed to go ahead!

The following week I met up with her in Wardour Street for what I thought was a preliminary meeting with Jimmy Young to talk over the content, prior to taping the advertisement.

I was wrong!

Saatchi's felt that the interview would come over far more realistically if I did not have time to consider my responses. With that in mind, they planned to record the commercial there and then.

In the studio, Jimmy Young was introduced to me, and the taped discussion started. I had taken part in many media interviews in the past and was wise enough not to find myself being caught out, by an unguarded response to a question from a probing inquisitor.

The conversation flowed naturally until eventually Jimmy Young came back at me with the query, "Why do Wrangler endorse Ariel?" I moved the conversation on without directly answering. He continued to try and obtain a definitive response, but I refused to bite.

Eventually, I stopped the tape and explained "I am not allowed to directly endorse the Ariel product but am willing to come up with a form of words that I think will be acceptable to all parties."

In the end, the finished radio commercial went as follows: -

> "**JY**: To talk to me about Ariel, I have got with me Robin Dilley. Advertising Manager of Wrangler UK. Hello Robin.
>
> **RD**: Hi
>
> **JY**: Your company sort of invented jeans as we know them today?
>
> **RD**: We pioneered the use of Sanforized finish which gave a pre-shrunk jean at a time most people were shrinking them in the bath.
>
> **JY**: Are there any particular tips about washing jeans, Robin?
>
> **RD**: A very important tip is to always wash the jeans inside out. First of all, it gives you an even fade and also it stops the creases fading white.
>
> **JY**: And the second tip?
>
> **RD**: We advise Wrangler customers to wash at low temperatures and Ariel washes very clean at low temperatures.
>
> **JY**: I was going to say, why particularly Ariel?
>
> **RD**: I always follow the advice my wife gives me. I find it's the best market research I can get.
>
> **JY**: And does your wife use Ariel on your Wranglers?
>
> **RD**: Of course, she does!
>
> **JY**: Background laughter."

My comments about Sanforized finish and sitting in the bath to shrink jeans to size, was a side swipe at Levi's. I had heard through trade sources that "shrink to fit" was integral to the content of their next commercial for 501's.

The last four lines were intended as a throw away because Jimmy Young wanted the interview to finish on a lighter note. The off-the-cuff remark did little for my credibility amongst my friends.

My wife was not particularly pleased either!

Eventually, the Ariel campaign ran for about three months, and I had more than my fifteen minutes of fame. It was a little bit of light relief at the end of a difficult period.

Tamara Ingram became one of the leading lights of the London agency scene and went on to become Managing Director of Saatchi and Saatchi. In 2018 she was working in the USA as global chief at J. Walter Thompson. Recalling the Wrangler and Ariel collaboration, she told me recently "It was, in its way, very modern to have a beloved influencer (Saatchi and Saatchi) connecting two great brands (Wrangler and Ariel). Funny, it seemed slightly old fashioned at the time."

During this period, discussions with CDP on a creative solution for our 1987 advertising campaign continued.

Moving agency at such a difficult time was not part of my agenda. There were already more telling issues to contend with.

Unfortunately, the advertising industry had other ideas!

An article appeared in Campaign, the key trade magazine. It claimed that Wrangler was looking around for a new agency. Before the magazine had even hit the newsstands in Nottingham, 12 agencies had contacted me. Before the end of the following week many more had followed suit.

I could take the hint!

Could it be that even though I did not want to look around, the CDP team thought perhaps I should?

In retrospect, the rumour mill may have been started by my collaboration with Saatchi & Saatchi on the Ariel radio campaign. The London advertising scene was then, and is now, a very small world.

To cut a long story short, I drew up a shortlist and visited a small number of agencies who I felt might be able to help us at this most difficult of times.

Batten & Barton & Durstine & Osborn (BBDO) stood out from the crowd. Not just because of the length of their name! Well known in America, they were keen to develop business throughout all their overseas subsidiaries, especially their London office. They had recently won the Apple account and a brand like Wrangler, even with a much-diminished budget, would be another great coup for them.

Exactly how I was feeling at the time was well articulated in an article that appeared in Campaign on 3 July 1987.

Under the heading "The client/agency split: is it worth all that trouble," I was pictured, adopting a rather apprehensive pose, and widely quoted, along with other client companies who had recently split from their agencies. I explained in the article that the market had shifted back to classic styling. "This meant that Wrangler jeans as a brand – rather than the range of fashionable styles had become a campaignable idea once again. This was not a change of direction, but a fine tuning in our advertising requirements."

The piece continued, "Having gone down this line with its existing agency – and Dilley says it may well have come up with what was wanted – BBDO came along with a particular campaign idea which Wrangler thought was right. Dilley says every company looks around in the marketplace to make sure they are getting the best on offer."

I was quoted as saying, "They may find that a new idea transcends loyalty. My door is always open to ideas as we are in the ideas market. Most people who come through that door say they have the big idea for you, but 99.9 per cent are really asking you what you want. It is a means to a pitch."

The article also alluded to the Wrangler relationship with CDP at that time. "Dilley also believes that if an existing relationship becomes too close, agency and client begin to second guess each other. The agency thinks: 'The client won't approve of that,' so good ideas are never brought forward."

Interestingly, another article appeared in the same issue of Campaign about clients who were enjoying the benefits of long-term agency relationships.

The main picture featured John Hart, then the sales and marketing director of Levi's Strauss. He is quoted as saying of his relationship with BBH, "The overriding point is that BBH has always given us very good work and very good service. But you always have to be consistent with people. If they are never given a chance to understand what the company is about, then we will never get the best service."

Looking back after all this time, I was surprised how understated his comments were. When the article appeared, the "Launderette" commercial was well into its run and, according to all the hype, was producing great results for Levi's. Perhaps the Wrangler initial take on the impact of the campaign was shared by the marketing team at Levi's? Could it be that at the time of the article it was too early to judge the true success of the 501 advertising? At the time of the two articles, John and I had never met. That would change sooner than I thought!

Towards the end of 1986, when we moved from CDP to BBDO, Campaign magazine had run an article with their own take on the events that led to our move. It read, **"Wrangler shifts to BBDO after clash with Colletts.** Wrangler jeans has moved its advertising account, likely to be worth around £1 million in the coming year (1987). For the past six years, the business has been with Collett Dickenson Pearce and leaves after what Managing Director David MacLaren describes as 'an honest disagreement.' David MacLaren is further quoted as denying speculation that the rift had come about over the problems resulting from the political issues surrounding the 'I Believe' commercial, produced for Wrangler by the agency."

A better story than the reality that the magazine published some eight months later but a concocted story nevertheless!

Chapter Eight

Batten & Barton & Durstine & Osborn (BBDO) 1987-1989

In the article in Campaign (3 July 1987) the writer articulates my view of the client/agency relationship as follows, "Dilley compares the client agency relationship with a marriage which no one takes on with a view to divorce: But sometimes it does happen, and not always through any fault of the partners. There is a drifting away, or maybe something traumatic happens which forces the couples apart," I was quoted as saying.'

This was certainly true in respect of our long-term relationship with CDP. We appeared to have drifted apart and the trauma of the VF takeover, coupled with changes in the senior management team at CDP, were certainly key factors that facilitated our move.

There was a temptation to take the Wrangler account to one of the so called "Second Generation" creative hot shops, who like BBH, were challenging the status quo. We were certainly approached by most of them, and had talks with a couple, but felt that the time was not right.

There was some uncertainty about how VF would position the Wrangler brand (then number two in the world) alongside the Lee brand (number three in the world).

What we needed was an agency who could work with us strategically to help us through a difficult initial period. Our new partner needed to provide a communications solution that would enable us to maintain a high share of voice with a dramatically reduced budget.

They should also be able to demonstrate their ability to provide creative solutions, across all media, that would help Wrangler to claw back any brand share that might be lost because of any short-term uncertainty.

BBDO had impressed us from our initial meetings.

Phil Slott, their American CEO, was the creative director who had been behind many great advertising campaigns in the BBDO New York office. He was also a great strategic thinker. He, and his team, instantly realised that the limited budget available, would have to work hard for us. National advertising through television was not a practical solution because of the high production cost and the low exposure that our budget would buy.

I had advised them, that we would be continuing our Sales Advancement Programme supported by staff and consumer incentives at the point of sale. This would be centred on our areas of weakest distribution.

BBDO's recommendation was to spend all our advertising budget on an outdoor campaign concentrated on the areas where Wrangler had strong distribution, namely Scotland, the north of England and the Midlands.

A strong account team had been put together by the agency. Phil Slott advised that he would be heavily involved in the overseeing of the creative execution. Marc Cox assumed the role of Wrangler Account Director with Tim Baynes as Account Manager.

Marc and Tim were both strong strategic thinkers. They had demonstrated, during the initial contact with us, they fully appreciated the position we found ourselves in, post takeover. They would be working with me to develop a communications plan that would be implemented as soon as all the uncertainty over brand positioning had been cleared up.

The BBDO offices were situated in Regents Park. The office building was in Chester Terrace, one of the neo-classical terraces designed by John Nash and built in 1825. The terrace has the longest unbroken facade in Regents Park and all the buildings are Grade 1 listed. The interior was equally grand although BBDO had been careful to ensure that, whilst the décor was sympathetic to the building's historical past, it also projected an image of modernity that visitors would expect from one of the world's leading advertising agencies.

Every staff member was connected to an Apple Mac (one of their newly acquired accounts) and the latest Apple technology was employed in all areas, including the creative department.

Today, such use of computer technology is regarded as the norm. In 1986/7, it was revolutionary!

I was working in something of a vacuum at the time, as a result, my recollection of the creative work produced for that first campaign is very sketchy. Recent conversations, with both Marc and Tim, have revealed that the passage of time has affected all our memories. What we could all agree on was that the creative work involved the use of a 'trompe-l'oeil' technique.

Now you may well ask, as I am sure I must have done at the time, "what the hell is that?"

The dictionary definition reads as follows, "Trompe-l'œil (French for 'deceive the eye') is an art technique that uses realistic imagery to create the optical illusion that the depicted objects exist in three dimensions."

We had asked that our campaign should continue to project Wrangler jeans that fitted well and looked great. In this way, we would continue to differentiate the Wrangler product from 'anti-fit' 501 that continued to be the 'star' of the advertising for Levi's.

The BBDO creatives had been working with a top fashion photographer. He had developed a means of changing a fashion shot by applying tints and overlays onto the original transparency. This 'jumbled' some of the image, to deceive the eye, whilst leaving other selective parts to almost stand out in relief. Using this technique, we produced two posters. One featured a man, and the other a woman. In both, the models, looking great in their Wrangler jeans, stood out three dimensionally from the background.

Whilst the change of agency and the campaign development process had been occupying a lot of my time, I had not given much thought to the implications of the VF takeover.

The only real sign of possible future change was the arrival of Tom O'Shea during the latter part of 1986. Tom had been an integral part of the Blue Bell human resources team in Greensboro. His new role at Calverton was to access the strengths and weaknesses of all the key players in the Wrangler team throughout all areas of the business. He would then report back his findings to the new VF Management.

We had heard from colleagues in Greensboro that the "new broom" had swept into the old Blue Bell operation and that the inevitable clash of cultures had caused some friction.

They talked about the "suits descending!"

Greensboro in North Carolina was a world away from the VF Headquarters in Wyomissing, Pennsylvania. For the Wrangler managers, formal wear was a pair of slacks, an open necked casual shirt and tailored jacket. The "suits" all wore business suits, white shirts, and red power ties. They talked the talk and, seemly, did not do a lot of listening.

This had not gone down well!

I had a lot of time for Tom O'Shea. As a result, when we sat down together to discuss my role and philosophy in respect of marketing communications planning, I was very candid about the way I worked and interacted with my colleagues.

The Blue Bell senior management team had always operated on a basis of complete trust in the ability of everyone to carry out their own individual tasks. The day-to-day interaction between us was of an informal nature. The whole group meeting two or three times a month to discuss how the company was performing against the business plan that we had all had provided input to, and collectively agreed.

It was clear from my discussions with Tom, the VF definition of team management involved a much more structured approach. To achieve this aim, there would be changes.

At Calverton, we were rarely visited by the European management team because all the key meetings took place in Brussels.

I can only recall only one visit by the Chairman of the Board from Greensboro. After picking him up from Manchester airport, I drove him to Calverton taking the scenic route by way of the Peak District. We chatted all the way about the scenery and not a lot about the business. Business, for the gentleman of Greensboro, was for the office.

He must have enjoyed the experience because he never came to see us again!

At Calverton, we used to joke: - "If we hear the helicopters, we know we are in trouble." Loosely translated this meant that we would only ever have the American management visiting us if we had really screwed up the business. We never had. They never did!

Then early in 1987, the Americans arrived in force! We had done nothing wrong. The VF senior management merely wanted to see for themselves some of the people that they had invested so heavily in.

Wrangler Limited (our new name) was now a subsidiary of VF International. We were introduced to John Johnson, President of VF International who was directly responsible to the VF Board for all the international brands including those previously under the Blue Bell banner.

He advised us that the old VF brand portfolio, including Lee jeans was overseen by the existing Vice President VF International. Another Vice President VF International was in the process of been appointed. He would be responsible for all the brands that VF had acquired as a direct result of the Blue Bell takeover. Dick Webzell would report to the new man and the existing Wrangler senior management team, including me, would continue to report to Dick.

There was only one problem. Under the Blue Bell regime, Dick was a Vice President of Blue Bell Europe reporting directly to the man who reported to the main board. Under the new set up, he was Managing Director of the Wrangler UK company. He would now be reporting to a man, who reported to the man, who reported to the main board. In the new company pecking order, every one of us had effectively been demoted.

Uncertainty still existed about the relationship between new company's two largest brand assets, Lee, and Wrangler.

I broached the issue head on when we were asked by John Johnson if we had any questions. "I am aware that on the face of it there is complete synergy between the brands of VF and Blue Bell. As you are aware, this is not the case in respect of Lee and Wrangler in Europe." The American contingent looked at each other, as I continued. "Are there any plans to reposition either one or both brands or are we to assume that we will continue to compete directly with each other?"

After what seemed an eternity, John Johnson replied. "You make a good point, Robin." he said. "We need to carefully consider how we develop the whole portfolio in the future. For the present, we ask you to continue in the same way you have in the past. We do not foresee any change of direction at least until after the end of 1988."

With the assurances that we had been given, planning could begin for the Autumn 1987 launch of the Spring 1988 product ranges.

The 1988 business plan, prepared by the senior management team, looked to place emphasis on increasing share in the geographical and retail distribution areas where the Wrangler brand was relatively weak. To achieve this, we agreed to maintain the existing SAP activity, particularly in the south of the country and to make a concerted effort to improve our presence within the larger multiple retailers.

Clearly, this was going to require an increase in our sales promotion activity, a more targeted public relations campaign, and a more visible, national advertising presence.

Whilst the total marketing budget had been increased, it was clear that we would still not be able to match the spend of Levi's. In addition, other competitors including Pepe and our sister brand Lee were already talking about increasing their future marketing spend.

With a new advertising agency in place, an opportunity existed to change the way that all our external marketing support companies inter-reacted. I made the decision to organise regular planning meetings. These were attended by the Wrangler account director at BBDO and the account directors at our Public Relations and Sales promotion agencies. Each was encouraged to provide input into what became the Wrangler Integrated Marketing Plan.

We decided never to use the acronym WIMP!

The approach was met with some resistance at first. Eventually, all participants began to realise that their early involvement in the creative development process was cutting out wasteful additional briefings and allowing more of the available budgets to be used to create more cost-effective outcomes.

In the middle of 1987, VF announced the appointment of Ralph Huschle as Vice President VF International. Ralph had previously been VP of Playtex in Canada.

At that time, only the UK & Ireland and Scandinavia remained as wholly owned subsidiaries. The rest of the International Division comprised of licensees responsible for major markets in Europe, the Far East, and South America.

Clearly, Ralph was faced with a steep learning curve. It was obvious that he would want to meet all the operational managers and immerse himself in the existing culture within the (now) VF owned operations. He would want to ensure that the key individuals would be able to adapt and prosper under his new management. To do this, he would have to meet with us individually.

We all faced, what could be construed as a new job interview!

Following on from my one-to-one meeting with Ralph Huschle, I had an opportunity to get to know him a little better when we travelled together to a meeting of Wrangler licensees in Germany.

He had a very clear idea of the priorities required to boost the performance of the Wrangler brand internationally. This involved ending some of the licensing arrangements in some of the key European markets, as soon as was possible, and developing a clear strategy for the brand internationally. Ralph was aware that I had broached the subject with John Johnson before he had come on board, and they had agreed that I should take on the responsibility for its production.

This would be on top of my specific responsibilities for the UK and Ireland!

During his time at Playtex, Ralph had developed a personal vision of the priorities required of a fashion orientated, marketing-based organisation. "Robin, as far as I am concerned, the four P's of marketing are Product, Product, Product, Product," he explained.

This concept sounded some alarm bells for me!

The number of product lines needed to fully cover the requirements of the women's underwear market was relatively small and very similar across different geographical regions.

In the jeans and jeans related tops market, Wrangler brought out two ranges a year covering the fashion requirements for men, women, and children. Some of the UK core lines were an integral part of the range offerings in other countries. However, a large proportion of the ranges catered for the different fashion requirements of consumers in each specific market.

Producing a successful, standardised jeans and related tops line would be difficult. Especially in the more fashion orientated international markets.

My focus remained on the development of the UK and Ireland marketing support programme for the whole of 1988.

The relationship with BBDO was progressing well. The availability of an increased budget enabled us to plan for a national advertising campaign. This would continue to provide most support for the Wrangler areas of strength but would also allow increased support to those areas where we were looking to increase our market share.

Around August 1987, I met the agency to discuss a new concept that the creative team had developed. The idea behind the campaign was, "cool, fashionable and adventurous people are wearers of Wrangler jeans." The concept centred on the exploits of a young stunt man and his ambition to pull off the ultimate crowd thriller. Instead of jumping a motor bike over a large number of buses, his aim is to jump a bus over a large number of bikes.

At the time, the well-known stunt rider, Eddie Kidd, held the world record for jumping a BIKE over 19 BUSES. Our hero planned to jump a double-decker London Routemaster BUS over 27 BIKES!

A sequence of set-ups would show our stuntman pulling on his Wrangler jeans, worn with a stylish leather jacket, before kissing his girlfriend and striding out into the night, climbing into the bus, driving it up a ramp and over the lined-up bikes. The commercial would hold on a freeze frame of the bus in mid-air over the bikes with the Wrangler logo highly visible.

The audience would be left in limbo. "Did he do it or did he not?"

I liked the concept. If we could pull it off, the commercial would be impactful. Its message would be clearly understood by the core market. Furthermore, the content, and the conjecture surrounding it, would help our Public Relations company to maximise the pre and post-publicity potential.

The go ahead was given to take the idea into pre-production.

Not long afterwards it was announced that Kevin Black, our merchandise manager would be leaving the company to take up early retirement. A few months later Dick Webzell himself also departed.

I had travelled to London with him to attend a meeting of key European marketing personnel representing both the VF wholly owned subsidiaries and the major licensees. We were both scheduled to attend a group dinner that evening but, during a break in proceedings he told me that he had been invited to a private dinner with John Johnson and Ralph Huschle. He would not be joining the rest of us.

The next day, everything appeared normal although he seemed subdued on the journey home on the Friday evening.

I had no inkling about the bombshell he was to drop when, on the following Monday, Dick called all the members of senior management team into his office. He announced he was leaving the company, with immediate effect, after clearing his desk and removing his personal effects.

We were all shocked at the brutality of the decision!

This was not how Blue Bell would have treated a man who had been at the helm almost from the start of the UK operation. "Dick was Mr Wrangler. The company had been his life for 21 years. If he could be culled in this way, how secure were the rest of us?"

The next day, a skip was brought in and placed next to his office window. Everything left in the office, apart from the furniture, was thrown into it. The skip was then taken away and with it all trace of the previous occupant, as well as a valuable archive of Wrangler memorabilia.

Ralph Huschle assumed the role of Interim Managing Director whilst a new Wrangler team was assembled. The Wrangler Ltd Organisation Chart had some notable vacancies. These included the position of Merchandise Manager and Managing Director. The Area Sales Managers had all reported to Dick Webzell and a decision would have to be made as to whether a National Sales Manager would also be needed.

Whilst all the disruption was happening, plans for the launch of the 1988 advertising campaign and Spring 1988 ranges were progressing at a pace.

In December 1987, BBDO had presented a detailed plan for the commercial shoot. It would be filmed outside the famous James Bond set at Pinewood Studios in Buckinghamshire. The agency had carried out extensive casting for the person to play the stuntman. They were recommending a 27-year-old male model by the name of Mark Beisiegel.

In reality. the bus would be driven by Rocky Taylor. He was well known for organising and carrying out stunts in many of the best action movies of the day, including the "Death Wish" trilogy.

I was assured that all the logistics had been carefully considered and the commercial could be made within the budget that had been agreed. The go-ahead was given for the shoot to take place in January 1988.

Immediately after the New Year holidays, I arrived at Pinewood studios for the shoot.

Filming had been split into three segments. The first being an indoor shoot of the interior of the "specially imported caravan." It featured Mark Beisiegel changing into his Wrangler jeans and kissing his girlfriend goodbye.

The second involved Mark climbing into the bus and preparing to launch it over the bikes.

The third element was the stunt itself.

The first two elements were reasonably straight forward because they were shot in a controlled environment. The stunt section was far less easy to control. It involved a large amount of risk. All the elements had to be set up outside to give the stunt coordinator, Rocky Taylor, the space, and necessary distance to pick up speed before hitting the ramp. The 27 motorbikes needed to be properly aligned beyond the take-off area.

The stunt had to appear to be taking place in a large floodlit arena. This meant that the positioning of the lighting was crucial. The Routemaster bus, weighing in at over 7 tons, needed to be hoisted into the air by crane and lifted, at the right angle over the bikes. Doing this correctly was critical to the authenticity of the stunt.

The motor bikes were supplied by the RAF display team who set them up in position. They were naturally very concerned. If Rocky got his angles and positioning wrong, all their bikes could be wiped out.

Practice went on throughout the daylight and into the twilight hours. Eventually, everyone signalled they were ready. Minutes later, the rain started to fall. There was no turning back. We had to carry on. Our tight budget would not allow us to come back and do it all again on another day.

Rocky was particularly keen to go ahead. Only later did I find out why!

He had been badly injured when a stunt went wrong, during the filming of "Death Wish III," nearly three years earlier. His injuries were so severe, he had been in danger of losing his life. Our commercial marked his comeback after a lot of adversity. He believed that the success of this stunt would provide a great launch pad for the continuation of his career.

Despite the wet weather, the stunt was executed perfectly. The result was stunning on the screen.

Our PR company were keen to capitalise on the publicity potential surrounding the finished advertisement. "Did he do it or did he not?" As a result, everyone involved was sworn to secrecy.

The press was invited to a pre-launch preview in March 1988, a week before the commercial was aired for the first time. The agency, the star and the stuntman all attended a press conference afterwards. I was assured all comments made would be closely monitored by our PR people.

A lot of positive publicity ensued!

On the 17 March 1988, The Sun newspaper carried a piece occupying more than half a page with the main headline "HOLD TIGHT ON TOP." Alongside this was the logo of London transport and a picture of the bus in flight measuring 21cm across 6 columns of the paper. A smaller headline at the top of the page read "Did bus really leap motorbikes in telly jeans ad?" Beneath this were three smaller shots from the shoot showing the bus at the end of the ramp, leaving the ramp and jumping the bikes. The explanatory copy read, "READY STEADY GO…the bus launches itself over 27 bikes in a £1million Wrangler jeans commercial. Did the double-decker fly or was it winched across by a crane?"

Under the large photograph was another caption, "CATCHING THE BUS…how you'll see the action when the commercial is screened next week. But it doesn't show the bus landing. Did it make it or did the adman fake it?"

Sun journalist, Pat Moore, wrote a great article to accompany the pictures and captions. In it she said, "the men behind the commercial – one of the most expensive ever – were remaining tight-lipped about whether the bus did make the leap. They admit that they had to winch the bus into the air on a crane to take some extra shots."

Rocky Taylor did not hold back and was quoted as saying, "It was one of the most amazing stunts I have ever done. There were (sic) a load of hairy moments. All I could see was a mass of open mouths below me. I think people were just staggered that it worked. With a stunt like that you shut your eyes, keep your fingers crossed and hope for the best."

The article quotes stunt rider Eddie Kidd, who at the time held the world record for jumping a bike over buses, as saying, "I'd rather jump the Grand Canyon than be on a bike under that bus."

A sentiment no doubt shared by the members of the RAF motorcycle display team on the night that it was shot!

The week after the commercial had first been aired, A JAK cartoon appeared in the Daily Mail. It featured a London bus, with Wrangler Jeans advertising on the side and back panels, jumping over an assortment of motorbikes at the roadside, complete with passengers and the bus conductor hanging from the door rail. The caption read, "COULD YOU LINE UP A FEW MORE BIKES? ARTHUR WANTS TO GO FOR A NEW RECORD."

At the end of the campaign BBDO presented me with a copy of the original cartoon. This still takes pride of place on my study wall at home.

These examples represent just a fraction of the great coverage that the PR agency was able to generate. The merchandising of the advertising through the PR and instore merchandising certainly contributed to high recall that the commercial generated.

As the campaign got underway, decisions were being made about the new structure of the management team at Wrangler Ltd.

Ralph Huschle had decided to fill the Merchandise Manager position, vacated by Kevin Black, with someone who had operated in a similar position with another, smaller competitor. This person would be responsible for the development of new product lines whilst I would continue, as Advertising Manager, to be responsible for all Wrangler brand communications output, market research and strategic development.

We would both report directly to the Managing Director.

True to his revelation, that to him that the 4 Ps of marketing were PRODUCT, PRODUCT, PRODUCT and PRODUCT, Ralph had changed the title of the new man from Merchandise Manager to Director of Marketing.

I was not happy!

Under the Blue Bell regime, there were only two Directors, the Managing Director, and the Financial Director. These titles were only used because as a UK Limited Company, there was a legal requirement to have Board Directors.

The new man's title would seem to imply, to the outside world at least, that he would be overseeing the whole marketing function, when, in fact, this was not the case.

Furthermore, it could also mislead people into believing that he was a Board Director of Wrangler Ltd, which of course he was not.

I raised the issue with Ralph who agreed that the title might lead to some confusion outside the company. "I understand your concern," he said. "Unfortunately, the offer has been made, and accepted under the Marketing Director job description," he continued. "What do you want me to do?"

After some discussion, we agreed that the PR announcement should be issued. This would clearly outline the responsibilities of the new man. I would be "promoted" to the title of Marketing Manager and my "elevation" would appear as part of the same press release.

With a new range to put together for Spring 1989, the new Marketing Director was under a major time constraint. His first range would be launched at the Men's and Boyswear (MAB) trade show in September 1988.

By the end of the Summer of 1988, the "Bus" commercial had enabled Wrangler to increase our share of voice despite being heavily outspent by Levi's. Other companies, such as our sister brand Lee jeans, Pepe and Lee Cooper were also using television and cinema campaigns.

Wrangler brand share remained static in a slightly increased market. Considering the traumas that had taken place within the company, I felt this was a good performance.

Every major brand of jeans was trying hard to be heard. Their advertising agencies appeared to be vying with each other to produce weirder and weirder pieces of work aimed at making their brands more acceptable to the core 16-24 consumers.

Wrangler and Levi's were being consistent in putting their product at the forefront of their creative concepts.

I explained to BBDO, that their role was to continue to focus their thinking on the idea that had influenced the creative work for the "Bus" commercial. The concept, that cool, fashionable, and adventurous people are wearers of Wrangler jeans, should continue to be the core idea behind our advertising message.

The BBDO team agreed that this was the right thing to do. The creative team went way to put on their thinking caps.

Meanwhile, in the Wrangler offices at Calverton, the fallout following the departure of Dick Webzell continued with the departure of one of the three Regional Sales Managers.

Ralph Huschle realised how important it was to stabilise the Wrangler salesforce. He had been in touch with some of the key sales personnel at Playtex in Canada. In quick succession, Messrs Wildgoose and Stone were recruited to take on the roles of Regional Sales Manager and Sales Director respectively.

Eyebrows were raised in the trade. The two new men in sales management team were UK born but neither had any recent knowledge of the UK retail market. In addition, neither they, or Ralph Huschle, the interim MD, had any experience of the jeans and casualwear markets.

Whilst Ralph was talking to possible candidates to take on the Managing Director role, it was taking longer than expected to bring the right man on board.

Clearly, Dick Webzell's shoes were taking some filling!

During this period, I was spending quite a lot of my time travelling around the country with Ralph Huschle visiting key clients, our advertising agency and PR company.

Like many Americans new to the UK, he found the pace of travel and the poor roads difficult to come to terms with.

On one journey, we were returning to Calverton from a meeting in London. I normally avoided long car journeys on a Friday evening. Londoners traditionally exit the capital in large numbers at that time. It was never a pleasant experience. Ralph had been insistent that the meeting should take place.

The journey from central London to the motorway had taken nearly an hour longer than normal because of the heavy traffic. Eventually, we entered the three-lane motorway and were travelling at around 70 miles per hour, a good distance from the car in front.

Ralph was clearly nervous. He asked me to slow down and not to drive as fast, or as close, as I was to the car in front. "Look out of the back of the car," I asked him. When he did, he was able to clearly see the car behind us. It was travelling at the same speed as us but was only inches behind. "If I apply the brakes only slightly, there is no way that he will be able to stop and there is nowhere for me to go," I continued.

Ralph went very quiet. He had realised that the three lanes of the motorway were, in fact, like a carpark. What was more, the carpark was travelling at 70 miles per hour, and would continue to do so for the next 100 miles.

He never asked me to organise a Friday meeting in London again. Mission accomplished!

On another occasion, we had travelled to the old Blue Bell jeans factory at Falkirk in Scotland. When VF took over Falkirk, they had acquired the factory which made Wrangler Jeans for the UK and the other European owned subsidiaries.

The staff at the factory were concerned that the new organisation might consolidate its production and that they might lose their jobs. Levi's had already closed a manufacturing plant in Scotland. VF themselves had closed a factory that had manufactured Lee jeans.

Dick Webzell had been able to assure them that there were no plans to close Falkirk. His departure had resurrected their anxieties.

Ralph wanted to personally reassure them that their jobs were safe and so the trip had been organised.

Divisional Manager, Frank Dimech, Ralph, and me, made presentations to every member of the workforce, having first split them into several quite large groups.

I explained our marketing plans to increase our share of the jeans market and how this would lead to more production in the future, not less.

Ralph, in his capacity of Vice President of VF International assured them that the Falkirk factory was very much at the forefront of the VF expansion plan.

Frank, then moderated questions from the shop floor.

A man close to the front put his hand up and asked the first question. "Canna ya tell us wither ya going ta meck enna changis ta wey we werk," he enquired in his broad Glaswegian accent.

Ralph looked puzzled. He had never heard a Glaswegian accent before. He was fluent in American English and German, but broad Scottish had defeated him. "Can you repeat the question?" he asked.

"Canna ya tell us wither ya going ta meck enna changis ta wey we werk," came the reply.

Ralph turned to Frank Dimech. "What did he say Frank?" "I'm Maltese," replied Frank. "I don't understand him either."

Luckily, I had lived in Scotland early in my career, and I was able to translate the question allowing Ralph to supply a full and reassuring answer.

I think it was Churchill who implied that "the UK and America were divided by a common language." The Falkirk experience demonstrated the benefits of good, clear communications that cross all the cultural divides.

Not long after the Falkirk meeting, Marc Cox the Wrangler Account Director at BBDO called me to set up a meeting. The agency creatives had come up with a "BIG IDEA" that they believe would perfectly fit the brief I had given them.

Ralph Huschle went with me to the presentation that took place in the BBDO offices in London. By this time, Phil Slott had returned to the USA. He had been replaced as CEO by the wonderfully named Art Unger. The creative department had been revamped by Art. This was the opportunity for the new boys to show us exactly what they could do.

Marc Cox began the build-up to the big reveal by explaining that the agency team believed it was important that Wrangler's American roots were central to creative idea. I groaned inwardly. My previous experiences had made me somewhat cynical. Such an opening pitch generally led to the inevitability of a "middling idea" that required a trip to the States to shoot a "middling commercial."

Marc continued, "The star of our advertising idea is the Wrangler product. A superbly fitting pair of Wrangler jeans worn by a great looking guy. The core message is great things happen to people who wear the Wrangler product."

The creatives, led by Andy Nichol, then presented the storyboard. "The location is a typical street in downtown Los Angeles. The hero walks down the street. We notice that he is being closely followed by a helmeted LA motorcycle cop.

As he passes a wire fence separating an open-air basketball court from the street, the cop pulls in front of him and orders him to "FREEZE." The cop dismounts from the bike and removes the helmet to reveal, not a man, but an attractive policewoman.

"Up against the fence," she commands. "Spread your legs." She says threateningly. The policewoman proceeds to frisk our hero in a very intimate manner (much to the amusement of the players on the basketball court). As she runs her hands sensuously up and down the inside and outside of his legs, the camera cuts in close to reveal the great fit and the Wrangler branding.

At this point our hero looks down towards her and says, somewhat wearily, "Susie, do you have to do this, EVERY time I wear my Wrangler jeans?"

The frame freezes on the jeans and the Wrangler logo."

The idea was simple, amusing and, if shot in a sensitive manner, it would be very effective.

Would the agency suggest a studio-based shoot in London, where complete control could be exercised, or would they opt for the riskier reality of the outdoor shoot in LA?

I already knew the answer!

I looked at Ralph. He nodded to me. We both liked the idea but expressed some reservations about the cost. Both of us wanted confirmation that the LA based shoot would leave sufficient of our limited budget, to ensure the commercial would be highly visible to our, notoriously difficult to reach, core target market.

Marc Cox explained they already had an American based director in mind. The use of an all-American crew, American cast, and extras, would ensure that the commercial came in at a realistic figure.

We agreed that the agency should check out all the logistics and get back to us with a full price breakdown. Once approved, the programme for the shoot could be agreed, and we could move forward very quickly. At the same time, the BBDO media people would put together a complete airtime proposal using a combination of television and, perhaps, cinema.

It was important to us that the salesforce would have as much time as possible to market the advertising to the trade. The realisation that Wrangler was supporting them, with a heavy, national advertising campaign, would help the sell-in of additional product.

I understood it would not be possible to produce the finished commercial in time for the Spring 1989 trade shows.

These were taking place in September 1988 and the shoot was unlikely to take place before the beginning of November. We planned to produce a highly finished story board and media plan, in time for the show. Also available, would be the complete airtime schedule.

When the commercial had been shot and edited, copies would be provided to the salesforce and our Field Promotion Representatives. This would provide the opportunity for them to not only sell in more product but also to book window and promotional space to support retail sales during the campaign period.

Several weeks later, I had a further meeting with the BBDO team to talk over, and sign off, the production cost for the commercial and the proposed media plan.

The commercial would be produced by the Ridley Scott Associates, production company in Los Angeles. It would be directed by one of their top commercial and film directors. Through them, a shoot location had been found in downtown LA that was perfect for our needs. The only major cost would be the replacement of the existing wire fence around the basketball play area. For filming purposes, something more substantial, than the one already there, was required and the necessary planning approval would have to be obtained.

The casting had taken place and I was shown photographs of all the proposed talent that had been selected. No fitting sessions had taken place, but the measurements of the lead character had been taken. Wrangler products would be sent out for fitting before the shoot. More would be taken out by the BBDO production people to enable a final fitting session to take place ahead of filming.

The top line cost had been calculated and, inclusive of a contingency, was within a budget that would allow us to buy airtime for a heavyweight campaign.

I was very happy, but before I could say so, Marc Cox announced that there was one small problem! "Unfortunately, there is only enough money in the budget for six people to fly out from the UK for the shoot," he said.

"What's the problem then?" I asked.

"We need to send that number of people from the agency so there isn't enough money in the budget for you to go," he replied, somewhat sheepishly.

"There is no way I am going to sign off such a large expenditure unless I am able to attend the fitting session and the shoot," I countered. "I am sure you will be able to trim the cost, or send one person less from the agency, so that the client can be accommodated," I continued.

The necessary savings were found!

Fitting and filming were scheduled. The agency booked my flight out to Los Angeles for Monday 14 November 1988. Agency personnel would go out a few days earlier to set up the fitting sessions and make last minute preparations at the location site.

Fitting sessions and final site inspections had been scheduled to take place on the Tuesday and the Wednesday. The shoot would then start on the Thursday and, if everything went to plan, would be finished on the Saturday morning.

Before I left on my trip, Ralph Huschle announced that he had concluded his search for a new Managing Director. John Hart, the former sales and marketing director of

Levi's Strauss, would be taking up the post that had been vacant since the departure of Dick Webzell.

On the face of it, John was not the obvious choice. He had served in various management positions at Levi's. He was the person holding the reins in the Marketing Department when the "501" advertising campaign was launched.

In the trade, it was felt that he was destined for one of the top jobs at Levi's. His move to Wrangler, the UK number two brand, had come as a surprise!

I knew several the Levi's advertising, marketing, public relations, and sales managers but I had never met John Hart.

It would be interesting to see his perspective on the future direction of the Wrangler brand.

When his appointment was made public, it was clear that, in one sense, John was coming home. His family lived in Nottingham. He had attended Nottingham High School at the same time as some of my acquaintances.

The date of my trip to Los Angeles had arrived. BBDO had sent through my return business class ticket. When this landed on my desk, I recall thinking that it was no wonder the agency had expressed some reservations about their ability to afford the cost of me attending the shoot.

If every member of the agency team had also travelled by business class, the total bill would be very hefty!

When I eventually arrived at the departure lounge at Heathrow, there was a huge queue at the TWA check in desk. After a waiting for 15 minutes, an announcement advised that another desk was opening for business and first-class travellers.

There were very few people at this desk, and I soon reached the front. The attendant took my ticket and looked at it closely and then entered some details into the system.

"I'm sorry Mr Dilley," she said. "Can you wait a few minutes?" before adding, "It will be worth your while!"

After a few more taps on her keyboard, the luggage tags were printed along with my boarding pass. My luggage disappeared, and the attendant handed over my passport and boarding card with the words that every flyer hopes they will hear, but very few do, "Mr Dilley, I have upgraded you to first class. Have a nice day."

It is a very long flight from London to Los Angeles but, if the journey is necessary, then first class is the best way to do it. When eventually the plane landed, I made my way through immigration and into the arrivals area. On entering, I saw a man holding a sign with the words, 'Robin Dilley, Wrangler jeans.'

He turned out to be the driver of a limousine the BBDO team had booked to whisk me off to the hotel where we were all staying. This was the iconic Four Seasons Hotel in Beverley Hills.

I should have been impressed but my only thought was how well we were all living, at Wrangler's expense!

After a flight of nearly 12 hours, all I wanted to do was to take a quick bite at the hotel restaurant and then go back to my room and catch up on some sleep.

It had been planned that, on the Tuesday morning, I would be taken to the location in downtown LA to meet the director and talk over the shoot.

The whole of Wednesday had been set aside for final wardrobe fittings and meetings with the cast, stylists and briefing the stills photographer. The latter would be working with me to produce shots for use in public relations and for point-of-sale material.

Work on the production of the commercial was planned to start on the Thursday morning and was scheduled to finish on the Friday evening.

Soon after I had checked in, I contacted the agency production people. I needed to finalise with them all the arrangements over the next few days. They explained that my original schedule had been altered slightly because "the clean-up of the location will not be completed until Tuesday afternoon."

Apparently, they didn't want me to see it until it was 100% ready!

I thought it strange that "the grimy downtown LA setting" we had come all this way to film in, was not considered clean enough for me to look at!

"No point in causing a fuss," I thought to myself. "I will just have to spend my time tomorrow morning sleeping off my jet lag by the pool. When they were ready for me, they would come and collect me."

Shooting television commercials is a hard life!

Next day, in the cab on the way to the shoot, Marc Cox explained the problems with the location. Apparently, the street chosen by the production company was frequented by people who slept rough there during the night.

"But surely that will not affect our shoot," I suggested.

It was then that the whole story unfolded!

Apparently for several weeks a serial killer had been at large in LA. He had been attacking people sleeping rough in the street. The killer had been given the nickname "The LA Slasher" by the local press. Just a few days before, two down and outs had been attacked and murdered at our location. It had been a police crime scene until that morning.

When I arrived, the new fence was in place and several extra street signs had been put in place by the production company.

The director went through the storyboard with us. He explained the shoot sequences and introduced his key people who were busy going through set up, lighting rig positioning and all the other technical intricacies.

I had only been to downtown LA once before. That had been nine years before. Arriving in the city during a return trip from the Far East, I had decided to pay a call on the Wrangler regional office. Driving my hire car from the relative safety of Beverley Hills, I had spent some time trying to find a car park. Eventually, I discovered one just across the street from my eventual destination.

Right next to the alleyway we would be using for our commercial shoot was that self-same carpark. Both locations were overlooked by the building that still housed the LA offices of Wrangler jeans.

Some coincidence! If I had time during the shoot, I would just have to give them a visit.

155

That night the BBDO team took me to a restaurant in nearby Santa Monica. It was a typical American/Italian eatery. Very informal and lacking the frills of the, somewhat stuffy, hotel environment, delivering great food and a fantastic atmosphere. It was just what we needed before the fitting and wardrobe sessions due to take place the following day.

The next morning, we took a cab to the offices of Ridley Scott Associates. I seem to recall they were situated in the grounds of one of the main studio complexes. Here we met all the other members of the crew including wardrobe, hair and makeup, all the actors and extras who comprised the cast.

I was particularly interested in seeing how well the Wrangler jeans looked on the actor who was playing the lead role. Thankfully, we had sent over several size and style options for the initial casting, and I had also taken some spares in my luggage. Without too much trouble, we agreed on the style and size that looked the best.

The female actress was a real stunner, even in her policewoman's outfit. Riding a police bike is not recommended for a novice but we were fortunate to have access to some of the best stunt riders in the business. Looking great and having no fear is a potent combination. The stunt rider chosen for the job met both criteria.

I was happy, the BBDO team was happy, and so was the Director.

We were ready to go!

The production company was aware still pictures were required for PR and point of sale purposes. It is important that a stills photographer and director can work together to ensure that one can step in, and do the business, when the other has finished.

The person chosen for the job was Joseph Viles.

He had already created a formidable reputation for himself in Hollywood, having worked on many major feature films. He was also the preferred portrait photographer for many of the top movie stars. Our director had worked with him before and was happy that they would be able to operate in tandem with each other on the Wrangler shoot.

Using the storyboard as a guide, I talked Joseph through what I was looking for, a mixture of black and white and colour shots. It was clear to me that we were on the same wavelength. I was confident he would "produce the goods" during the shoot.

These were the days before digitisation. Photographers still used film. If the results didn't meet expectation, or some technical gremlins had caused problems, there was no way we could go back and take the shots again. Trust was all important.

Joseph Viles was someone in whom I had complete faith!

That evening it was decided to splash out on top class restaurant for a meal, for me, the agency team, and key people from the production company.

Once shooting started, we would all be heavily involved. Although to the outsider, filming can seem a bit like "watching paint dry," it is time consuming and very tiring. Location catering and then an early night would be the order of the day on the Thursday and Friday.

The restaurant scene in Los Angeles, and particularly Hollywood, relies very much on word of mouth. You can't look in a phonebook or restaurant guide and just call and reserve a table. The restaurants to be seen in, are not always those who produce the best food.

Thankfully, our production company was very well connected. They had used their influence to book a table in one of the new up and coming restaurants in town. We were assured it was frequented by the great and the good and that the food was excellent.

When we arrived, Joan Collins was seated in the best table adjacent to the window. Her escort, I was reliably informed, was Bill Wiggins. Apparently, for reasons I will not go into here, he was well known in the UK tabloid newspapers as "Bungalow Bill." The restaurant was crowded with 'A listers,' hangers-on and film production personnel like us. The environment, the service and the food did not disappoint!

The next morning, we arrived at the location early.

Even though "The LA Slasher" was still at large, the first few hours of set-up also involved moving out the itinerants who had taken up residence overnight, and then cleaning up the mess they had left behind.

I was surprised to find that there were four LAPD cops with motorcycles on set. In addition to our actress and stunt policewomen, there were also two real policemen.

In Los Angeles, a lot of films and commercials are shot. As a result, the LAPD set up special film division. Comprised of retired or part time officers, its role is to provide security, crowd and traffic control services to protect films crews, and the public alike.

In the case of our shoot, our "pretend motorcycle cop" was required to ride her bike along one of the busiest streets in downtown Los Angeles and then turn into the alleyway where all the main action was taking place.

The Director of the commercial and his Assistant Director needed to work in close liaison with the two officers allocated to our shoot, to minimise traffic disruption. In the UK, the flow of traffic has precedence over the requirements of a film crew. For this reason, most traffic sequences are shot in the early morning when little traffic is around.

In LA, the opposite is the case!

If a film crew has the required licences to film and have paid for police office support through the special LAPD Film Division, they can shoot whenever, and virtually, wherever they want.

Our director wanted heavy traffic and chose to shoot during the peak lunchtime period. That presented no problem to our officers.

When our director was ready to shoot, he assumed full control of the traffic flow along the street, which had to do what he and our police support officers wanted them to do. On the call of "Action," the traffic controls were applied, sometimes bringing all movement to a complete standstill. When he said "Cut" the officers lifted their controls.

For nearly three hours, the movement of all traffic in downtown LA was under the complete control of a man directing a Wrangler television commercial!

A lot of people were inconvenienced but there was no hooting of horns and no heated arguments. The population of "film city" were used to such things. They simply took it all in their stride.

During a lull in shooting, I went to visit the Wrangler offices which were just a block from the film location. I was made very welcome and shown around. Explaining that we were shooting a Wrangler television commercial, for the UK and northern Europe, just a few hundred yards away, the Divisional Manager showed some interest. Not enough however to accept my invitation to visit the scene of the shoot.

Just another day of filming in LA for him!

On day one, we had completed all the motorcycle sequences to everyone's satisfaction. Our police support officers were no longer required to control the traffic. Their hands were now full preventing the down and outs from entering the alleyway, to claim their sleeping slots for the night, while the film crew were still dismantling their expensive equipment.

I was happy with the playbacks I had seen. Joseph Viles had worked well with me, and the director, to capture still shots of the main action. We would be able to look at contact sheets before the shoot started the next day. The first day had gone to plan and we were all able to return to our hotel.

The important product shots and the interaction between the two main characters were scheduled for the next day.

Shooting on the final day went to plan and with no major hitches. I had an opportunity to sit down with Joseph to look at the contact sheets of shots he had taken the day before.

We also talked over the importance of the product shots that were required and agreed he would load two cameras for each set up. This would allow him to take black and white pictures for PR purposes and colour for subsequent point of sale material.

During the day, I was impressed with how he and the director and the main characters interacted. When the director was happy with a set up and called "Cut," Joseph would step in and control all the action. He instinctively, seemed to know which shots to take during filming and never got in the way of the process. A true professional!

The playbacks looked great, and we were all very happy. The director indicated there were a small number of technical elements that needed attention. He would be bringing the crew back on the Saturday morning to shoot a little more film, from slightly different angles.

It was agreed, there was no need for me to attend. Instead, I had arranged to meet up briefly with Joseph at the hotel to look at the remaining contact sheets and organise dates for delivery of the chosen prints, along with transparencies of the colour work.

This left me with some spare time on the Saturday afternoon to really look around the Beverley Hills area. This included a visit to the fashion shops of Rodeo Drive from where the Wrangler merchandise team gathered a lot of inspiration for their jeans related clothing ranges.

Marc Cox was keen to organise a last night dinner for me and the BBDO production team. The creatives were going to RSA to look at rushes after the morning technical shoot and would be eating out with the director afterwards.

Aware of the difficulties of booking a decent restaurant on a Saturday night, I suggested that a good American steak house might be ideal. I figured this would be more cost-effective. To go all the way to California and not have a classic American steak, with all the trimmings, would be a grave omission.

Marc said he would ask the concierge to recommend a place to go and make the booking. That evening we met up in the hotel lobby. The concierge had been very helpful and had organised everything, including the cab.

As we piled in and the driver, who turned out to be Irish, asked Marc where we wanted to go. "You want to go THERE!" he said incredulously in his lilting brogue.

"Yes," said Marc. "We wanted a lively American steak bar with good food and lots of atmosphere. This was the one recommended, is it OK?"

"To be sure, I'm told the food is very good and the place has a REAL American feel," the driver replied.

We soon arrived at our chosen venue and, after Marc had paid the driver his parting words were, "Have a great night. I HOPE you enjoy yourselves."

We were intrigued. What were we letting ourselves in for?

Outside the restaurant was a billboard announcing that this was "a real New York Steak Bar." This seemed a strange thing to say given that it was located at Beverley Hills in Los Angeles. Of course, Hollywood has many unique places to visit. Our "New York Steak Bar" proved to be no exception.

When we went inside, there was a huge queue waiting patiently for a table to be allocated to them. There were plenty of empty tables. We assumed that these were reserved for the people who had booked beforehand. One of them was presumably ours.

The people in the queue had obviously walked off the street without a booking. This was surely a good sign. The food must be excellent.

We followed Marc through to the head of the queue where we were halted by the officious sounding Maître D. "Buddy, where do you think you're going," he snarled, in an apparently authentic New York way.

"We have booked a table for four in the name of Cox," Marc explained.

"Booked a table," the man spluttered. "We don't take no bookings here," he continued. "Get your asses to the end of the queue and wait your turn," he snarled,

Marc was gobsmacked. He wasn't used to been spoken to like that. He also did not understand why all the other people waiting found it so funny.

I suddenly twigged what was going on. This was Hollywood. The other customers were used to people being servile to the point of being sycophantic. Our venue was LA's idea of a New York restaurant. New Yorkers had a reputation for being forthright and rude. It was my guess that all the staff were out of work actors pretending to be New Yorkers.

I decided to play them at their own game.

"Are you really from New York?" I enquired of the Maître D. He looked puzzled and I continued, "We are from England. My three companions are from London and don't like making a fuss. I am from the wilds of Yorkshire. We don't suffer fools gladly. You wouldn't like to get on the wrong side of a Yorkshireman. Let's not mess about. Please take us to our table!"

The people at the front of the queue broke into spontaneous applause. I think they thought it was all part of the evening's show. Our pretend New Yorker saw the funny side too. He took us immediately to one of the best tables in the house.

After that, our party really entered into the spirit of the night and enjoyed excellent service, great food and a fantastic atmosphere.

Back in the UK, John Hart was getting to grips with the complexities of his new role. He was working, in tandem with Ralph Huschle, to bring together a new team.

As far as I was concerned, I had a commercial to sign off, support material to develop, a PR support programme to brief and the launch of the Spring 1989 ranges to plan.

There was too much to do, for me to be unduly concerned with the politics and possible restructuring of Wrangler Ltd.

It was clear to me that John Hart would want to surround himself with his own team. As a result, there would be changes. I would just have to wait and see whether there was still a role for me.

A few weeks after my return from LA, the finished version of the "Frisk" commercial was presented to me, John Hart, and Ralph Huschle. The final cut worked very well. We were all in agreement that it be signed off along with the media plan.

The stills shots from Joseph Viles provided a rich vein of material to help the PR company to merchandise the advertising and for our promotions company to produce some stunning point of sale material. Joseph also sent me a framed and signed hand tinted print of the Wrangler clad hero standing against the wire fence.

I still have it hanging in my house today.

The Wrangler salesforce was also enthusiastic about the commercial, the media schedule and the support material. Presentations to key retailers enabled us to increase sales and book incentive programmes, window, and indoor support to help facilitate the sell-out at the point of purchase.

When a vacancy for the position of Marketing Director became available, it was filled by Robin Hollick who had worked with John Hart at Levi's.

From being the only Robin in "marketing," I was now being referred to as one of the "the Two Robin's." This led to some confusion when talking to suppliers and during management meetings. Every time someone asked a question of Robin, neither of us was too sure who they were referring to. Often, we either both remained silent thinking that the other should reply, or we both answered in unison. Often, with a different answer!

As the year progressed other senior appointments were made in the merchandise department and in sales management. All the new people also came from Levi's. A pattern was emerging.

In our strategic development meetings, it was becoming clear that my ex-Levi's colleagues were looking to change the positioning of the Wrangler brand. They felt it was too pristine. The American imagery needed to be more of today, and less retro, than that of their old company.

I partly agreed with their observations but pointed out that changing the image would be a long-term project. After all, "Rome was not built in a day."

My colleagues had the benefit of a perception of the Wrangler brand as seen through the eyes of the major competitor. They would also have been privy to consumer research in the Levi's areas of strength which tended to be the Wrangler areas of weakness.

John, and the "other Robin," also believed that BBDO was not the agency the deliver the edgy creative solution they felt was required.

John had worked with BBH for several years. He had been part of the Levi's team that had taken a risk on them, at a time when they were perceived as the leaders of a "new wave" of creative agencies. Perhaps, he thought, we should seek out the next creative hot shop and move the Wrangler account to them?

At this point in time, I had been custodian of the Wrangler brand for over 14 years. A consistent strategy to brand development, had helped Wrangler maintain its market share despite the upheavals of the past couple of years. I was not convinced that this was the time for a complete change of direction.

We had a vote. I lost by two to one!

My case was not helped by the upheavals that were taking place at BBDO. Most of the Wrangler team at the agency had already left or had signalled their intentions to leave soon. The job of advising BBDO of our plans was left to me. They were given the option of being part of a pitch working on the new brief. They chose not to do so.

I think they felt they had enough problems of their own at the time. Possibly they realised the new Wrangler team was really looking for a complete change of direction and that, whatever they did, the Wrangler account would be on the move.

Over a period of many months, I had been contacted by one of the new kids on the block called Simons Palmer Denton Clemmow & Johnson Ltd (Simons Palmer). They had sent me a series of postcards.

The first, posted to me on 8 December 1988, had a poster they had produced for Greenpeace on the front.

It featured a car number plate that read, "MICHIGAN F-U-GB HAVE A NICE DAY!" Underneath were the words, "A Ford in Britain pumps out 100% more toxic fumes than a Ford back home in America."

Beneath this was the Greenpeace logo

The hard sell on the back of the post card was a quotation from the Campaign magazine – "controversy helps a small budget stretch a long way." The call to action was a simple message. "To make your money go further call PAUL SIMONS on (telephone number)."

Another post card arrived on 13 December 1988. This featured, on the front, a poster for their client Heineken. On the reverse was a couple of citations from the Campaign Poster Award 1988. These heralded the fact that the Simons Palmer posters had received a Gold Award for Best Individual Poster and another Gold Award for Best Campaign.

This time the call-to-action message was "for outstanding advertising call PAUL SIMONS…."

On the 22 May 1989, not long before our internal Wrangler brand development meeting, I had received yet another postcard. This featured a picture of one "stuffy man," one "cool man" and a very attractive woman on a flight. The woman is using her compact mirror to gaze at the "cool man" sitting behind her.

The reverse featured a quotation about the Campaign magazine 'Choice of the week' 21.01.89. "Simons Palmer Denton Clemmow and Johnson prove that insurance ads need not be dull." The call to action this time suggested "to insure yourself against dull advertising call PAUL SIMONS…."

I had spoken to Paul Simons on several occasions and told him that we were happy with our current agency. The situation had now changed. I picked up the phone to talk to him again.

From my previous discussions, I was aware Simons Palmer had a clear idea of how they felt they might be of assistance to Wrangler. I was also aware that they were keen to work with us. Good work for a brand like ours, could only further enhance their growing reputation!

An appointment was made on a date that was convenient for me, John Hart, and Robin Hollick. Before the meeting, I had several further conversations with Paul Simons who was keen to glean as much background information as possible ahead of our first meeting.

Eventually, I received a call from Paul advising that they were ready to talk. They had some concept suggestions to make the Wrangler brand more appealing, in image perception, to the extremely volatile, 16-24 age group, who represented 50% of all jeans sales.

I had already assessed the market and carried out some independent research on the "Frisk" commercial produced by BBDO.

Although Wrangler had been brand leader at the end of the 1970's and into the 1980's, we had lost brand share to Levi's. This was due to several factors, the most important of which was the lack of investment in the brand during the mid-1980's, firstly, as the result of the Blue Bell management buy-out, and then, following the subsequent sale to the VF Corporation.

Despite this, Wrangler remained a strong brand but with a divided image. To succeed, I felt it important "that we improve the perception of the Wrangler product to the more fashion conscious, younger consumers, taking care not to alienate the loyal, but older Wrangler consumer."

Our post-advertising research showed that the BBDO "Frisk" commercial had struck a chord across both markets. The company, who carried out the research, reported back to us with their findings. "We carried out several group discussions amongst the key target market. Those interviewed liked the element of realism portrayed. They bought into the street tension that built to the conflict tension amongst the two key characters. They loved the way that the sexual tension built up and the way this was turned into relief, rewarded by permission to enjoy," they explained.

During our first meeting with Simons Palmer, the question of realism was explored. The new members of the Wrangler marketing team had wondered whether the "Frisk" concept was real enough. Simons Palmer was adamant that they didn't think it was.

The agency felt they could build on the strengths of the "Frisk" commercial, to produce something altogether more reflective of a gritty street realism, that the key sections of the market could relate to. Furthermore, they were convinced such an approach would move the Wrangler image even further away from the "Hollywood style of America," employed by our key competitor, and strike a chord with the UK fashion innovators.

If they were lucky enough to be given the chance, they would develop the concept through some further research. This, they believed, would give us some directional pointers for a creative concept that would take the Wrangler brand into the 1990's.

Back at Calverton, John, the other Robin, and myself agreed to move the account to Simons Palmer. It was accepted that this was a risk but a risk that, hopefully, would be worth taking.

Only time would tell!

Chapter Nine

Simons Palmer Denton Clemmow & Johnson Ltd - 1989 to 1991

At our first meeting since we had appointed Simons Palmer as our advertising agency, we were introduced to the team that would be working on the Wrangler account. In effect, this included all the agency partners, plus Mike Perry, who would be my day-to-day contact and the Wrangler Account Manager.

Simons Palmer did not have an in-house media department. All their media planning and buying had been assigned to one of several media buying companies. It was a long time ago, but I have a strong recollection that CIA Billet & Co was the chosen agency, and that Colin Gottlieb and Nick Manning were the account directors on our account.

Simons Palmer had carried out the group research that we had discussed at the 'pitch' meeting. Both the agency and Wrangler marketing teams were keen to determine the key factors that made a brand "cool" in the eyes of the target market.

Previous research had determined that the Wrangler customer age profile differed dramatically across the 15-25 key consumer group. This clearly indicated that what turned on the 15-19-year olds, was a turn off to 20-25-year-olds. They had totally different values! To the younger group, someone who had reached the age of 25 was regarded as positively geriatric.

There was, however, a common thread running across the whole age profile – Style! We needed to find out what they all meant by style and who they all thought had it. Simons Palmer had selected some film clips which they felt showed people who had style. Magazine cuttings were also used as a stimulus.

During my early telephone conversations with the agency, we had agreed that contemporary America (as used in the BBDO "Frisk" commercial) was the correct positioning for the Wrangler brand.

How to best portray it moving forward, was another problem!

To try and solve this dilemma, the agency put together two film clips. One represented what they described as adman America. The other projected something they regarded as close to the real thing.

The research groups had been exposed to both.

After analysing the responses, the research agency concluded that what they described as "eighties design culture" was out. It was perceived as creating "clichéd and predictable imagery" which the Wrangler target consumer saw as no longer aspirational or believable.

Simons Palmer was convinced that the way forward had become clear. The portrayal of "reality" was the way to connect with the consumers of the nineties!

Chris Palmer and Mark Denton believed they had come up with the "BIG IDEA" that would move the Wrangler brand image forward. They had cut together some rough clips of real people through the window of a vehicle crossing New York. This was over-played with a little-known, heavy beat track, by Jimmy Hendrix, called "Crosstown Traffic."

"The story board showed New York as seen through the eyes of a New York cab driver. He has become disillusioned with the hustle and bustle of 'THE BIG APPLE' and abandons his cab in the rush hour traffic. Catching the subway to the airport he boards a plane and flies out of the big city to join his family."

I liked the proposed payoff line, "Be more than just a number." It worked at several levels. As well as reflecting the desire for individuality, that younger consumers increasingly identified with, it also represented a challenge to Levi's 501 advertising and a declaration of our challenge to their number one position in the jeans market.

I was not happy about the proposed background track, or the amount of exposure of the Wrangler product.

Robin Hollick loved the music. Both he and John Hart felt that the idea would break new ground, just as the "Laundrette" advertisement had done for Levi's.

Chris and Mark sought to reassure me. "We believe that the Hendrix track could prove an inspirational choice if we can obtain permission to use it," they said. "Our hero has style which comes from his actual experience of life," they continued. "The scenario we propose reeks of reality. It is not so much an advertisement; it is more a mini document of New York life."

Hendrix had never been one of my favourite artists. I believed his music could polarise opinion amongst our target market. It seemed to me that the creative idea, rather than the Wrangler product, could easily become the star of the commercial.

I understood that I was not a part of the age group that we were targeting. As a result, I agreed with my colleagues that the agency should move to the next stage of pre-casting both a director and the main characters.

Simons Palmer, in turn, agreed that they would take on board my concerns about product visibility.

The media schedule would be drawn up to include TV and cinema alongside a campaign in the magazines read by the style leaders.

A couple of weeks later, we were back at Simons Palmer for the pre-production meeting. Paul Simons advised us they were proposing that Roger Lyons direct the commercial. This was perhaps a master stroke on their part. Roger had directed the "Laundrette" and "Bath" commercials for Levi's when John Hart oversaw the company's marketing. The argument being, "He produced the goods for Levi's, he can do it again for Wrangler!"

They wanted to cast a 40-year-old actor called Paul Garcia as the taxi driver. Apparently, he had done a stint driving a New York cab between appearing in minor roles in "Jaws 2" and "Trading Places." "Does he look good in a pair of Wrangler Jeans," I enquired.

"If you like him, we will go out to New York and do a fitting session," came the answer. "We have excellent news about the music," Paul continued. "Hendrix music has never been used in advertising before, so we never expected to be able to use the original. We have been lucky, the Hendrix family like the idea. 1990 marks the anniversary of his death and his music is having a revival. It can only represent a win, win situation for both parties," he concluded.

Cynically, I thought to myself, "The use of the track is going to cost 'big bucks.' I'm not surprised that they like the idea."

I was unhappy about casting Paul Garcia without having seen him in the flesh, so to speak. If we went ahead with the recommendations, we would need to ensure that he looked good in the product. Simons Palmer agreed to ensure that this was done, and to provide an accurate quotation for the use of the Hendrix music, and production of the finished commercial.

CIA Billet & Co were asked to develop the media schedule to comprise the use of television, cinema, and a product-based magazine campaign, "to specifically increase credibility of Wrangler merchandise amongst style leaders."

To cut a long story short, Paul Garcia was contracted to take on the taxi driver role. Roger Lyons was appointed as director.

The Hendrix management did ask for mega bucks for the use of the "Crosstown Traffic" track. They were not prepared to negotiate and, because it was felt to be central to the creative idea, we reluctantly agreed.

The downside of the higher-than-expected production costs was that the product-based magazine campaign had to be abandoned to provide a contingency for any additional strategic activity, that might be deemed necessary, as the "Crosstown Traffic" campaign unfolded.

Because of the loss of the magazine campaign, Simons Palmer had asked CIA Billet to fine-tune the TV schedule to concentrate the expenditure by following a single-minded approach to reach the 'style influencers.'

This was a high-risk strategy as they were known to be light viewers!

Furthermore, this meant that 50% of our TV spend would go behind the London area (a weak area for Wrangler sales) at the expense of visibility to the wider market outside London (the Wrangler areas of strength). It was also likely that we would be outspent by Levi's who were also using a similar buying strategy.

I had made my views known but I was in a minority of one!

The agency was confident in the strength of their idea and the ability of the production company and chosen director to deliver it. "The competition will be blown out of the water," they predicted.

There are times when the realisation that you are never going to win the argument sets in. This was one of those moments!

Approval was given to all the recommendations and the shoot date set.

At the end of November 1989, I found myself flying into New York to represent the company during what would prove a very complicated, and difficult shoot for me to follow. The only areas I could really influence would be those elements involving the relatively few, static product shot moments.

New York, like LA, is used to the invasion of TV cameras. As a result, provided you have the correct licenses, the director is given a long rein. Unfortunately, Roger Lyons, like all great directors, wanted to stretch the limit of the approvals he had been given to the absolute maximum, and beyond if possible!

The opening shot of the commercial needed to establish where all the action was taking place. The iconic shot of the Brooklyn Bridge from the Brooklyn side of the river was therefore the obvious choice.

We had a permit to shoot by the riverside, so this should have been a straightforward exercise. Unfortunately, entry on the site was controlled by two ex-cons who had constructed a huge wooden structure which they inhabited along with two large, and very fierce looking dogs.

They made a good living by extorting an entry fee on to the land from anyone wishing to film there. "If you wanna film here you pay $100 a day, or you don't come in," one of them informed the Assistant Director when we arrived.

His tone was threatening, his presence was intimidating, as was the hound he was holding on a tight leash.

The AD paid over the money. Two days of entry fees, in cash of course!

Mike Perry took an interest in them. He discovered that both men had spent many years in prison for violent crimes. They had not been able to get a job, or a home, when they came out. Starting out sleeping rough underneath the bridge, they had discovered its potential as a commercial venture almost by chance. The police turned a blind eye to their activities. In turn, they ensured that only "desirable, paying customers" came onto their patch. The two of them were now established as part of the New York tourist trail.

Tourists came to film the bridge. They paid the fee. They would also ask to have their photographs taken with the men. An extra fee applied of course. Mike Perry had taken some photographs of one of the men and sent me a framed print after the shoot as a memento.

A lunch break had been set up at a small boat moored just beyond the Brooklyn Bridge.

Film crews and actors always eat well on location. The buffet spread laid out for us that day was no exception. The food and hot drinks were very much appreciated. Standing around in the open in New York, on a cold mid-November day, is not to be recommended.

Out of the corner of my eye, I saw Mike Perry going around the buffet, selecting some of the more succulent items and putting them into a large paper sack.

"What are you doing Mike, you're not that hungry are you?" I enquired.

"I'm just getting some food for the two guys by the bridge," he replied. "I thought they would appreciate something good to eat."

"Take it if you like, but I will lay odds that they are earning more, and living a better life, than you think they are," I suggested.

When we went back to the bridge site for the next session, I followed him to the wooden structure where "the custodians of the bridge" were living. We were invited into a large kitchen area. There, over a large open fire, was half a side of succulent beef slowly roasting on a spit.

Mike handed over his goody bag from our buffet.

"Well thanks man," the men chorused. They both had a puzzled look on their faces.

"I'm sure that they will not be eating your buffet tonight, Mike," I said to him after we had left. "I imagine that the dogs will eat well though!"

Roger Lyons had been driving around New York taking footage of everyday life in the city to be cut into the commercial. He had spotted a young man, aged about 13, who was using two upturned and empty paint tins as a makeshift drum kit. His exertions had drawn a large, appreciative crowd of people.

"It sounded great," Roger explained to the creatives Chris Palmer and Mark Denton. "I know it's not on the shoot plan, but think that using him playing his 'drums,' along with the opening bars of the music, will make a fantastic start to the commercial," he enthused. "I have asked him to come here early tomorrow morning and we can get the footage in the can ahead of what we have already planned. If we can't find use for it in the final cut, so be it. Nothing ventured, nothing gained."

Chris and Mark thought it was a great idea. Great creative minds, working together, can visualise how a different concept can enhance the original idea. This was a case in point.

At the end of the first day of shooting, everyone seemed to be pleased with the outcome.

Roger, Chris, and Mark went off to look at the footage. The rest of us went back to the more civilised surroundings of our hotel, overlooking Central Park, to thaw out before dinner.

Bright and early the next morning, we were back at the Brooklyn Bridge location to meet the young drummer and to shoot sequence that Roger, Chris, and Mark had talked over the night before.

The drummer arrived complete with drumsticks, empty paint tins and a very large minder who he introduced as his agent. Addressing Roger, the agent's opening remarks went something like, "Man, we understand what you want. We will be happy to oblige, providing we can agree the right price and buyout rights on behalf of my client."

It was clear the "agent," probably the father of our young drummer, had been approached by film makers before. He knew the score and had a good idea of his "client's" worth. A mutually acceptable fee was agreed and paid.

Roger played the opening bars of "Crosstown Traffic". The young drummer took up the beat and the resultant sequence was stunningly executed.

That afternoon, the production team had planned to secure the service of a private helicopter to enable Roger and his camera team to take some aerial shots of New York. They wanted these to create more atmosphere during the opening sequence. The aerial sequences would be spliced into the footage they had already taken on the ground.

This had proved difficult because the private hire of a helicopter was expensive and the insurance for filming usage was prohibitive.

The production team had come up with a cunning plan!

A commuter helicopter shuttle service ran from JFK to Manhattan. It enabled busy executives to cut the travelling time from airport to their offices or hotels.

The production company had booked six seats. Three were for Roger, his Assistant Director, and the cameraman. Two were for the creative team of Chris Palmer and Mark Denton. The other was for the client – me!

Thinking about it later, I deduced that I was there to give the party some credibility. Whatever the reason, I had never flown in a helicopter before. This was going to be a new experience. Quite how much of an experience, I had no idea!

We were driven out to JFK and into the heliport terminal. Waiting for the next flight was our party of six and two be-suited Japanese businessmen. They had just arrived on a flight from Tokyo.

The production company must have warned the shuttle company what we intended to do on the flight. It was probably something not entirely new for them. The pilot was obviously aware because access from the cabin to flight deck intercom had been arranged beforehand.

The only people not in on the arrangement were the two Japanese businessmen, and ME!

The helicopter took off. As we approached our destination, out came the hand-held camera and Roger started issuing directions to the cameraman. They were rushing from one side of the cabin to the other to get the shots they wanted out of the windows.

I was nervous because, as a first-time helicopter flyer, I thought that their antics were making the aircraft unstable. The two Japanese remained inscrutable, sitting upright in their seats, gripping their briefcases on their laps, and ignoring the mayhem going on around them.

Roger pressed the intercom and began directing the pilot. "Can you get closer to the Brooklyn Bridge," he shouted above the noise. The pilot turned out to be a Vietnam veteran. He was only too happy to oblige. "I'd like to get closer to the buildings before you land," Roger requested. "I want a close-up of the Manhattan skyline." Again, the pilot obliged.

I was glad when we finally landed!

The two Japanese businessmen were delighted. Apparently, they had thoroughly enjoyed themselves. What a story they had to tell their families back home and their associates in New York.

Roger had secured the shots he wanted. I have never flown by helicopter since!

That evening, by way of compensation, the agency treated me to dinner at "Grand Central Oyster Bar & Restaurant." Situated just off the main concourse at Grand Central Railway Station, it is acknowledged to be one of the best fish restaurants in New York City, if not the world. After dinner, we all had an early night. The shooting schedule for the next day, required a very early start.

The location was JFK, at the TWA terminal. Here we would be shooting the scenes of our taxi driver hero checking in at the departure lounge before flying out of the city.

The set-up required a TWA 747 to be pulled up to the stand. Passengers would disembark. Then our hero, and the rest of the passengers for the outgoing flight, would present their boarding passes at the departure gate.

When the agency team and I arrived at about 5.00am, the crew had already been working on the set up for several hours. At that time in the morning, the terminal was closed. We had less than three hours to complete all the filming required.

With the cameras rolling the 747 was pushed into place.

There were around forty people on the set. We had to provide the illusion of several hundred passengers leaving the aircraft. To achieve this, everyone was called into action. We had to form and orderly queue and stroll up the walkway from the aircraft. When we reached the end, everyone had to sprint back behind the camera to join the other end of the queue and stroll up the walkway again.

This continued until Roger called "Cut" and the sequence was in the can.

The next set-up featured Paul Garcia having his boarding card checked in at the departure gate. All forty crew and bystanders were called into action again. There were two air hostesses at the check-in desk, and they needed a "volunteer" for a "supporting role" as the person checking in with his own boarding pass, next to the star of the commercial.

Roger wanted a contrast between Paul, who was casually dressed in his Wrangler jeans and leather jacket, and a more formally dressed businessman type. I was the only person on set who was anywhere near what could be classed as formally dressed.

The creatives and the director wanted me to do the honours. I very reluctantly agreed.

An unwritten rule existed amongst advertisers that, as the client, you should never accept the offer of a cameo roles in commercials being produced on your behalf. This was regarded as the sole prerogative of directors like Alfred Hitchcock. Amongst the senior managers at Wrangler, appearing in any company related photograph, was regarded as a "harbinger of fate" to be avoided at all costs.

Time was short. The decision was holding up filming. I felt I had no choice but to "step up to the plate," despite the possible negative portents.

This was my first "acting" role since my school days. Roger wanted me to say a few words to the air hostess as I presented my boarding pass. I can't remember what I said. It was barely audible when viewed on the playback.

Eventually, the scene was completed to everyone's satisfaction. The area returned to normal just minutes before the terminal opened.

The afternoon shooting schedule involved hand-held camera work featuring Paul Garcia and a small number of extras taking the subway from downtown Manhattan to JFK.

Effectively, apart from the post-production meeting scheduled for the next morning, my work was now done. I had some time to myself to look around New York and do all the tourist things such as taking the Staten Island Ferry, going to the top of the Empire State Building, walking around Times Square, visiting Battery Park, and buying some presents for my family back home.

That evening we all celebrated the completion of the shoot with a great New York meal in a restaurant in the Soho area of the city.

At our post-production meeting the next morning, Roger Lyons announced that he and the team were very happy with the material they had in the can. The cutting and editing process would be starting as soon as everyone was back in London.

The final cut would be available before the Christmas period was underway and, assuming this was approved, the broadcast quality versions would be available at the beginning of the new year.

This was particularly important to me as the PR, Sales promotion and merchandising campaigns had to be briefed in and campaigns produced ahead of the Wrangler Sales meeting which was scheduled to take place January 1990.

Back in the UK, it was "all hands to the pumps" to bring together all my external agencies. It was important that they all worked together to ensure the whole marketing support programme was fully integrated.

Early in December 1989, Simons Palmer presented the director's final cut.

Two different versions had been produced. The first included the extended opening sequence featuring the boy drummer. It was recommended that this be used during the first week of the TV campaign and in the cinema. The shorter version' without the drummer, was to be used in all other slots on television.

Roger Lyons had produced two pieces of imagery that, in the words of Simons Palmer, "project the inner style of the contemporary America of the 1990's."

Everyone loved the two versions. Even I had to agree, that the commercial was hard hitting and strikingly different. The 'gritty reality' that we had been promised had certainly delivered - in bucket loads!

Would it sell more Wrangler jeans? The jury was still out on that one!

I still had some reservations about the limited visibility of the Wrangler product in the commercial. Furthermore, the section that I appeared in had made the final cut. This would result in my receiving some "stick" from family, friends, and work colleagues, when the advertisement finally appeared.

With the help of our sales promotion agency, we hired some video ports. Every member of the sales force and each of the field promotion representatives had been tasked with visiting each of their key retailers to present both versions of the commercial.

We hired a London based design company to work with Chris Palmer and Mark Denton. Their brief was to design a collection of promotional items to merchandise the advertising at the point of sale. Featuring a selection of stills from the TV commercial, the final package included window back drops, window cubes, posters and show cards and advertising slogan signs.

Simons Palmer had held meetings with Polydor, the Hendrix record company. They were so impressed with the commercial that they announced they would be reissuing "Crosstown Traffic" as part of a small compilation of Hendricks classics to include "Voodoo Chile," "All Along the Watchtower," and "Have You Ever Been."

Even better, they wanted to use the same imagery we were using on our own point of sale material, including the Wrangler logo, on the covers of the 7" and 12" vinyl,

CD, and cassette versions of the release. Additionally, Polydor wanted to order a further run of our campaign posters so that they would be able promote the track, and its Wrangler association, in record shops around the country.

When our sales meeting took place, just weeks before the International Men's & Boys Exhibition (IMBEX), I presented the full package of advertising and support activity that would be launched during the exhibition and continuing throughout the year.

The salesforce had already made initial presentations of the TV commercial to their key retailers.

The feedback had been mixed but I was able to use this to our advantage during my presentation at the sales meeting. "I think you will all agree that, whether the reaction has been positive or negative, there has been a reaction. 1990 will see Wrangler closing the gap on our major competitor by positioning ourselves as THE urban, contemporary jeans brand with the best range of styles around." I announced.

My call to action was a strong message, "We will increase our share of the jeans market through an aggressive sales programme carried out by the best salesforce in the business. Wrangler is more than just any number. Wrangler is the brand that thinks, acts and will be number one. Let's go out and make it happen!"

The salesforce moved on to IMBEX, the main selling platform for the Autumn 1990 ranges, fired up to sell forward. IMBEX also presented the perfect opportunity to create additional jeans sales to support the advertising campaign. The TV and cinema advertisements, backed by the strong support package, was available for their customers to see on the Wrangler exhibition stand.

All the tools were in place. It was now up to the Wrangler salesforce to do the business.

As the advertising campaign began, the public relations agency also swung into action. They had obtained profiles about the Wrangler advertising campaign in style magazines such as 'Blitz'.

This neutralised the fall-out arising from the "shock horror" reaction from some older viewers and calls that the advertisement should be censored or even banned.

Apparently, some of the tabloid newspapers were "shocked by the reality of the content."

This seemingly negative press, generated interest, and coverage in wacky, news programmes such as the 'Media Show' and 'Reportage.'

The music press was intrigued by the Wrangler and Hendrix partnership and a lot of speculative coverage ensued.

I was advised that our hero Paul Garcia, was perceived as being a quirky, sensitive, 90's man. "Women journalists love him." I was assured by the PR team. "Are they our target market?" was my response to those comments.

When Simons Palmer initially presented the concept, they assured us that it would polarise opinion.

It was certainly doing that!

Whilst all this was going on, further changes were taking place within the management structure of Wrangler Limited.

Ralph Huschle had moved on from VF. John Hart took his place as Vice President of VF Europe. He appointed Alf Evans as Managing Director of Wrangler Limited but maintained an overseeing role.

I appointed Gary Hodder as Sales Promotions Manager. Gary was tasked with increasing the Wrangler presence within retail outlets and controlling the activities of the Field Promotion Representatives.

Meanwhile, Simons Palmer had been working with our public relations people to further exploit the marketing potential of the "Crosstown Traffic" commercial and "the Jimi Hendrix backing track."

The first concept involved recreating the taxi driver sequence from the commercial at Piccadilly Circus in London. To achieve this, it was suggested that Paul Garcia should be brought over from the USA, a New York yellow cab would be hired for him to drive around central London, and an on-street press conference organised in Piccadilly, close to the offices of Polydor.

Invitations to this would be sent out to a special selected press list including the influential music and style magazines, selected national press journalists and national radio and TV news representatives.

I was assured that the effort involved would be worth all the expenditure that would be incurred. "The coverage that we will achieve will be worth several times the outlay. Despite all the effort, and cost, we are confident it will all be worthwhile."

Paul Garcia was approached, through his agent. His participation would be assured providing certain conditions were agreed to. One of his main "conditions" was that we book him into Blakes Hotel in Kensington for his three-night stay. Designed by, ex-model and designer, Anouska Hempel, the five-star boutique hotel had not been open long. It was fast becoming the favourite haunt of film stars and the rich and famous.

This condition was accepted by the PR people who, perhaps to stave off a potential backlash later, booked me into the same hotel for my one-night stay.

The turnout for the Piccadilly event was not as large as I had expected but several "exclusive" interviews had been set-up by our PR people before-hand. As a result, "live" interviews with Paul Garcia for the radio and television news were broadcast on the day. Good press coverage was also obtained in the national, local press, trade and special interest magazines in the weeks and months afterwards.

A second concept was dreamed up by Simons Palmer and the media team at CIA Billett. The recommendation included the short-term booking of a 96-sheet poster (10 feet x 40 feet) super site in Piccadilly Circus in the heart of London. Then, and now, these sites are the most sought after in the whole of the UK.

With their huge buying power, CIA Billett had received information that one site would soon become available. They had approached Simons Palmer to see whether there might be any interest in taking advantage of the opportunities this might provide. The site was only available for two weeks but would be seen by tens of thousands of people.

Whilst they had been filming the "Crosstown Traffic' commercial in New York, Chris Palmer and Mark Denton had come across a lot of "Graffiti Art" adorning closed-down buildings and walls across the city. One graffiti artist, with the tag name of "CHICO," had particularly impressed them. They had tracked him down with a view to working with him in the future.

The Jimi Hendrix soundtrack on the Wrangler commercial and the resultant tie in with Polydor in the months leading up to the anniversary of his death, meant that Hendrix was becoming a hot property again.

They sounded out "CHICO" to see whether he would be interested in coming to London "to produce the biggest and most visible piece of graffiti ever seen in the capital."

Naturally, he jumped at the opportunity.

They asked for a meeting with me to discuss their ideas. Basically, they wanted permission to book the supersite at a cost of around £20,000 for the two weeks. "CHICO" would spend a whole day on a scaffold using his spray paints to produce the ultimate homage to Jimi Hendrix and the link to the Wrangler "Crosstown Traffic" commercial.

"The agency believes that the idea will work on several levels," Paul Simons enthused. "There will be a lot of interest in the creation of the imagery from both the public and the media," he continued. "What's more the controversial nature of graffiti, as an art form, will generate both negative and positive comments that the PR people will be able to exploit."

The idea had legs and it was agreed that I would find additional funds from my budget to cover the media costs that would be incurred.

Unlike Paul Garcia, the star of the "Crosstown Traffic" commercial, "CHICO," real name Antonio Garcia (no relation), had no pre-conditions. He was more concerned about the possibility that he might lose credibility, as part of the New York anti-establishment art movement, by undertaking such an overtly "commercial" commission as ours.

His background was particularly interesting. Antonio had moved to America from Puerto Rico with his family as a young boy. Realising he had artistic talent, he had started practicing in New York train yards before graduating to painting on the streets. By time he was 18 his work, and "CHICO" tag name, was appearing all over the city. When he arrived in London, he was generally recognised as the number one street artist in New York.

The set-up of the scaffolding and pasting up of the white background sheets, had been organised by the poster site contractors, under the direction of CIA Billet and Simons Palmer.

Our PR company had been active in creating pre-event publicity and organising a press photoshoot on the day. As a result, quite a crowd had gathered when "CHICO" climbed on to the scaffolding. First, he sketched out the basis of his design idea, then got to work, with a vast array of spray cans, to bring his concept to life.

Throughout the day, media representatives, visitors to London, businesspeople and Londoners just going about their daily lives, stopped everything just to watch what was going on. It would be an exaggeration to suggest that Piccadilly came to a standstill, during the hours that "CHICO" was working, but, at times, it came very close.

The result was stunning. Everyone was delighted including Polydor, the Hendrix record company, whose offices overlooked the site.

Resulting publicity was everything we had expected. Glowing articles appeared in the youth orientated magazines, national and local press. The airwaves were filled with news coverage on the radio and TV.

Several Conservative Party MPs were vociferous in their condemnation of Wrangler for encouraging vandalism. "What did they think they were doing allowing a New York graffiti artist free rein on the streets of London?" was their outraged cry. To them, graffiti art was represented by the tags left on walls and the messages scrawled on carriages on the London underground system.

I would be surprised if any had even bothered to venture to Piccadilly to see for themselves what all the fuss was about. That didn't really matter. The more the perceived "establishment" criticised us, the more our target market appeared to leap to our defence.

Before he left London, "CHICO" produced a miniature version of the portrait of Jimmy Hendrix used in his Piccadilly masterpiece. The artwork was used to print a limited run of posters. These were used as part of Wrangler in-store displays in key outlets all around the UK. A small number were framed along with a biography of the artist complete with his signature. These were provided as promotional prizes, in Jimi Hendrix inspired competitions, organised by the Wrangler field promotions team, throughout the UK.

Simons Palmer had thoroughly researched other promotional possibilities in the lead up to the 20th anniversary of Jimi Hendrix death at his flat in Kensington, London, on the 18 September 1970.

They had come across some footage of Denny Dent, who had developed a stage act during which he created speed painted portraits of famous personalities of the time. Delving through his archive they had found some film of Denny painting Jimi Hendrix. Simons Palmer were so impressed with it, they had obtained permission to edit the footage into a short commercial complete with "Crosstown Traffic" soundtrack and Wrangler logo.

CIA Billett had discovered that, around the time of the anniversary, several Hendrix inspired programmes were being planned by commercial television companies. Together with Simons Palmer, they had come up with a media plan that they felt would extend the coverage of the "Crosstown Traffic" TV campaign whilst making the Wrangler connection with Jimi Hendrix more visible to the older, traditional Wrangler jeans wearer.

Everyone at Wrangler liked the idea. Unfortunately, this required me to delve even deeper into my marketing budget reserve. The money was eventually "found." The go-ahead was given to adapt the film footage and book the media schedule.

Back at Calverton, the management changes continued. In October 1990, Financial Director and Company Secretary, Bob Radford left the company. Of the senior management team that was in place when I joined the company in 1975, I was one of only two remaining, the other being Credit Controller, Tony Fleet. Several long-serving, key members of the salesforce also moved on.

The writing appeared to be on the wall. "Could it be that I would be next?" For whatever reason, there appeared to be a policy of purging senior members of the original Blue Bell team. Or was I just being paranoid?

Only time would tell!

By the middle of September 1990, I had begun tentative discussions with Simons Palmer about the development of a marketing communications plan for 1991.

The month before, changes were announced at our media buying agency. Colin Gottlieb, our account director had left the company and joined forces with Nick Manning with a view to setting up his own agency. Colin came up to Calverton to break the news to me personally. Over lunch, he sounded me out about the possibility of the Wrangler account moving to his new operation, once it had been set up.

I wished him well but made it clear that I had no plans to change the CIA Billett and Simons Palmer arrangement. "If for any reason, we find a need to change our media buying strategy, I will certainly bear you in mind," I assured him.

At the time, I was harbouring concerns that, despite all the efforts of Wrangler salesforce and field promotion representatives, Wrangler share of the UK jeans market had not increased.

A Gallup post advertising awareness survey indicated that the Wrangler brand had experienced some small positive shifts in advertising awareness and image. Unfortunately, spontaneous recall of the "Crosstown Traffic" commercial was disappointing. The research company could find no clear measure to indicate that the Wrangler commercial, they claimed to have seen, was in fact the "Crosstown Traffic" commercial they were measuring.

Of more concern was the fact that preference to purchase scores were very low.

Our media buying strategy had apportioned 50% of our TV spend behind London. The programming involved a single-minded approach to reach style influencers, who we knew were extremely light TV viewers. This had been done at the expense of visibility to the wider Wrangler market.

Our original media schedule had employed the use of a press campaign. This was intended to work against the style leaders to establish product and style credibility for the Wrangler brand. This approach had worked well as a back up to the "Frisk" campaign produced by BBDO.

I felt that the lack of the press campaign could have weakened the Wrangler product message against these key consumers.

CIA Billett had been asked to analyse the expenditure of all the major Jeans brands in the year to date, and to indicate where the money had been spent.

The resultant breakdown of information was very revealing.

Total expenditure across the leading jeans brands of Wrangler, Levi's, Lee, and Pepe amounted to nearly £5.5 million. Of this, £3.8 million had been spent on TV, £1.5 million on cinema. Television was the dominant medium, with 70% share of spend, cinema accounted for 28%.

Only Lee, our sister company, had not used TV during the period measured. All the key brands had a presence in the cinema. In both main media used, Levi's were shown to be the dominant player. They had 67% of spend on TV. Wrangler trailed a distant second with 24%. Cinema was very hotly contested but again Levi's were the largest spenders. Their share was 37%, with Wrangler and Lee on 28% each.

The post-mortem, I had conducted, showed that Wrangler needed to work harder to increase distribution in its areas of weakness.

The media buying needed to be less focused on reaching just the style influencers and broaden its scope to cover the Wrangler core consumers also. It was my stated belief that, "Our media plan should be creative, to outflank the opposition and, at the same time be highly visible to both our prime consumers and the trade."

I felt that some focus groups needed to be set up by an independent agency. Their purpose would be to determine whether there might be a case to use the "Crosstown Traffic" commercial again in the early part of 1991, possibly in a recut form.

Group research was given the go-ahead. Conducted by Graham Hall Research, the feedback indicated the "Crosstown Traffic" commercial had not experienced the levels of exposure that had been intended. A lot of the people in the groups had never seen it before. When they had seen it, they liked it. There was surprise expressed when they saw it was for Wrangler Jeans.

Feedback suggested that some changes might improve the message. This included more Wrangler product visibility and additional female content to offset the perceived, over-aggressively male, street footage in New York.

During the shoot in New York, an awful lot of footage was taken that had never reached the final cut. I felt confident there was enough material available to ensure that a new edit could take on board all the views expressed.

At the end of October 1990, I developed a strategy document in which all my views on the research findings were laid out. It questioned the validity of the 1990 strategy that we had all bought into. I suggested that "Wrangler must accept what we are and build on our product, image, and distribution base to make Wrangler more acceptable to a wider range of consumers. All aspects of the marketing mix will have a role to play."

My brief to Simons Palmer was very clear. It stated that, "We must continue to project the differentiated creative strategy, started by "Frisk" and continued by 'Crosstown Traffic," in the projection of the brand (Wrangler) image to a wider audience. The advertising needs to ensure that the style influencers are aware that the Wrangler product is good enough for them to try."

In 1990, we had bought into the concept of concentrating our efforts both creatively and media-wise on reaching, and communicating with, the style influencers. This had been carried out, almost to the exclusion of the rest of the market. All our research had shown that we did not have a large enough budget to successfully achieve our market development aims. We had simply been swamped by the larger spend that Levi's had at their disposal.

Creatively, there was a need for a Wrangler brand campaign projecting an advertising effect "top down" to include style influencers, style leaders and early adopters. At the same time, it was accepted that there was a need for a hard-hitting, effective, product orientated campaign (probably in the youth press). This would ensure that the product advertising message would capture the attention of the style influencers and style leaders.

As far as media buying was concerned, I suggested, "The plan needs to be creative, to outflank the opposition, and avoid the Wrangler message being swamped by the larger spending power that Levi's have at their disposal. At the same time, we need a campaign that will be highly visible by our target consumers and the retail trade."

The strategy was signed off by the rest of the Wrangler team, and the account teams at Simons Palmer and CIA Billett.

Or so I thought!

In November 1990, Colin Gottlieb and Nick Manning set up their own media buying shop called Manning Gottlieb Media. It was not until many years later that I found out that one of their backers in the new venture was Simons Palmer.

Early in December 1990, after several planning meetings with Simons Palmer, I was sufficiently confident that the Wrangler Team and the agency were all singing from the same hymn sheet. So much so, that I had published a document, "1991 Strategy for Marketing Support." It was issued to the Wrangler senior management team, internal public relations and sales promotion managers, Simons Palmer and CIA Billett account teams, internal and external public relations, and sales promotion agencies.

The overview made it clear that the main thrust of our activity for 1991 should be directed "to maintain/increase our (product) unit sales (particularly of jeans) in what we expect to be a very difficult market." I suggested, that to achieve our objectives "we will have to adopt a more focused approach to our strategic planning to ensure that all aspects of the marketing mix work together to maximise our efforts."

It was clear that Levi's "will be spending more money than we are and that their activity will last for the whole year.. Clearly, we cannot match their spend but we will be able to ability to utilise our resources more effectively – if we all work together as a team." I concluded.

In our discussions with Simons Palmer, it had been agreed that we would continue with the strapline "More than just a number" and the thought behind it. An outline communications plan had been discussed and approved. It was based on a need for a year-long, product support-based campaign using a mix of media to reach the key style sectors of our core market.

Whilst the creative direction was still being developed, it had been suggested that, during the early part of 1991, our advertising would be projecting the strapline via the use of a 4 sheet "W" campaign and/or a 40/60 second recut version of the "Crosstown Traffic" commercial.

This would be supported by a campaign in the 'style press' promoting the "Authentic Wrangler" product line during, March and April, and a "Classic Wrangler" range campaign in May and June. This would be followed by a "Generic Wrangler" jeans campaign from September – November.

To build on the initial momentum, it had been proposed that a new commercial might be created. This could be used as part of a cinema campaign in June, September, and October and on television from September through November 1991.

A strong public relations programme was needed that aggressively followed a policy of pro-active and re-active media support to increase the Wrangler product coverage. The intended result of this activity was to make the Wrangler brand "the authoritative voice in the jeans market."

In addition, the PR team would be required to develop activity to support not only the advertising but also the product ranges featured in it. This would need them to work closely with the account team at Simons Palmer. The approach would ensure that the PR campaign could be strategically timed to maximise overall Wrangler product awareness.

A sales promotion package was needed to aggressively support the Wrangler sales team in meeting pre-determined sales targets. This would be achieved by supporting the sell-in through buyer and sales staff incentives in retail outlets and, where necessary, the Wrangler consumer.

Our in-house and external sales promotion teams would also be required to maintain close contact with their PR team colleagues and the account team at Simons Palmer.

In this way, their planned activity would dovetail into the advertising supporting "Authentic Wrangler," the "Classic Wrangler" and "Generic Wrangler" campaigns.

The in-house sales promotion team were already working together to produce a comprehensive set of point-of-sale packages. These would be used to merchandise the advertising of the Wrangler brand, and product ranges featured.

To maximise the effectiveness of all the integrated activity, it was important that all parties could develop their own individual activity programmes so that they could form part of an approved, comprehensive marketing activity programme, as early in 1991 as possible.

The Simons Palmer creative proposals, backed by the CIA Billett media plan, were pivotal.

Until the approval for the advertising creative concepts had been given, it would not be possible for CIA Billett to gain approval for the advertising spend. Any delay would seriously compromise the finalisation of the PR and sales promotion support programmes.

As the document was circulated during the first week of December, I was confident that the Integrated plan would be brought together on time and on budget. The key players were all on board and, although the Simons Palmer creative concept was still in the pipeline, I was assured that there were no problems with the brief or the agencies understanding of what was required on them.

What could possibly go wrong? The answer, it turned out, was practically everything!

In January 1991, a meeting with Simons Palmer took place to discuss their interpretation of the marketing brief. It became clear, that the creative team were reluctant to let the Wrangler product get in the way of the development their ideas. A gulf was emerging between the Wrangler marketing team and the agency. We were looking for an advertising campaign that projected the Wrangler brand and products in a creatively progressive way.

The agency was suggesting a more anarchic approach to the task. They claimed, "this will make the Wrangler brand, and then the product, more appealing to the style influencers whilst distancing the brand from all its major competitors."

I suggested that the results from the "Crosstown Traffic" campaign in 1990, had demonstrated the failure of a top-down approach to stimulate the volume buyers to buy more Wrangler products.

My briefing sought to explain our marketing expectations, "What we are looking for is a campaign that will sell our product and improve the image of Wrangler amongst style leaders, without alienating the core Wrangler market who deliver our volume sales. The success of Levi's 501 advertising has demonstrated that this approach, if done well, can be extremely effective,"

The proposed media planning campaign was broadly agreed. It would start with a four-sheet poster campaign promoting the tag line 'More than just a number' that had featured in the 1990 advertising. Following this would be a product campaign in the style press featuring "Authentic Wrangler," "Classic Wrangler" and "Generic Wrangler" jeans advertisements. A new commercial would be developed for Wrangler jeans, to run later in the year, on television and in the cinema.

Simons Palmer would now move forward to develop the creative work, bearing in mind all the points made during our discussions.

Before the next meeting with the agency could take place, it was announced that Wrangler Managing Director, Alf Evans was leaving the company. Frank Dimech, Divisional Manager responsible for the production plant at Falkirk, replaced him.

One Managing Director for over twenty years and then three in a period of just over two years. This was not at all good for the image of the company and quite destabilising for all the staff.

Winston Churchill would say, about every crisis that occurred during the second world war, despite adversity "you just have to keep on going." It was said that he used the acronym KBO ("Keep Buggering On") to end all his phone calls.

In our circumstances at the time, "KBO" seemed like sound advice!

The deadline that I had set myself to finalise the comprehensive marketing activity programme was long past and still the creative work from Simons Palmer had not been presented or signed off.

Then, around the middle of February, the agency announced that they were ready to present their proposals for the new campaign. Robin Hollick and Frank Dimech joined me for creative presentation at the Simon Palmer offices in London.

The original briefing meeting in January had highlighted that there were some divisions between us. We had left that meeting with a clear understanding of what we expected the advertising to achieve and the products that we required to be featured.

It was our belief that Simons Palmer were on board and that their creative solution would reflect the brief. We were in for a real surprise!

Paul Simons fronted the meeting. His opening comments went something like, "At our last meeting, we agreed that the advertising for 1991 will be three-tiered."

"So far so good," I remember thinking.

"The creative work we will be recommending is hard-hitting, progressive and impactful." Paul continued. "We believe that it not only meets the brief, but it will also open a clear gap between Wrangler and the rest of your competitors."

At that point, the creative team of Chris Palmer and Mark Denton took over. "We strongly believe that it is important to create a clear association between the "W" branding (that appears on nearly all the Wrangler jeans and jeans related products) and the line "Be More than just a Number" used in the 1990 campaign." Chris Palmer asserted. "Our creative ideas, for the four-sheet poster campaign, seek to do this in an amusingly, progressive and hard-hitting way that will get people talking," he concluded.

I began to feel uneasy!

Mark and Chris then presented five ideas.

The first featured "a black superhero type character with a 'W' on the facemask of his outfit."

Second was a "cartoon dog character with a W for its mouth.'"

This was followed by "a pipe smoking man wearing just 1930's style underwear and socks with male suspenders and posing provocatively."

Next was a "dodgy male character with glasses with one lens blocked out by a W on a white ground."

The last image paid homage to Man Ray, the famous artist and photographer. "It showed a man smoking a pipe with his back to camera and the hair on the back of his head shaved in the form of a W."

Each poster featured, in addition to the Wrangler logo, the payoff line "Be more than just a number." A different type face was used for this on each poster.

If the agency team were expecting ecstatic laughter and a positive reaction, they were disappointed. The Wrangler team looked at the ideas and then each other. This campaign was intended to get people talking. It had stunned me, and my colleagues, into complete silence!

The Simons Palmer team appeared undaunted and moved on to the creative work they were recommending for the style press campaign. "Before we show you the work, we need to explain some of the context behind it," Paul Simons announced.

In my experience, this is always a bad sign. If explanations are required beforehand, it generally means the content is controversial, difficult to comprehend, or both.

"We have produced three advertisements covering Wrangler Authentic and Classic jeans plus a generic advertisement for Wrangler jeans." Paul continued. "The readers of the magazines we are using are progressive in their approach to fashion. Many do not consider Wrangler to be the brand to be seen wearing. For this reason, our creative approach has selected characters, to represent the brand, that might not necessarily fit the Wrangler profile."

The creative team took over at this point. "Our idea for authentic jeans advertisement is to obtain an endorsement for the Wrangler product from a most unlikely source. We have chosen "Tank Girl" from Deadline Magazine."

Neither I, nor the rest of the Wrangler team, had any idea of what they were talking about. Sensing our bemusement, they explained the background behind their choice.

Apparently, in 1988, artists Jamie Hewlett and Alan Martin created "Tank Girl" for Issue One of Deadline Magazine. "Tank Girl," with its post-feminist and post-apocalyptic vision of a not-too-distant future, stood out and had become a cult figure amongst its readers.

According to Simons Palmer, "Tank Girl" this anarchic symbol of the anti-establishment, was an ideal vehicle to promote, and enhance the image, of our core product line!

They then presented their proposed advertisement. This featured a model wearing Wrangler jeans but otherwise dressed as "TANK GIRL." She was holding a large club with nail through it and had adopted a menacing pose.

At the top left of the picture was 'W BE MORE THAN JUST A NUMBER' in an anarchic style of lettering. Under the picture was a small Wrangler logo followed by the words, "Authentic jeans. If they're good enough for Tank Girl they're good enough for you."

I just didn't know what to say, the concept was so far out of our comfort zone!

Breaking the silence, Chris Palmer moved on to the next concept board. "To promote Wrangler Classic jeans, we have taken up a cowboy theme," he said.

A black cowboy was seated on a horse (obviously not a live one). He was dressed in a flamboyant red, white, and blue western top of the type normally only seen in stage shows such as "Paint your Wagon." The location was obviously studio based with a backdrop showing a typically American, outdoor western desert scene. A chandelier was visible above the cowboy's head.

The words "W BE MORE THAN JUST A NUMBER" were depicted in a 'rope' style of lettering. Under the picture, the small Wrangler logo was followed by the words, "Ruggedly constructed for rugged chaps."

I understood the message the agency was trying to put over. I just did not find it at all amusing or pertinent, on many different levels!

The agency struggled on. "We have continued the theme of unlikely advocates for Wrangler into our final concept. For generic Wrangler jeans, we recommend the use of Father Bill."

"Father Bill" meant nothing to the Wrangler management trio comprising a Yorkshireman, a man from Leicestershire and a former Maltese football international. Once more, the agency had to provide background information to explain the significance of their choice.

Father Bill (the Reverend Bill Shergold), apparently enjoyed unusual celebrity in the London scene of the 1960s when he was known as the "ton-up vicar" or the "biker priest." Decked out in black leathers and sitting astride his trusty Triumph motorcycle, Father Bill ministered to the rocker fraternity in East London as leader of the 59 Club.

In 1991, he was into his 70's, but Simons Palmer were convinced he was just the man to promote our core denim products.

Before putting their proposal to the Wrangler team, they had spoken with Father Bill. He in turn had sought the advice of his rector, who allegedly advised him to go ahead on the basis that it would be, "Good for the Church to be seen doing ordinary, rather silly things."

The Simons Palmer creative approach featured a picture of Father Bill, complete with old fashioned helmet and goggles. Sitting astride his trusty Triumph motorcycle, under the pier at Brighton, he was wearing a Wrangler denim jacket, under his biker leather top, and a pair of Wrangler jeans.

The "W be more than just a number" wording featured a "biker" style of lettering. The payoff line, after the Wrangler logo, at the bottom of the advertisement read, "Authentic jeans and classic denim jacket worn by Father Bill the 'Ton-up' vicar."

We had been in the presentation for several hours by this time. There was still a storyboard for a proposed TV commercial to be seen. The ideas for the outdoor and press had proved controversial. There was no reason to suppose that the proposals for the television commercial would be any less so!

I think at the time, that we were all in London for a few days attending the IMBEX trade fair. We needed time to consider the proposals made so far. Prolonging the session might prove counterproductive. Another meeting was scheduled for later in the week, on the day after the close of the exhibition.

Discussing afterwards what we had seen during the session, it was clear that we were all of one accord. The proposals had stretched credibility several steps too far. From the lack of positive response from us, Simons Palmer must have been aware of our concerns.

"Perhaps they might have second thoughts?"

We agreed that the agency would be asked to present the TV storyboard at the beginning of the next meeting. When this had taken place, we would then be able judge the whole campaign "in the round."

To say that I was concerned, with the direction that Simons Palmer was proposing, would be an understatement!

When we reconvened, Simons Palmer presented a storyboard for a commercial with the working title "Junk TV."

Despite all our conversations about building the imagery around the product and with a clear storyline, the storyboards seemed to me to be all about imagery. The Wrangler product appeared to be very much a bit player with a walk on role. Taken alongside the outdoor and press creative work, in my opinion, the recommendations were putting Wrangler in a place that I did not want the brand to be.

When asked for their reactions my colleagues appeared to agree.

We discussed at length the reason for our misgivings over the creative direction we were being asked to buy into. The agency appeared to reject our concerns at every turn. They argued that they knew the target market better than we did. Their way was the right way. "Instead of putting up resistance to our ideas, why not just trust us?" they appeared to be saying to us.

Over nearly sixteen years of working with some of the most creative advertising "hot shops" in the world, I had acquired a wide knowledge of the jeans market as well as the strengths and weaknesses of the Wrangler brand. I had been at the forefront of developing research techniques in customer segmentation and brand perceptions of all the key jeans brands across Europe.

In addition, I had a track record of taking risks on creative concepts developed by several of our advertising agencies. Taking risks had reaped dividends, but only where I felt confident that the creative risk would not damage sales of the Wrangler product and/or the perception of the Wrangler brand.

Up until now, I had nearly always been prepared to trust the judgement of my advertising agency on creative matters, because they had always trusted my judgment on everything else. What Simons Palmer was demanding approval on was, in my opinion, a step too far. Furthermore, it seemed to me that the key element of trust, required between agency and client, was in danger of breaking down.

We were going around in circles and getting nowhere!

It seemed better that, after many hours of somewhat fruitless discussions, we should call a close to the meeting and carefully consider our next move.

Within a week of returning to the office, we discovered that Paul Simons had been cultivating a relationship with John Hart who was keen to develop marketing strategy that could be rolled out across Europe.

When the VF Corporation had acquired Blue Bell, I had been given the task of creating an international brand strategy. My recommendations had been submitted six months before our ill-fated meeting with Simons Palmer. My report had identified that with licenses in place in key markets, and no common international core product line, it would be nearly impossible to produce a consistent marketing campaign across all international divisions.

In Europe, many of the licensee agreements were coming to an end. John Hart was keen to establish a European marketing and communications strategy that could be coordinated through his office in London.

Perhaps with one eye on the possibility of Simons Palmer being appointed to the European advertising role in the future, Paul Simons had decided to go over the heads of the team at Calverton. He wrote a letter to John Hart in which he tried to imply that the Wrangler UK team did not know what we were talking about. It was further implied that the campaign, we had all but rejected, should be adopted - because the agency was right, and we were wrong!

As a case study on "how to win friends and influence people," this response was, in my opinion, very high up the ratings list.

The first I knew about the letter was when a copy landed on my desk from John Hart, asking me to comment on the salient points that Paul Simons was making.

I was incensed but bit my lip before sending through a considered reply!

Because of an association with a large College of Further Education in Nottinghamshire, I had, only days before, accessed the opinions of 40 students in the 16-24 age bracket.

These members of the core Wrangler market were shown the "Crosstown Traffic" commercial, that appeared in 1990, together with the new advertising concepts proposed for 1991. I had felt that it was important to gauge the reaction of consumers to whom the proposed advertising was to be targeted.

In my response to the comments made in Paul Simons letter, I suggested that it was, in some respects, "as naive as it was predictable." I made it clear that he had also side-stepped the issues which had caused us not to accept the creative work submitted – despite 7 hours of discussion.

Paul had asked three questions which he felt were at the heart of the problems the agency had with our reaction to the work they had presented. Frankly, I thought that it was patronising of him to suggest that the Wrangler team, who had expressed concerns about the creative direction the agency was recommending, might be ignorant of the market to whom the advertising was aimed.

After all, the marketing strategy had been developed by me, as part of the creative brief, and agreed by my colleagues at Wrangler and the account team at Simons Palmer.

I had been asked to respond and so, holding back my anger, I did!

To the question, "Who are we writing the advertising for?"

I confirmed that the Wrangler target market "was primarily the 16-24-year-olds throughout the UK. Not just the 'super-trendies' in the southeast of England (an area of Wrangler weakness) but also the more down-to-earth versions who lived in

Glasgow, Manchester, Liverpool, Leeds, Nottingham, Birmingham etc. (All areas of Wrangler strength)"

In citing the reaction to my meeting with the Nottinghamshire College students, I explained that they had liked the Wrangler "Crosstown Traffic" and the latest Levi's television commercials. They were aware of magazines such as iD, The Face and Viz but they knew nothing about "Tank Girl," "Deadline Magazine" or "Father Bill."

To the question, "What do they (The Wrangler target market) think?"

I explained that the 16-24-year-olds market was very wide. It contained many sub-groups and, because they purchased 50% of all jeans sold, they were extremely important to Wrangler. All our previous research had indicated that "their thought pattern was complicated. It was influenced very much by their individual lifestyle and environment. Over many years, Wrangler had been at the forefront of lifestyle research. As a result, we had lots of information and so were well qualified to know how they thought."

To the last question, "Who is best equipped to decide whether the proposed advertising is relevant or not?"

I had presumed that Paul Simons was trying to make the point that the advertising agency were better qualified to assess how the core Wrangler consumers might react to Simon Palmer's progressive advertising approach.

In my reply, I suggested that "the relevance of the advertising would always be decided by the consumer at the point of sale. Good advertising always created a propensity to purchase that encouraged core consumers to take positive action and look at, and hopefully buy, the Wrangler product."

I went on to explain that "whilst there was some evidence that 'Crosstown Traffic' had begun to change attitudes to the brand image of Wrangler, the reality of the situation was that it had not led to an increase in sales."

It was this latter point that was the crux of our uncertainty about the creative direction.

The reason for our unease about the "progressive" work presented by the agency (the outdoor, the press and the "Junk TV" commercial) was not that it was "progressive," and therefore a risk, but that, despite our agreement on objectives and strategy, the product was not king.

I then reiterated the communications objectives we had agreed. For Wrangler, "the requirement was that the product should be projected to the consumer in a hard-hitting, 'progressive' and impactful way. It was important that the story line should spring out of the product in a way that would make the consumer aware that we were saying something positive, not only about the Wrangler image, but also the product to which that imagery was being applied."

The relevance of the outdoor campaign being used to create a link between the strapline of "Crosstown Traffic" and the "W" symbolism was understood, although some of the imagery used was contentious.

The press and TV executions were more difficult to accept because the product was, in our opinion, secondary to the creative idea. "Father Bill," "Black Cowboy" and "Tank Girl" were all individuals who were wearing Wrangler jeans – but would the consumer feel the desire to buy (Wrangler product) having seen the advertisements featuring them?"

Similarly, our concern with the "Junk TV" commercial was that "the Wrangler product was becoming lost within the creative idea."

I suggested that the differences we had with Simons Palmer were nothing to do with objectives or strategy. "They were everything to do with balance."

To end, I posed a question of my own, "Will the consumer react positively (to the proposed advertising) towards Wrangler jeans, or will they like the advertising imagery but not purchase the product as they had apparently been the case with Crosstown Traffic?"

My response was circulated to John Hart, Robin Hollick, and Frank Dimech on 8 March 1991 just before I left on a week's holiday.

My recommendation was clearly outlined in an accompanying memo. In it, I expressed the opinion "that we had carried out enough research and done enough talking. I believed that our original brief was clear, our objectives realistic and the strategy we wished to employ was correct."

I concluded with a question of my own.

"Perhaps it's time for a change?"

The following day, I went on holiday, happy in the knowledge that my comments accurately reflected the opinions of me and my colleagues following our failure to accept Simon Palmer's creative recommendations.

When I returned from my break, I was refreshed and eager to move forward, with Simons Palmer, or another agency.

There had obviously been some major discussions whilst I was away. In the end, it appeared that all the recipients of my memo had accepted my recommendation that "Perhaps it's time for a change?"

I had barely got my feet back under the table when I was called into a meeting to be informed that I was being made redundant!

This came as a slight surprise as, only a few months earlier, I had been advised that my good work in 1990 had earned me a pay rise and a bonus.

Could it be, that the real reason behind the decision was something to do with the disagreement, over creative development, with Simons Palmer?

I was puzzled that it had also been decided to make Lindah Kiddey, the Wrangler Public Relations Coordinator, redundant at the same time. This VF management decision meant that there were no professional advertising or PR professionals remaining in the company within the European division. The company would have to rely solely on the good offices of its external PR and advertising agencies to control creative output and the effective expenditure of their own budgets.

To soften the "blow," I was offered a generous payoff and the use of my company car for an extended period. On top of this, I also received a plethora of additional redundancy 'perks.'

True to form, the VF management asked me to immediately clear out my desk and leave the office as soon as I had done so. Sixteen years of loyal service apparently counting for nothing!

In a final act of defiance, I made it clear, that because I had been away, there were loose ends to be tied up and I did not want to leave my remaining, loyal staff, in the lurch. As a result, I returned to Calverton for a few hours the following morning to brief my remaining staff and to say my goodbyes and to take away my personal belongings.

My departure signalled the final breakup of the Blue Bell marketing triumvirate, that I had become a part of when I joined the company in 1975.

This team had worked harmoniously together to make the Wrangler brand and product ranges market leaders in the UK and Ireland.

In a way, the decision was a huge relief. Blue Bell had been run as a friendly team with everyone working together for a common aim. VF on the other hand, appeared to me to be run at arms-length with too many decisions made for apparently political reasons.

As part of my long-term career plan, in the event of my leaving VF, I had decided that I would opt out of the corporate rat race.

Staying in the industry, in a senior management capacity, would have meant a move to London or Brussels. It would also have required a continuity of a high-flying lifestyle, travelling around the world, and leaving my family at home.

I had created an outline marketing plan that involved the setting up my own marketing service company. Working from home, I believed, would enable me to make a good living, in a stress-free environment and allow me to spend far more time with my family.

After leaving Wrangler, I heard nothing from the Simons Palmer team. I suppose as far as they were concerned, I was just an obstacle that had now been removed.

All my other suppliers were quick to offer their support!

CIA Billett had invited me to join them, as one of their guests at the Middlesex Rugby Sevens before I left Wrangler. They contacted me to say that the invitation still stood, despite the change of circumstances, and would be delighted if I was still able to attend.

On the 11 May 1991, I travelled down to London to join them, and a selection of their clients, at their offices in London. From there we travelled to Twickenham in a specially converted double decker bus complete with fully hosted hospitality. The bus was parked in the carpark at the ground. Its proximity to the rugby action provided us with an all-day food and drink bonanza and fantastic action on the field. As far as I can remember, London Scottish beat Harlequins 20 point to 16, in a closely contested final.

Design Associates, who had worked with me producing brochures and point of sale material, developed designs and artwork for the stationery for my new venture. This provided me with world class material at a fraction of the price they would normally have charged.

Hawthornes Colour Printers was kind enough to produce the initial print run of my letterheads and business cards. They were to become one of my first clients.

Three months after I had left VF Corporation, Robin Dilley Associates opened its doors with a small client base and a lot of ambition.

Even though I still lived and worked only 8 miles down the road from the VF offices in Calverton, life after Wrangler had well and truly begun!

PART THREE

THE ART OF SPONSORSHIP

Chapter Ten

Developing Sponsorship Rules

From my very early days at Blue Bell, it was clear that many people in other organisations assumed the Wrangler brand was a potential "cash cow" just waiting to be associated with them.

Commercial sponsorship was still very new and, as a result, no clear ground rules had been laid down either by those looking for sponsor's cash or, for that matter, by potential sponsors themselves.

Nearly every day, I was receiving calls from people who clearly believed that I would just hand out money to them, no questions asked!

The list included music companies, agents for big bands, sports stars, film and television producers, charities as well as struggling potential star names seeking vital funding support to move their careers to the next level.

Blue Bell Inc. had entered into many sponsorship agreements in the United States. These had met with varying degrees of success.

Some of my colleagues in other European markets had dabbled but many had had their fingers burned.

When I joined Blue Bell Apparel in 1975, I had inherited a small number of sponsorship deals. The major one of these involved the support of The International Country Music Festival at Wembley. I suspected that the decision had been influenced by the fact that Wrangler in the USA had a sponsorship contract with the country and western superstar Willie Nelson. It was questionable how relevant the arrangement was in the UK market.

It was clear that there needed to be a clear strategic reason for entering into any sponsorship arrangement. I set out to determine some clear criteria that could be used as a measure of the worth of any bid received.

- Each sponsorship request was to be carefully scrutinised on merit.

- Care needed to be taken to avoid supporting activities of specific interest of me or any other members of the senior management team (unless the case for involvement was particularly compelling).

- A sponsorship budget was to be set aside as part of the overall communications spend and care was required to ensure that this was never exceeded.

- The total cost of any sponsorship undertaken was to include all additional activities needed to ensure that objectives could be met.

- The end outcome of any sponsorship activity must be measurable and, above all, enhance the credibility of the Wrangler brand as well as the marketing objectives set.

I made a calculation, not scientifically I might add, that for any sponsorship activity to be successful, it was important those elements of the target audience for whom the association would be of interest, would need to be made fully aware of the Wrangler brand involvement.

To make this possible, I came up with a 1:2 spend ratio calculation. This ensured, that built into the overall sponsorship price, was an additional cost of £2 of promotional spend for every £1 of sponsorship money requested.

Talking to my colleagues in other European markets provided more proof that sponsorship can be a hit and miss affair.

The head of advertising in Scandinavia had been very creative in his approach. He had sponsored the Danish heavyweight boxing champion and agreed that he would have the Wrangler logo stencilled across his back for a non-title, televised fight, in Copenhagen.

"What happens if he gets knocked out during the fight"? I queried. "He has been given strict instructions to fall face down," came the tongue in cheek reply.

The same individual had received a direct contact from a young tennis player from Sweden who was looking for some help to further his career. Because he was only 17 and had no real track record of success on the tennis circuit, his request had been turned down. Bjorn Borg, the young player in question, went on to become one of the all-time greats of the sport. He won numerous Grand Slam titles and became the number one ranked player in the world.

The moral of this story?

It is sometimes worthwhile to play the "long game." Taking a gamble on a young unknown can be relatively inexpensive at the start of the relationship. The real rewards will come when their potential is fully realised. "

I continued to receive requests for sponsorship. Applying my strict criteria to each enquiry inevitably led to some excellent potential opportunities being rejected.

Late in 1975, I received a telephone call from an "agent" claiming to be acting on behalf of a young up-and-coming motorcycle racer. "Watch the TV sports programme tonight at 9.00pm," he advised. "I think you will agree that my client is a very exciting prospect. What's more, I am convinced he will be a perfect fit with your core target market. I am certain we will be able to develop a cost-effective, long-term relationship."

I agreed to follow his advice and arranged that he would call me back the following day with a view to taking our discussion further.

That evening, I watched the programme. It included a mini documentary featuring the sponsorship prospect, whose name was Barry Sheen.

Racing around the Daytona circuit in the USA, he lost control of his bike at over 170mph and crashed breaking numerous bones in his body.

The next morning, I received a follow up call from the agent. "I assume you saw the film," he exclaimed. "What do you think?" "Yes, I saw the film. Your client crashed and was badly injured. He may never race again," I responded.

The sponsorship discussion was never pursued!

With the benefit of hindsight, I had underestimated the ability of Barry Sheen to recover from his injuries. I also failed to recognise that the raw talent he exhibited before the crash and his obvious will to succeed against all the odds, would propel him to greatness on the racing track. He retains a cult status even to this day.

You win some! You lose some!

During my 16 years with Wrangler, I was involved in a whole host of different sponsorship deals across a wide range of activities. Some were very successful, others less so. Over the time my hands were on the purse strings, many now famous names slipped through the net and many potentially lucrative deals fell at the last hurdle.

Chapter Eleven

Motor Sports

Barry Sheene might have slipped through the net in 1975, but he and his associates crossed my path several times in the late 1970's and early 1980's.

In the book, "Barry: The Story of Motorcycling Legend, Barry Sheene," co-written by Steve Parrish and Nick Harris, reference is made to the "Squadron" made up of Barry and his circle of close friends. He was the "Wing Commander", Jeremy Paxton was "Fols," Julian Seddon was "Raj," Steve Parrish was "Stavros" and Andrew Marriott was "Count Jim Moriaty."

It was probably Andrew Marriott who made contact me after the Daytona crash. He was involved with CSS Marketing Company at the time.

In 1976 Barry Sheene became 500cc World Motor Cycling World Champion.

In March 1977, I was at a shoot for one of the first Mr Wrangler commercials at film studios near London (Twickenham or Elstree). Watching, was a larger-than-life character who had some connection with one of the female models on the shoot.

Between takes, he introduced himself as Julian Seddon ("Raj"). "I am a great friend of Barry Sheene" he announced. "I worked with his people to secure his TV commercial contract with Brut (aftershave)." We discussed how I had also been contacted with a view to developing some sort of relationship between Barry and Wrangler. He seemed very interested.

Shortly after lunch, Julian donned his leathers and helmet and roared off on his powerful motor bike. "I have to pick up a friend at Heathrow," he said as he left. "I will be back later."

As the shoot continued and the hours passed by, I assumed that Julian would not be returning. Much to my surprise, at around tea-time he appeared. He was not alone. With him was a sun tanned, denim clad figure that everyone on the set recognised instantly.

The friend he had picked up at the airport was none other than Barry Sheene, fresh from winning the first 500cc Grand Prix of the 1977 season in Venezuela. His teammate in the Suzuki team was Steve Parrish ("Stavros"). The Grand prix had taken place on Sunday 20 March 1979 and yet here he was at our shoot only a couple of days later.

No Chauffeured limousine for World Champion Barry, just the pillion seat of a friend's powerful motorbike. There was no side to him. What you saw was what you got!

We briefly discussed the sponsorship possibilities and I think I took his measurements and supplied him with a complete Wrangler outfit of jeans, shirt, and jeans jacket.

It would be 7 years before we would meet again.

Dave Taylor – The "Wheelie King"

I was forever receiving telephone calls from motor cycling hopefuls optimistically hoping to tap into the pot of sponsorship gold they thought I had by my desk.

None of these led anywhere until, in the latter part of the !970's, I received a call from Dave Taylor. "I'm known as the "Wheelie King," he told me. "I hope you might be interested in sponsoring me," he continued.

"What exactly do you do?" I asked. I was not a biker and had no idea what a "Wheelie" was.

"I am a display rider," he explained. "I ride all the way round racetracks balancing on one wheel. Last week I completed whole circuit of Brands Hatch without dropping the bike," he proudly announced.

I did not quite know what to say, but the germ of an idea was formulating in my mind. I wanted to bounce this off my PR agency before taking the matter further. I agreed to meet up with him the following week. Meanwhile, I did some research on Dave. This confirmed that his motorcycling skills were unique to him, and he was held in high esteem amongst the motor cycling fraternity.

He had some limited sponsorship from bike and kit suppliers. To make ends meet, he worked as a proof-reader for the printers of "Hansard," the printed verbatim report of proceedings of both the UK House of Commons and House of Lords.

The modest sum of money he was asking for, would allow him to develop his skills on a full-time basis.

I was not interested in investing in a display rider whose "act" might be mimicked by younger, less skilled, individuals who could do themselves harm. My idea was to get Dave to display his skills in a more positive manner, to school age budding motorcyclist, as part of a motorcycle safety campaign.

Dave would demonstrate his skills in school playgrounds across the country. He would then explain how it was necessary for potential motor bikers to develop on road skills if they were to ride a motorbike properly and avoid accidents.

I felt that most road safety campaigns directed at the teenage market talked "AT THEM" not "TO THEM." As a result, they were seldom successful. My gut feeling was that Dave Taylor could provide the catalyst for a campaign that could be very effective.

Our PR agency agreed.

We met up with Dave and we were all very impressed by his unassuming manner. He in turn, appeared genuinely interested in the programme we were presenting to him.

Dave registered some concerns. Never having done anything like we were suggesting before, he did not know where to start.

We reassured him that we would develop a basic script for him to work with and arrange some presentation skills sessions to prepare him to speak in front of an audience. It was stressed that the success of our idea would revolve around his ability to be himself and maximise his role model persona.

Whilst the agency was developing the content of the programme with Dave Taylor, I took on the task of selling the programme to road safety officers throughout the country. I was advised that individual local authorities were only likely to endorse the programme if it had been already run successfully by another authority. Luckily, road safety officers in all the local authorities had their own association.

The road safety officer at Nottinghamshire County Council, was on its National Executive Committee.

If I could convince him of the validity of the programme, he would be able to recommend it to the rest of the executive and the programme would be given national approval. If the relationship went well, it might then be possible to obtain the endorsement of The Royal Society for the Prevention of Accidents (RoSPA).

I held a meeting with the Road Safety Manager at Nottinghamshire CC and the regional representative of RoSPA during which I presented the programme. Both were enthusiastic bikers and already knew about Dave Taylor. They were also in agreement that our proposed Motorcycle Safety Programme would be ideal for pupils in the Sixth Form of Schools or in Colleges of Further Education, although clarification was needed on several points.

The first was predictable, "How much will it cost us?"

"It will cost you absolutely nothing," I was able to assure them. "Wrangler will organise the programme and pay all the travel and accommodation expenses incurred by Dave Taylor. It's all part of our sponsorship package with him," I added.

The second question took me aback.

"What is in it for Wrangler?" I was asked. "Each year the Blue Bell company selects a good cause to support. We can think of no better cause than the Dave Taylor Motorcycle Safety Campaign." I replied.

"But what is in it for Wrangler?" I was asked again.

It was becoming obvious that the kind-hearted corporate reply cut no ice with my two inquisitors. There must be some good commercial reason why we were prepared to put so much time, effort, and money behind the programme. "OK," I said. "16-24-year-olds represent a prime market for Wrangler jeans. 16 to 18-year-old motorcycle riders are more likely to be involved in a fatal or life changing accident than any other demographic. By targeting this segment through the programme, we hope to prevent members of our core market from being killed or badly injured."

"Ah, now we understand," was the response. "We love the programme and subject to a trial run at a Nottinghamshire school, we will endorse it to the members of both organisations."

The trial took place, not long afterwards, at three schools in Nottinghamshire. It proved to be a great success. Dave's easy manner and skilful demonstrations struck a chord with his young audiences. This was not someone in a suit banging on about road safety.

Dave was a role model who had the ability to put over an important message, in a way that was sincere and convincing.

Soon requests were coming in from schools all over the UK!

Our PR agency organised a whole programme of activities that included appearances on several children's TV programmes.

At my request, the Wrangler involvement remained low key. It was important that the campaign was focused on road safety, with Dave Taylor the bearer of an important message. We did not want it to be perceived as some sort of PR stunt to promote the Wrangler brand.

You could say that the programme developed a life of its own. It became almost a full-time activity for several members of my staff.

The racing fraternity was beginning to take an interest. When a sponsor from the motorcycle industry offered to take over and expand the campaign, we were happy to give Dave our blessing.

Some years later, Dave was awarded an MBE for his services to motor cycling road safety. He also set up the country's first Trail Park near Dartford.

Sadly, he died in 1996. His memory lives on through the Motorcycle News 'DAVE TAYLOR LIFETIME ACHIEVEMENT AWARD." Past winners have included John Surtees, Evel Knievel, and Barry Sheene.

The Wrangler-Which Bike Yamaha RD350 Pro-Am Series

Late in 1982, an approach was made to see if we might be interested in sponsoring a Yamaha RD350 Pro-Am motor cycling series in conjunction with Which Bike magazine and Yamaha.

Designed to promote the best up and coming riders on the circuit, every race was being televised live on ITV. In return for covering the prize money for the whole series, the lead sponsor would have their brand decals on every bike. The lead bike would be fully customised in the sponsors colours and decals.

The format was particularly appealing because every bike, in every race, had the same specifications. It was planned that the keys for each participating bike would be drawn out by each rider on the day of each race. As a result, the skill of the individual rider would a key factor in determining the result of every race.

This would apply to the whole series except that the series leader, after race one, would ride the Wrangler customised bike.

Our participation was a "no brainer!"

The motor cycling fraternity was part of the Wrangler core market profile. This meant that there were plenty of opportunities for retailer promotional participation.

For a relatively small investment, we were guaranteed a lot of exposure through the live TV coverage, on-track promotion, and press coverage through "Which Bike" magazine.

I signed on the dotted line for what would prove be an extremely beneficial two-year relationship.

Just to make things clear, at that time, I was not aware of just how big the sport was and how many people attended the events.

"The Wrangler-Which Bike Yamaha RD350 Pro-Am Series" was one of a selection of races that were televised live by ITV's "World of Sport." Other events included the "World of Sport Superbike Challenge" and the "Shell Oil's 350cc Promoters Championships."

The prize money was poor by today's standards. This did not prevent some of the top names in the sport participating at the meetings.

In line with our sponsorship policy, the series was supported by a comprehensive public relations campaign. Point of sale material was made available in store and at the events and a specially designed "Yamaha Wrangler Which Bike? Pro-Am" pin badge was produced as a give-away item.

We also organised many competitions though retailers enabling customers to attend race meetings that featured our sponsored event and giving them the opportunity to enjoy a VIP experience, as the guests of Wrangler and Yamaha.

A national competition was developed for key retailers in major towns and cities around the UK. Entrants were asked to "Spot the Wrangler Rider" on a map of the Donington Racing Circuit. They were told that a typical Pro-Am rider would complete a lap of Donington in 1min 26.4 seconds. Entrants had to use their skill and judgment to choose a spot on the map that the Wrangler bike would pass in 19.7seconds. They were also required to tick the correct answer to the question, "Where did denim originate?"

Winners at store level received a Wrangler outfit and tickets to one of the Wrangler/Yamaha races, runners up received a Yamaha Travel bag and a subscription to Which Bike? Magazine.

A Grand Prize Draw took place in which correct entries from around the country were entered. The lucky winner received a Wrangler customised Yamaha 125cc motorbike, a Wrangler customised crash helmet and 2 tickets to a "Wrangler/Which Bike? Pro-Am" event.

The competition proved to be a great success. It not only helped to generate extra sales for Wrangler product, but it also created lots of publicity at a local and national level.

I had acquired a pick-up truck and had it fully customised in Wrangler livery. This was used by our Field Promotion Representatives for carnivals and other similar events around the country. With the permission of the race organisers at the host race tracks, the Wrangler FPR's would drive this around each circuit prior to our sponsored event.

One of the early events took place over the weekend of the 16 & 17 April 1983 at Donington Racetrack. Because it was close to the Wrangler offices, I was invited by Yamaha to go along with my family, as their guests, on the race day.

During the day, we had access to areas of the track, including the pit area. Here we met some of the riders and soaked up the atmosphere.

The Yamaha box at Donington was ideally placed adjacent to the last chicane on the track. Not only were we able to sample great hospitality we also witnessed first-hand exactly how exciting the races were. I was amazed by the enthusiastic reception the riders were receiving from the tens of thousands of potential Wrangler customers, who were watching from vantage points all around the track.

The "Wrangler/Which Bike?" race was very exciting with 20 riders competing as if their lives depended upon it. This was amazing considering that the winner of each race received the princely sum of £200, with the prize money decreasing incrementally and the 10th placed rider going home with just £20. I presume the 10 non-placed riders received absolutely nothing!

Amongst the star riders we were introduced to was Steve Parrish. Steve was a close friend of Barry Sheene and had been his racing partner during his world championship racing season. He was contracted to Yamaha and had some involvement in the "Wrangler/Which Bike?" programme.

"I'm a great fan of Wrangler gear," he explained as we were talking.

It was agreed I would send him a pair our jeans. I also offered him a facility to purchase products from us, for him and his family members, at a very favourable rate. He was happy to take me up on the offer and we were still in contact many years after he retired from racing.

Another person we met that day was a very young 250cc grand prix rider called Alan Carter. He was part of a very famous biking family from Halifax in Yorkshire, becoming the youngest rider ever to have won a 250cc Motorcycle Grand Prix when he had triumphed in his first ever Grand Prix at Le Mans, in France, only two weeks previously.

I think he was still in a state of shock and totally overawed by his new superstar status. I have a photograph of him with my daughter who was only 10 years old at the time. She looked young but so did Alan.

He did participate in the "Wrangler/Which Bike?" race but was shown no favours by his older, and more worldly-wise, fellow competitors.

Sadly, Alan was never to win another Grand Prix and suffered series of personal traumas. His best season was 1985, when he finished seventh in the 250cc World Championship, and went on to compete in 54 GPs until he retired in 1990. Eventually he wrote an autobiography, "Light in the Darkness," In it, Alan revealed the truth behind his meteoric rise and fall and all the many contributory factors that helped shape his life.

In the weeks and months of our sponsorship, we started to receive requests from all over the country for Wrangler decals.

At first, I was puzzled. Everything became clear at a meeting with my FPR's. They advised me that budding racing bikers were keen to customise their own bikes in the same livery as the lead bike in the "Wrangler/Which Bike?" races.

They could not afford a costly paint shop makeover, but blue and yellow spray paint and "genuine" Wrangler decals were the next best thing!

My next visit to the Yamaha box at Donington was on Monday 30 May 1983. The track was hosting the British rounds of the F.I.M European Championships with races from 80cc, 125cc, 250cc, 500cc and Sidecars. A whole day of fantastic racing featuring the best that Europe had to offer.

This, however, was not the reason that I was once again enjoying Yamaha's hospitality. The Austin Rover Group had been persuaded to sponsor a "2-4 Challenge." This was to be the final event of a very memorable day. The "2-4 Challenge" was a unique motorsport event consisting of a two-leg race featuring 10 of the top riders from the "Wrangler/Which Bike?" series.

In the first leg, the entrants would be riding 10 laps on the Wrangler liveried, Yamaha RD350 motorcycles. They would then switch to MG Maestros, provided by Austin Rover Group, for the second leg of 10 laps.

Points would be awarded to the finishers in each race based on 10-9-8-7-6-5-4-3-2-1. The competitor accumulating the most points over the two legs would receive a £750 prize. In the event of a points tie, the competitor with the best placing in the car race would be declared the overall winner.

I was relaxed about the whole affair, after all this extra event had not cost Wrangler anything and yet we would have all the kudos of exclusive branding on the bikes.

My opposite number at Austin Rover Group had borne the bulk of the cost of the sponsorship. His company had also provided 10 brand new MG Maestros, with souped-up engines, and a team of mechanics for each rider.

He appeared far from relaxed!

In the Yamaha hospitality suite, the food and drink flowed. Everyone was enjoying a great day of exciting racing. Everyone, except the marketing director of Austin Rover Group.

He confided in me, "I am a little nervous about the "2-4 Challenge" race. I hope that everything runs smoothly and there is not too much damage to the cars." I tried to reassure him. "These are professional racers. They are always on the edge, but they do have respect for the machinery they are driving."

As I spoke the words, my fingers were tightly crossed!

The 10 laps on the bikes passed by quickly and were full of incident, near misses and a couple of crashes. I glanced across the room. The Austin Rover contingent were looking a little tense as the cars were lined up on the grid. The best placed riders on the bikes taking the best places on the grid.

As the start light went out, the crunching of gears was clearly audible. The leaders were wary into the first corner as they tried to evaluate the different racing environment, they found themselves in.

As they gathered more confidence, they became more carefree, throwing caution to the wind. There is a world of difference between bike and car racing. Our challengers were driving their cars in the same manner they had just ridden their bikes.

Approaching the chicane for the first time, in full view of our box, it was clear that one driver was well clear. The four drivers behind him were four abreast as they might compete on their bikes. Only one car at a time would be able to get through safely. Cue screeching of brakes and crunching of metal.

The people from Austin Rover had gone very quiet!

With one lap to go the only car unscathed was that one that had led from the start. The rest showed clear signs of damage or were obviously suffering from major mechanical problems. The leader came through the final chicane well clear and entered the final straight to the cheers of the crowd.

I may have imagined it, but I swear he tried to do a "wheelie" in his car. Whatever the reason, he lost control as he went through the finishing line and crashed into the corner at the end of the straight.

The spectators loved it. The members of the Austin Rover Group Management Team were clearly not amused!

To the best of my knowledge the "2-4 Challenge" was a one-off experience!

On Saturday 22 September 1984, I was back at Donington for the World of Sport Superbike Challenge Meeting. The first race was the final round of the "Wrangler-Which Bike? Pro-Am series." The race included stalwarts such as Kenny Irons (who was to top the final standings), Roy Swann, Kurt Langan, Andy Watts, and Kevin Mitchell.

As usual, it was full of excitement and set the scene for an excellent day of motorcycle racing.

"The World of Sport Superbike Challenge" was the main event of the day. It featured some of the all-time greats of the sport. These included Ron Haslam, Joey Dunlop, Steve Parrish, Wayne Gardner, and the incomparable Barry Sheene.

My programme for the day records that Ron Haslam won the race and clinched the series. Barry Sheene took second place, with Joey Dunlop third, Wayne Gardner forth, Roger Marshall fifth and Steve Parrish sixth.

After the race Steve Parrish came back to the Yamaha box bringing his buddy, Barry Sheene with him. I renewed my acquaintance with the great man who no doubt reminded me of the mistake I had made by not signing him up before he became a two-times world champion. My son was with me, and Barry signed his Hospitality Suite ticket for him as a memento of the day.

The "Wrangler-Which Bike Yamaha RD350 Pro-Am Series" only ran for two years but left a lasting impression on fans of motorcycle racing who still relive the series over thirty years after the final race. Indeed, I learned in 2016, that motor cycling fanatics were still spraying their bikes in the Wrangler lead bike livery.

I am not quite sure why the series did not continue.

It might have been that ITV decided to reduce their coverage of the sport, or Yamaha may have decided that their priorities lay elsewhere. Whatever the reason, the "World of Sport Superbike Challenge Meeting," in September 1984, marked the end of the Wrangler brands involvement in motorsport on two wheels.

During the 1970's and 1980's the prospect of Wrangler involvement in motor sport of the four-wheeled variety was considered on several occasions.

P34, six-wheeled Tyrrell-Ford Racing Car

In early in 1976, an approach had been made to the Blue Bell office in Brussels enquiring whether Wrangler might be willing to consider sponsorship of the, Derek Gardner designed, P34, six-wheeled Tyrrell-Ford racing car. The car had been developed to race during the 1976 Grand Prix season and its revolutionary design was the talk of the Grand Prix circuit at the time.

The lack of a main sponsor meant that it had been largely funded from Ken Tyrell's own pocket. He was naturally anxious to bring a sponsor on board as quickly as possible, to ease the financial burden. His son, Bob Tyrrell, was the Business Development Director of Tyrell Racing at the time. He had been tasked with negotiating with possible sponsors to have some minor involvement during the 1976 season with a view to a full-blown relationship in 1977.

Tyrell Racing was based in the UK. I was involved in all the early discussions as we explored how the Wrangler brand might benefit from such a deal.

Blue Bell Inc. in the USA were keen for their European operations to go ahead with the project. They even pushed for Randy Lewis, then a promising Formula Three driver in Europe, to be appointed as one of the drivers. Randy was born in Charlotte in North Carolina, and I presumed "someone knew somebody."

Keen as they were with the concept, our American colleagues made it clear that they were not prepared to provide any funding!

The main obstacle to moving forward, in the short term, was that each country in Blue Bell Europe was responsible for its own marketing budget. When negotiations had begun, much of this was already committed.

Even back in the 1970's, a seven-figure sum was required for the full-blown sponsorship for the 1977 season. Allocated on a country-by-country basis, this would have created a considerable hole in everyone's budgets. In addition, race and media coverage was not as extensive as it is today. The potential publicity exposure was therefore much lower.

My UK budget was the largest in Europe but without the significant input from all the other European subsidiaries, it was not affordable for the UK to go it alone.

The European Marketing Manager operating out of Brussels wanted to convene a Pan-European meeting to allow Bob Tyrrell the opportunity to present his case to all the countries operating in Blue Bell Europe.

This was planned for 7 May 1976 in Vienna, Austria.

A dinner had been organised at our hotel, The Vienna Hilton, for the evening of 6 May. I had booked a flight that was scheduled to arrive at around 6.30pm. This gave me ample time to travel from the airport to the hotel and freshen up before the dinner.

In the event, my flight from London was delayed by several hours owing to problems at Vienna airport. I eventually arrived at the hotel just as my colleagues were going down to the bar for a nightcap. They informed me that there had been a major earthquake whose epicentre was in neighbouring Italy. The shockwave and aftershocks had been felt in Vienna at around the time that my plane was due to have landed.

A delay owing to an earthquake and no dinner. Not a great start to a meeting that could have "seismic" consequences!

Blue Bell Europe had provided a huge Scalextric track in the lobby outside our conference room and Randy Lewis had been flown in to support Bob Tyrrell's presentation.

The first outing of the Tyrrell six-wheeler had taken place at the Spanish Grand Prix only a few days earlier. Bob Tyrell announced that this had been very promising. Firstly, the car had been passed to drive in the race by the authorising body. Secondly, against all expectations the driver, Patrick Depailler, had managed a third place on the starting grid. The car was looking good for a podium finish when it crashed out at the half-way point.

"This proves that the revolutionary design is not only causing a stir amongst racing circles, it is also extremely competitive," Bob announced. "We at Tyrrell, are convinced that a partnership with Wrangler will be a win, win for both parties," he continued. Bob answered all the questions he received from my European colleagues, but it was clear that the funding he was hoping for would prove to be a major stumbling block to moving forward.

Randy Lewis presented himself as an up-and-coming driver in whom Tyrrell expressed the utmost confidence. His ultra-competitive nature was well demonstrated when he beat all comers in the organised Scalextric racing that took place during a break in the formal proceedings.

Unfortunately, after the meeting the consensus was that the investment was too much for the perceived return.

The P34's golden moment came the following month in the Swedish Grand Prix, which took place on 13 June 1976. Jody Scheckter and Patrick Depailler finished first and second, Scheckter is the only driver ever to win a race in a six-wheeled car.

He left the team at the end of the season, allegedly insisting that the six-wheeler was "a piece of junk!" Scheckter probably realised that the car could only be temporarily competitive. The special Goodyear tyres had not been developed enough by the end of the season. Ultimately, it was this that finally scuppered the six-wheeled concept.

Randy Lewis never fulfilled his ambition to be a Formula 1 driver. He returned to the USA to compete in the Formula 5000 and Can-Am series. He was a five-time starter in the Indianapolis 500 with a best finish of 14th in 1990 and 1991.

He finally retired 1991 setting up Lewis Cellars, in the Napa Valley, with his wife Debbie in 1994. Today, Randy Lewis prefers to be known as a quality winemaker.

Who knows what might have been had the decision taken in Vienna in 1976, gone the other way?

With the benefit of hindsight, the conclusion of the delegates at the meeting turned out to be the correct one.

Le Mans 24-hour Race

One of the partners of the Blue Bell solicitors in Nottingham, was extremely keen on motorsport. He had close connections with a team of privateers who raced a Porsche 956 at the Le Mans 24-hour race in France, with some success. We had provided a small amount of support in the form of Wrangler merchandise but had not considered any kind of formal sponsorship arrangement.

Early in 1980, they approached us with a full-blown sponsorship deal. This included the possibility of their hiring Mark Thatcher, son of the then Prime Minister, Margaret Thatcher, as one of the drivers. He had some experience in sports car racing but was keen to take the next step up. Le Mans was the "real deal" with cars capable of travelling at speeds of over 200 mph.

The son of the Prime Minister, driving a Wrangler liveried car at one of the most iconic motor racing events in the world, was worthy of consideration. We made it clear to our contact that, in view of the sponsorship money they were looking for, we would only go ahead if the car had a real chance of winning its class – if not the race itself.

The involvement of Mark Thatcher would create some publicity before the event because of who his mother was. He would need to convince both us and the racing team, that he could compete at the high level required to be successful.

A meeting was arranged at the Wrangler showroom in central London with representatives of the team and Mark Thatcher himself. To say he was not lacking in confidence would be an understatement! What was not clear, was whether he would be able to match his faith in his own ability, when the chips were down during a super competitive event like Le Mans.

I particularly needed to satisfy myself that he was not simply trying to exploit his mother's position as Prime Minister and that he would be able to act as a true ambassador of the Wrangler brand.

After a short time, it was clear that he felt that HE was the key player in the proposed relationship and that everyone else was of little importance. His approach was very much "me, me." He came across as brash and over-confident in his own ability to succeed and was clearly of the opinion that his presence in the Wrangler funded racing team, would create a media storm.

"You realise that even if the team wins there is no guarantee of large-scale media coverage. Even a small world crisis will reduce the impact from a major headline to a few lines on the back or inside pages." I suggested. He laughed and replied, "Don't worry the Boss (referring to his mother, the Prime Minister) will take care of that."

At the time, we thought he was joking but, with the benefit of hindsight perhaps he was not!

Anyway, we did not take our sponsorship discussions any further.

In 1980, Mark Thatcher did contest Le Mans 24 Hours alongside racing driver Lella Lombardi, the only woman to score points in Formula 1. Dropping out after 157 laps, Mark was back in 1981 driving a Porsche 935. This time, he retired after 260 laps. To put his performances in perspective, the number of laps normally covered by the race winner is in the region of 380.

In 1982, Mark Thatcher took part in the Dakar Rally with Ann-Charlotte Verney as co-driver. They were competing in a Peugeot 504 sponsored by Lois Jeans. On 9 January 1982, they and their mechanic went missing for six days in the Sahara Desert. A large-scale search including six military aircraft from three countries and Algerian ground troops was launched at the instigation of his mother.

In his autobiography, Mark Thatcher admitted his thought process, before the race, was, "I've now raced in Le Mans and other things – this rally is no problem." He continued, "I did absolutely no preparation. Nothing!"

Having praised his mother for using her influence to set up the search, he then blamed the other competitors, who stopped when his car broke down, for giving the race organisers the wrong co-ordinates. He went on to claim, "The biggest story of 1982 was the Falklands war. The second biggest also involved my mother... and me."

Clearly, the assessment we made in 1980, in respect of the Le Mans sponsorship, was 100% correct!

Lombard RAC Rally

In 1985, I was approached via a retail contact to see if Wrangler might be interested in a low-key sponsorship of car in that years Lombard RAC Rally.

Normally, there would have only been one answer, but that year the Rally was scheduled to start and finish in Nottingham. Furthermore, the team in question had acquired the services of a former world champion driver. They did not stand much chance of success against the works teams, but they were confident they would put up a good show.

There were several stages in Nottinghamshire. The opening stage was in Wollaton Park and another off-road stage at Clipstone Forest. Our offices at Calverton were about halfway between the two.

A small sponsorship fee passed hands and some Wrangler merchandise was supplied to the team members. For this, we had Wrangler decals on the car. Unfortunately, our team never made it out of Nottinghamshire. The car suffered a major mechanical breakdown during the Clipstone Forest stage.

The unsuccessful experience marked the end of the Wrangler UK involvement in motorsport. At least during my tenure!

A missed opportunity in Motor Sport

During the 1980's several budding young racing drivers contacted me with a view to obtaining sponsorship from the Wrangler brand. Among them was a certain Damon Hill who introduced himself as the son of the late Graham Hill, a two-time Formula 1 world champion.

These were the days when up and coming drivers had to find quite large sums of money to secure a drive. Being the son of a famous father cut no ice in a super competitive sport. At the time, Damon was not regarded as a high-flyer although he had experienced some minor successes.

We were unable to help. I believe he managed to obtain a loan that secured a drive and eventually his progression to Formula 3000 Championship racing. He got his big break as test driver for Williams in 1992 and was promoted to the race team the following season. He became world champion, like his father, in 1996.

Chapter Twelve

Team sports

Nearly everyone will have participated in, or been a spectator at an event involving a competition between teams of people.

Team sports uniquely set themselves apart from most sporting activities because they generate a fierce competitive spirit, not only between the teams competing, but also amongst the spectators supporting them.

Anyone who has gone along to watch a son or daughter representing their school in a team sport will testify that, even the mildest of individuals, can undergo a change of persona and descend into the sort of loutish behaviour that they would roundly condemn in others. This descending "red mist" manifests itself in many ways. It ranges from righteous indignation, when they feel that their loved one has been wronged, to actual physical assault on the perpetrator.

In some sports, a sort of tribal loyalty exists that transcends everything. As a result, rival spectators spend more of their time hurling insults at each other than they appear to spend following the activity they have paid good money to watch.

For a potential sponsor, team sports can become a poisoned chalice. The fiercer the competitiveness of the sport, the greater the possibility that involvement can do more harm than good.

In my 16 years promoting the Wrangler brand, I developed an instinctive feeling for the handling of sponsorship in team sports. I am not saying that we got it right every time. The scars are still visible from the areas where mistakes were made.

In most cases, the experience proved positive, for both Wrangler and the teams sponsored.

Great Britain's Athletic Team – 1976 Olympics in Montreal

At the beginning of 1976, I received a telephone call from a Tom McNab. He introduced himself as one of the coaches for the Athletics team that was in the process of being selected to represent Great Britain at the 1976 Olympics in Montreal. Tom asked if he could come up to Calverton to discuss the possibility of some "low-key" sponsorship activity.

At this point, I admit that my judgment was somewhat clouded by the fact that I had been an athlete myself and was a great fan of the sport.

Later in my career, I would probably have declined and applied my unwritten rule never to consider a sponsorship request from a representative of a sport that I was particularly keen on.

Tom's contact had come when I was less than 12 months in the post. I was still a little green behind the ears and agreed to meet him.

Even after all these years, I still recall what a formidable character he was.

A Scotsman trying to extract cash from a Yorkshireman. It should have been a close fought contest. It was not!

"What exactly have you got in mind?" I asked him.

Tom explained that he was working with a small group of young athletes who, whilst being selected on merit for the Games, were unlikely to "set the world alight" this time around. The 1976 Olympics would enable them to gain experience in a major event. Some were tipped to make a major impact on the sport in the future.

"The British Olympic Association have organised official team uniforms for all occasions, but my young athletes like jeans and casual tops when they are relaxing. They particularly like Wrangler products," Tom enthusiastically declared.

"So, what is the proposition and how will Wrangler benefit from involvement?" I enquired.

Tom was very honest with me. The arrangement would only be "semi-official." He wanted me to supply a Wrangler outfit to each of the team members in his group of athletes. Wrangler would not receive any credit in any of the team literature. We would not be able to use the link up for publicity purposes for fear of jeopardising the amateur status of his group of athletes.

In other words, he wanted me to authorise the supply of outfits as a "goodwill" gesture for which there was no hope of any material benefit for the Wrangler brand. His enthusiasm was infectious. Despite my obvious misgivings, I found myself agreeing to his request.

The measurements were sent through, and the outfits despatched before the team departed for Montreal.

During the Games, I received a postcard from the Olympic village. It read, "Best wishes from Montreal. The team loved the gear. Tom McNab."

As he had predicted, the performance of the Great Britain Team in athletics was not very inspiring. Only one athlete won a medal, a certain Brendan Foster, who earned a bronze medal in the 10,000 metres. Tony Simmonds and Bernie Ford were 4th and 8th in the same race.

Other performances of note included appearances in finals for Steve Ovett (5th 800m), Frank Clement and Dave Moorcroft (5th & 7th 1500m), Alan Pascoe (8th 400m hurdles), David Jenkins (7th 400m), Andrea Lynch (7th 100m), Women's 4x100m relay (8th) and Women's 4x400m relay (7th). A young thrower called Tessa Sanderson came 10th in the javelin whist the youngest member of the team, 18 years old Daly Thompson, finished 18th in the decathlon.

Many members of the team went on to future success.

Steve Ovett set world records for the mile and 1500m. He won Olympic gold (800m) and bronze (1500m) in Moscow in 1980. Daly Thompson won decathlon gold in Moscow in 1980 and repeated the feat in Los Angeles in 1984. Tessa Sanderson competed in a further five Olympic Games winning gold in the javelin in 1984 in Los Angeles. Dave Moorcroft broke the world record for 5000m in 1982.

The formidable Tom McNab is still very well known for his coaching career in athletics and other sports, including the British Bobsleigh team at the 1980 Winter Olympics in Lake Placid.

Away from athletics, in 1981 he was technical director for the film "Chariots of Fire." During filming, he was responsible for coaching the actors so that they could perform like real runners when the camera was rolling.

In addition, he wrote three excellent books. "Flanagan's Run" in 1982, "Rings of Sand" in 1984 and "The Fast Men" in 1986.

I still have the copy of the Official Handbook of Great Britain's Team for the Montreal Olympics that he sent to me after the event. He had signed it, as had most of the Athletes who participated in his training squad.

Great Britain Rugby League Team in Australia 1977

When I was nine years old, I was introduced to rugby league at my primary school in Leeds. I played for the school team until I left for secondary school aged eleven. From then, until I left school in 1959, I played rugby union. Despite this fact, the Leeds Rugby League Club was always the first result I looked for in the sports newspapers.

At the age of 16, I became a founder member of West Park Old Boys RUFC (now West Park Leeds) and during the 1960's I played first team rugby union for them, Edinburgh Northern and Moortown RUFC.

In 1968 a serious injury curtailed my active participation in the sport.

At primary school, I was lucky enough to attend two rugby League Challenge Cup finals at Wembley Stadium, in London.

There was a huge divide between the two codes of rugby during this period because rugby league players were paid to play. Rugby union players were not.

In the north of England, the stronghold of rugby league, the "cultural divide" between union and league players was less pronounced. I knew quite a few players who had crossed codes before their 18th birthday (this was allowed) and had played with distinction at representative level for both county and country.

In the early 1960's, I worked for a large advertising agency in Leeds called Nevin D. Hirst. When they moved their offices to the Chapeltown district of the city, one of the agency's close neighbours was the headquarters of the Rugby Football League.

As a result, during this time, I came to know some of the games administrators.

At the beginning of 1977, I received a call from David Howes who was Public Relations Officer of the Rugby Football League. He worked closely with David Oxley the Chief Executive. Their task was to change the perception of the sport, increase its penetration nationally and internationally, and to break some of the taboos that existed between the two codes of rugby.

"The Two Dave's," as they became known, were aware that the sport needed to become more business-minded and to embrace commercial sponsorship if it was to survive and thrive.

Ironically, rugby union, the so called "amateur code" had been more successful in raising funding in this way. This was probably because of their extensive network of current, and ex-players, operating within the business community.

I met up with David Howe to discuss how we might work together. During that first meeting, I suggested that he did not need to sell the rugby league concept to me. His aims were fully supported.

David explained he was not looking for sponsorship money, but the provision of merchandise on much the same basis that I had supported the Olympic Athletics team the previous year.

The GB Rugby League team had qualified for the Rugby League World Cup finals. These were being held in Australia during the summer of 1977. They would be competing against the hosts Australia along with New Zealand and France.

David had established suppliers for match shirts and tracksuits. Arrangements had also been made for the supply of suits, shirts, and ties at all formal occasions. He felt that the support of a major jeans and casualwear brand would help to improve the image of Rugby League amongst younger potential players and supporters.

Blue Bell International was in the process of developing the Wrangler brand in Australia and New Zealand and had a subsidiary in France. I expressed the opinion that press interest of the team, outside coverage of the games, would be minimal in the UK and France but that wider media coverage could be expected in Australia and New Zealand.

We selected a red, white and blue coloured themed outfit that consisted of jeans, Tee shirt and casual jacket. This was approved by David Oxley and the RFL board.

I encountered some difficulties accommodating the larger members of the team during the fitting session. This took place, in the dressing rooms of Leeds RFC, at the famous Headingley Stadium. There were one or two grumbles about tight jackets and even tighter jeans but overall, the team was delighted with the product we had provided.

The tour went ahead, and the GB team reached the final. They were unlucky to lose to Australia. The team management ensured the casual "uniform" was worn at every possible opportunity.

Because of the media coverage received, the management of Blue Bell in Australia, then led by Jack Hill, an American who had previously been a VP in Blue Bell Europe, was delighted.

"The Two David's" reported back that they were very happy that the Wrangler involvement had proved a win, win situation for all concerned.

At the beginning of 1978, Jack Hill, who was visiting the UK at the time, attended a Wrangler UK sales meeting in Nottingham. I presented the results of our most recent advertising campaign. "Top of mind awareness of the Wrangler name is now 75% with prompted awareness standing at almost 100%," I explained.

Jack then presented the figures for Australia. "Top of mind awareness 0% and prompted awareness now peaking at around 5%," he announced to the audience, amid much laughter. "Only joking," he continued. "We still have a long way to go before we reach your levels of awareness, but the Rugby League World Cup sponsorship worked very well for us."

Apparently, the team management had been as good as their word. The GB Team had worn the Wrangler merchandise on all possible occasions. Our product was heavily branded and featured prominently in press and on TV. This helped the salesforce in Australia to increase their distribution considerably.

For the next three years, my wife and I attended the Rugby League Cup final at Wembley as VIP guests of the RFL. We enjoyed the opportunity to watch the matches and mingle with the great and the good. I remember the President of the RFL at the time was the Earl of Derby. All the named guests, attending the VIP lunch before the game, were listed alphabetically in a printed souvenir brochure. In the 'D's' "Derby the Earl of" was followed by "Dilley, R M."

The three games we attended proved to be great advertisements for rugby league.

In 1978, we were present to watch our home club, Leeds defeat St Helens 14-12.

The 1979 final celebrated the 50th Anniversary of the first Wembley final when Wigan beat Dewsbury. Some of the players from Dewsbury who played in that final were seated at our table during the pre-match lunch. That year Widnes beat Wakefield Trinity 12-3 to claim the trophy.

In 1980, we watched the local derby between Hull and Hull Kingston Rovers. Hull KR came out the winners by 10-5. Queen Elizabeth, the Queen Mother presented the trophy to the winning captain Roger Millward. In the 1977 Rugby League World Cup, Roger Millward had captained the GB side so narrowly defeated in the final by Australia. The coincidence neatly rounded off our association with the sport!

David Oxley and David Howes worked together at the RFL until 1992 and were responsible for transforming the image of the game.

Nottingham Ice Speed Skating Club – Open Meeting 1979

In 1979, I was approached by Pauline Jordon who was working as one of the Wrangler sales administrators in Calverton. Both she and her husband Dave, were very much involved with the sport of short track speed skating.

At the time, it was not an event at the Olympic Games, but Dave Jordon was keen to increase its profile so that it would be accepted. It was his hope that this would occur in the "not too distant future."

Pauline and Dave were organising an open event at the Nottingham Ice Rink and wondered if Wrangler might be able to provide some backing. Dave explained that short track speed skating was an amateur sport, and the opportunities were very limited. He was more interested in the publicity that the involvement of a brand like Wrangler would generate. This in turn, might encourage more young people to get involved and perhaps join a club in their area.

We were happy to get involved. From memory, I believe we covered the cost of the ice time, pre-publicity, and stewarding.

Our efforts paid off with considerable interest from the sports press and a large enthusiastic crowd on the night. The Nottingham team was very strong but was facing major competition from the team from Birmingham.

One of the highlights of the night was the 500m. This was won by an up-and-coming star from Birmingham called Wilf O'Reilly. Nottingham favourite, Stuart Horsepool was runner up in an exciting and close fought race. Recently I found a photograph of my wife and myself handing out a trophy on the night and presenting a Wrangler boot mirror to the club.

Both Wilf and Stuart were to become stalwarts of a Great Britain Team managed by none other than Dave Jordon.

In the 1988 Olympics, short track speed skating was admitted as a test sport. Wilf O'Reilly, who had won the main race at the Wrangler sponsored open meet in 1979, was the winner of both the 500m and 1000m. Stuart Horsepool was a member of the relay team that came 6th in its final. He went on to become Performance Director of the GB Short Track Speed Skating Team.

At the event in 1979, Dave introduced me to a rather nervous looking, young ice dancer by the name of Christopher Dean. With his partner Jayne Torvill, they had just won the British Ice Dance Championship and it was felt by many people, that they were on the brink of success on the international scene.

Christopher had been born in Calverton and attended the Colonel Frank Seely School that was opposite the Blue Bell offices in the village.

"He would like to talk to you about possible financial support for Jayne and himself," Dave said.

"We are both working full time. Currently, I'm a policeman. Jayne is working in an office. If we are to compete against the very best, we need to train full time. Basically, we need to find a way of covering our living expenses, a least up to and including the 1984 Olympics," Christopher explained.

Around this time, there were some professional ice dancers. They were prevented from participating in the British, European, World championships and the Olympic games. These competitions were for amateurs only.

Some countries seemed prepared to "bend" the rules either through state sponsorship, as was the case in Russia, or the college scholarship system that operated in the United States. Athletes in these countries enjoyed the best full-time facilities that were available, the best coaches and full cost of living support, without compromising their amateur status.

To compete successfully, on a level playing field, Christopher and Jayne needed to find some means of doing the same.

"I calculate that you will need at least a five-figure sum to cover the necessary outlay over the next four years. I would like to help, but the Blue Bell shareholders would need a positive return for such an investment. This is not possible because the sport's governing bodies will say that you are receiving money from a "commercial sponsor." This would make you both professional in their eyes," I explained. "The only way I can see that you can move forward is to approach local or national government to obtain some sort of loan or grant."

Christopher was obviously disappointed but agreed that commercial sponsorship was probably out of the question. Apparently, he had received similar advice from other sources and had already made soundings with the Nottingham City and Nottinghamshire County councils.

The following year, Torvill and Dean were given a grant by Nottingham City Council. It was controversial at the time but perceived as no different from the type of help offered to their major competitors from other countries.

The rest is history!

They competed in the 1980 winter Olympics at Lake Placid, where they were placed 5th. Following this, they were 4th in the 1980 World Championships. After which, they won every competition they entered including their "maximum score," for their now famous gold medal winning performance of Bolero, in the 1984 Olympics.

Nottingham Forest Football Club – 1983/4

Prior to the 1983/4 football season, there had been club sponsorship deals in the English Leagues. In theory, sponsors names had been allowed to be displayed on football shirts. Unfortunately, the major television companies had refused to allow clubs to use shirts with sponsors names on them for games that were being televised.

It was rumoured that this rule was to be dropped. Not only would sponsors names be allowed, at a size that could be identified on screen, but there would also be live coverage of some of the key games.

To the marketing community, it was clear that if this rumour became a reality, there would be a rush to be involved. This could send the price of shirt sponsorship spiralling!

In July of 1983, only weeks before the start of the new football season, many clubs had still not negotiated club or shirt sponsorship deals because of the uncertainty that existed.

I had not contemplated any promotional involvement with a football club. The game was traditionally "tribal" with supporters being fiercely loyal to the club that they followed and antagonistic to the supporters of all other clubs.

As a leading national and international brand, we had been careful to ensure that any use of the Wrangler name in advertising and/or sponsorship would be beneficial to the brand. There was a feeling that supporting a specific football club, or international side, might affect our relationship with customers of the brand from every other club/country.

When I received a call early in July 1983 from Nottingham Forest, enquiring "would Wrangler be interested in discussing the possibility of a club sponsorship deal," it was true to say that I was a little "lukewarm" about the idea.

There were two football clubs in the city of Nottingham. Both were in the top division of the English Football League.

Notts County, the other team, were proud owners of the title "the oldest professional football team in the world" having been formed on 28 November 1862. For years they had held the "bragging rights" in the city.

In more recent times, Nottingham Forest had become pre-eminent. Since the arrival of Brian Clough in 1975, they had enjoyed almost continuous success and had been European Cup Winners in the 1978/79 and 1979/80 seasons.

To side with one club against the other would be to risk alienating, not only half our own city, but also a large proportion of our own workforce in Calverton.

After a conversation with Dick Webzell about the approach, we agreed that I would start negotiations with the Nottingham Forest board to determine what sort of deal was on the table, and level of sponsorship funding they were looking for.

Any proposal would be put in front of the Management Team before a final decision was made.

Football held little appeal for me personally. I was a rugby man. What's more I came from Leeds, the club that Brian Clough had managed for a disastrous 44 days before leaving to take over as manager of Nottingham Forest. I had no axe to grind one way or the other. This would ensure my complete impartiality in every part of the decision-making process.

The Chairman of Nottingham Forest at that time was Geoffrey MacPherson. He owned a company that provided embroidery and screen-printing services to the textile and clothing manufacturing industries.

Blue Bell Apparel Ltd. worked with the company. Geoffrey's son, Neil, ran Macpherson Meistergram Inc. in the United States. One of its largest customers was Blue Bell Inc. and its company headquarters was also in Greensboro, North Carolina.

Because of his association with Blue Bell, Geoffrey had decided to take no part in the early negotiations. He appointed fellow directors Maurice Roworth and Irving Korn to liaise with me to see whether a mutually beneficial deal could be hammered out.

I had gained a lot of experience in negotiations of this kind but had never been involved in football. Added to this, football club sponsorship deals were not as an essential part of the sport as they are today.

No real value had been attached to shirt sponsorship packages.

Maurice and Irving were anxious to finalise a deal before the start of the season. It was clear, from early on in our discussions, that there was nobody else in the frame.

"What sort of money are you looking for and what will that buy us?" I enquired.

They gave me an opening figure and explained, in addition to the Wrangler name on the shirts at every game, we would have two perimeter advertising sites at the Forest ground, an allocation of seats in the members stand for every home game and two executive boxes. Forest had also qualified for European football in the seasons UEFA Cup. Two tickets and travel to every away game would also be included.

I advised that the way I assessed sponsorship deals was to allocate the true cost of every element including the cost of the shirt deal, seats allocations etc. "Whatever difference there is between the actual value of items we are been offered and the sponsorship figure you are asking for, will be classified as goodwill." I explained.

I knew that the stand seats, executive boxes, perimeter sites were easy to evaluate as the costs were already calculated. Seats at the European away matches would depend on how successful Forest would be in the UEFA Cup competition.

The shirt sponsorship was the most intangible item!

As things stood, at the time of our initial talks, exposure of the Wrangler brand would be limited to the sports pages of the press, and football supporters attending home and European matches, and any resultant coverage on TV news channels.

If the TV deal went ahead, the visibility and resultant value would increase considerably!

I was keen to ensure that, if the sponsorship was given the go ahead, we would be able to include the supporters of the other clubs participating in the league. To do this, I assessed that for every pound spent on the sponsorship itself, another two pounds would be needed for this additional activity to cover public relations and sales promotional support.

The total sum was a six figure one. This is considerably less than companies are prepared to pay for similar deals today. At the time, it represented the largest sponsorship deal that Blue Bell Apparel Limited had ever contemplated for the Wrangler brand in the UK.

We played hardball during negotiations. I insisted that we needed to trim the sum that Forest were seeking whilst they tried to dig their heels in. In the end, time was not on their side and a fee was agreed that was closer to the Wrangler evaluation. Dick Webzell, and my fellow members of the senior management team, were happy to go ahead and a contract was drawn up for signature.

Bob Radford, Financial Director of Blue Bell Apparel Ltd and myself went along to a specially convened meeting of the board of Nottingham Forest. Only one item was on the agenda, this was to formally confirm agreement of the sponsorship deal. For reasons that I cannot recall, this had been organised to take place on a Sunday morning around two weeks prior to the start of the 1983/4 football season.

Bob and I were seated at the head of the boardroom table opposite Geoffrey MacPherson. The rest of the Forest board were seated down the other two sides.

Geoffrey welcomed us to the meeting and proceeded to read out the sponsorship details agreed by us with Maurice Roworth and Irving Korn. "Shirt sponsorship, two executive boxes, forty seats in the main stand for each game, two perimeter advertising signs."

His voice changed pitch as he read out the rest of the agreement!

Either he had never seen it before, or he was simply trying to force up the price by suggesting that the board might not ratify the deal.

I looked at Bob, pushed back my chair, looked around at the members of the Nottingham Forest Board and then made direct eye contact with Geoffrey. "Gentlemen, we have not come here to renegotiate any aspect of the contract," I announced. "If you are not happy, we are quite prepared to walk away from any deal,"

"No, no we are very happy with the agreement and will work with you to make it mutually beneficial to all parties." Geoffrey hastily replied.

The Forest Board gave their unanimous approval, and the contract was duly signed!

Two weeks later, the TV deal to allow shirt advertising was ratified. The sponsorship package, we had signed and sealed, had become an even better deal!

There was a slight delay with the shirt printing as far as I recall. This meant that the Wrangler name did not appear on the Forest shirts for the first home game. We had always felt that this might be the case, because of the last-minute nature of the negotiations.

Before long, the Wrangler name was clearly visible on the shirts, we began to reap benefits from all brand coverage that the arrangement was creating.

We had worked hard with the commercial departments of all the other clubs in the league and retailers of Wrangler products across the country. As a result, competitions had been organised in the match programmes of each team. Prizes included Wrangler products and tickets to their away game in Nottingham. The winners would meet some the players and enjoy VIP hospitality in one of the Wrangler VIP boxes.

Key retailers could enjoy the same experience when their team was playing at Nottingham Forest.

I had met Forest manager, Brian Clough, during the negotiation period. He was the same larger than life character that was portrayed in the press, during radio and TV interviews.

Under the chairmanship of Geoffrey MacPherson, the impression I had formed was that Brian Clough looked after the team, and the board oversaw everything else.

At the beginning of the 1983/4 seasons, Geoffrey's term in office came to an end and Maurice Roworth was appointed Chairman in his place. Initially, it seemed that Maurice was in awe of his manager and Clough, being Clough, took full advantage. This was to cause some friction between club and sponsor as the season progressed!

During the honeymoon period, everything was going to plan. On the 10 September 1983, Queens Park Rangers, were the visitors. It had been arranged that the Wrangler sponsorship would be officially announced by way of an on the pitch presentation before the game began.

QPR were managed by Terry Venables an ex-player, England international, and another high-profile manager. The previous season he had guided QPR to promotion to the top-flight. Media talk suggested that he and Brian Clough did not get on with each other.

While waiting to go on to the field they were engaging with good-humoured banter with me, and with each other. Nothing I saw, suggested that any antagonism existed between them.

I went on to the pitch, in front of a crowd of nearly 15,000 people. There, for the benefit of the attending media, I presented a mocked-up contract to the new Forest Chairman.

The whole episode was met by a mixture of booing (from the QPR away support) and chanting and cheers from the home supporters.

The match ended in a 3-2 home win for Forest, resulting in Brian Clough claiming bragging rights during after-match drinks with Terry Venables, that I am sure they both enjoyed!

The Nottingham Forest UEFA Cup campaign began with a match against German team, Vorwaerts. The home leg took place in Nottingham on the 14 September which Forest won 2-0. As part of our sponsorship agreement, we had been given two tickets enabling recipients to fly out with a Forest supporters club group and take their seats in the stand at the game.

We decided to hold a draw for all interested members of the Wrangler workforce at Calverton. This was won by two members of our warehouse staff. They travelled to Germany on 28 September to watch Forest win the match 1-0, and the tie 3-0 on aggregate.

The first ever live televised match in the sponsorship era was between Nottingham Forest and Tottenham Hotspur at White Hart Lane in London. This was a major coup for Blue Bell because, at the time, Spurs did not have a shirt sponsor. As a result, the Wrangler brand was the only one visible on the field of play.

I had asked my father-in-law, who I knew would be watching the match, to give me some feedback after the game. "How did it go?" I enquired the following day. "Oh, Nottingham Forest lost 1-2. It was a really good game," he replied.

"How visible was the Wrangler logo?" I queried. "What Wrangler logo?" he responded. "The one on the Nottingham Forest players' shirts," I exclaimed. "I didn't notice it," was his puzzled reply.

Feedback from one person is not a scientific piece of research. Thankfully, most other people who watched the match, including many retail buyers, had seen the exposure the Wrangler name had received and were most impressed.

During the first part of the season Nottingham Forest had been playing well in both the league and the FA Cup. In the UEFA Cup competition, apart from Vorwaerts, they had beaten PSV Eindhoven and Celtic and had advanced to the Quarter Finals. Because of this, Forest had been receiving a lot of additional media coverage right across Europe.

All great for the exposure of the Wrangler brand!

In addition, the competitions in away team programmes had drawn large entries and achieved a lot of good will amongst away supporters.

I had been anxious to include the Forest players in some of the promotional activity. This had been promised as part of the overall sponsorship deal. Our PR people had come up with several possibilities, but all had been blocked by the Forest Board.

The response was always the same, "Sorry, but Brian (Clough) says he can't allow it."

I was beginning to become very frustrated about this aspect of the sponsorship. After all, everyone at Wrangler had more than played their part to make the relationship work.

Early in 1984, matters came to ahead and I decide that more direct action was needed. I rang Maurice Roworth and asked him to set up a one-to-one meeting with Brian Clough to enable us to iron out the perceived difficulties.

A week or so later I went down to the Forest ground for the encounter. I was suited for a business meeting. Brian was wearing his iconic green football shirt, tracksuit bottom and trainers. We had met several times before and I reminded him that we were both from Yorkshire and that Yorkshiremen were well known for calling "a spade a spade." I had some difficulties with the sponsorship deal and he, according to the Forest board, was the cause.

He looked at me and smiled, "Well young man, what do you want me to do?" he asked.

"I would like to engage some of the players in what we are doing. A photoshoot in Wrangler gear and some personal appearances at Wrangler events. Nothing too demanding," I suggested.

Without pausing, he countered, "I am happy to go ahead with anything like that. Just give me a call and it will be sorted out. The only thing I will never allow, is a band from the armed forces marching up and down on MY pitch."

True to his word, everything I asked for after the meeting, was agreed to by him!

Many of the top players, their wives and children took part in a photoshoot. There were no tantrums about endorsement fees or image rights. Back in 1984, if a manager of the stature of Brian Clough asked a player to do something on behalf of the club, they just did it without question.

As a result, Garry Birtles and his wife Sandra, captain Ian Bowyer's children, twins Paul and Lisa and son Garry, Paul Hart and wife Vicky, Steve Hodge and Dutch stars Hans Van Breukelen and Frans Thijssen, were all happy to participate and receive the Wrangler merchandise they had posed in.

The resultant shots were used for PR purposes and to form part of an advertisement in the Nottingham Forest club programme. The headline ran, "Wrangler Sponsoring Nottingham Forest … with the team, their friends and families stepping out in great Wrangler gear for Spring/Summer 1984."

A list of the best local stockists in the Nottinghamshire area was also featured.

Garry Birtles, Forest centre forward, spent a day chatting to retailers on the Wrangler stand at the MAB exhibition in February 1984.

The same month the Wrangler logo on a Forest shirt made the headlines when a Forest substitute, I think it could have been Peter Davenport, was sent off to change his shirt because the Wrangler logo on the original was deemed "too big" by match officials.

I saw Brian Clough briefly after one of the Forest games that I attended not long afterwards. He winked and said, "Hello young man, did you hear about the logo on the shirt? Don't tell me I don't help promote Wrangler."

I am sure that the incident referred to, resulted from an unenforced error but then, knowing Brian Clough's reputation, perhaps it did not!

The Nottingham Forest board invited Bob Radford and me to travel with the team, for their UEFA Quarter Final second leg with Sturm Graz in Austria.

Brian Clough had booked a training ground just outside the town. This meant that we would be flying out on Sunday before the game and flying back just after the match on Wednesday evening.

Whilst the players were in their training camp, the rest of us would be staying in a hotel in the centre of the old town area. The Directors of Sturm Graz had organised a series of events, but the Tuesday before the match was a free day.

During the flight out, our party was jubilant. Forest had won the first leg 1-0 and were confident in their ability to progress to the next round. The fact that the match coincided with Brian Clough's 49th birthday was believed to be a good omen.

Graz is situated about 120 miles from Vienna. The two cities are connected by an excellent rail service over the mountains. Blue Bell had only recently set up a subsidiary in Austria with headquarters in Vienna. I knew the Managing Director who had previously worked as European Marketing Manager from our office in Brussels. This presented an opportunity to catch up with what he was doing, and for Bob Radford to see the city for the first time.

I booked tickets for the train and set up a meeting at the office of Blue Bell Austria.

On Monday, the directors of Sturm Graz had organised several events for our party that included the player's wives. Highlights included a guided tour of the city sights, and the medieval old town, said to be one of the best preserved in Central Europe. This was followed by a civic reception and dinner in the evening.

Bob and I were up early the following day to catch our train to Vienna. On our arrival, we were cordially greeted by our Austrian colleagues who updated on the progress of the relatively new Wrangler subsidiary. Afterwards, we were treated to a tour of the major sights of the Austrian capital, before returning to Graz.

The build up to the match was enjoyable because the weather was good, and both sets of supporters were mingling together without incident.

For Sturm Graz, this match was one of the biggest games in their history. Brian Clough had a legendary status and Nottingham Forest were two-time winners of the European Cup. The small ground was bursting with 22,000 enthusiastic fans!

Before the game local press photographers were keen to take pictures of the Nottingham Forest manager. Brian had other ideas! He simply wanted to complete his pre-match preparations. When one photographer got too close, "Cloughie" pushed him away. The Austrian supporters in the main stand were far from happy and expressed their annoyance. Someone may have launched an empty beer can over the fencing separating the spectators from the field of play. Brian made out that he was going to scale the fence, only to be restrained by the other occupants of his bench.

It was clear, even before a ball was kicked that the game was going to be very competitive!

Sturm Graz scored first. The match was now 1-1 on aggregate. Forest had to score the all-important away goal. If they succeeded, even if Sturm Graz equalised, they would go through on the away goal rule.

In the event, the Russian referee handed Nottingham Forest a controversial penalty that sent Forest through 2-1 over the two legs.

Without delving too deeply into post-war politics, it would be true to say the Russians were not very popular during the allies' occupation of Austria. The penalty decision brought back these memories, and the pre-match goodwill that existed between the two sets of supporters, quickly evaporated.

We were glad to board our coach to the airport where we met up with the players for the flight home.

By this time "Cloughie" was well into birthday celebration mode. He made a point of planting a kiss on everybody before they boarded the plane.

Yes, I can claim that I was once kissed by Brian Clough. It was not an enjoyable experience!

During an eventful day, we had witnessed the contradictions in the make-up of the man. These included his explosive temperament before the match, the jubilation bordering on manic at the final whistle, and his over-the-top birthday celebrations at the airport.

On the flight back to Nottingham, we caught a glimpse of Clough the family man intent on sitting with his daughter irrespective of inconvenience to others.

We also witnessed his hard-handed man management style when he insisted that the 19-year-old Chris Fairclough, an England under 21 International and one of the stars of the game, help to serve the in-flight refreshments to his fellow passengers.

Brian Clough might have been something of an enigma but there is no doubting he was the most successful manager that Nottingham Forest have ever had and one of the true legends of the game.

The UEFA Cup semi-final took place on the 11 April, against the Belgian club Anderlecht, at the City Ground in Nottingham. Forest won the match 2-0 and went into the return match as the hot favourites to reach the final.

In Brussels, Forest lost controversially by a debatable extra-time penalty allowing Anderlecht to win 3–2 on aggregate. It was later alleged that Anderlecht might have bribed the referee to ensure their passage to the final.

At the end of the 1983/4 season, Nottingham Forest had performed well in Europe and finished third in the league behind champions Liverpool and surprise package Southampton. By contrast, the other Nottingham Club, Notts County had been relegated to Division Two of the league.

In the closed season, we had assessed the benefits of the association with Forest and concluded that we had achieved excellent value for money. This was largely because of the team's success on the field but also because of the funding we had ploughed into PR and Sales Promotion support.

We certainly felt that the association was worthwhile continuing, but only at around the same level of expenditure.

Unfortunately, Forest had received interest from other sources. We were informed they had received an offer that was more than Blue Bell had paid them for the 1983/4 season. It was implied that if we exceeded this, Forest "might be willing to continue the association."

After conversations with Dick Webzell, it was agreed that we would not enter an auction process. The other party, a national brewery, had much deeper pockets and would inevitably outbid us.

I must admit, we were somewhat aggrieved with the way that our association with Forest had ended. Wrangler had more than fulfilled our part of the deal and felt that we were been used to help "bump up" the eventual sponsorship fee.

On the other hand, we were aware that the ground rules had changed. Our successful approach to the sponsorship had been noted by others.

At the beginning of the 1983/4 season, football sponsorship had been regarded as a big risk. Companies prepared to take a chance held most of the cards. The stakes had changed. Clubs now believed that they could name their own price.

"Cash up front" was obviously their overriding priority!

Notts County Football Club – 1984/1987

Following the failure to renew the Nottingham Forest club sponsorship, I had no plans to get involved in a similar arrangement with any other club.

In the summer of 1984, I was approached by Neal Hook, Managing Director of "the other Nottingham based football club," Notts County. I knew Neal quite well through the local branch of the Institute of Marketing of which we were both members. "I have heard through the grapevine that Forest have acquired another sponsor for 1984/5. Might you be interested in some sort of arrangement with County?" he enquired.

I said that I would give it some thought and talk it over with my marketing team and the Blue Bell Management Group.

Whilst Forest had enjoyed an excellent season in the First Division of the Football League, County, nicknamed "The Magpies," had endured a torrid time and had been relegated to the Second Division

Notts County, established in 1862, had the distinction of being the oldest professional football club in the world. For years, they had been the predominant football club in Nottinghamshire but with the rise of their city rivals, Forest, they were very much considered underdogs.

The club did not have the money to entice top players. Instead, they had invested in a policy of bringing on youngsters through their youth academy and signing seasoned professionals nearing the end of their playing careers.

Relegation would have a massive impact on the club's income. Anticipated gates for some home matches would struggle to reach 5,000. They would be very lucky to achieve the 15,000 gates they needed to break even.

Whilst they were ambitious to "bounce back" immediately to the top league, Neal had to admit that with big money teams such as Leeds United, Birmingham City, Wolverhampton Wanderers, Middlesbrough, and Manchester City all harbouring similar ambitions, this was going to prove very difficult.

On the positive side, several top names from their team who had competed in the higher league, such as Justin Fashanu and Martin O'Neal, would be staying with the club.

The club sponsorship package included Wrangler branding on the team's shirts, an executive box, and a quota of seats in the main stand. Neal was realistic, he was looking for was much less than we had spent with Forest. He felt that a "big name club sponsor" would encourage other companies to get involve as match sponsors, executive box holders and advertisers in the match programmes.

I discussed the proposal with Dick Webzell and the other members of the Blue Bell management team. To my surprise, they were very receptive to the idea. Retailers had provided very positive responses to the match day package that we were able to offer them at Forest.

With so many big name, big city clubs fighting it out for promotion, it was felt that the opportunity existed to continue the successful format, at a fraction of the sum we had paid the previous year.

This was the start of a relationship with Notts County that was to last for three seasons!

At Forest, it had taken several months before manager and players became fully involved with the Wrangler sponsorship. At County, the involvement began on day one.

Larry Lloyd, a former Forest favourite, had been appointed to take charge of the team in July 1983. He was being mentored by former manager, Jimmy Sirrel who was Director of Football.

At the beginning of September 1984, I received a request from a retailer in Sutton on Trent who was, with a little support from our co-operative advertising programme, sponsoring a local youth team of 13-15-year-olds. The deal involved shirt sponsorship using the Wrangler branding.

"I wondered whether, the other Wrangler shirt sponsored team (Notts County), will be willing to send a player to meet my team of young footballers," he asked.

I contacted Neal Hook and asked the question. "No problem," was his instant reply.

A couple of weeks later, I drove down to Meadow Road and picked up Larry Lloyd and his number one striker, Justin Fashanu.

Larry Lloyd had started his playing professionally at his home club, Bristol City. During an illustrious career, he had won major honours under two of the most famous managers in football, Bill Shankley at Liverpool, and Brian Clough at Nottingham Forest.

He had replaced Howard Wilkinson as manager of Notts County at the start of 1983/4 season during which the club had suffered relegation.

Justin Fashanu had become famous as a player at Norwich City when one of his goals was named "BBC Goal of the season for 1980." An England under 21 International, he was signed for Nottingham Forest for a £1 million fee in August 1981.

His relationship with Brian Clough was fractious and he never fulfilled the potential for which Brian had paid such a large fee. He fell out of favour at the City ground and, after a short loan period at Southampton, he was transferred to Notts County in December 1982 for a fee of £150,000.

During our trip to Sutton on Trent, Larry sat next to me in the passenger seat with Justin sitting in the back. I remember the journey as though it was yesterday. Larry was full of optimism about the ability of "The Magpies" to bounce back into the first division.

Justin recalled all his past moments of brilliance and was confident his goal scoring would be the catalyst that would ensure his manager achieved his goals.

When we reached our destination, both men performed their PR duties with aplomb. The young players were delighted to meet them, the local media got their interviews and took their pictures. Our retailer was able to bask in all the reflective glory. Everyone was very happy!

As the season progressed, the team performance of Notts County failed to achieve the same level of excellence. On the back of their relegation, the club lost nine of their first thirteen fixtures in the second tier of the Football League. Justin Fashanu scored only once during this dismal run.

On 21 October 1984, the day after a 1-3 home defeat to Birmingham, the County board ran out of patience. Larry Lloyd was dismissed!

On the 5 November 1984, he was replaced as manager by Richie Barker. If the Notts County Board of Directors and the club's loyal supporters were expecting fireworks, they were to be disappointed.

In a match programme for the game with Shrewsbury Town, on 2 February 1985, Notts County was languishing at the foot of the table with only 17 points from 25 games.

In his programme notes for the game, Richie Barker stated, "we………are suffering from an acute shortage of goals (Justin Fashanu had scored only twice in the eighteen games he had played in). But, while people have been quick to point out that we have failed to win any of our last six League games, there are two sides to the coin. It would be wrong to overlook the fact that we have lost just two of our last seven fixtures and no one can dispute that represents a considerable improvement."

The notes went on to state that stage 1 of the improvement plan had been achieved and the onus was now on everyone to put stage 2 into operation. He called for an all-round effort from his players whilst acknowledging that it would be difficult "because players who have grown accustomed to struggling tend to lose the ability to "kill off" the opposition."

He was happy with his defence and confident that his attack would come good "providing we continue to apply the amount of pressure we have in recent home games the goals will come."

Reading the notes, many years after the event, they seemed like a plea from a desperate man who was seeking a way out of an impossible situation.

There was no improvement in the on-field performance and Richie Barker was dismissed on 19 April 1985 with only five fixtures remaining to be played. Director of Football, Jimmy Sirrel, took on the managerial role, but it was too little, too late and Notts County suffered the indignity of a second relegation in successive seasons.

As for Justin Fashanu, he moved to Brighton & Hove Albion in June 1985 for a fee of £115,000 having scored 20 times in 64 games for "The Magpies."

It would have been easy to walk away from our involvement with Notts County after their relegation. After all, the third tier of the Football League did not appear to present many opportunities for national media coverage. Having said that, at the start of the 1985/6 season, Division 3 also featured clubs such as Reading, Wigan, Derby County, Cardiff, Swansea, Wolverhampton Wanderers and Bournemouth.

Despite their on-field performance during the previous season, we had been impressed by the way the club had "gone the extra mile" to cooperate in every aspect of their dealings with us. Retailers had provided feedback to us about how well they had been looked after on match days and the efficient and friendly atmosphere that they had encountered.

Initial conversations with the club revealed they were prepared to offer the same level benefits to us that we had enjoyed previously. They levelled with us about the dire financial position the club found itself in and understood that the asking price would be lower than it had been in Division 2.

It was acknowledged that they needed the Wrangler brand more than we needed them!

We were guaranteed the same level of inputs and outputs that we had enjoyed before, despite the lower sponsorship fee. This meant we would still be able to offer our retailers the same excellent level of hospitality, at home matches, that had been so well received the previous season.

I recommended that we maintain the links and a new contract was signed.

During the 1984/5 season, we had used some of our ticket allocation to invite pupils of Nottingham schools to attend home matches as our guests.

At the same time former County player, Iain McCulloch, was running the Evening Post Junior Magpies scheme. Members had their own secure enclosure at Meadow Lane for home matches. They had a special page in the match programmes which included competitions for them to enter. Other benefits included behind the scenes visits to the dressing rooms before each match and the opportunity to be ball boys during the games.

After discussions with our PR team and Iain, a project called the "Wrangler/Magpies Schools Project" was developed.

It was planned to involve around 20 schools during the season. Each school would be invited to involve pupils in a special project related to any aspect of football. When completed, each project would be submitted to the club and judged by a group of independent assessors.

At the end of the process, Notts County agreed to hold and exhibition of all the work. The school producing the most interesting and lively project would collect an award and a major prize of £200, courtesy of Wrangler. This would be used in purchasing educational equipment and a complete new set of football kit for the school team.

As the project idea developed, the Notts Schools FA became heavily involved and were instrumental in giving the scheme their approval. They also helped to launch it across the whole county.

It was agreed that pupils, teachers, and parents of the participating schools would be invited to attend a match as guests of the Junior Magpies. This would be followed up by a visit to the school by some of the Notts County coaching staff and players.

After staging a coaching session, they would then make themselves available to answer questions that would help the participating pupils to develop and complete their project.

All pupils involved would receive a specially produced tracksuit badge featuring the Wrangler and Magpies brand logos and the legend "THE WRANGLER/MAGPIES SCHOOLS FOOTBALL PROJECT."

The project was formally launched on Saturday, 28 September 1985, at the Notts County versus Bury match.

50 pupils from Hucknall Holgate School, accompanied by teachers and parents, were warmly welcomed into the Junior Magpies enclosure and, in front of a crowd 4,622 people, witnessed a thrilling 2-2 draw. The following week, Iain McCulloch, Mike Walker, and several of the players visited the school for the coaching and question and answers sessions.

The project proved to be a great success as more and more schools joined the programme!

On the pitch, Jimmy Sirrel had worked his magic. With limited resources, at the turn of the year the team were in the position of having an outside chance of promotion. Ian McParland was hitting the net on a regular basis and the other players around him had responded accordingly.

In the FA Cup competition, they reached the 4th round. Playing against First Division side Tottenham Hotspur, they held them to a creditable 1-1 draw in front of a crowd 17,546 at Meadow Lane.

The replay at White Hart Lane resulted in a 5-0 defeat for the Magpies watched by another crowd of over 17,000.

Unfortunately, injuries, dwindling support at home matches and lack of funds to buy new players had finally taken their toll. In the latter part of the season, results did not go in their favour and Notts County fell out of contention for promotion. When all their matches had been played, they had accumulated 71 points scoring 42 goals and conceding 26 for an eighth-place finish.

I had intended to finish our association with Notts County at the end of the 1985/6 season as I cut back the below-the-line marketing spend to enable top line advertising to be maintained at a highly visible level.

Discussions with the club, during the season, had revealed that it was losing money and its finances were in a perilous position. Two successive relegations, and failure to achieve promotion out of the third tier, had left them with a massive debt pile.

There was talk of a "white knight" coming to the rescue of the club, but they needed to reassure the potential buyer that they would continue to receive support from sponsors, box holders and the 'hard core' of their supporters.

I talked over the situation with Dick Webzell, and we agreed to maintain our support as Club and "Wrangler/Magpies Schools Football Project" sponsors for one more year.

At the start of the season, fans of the club had no real idea just how perilous the Notts County finances were!

In his match notes in the match programme for the first match of the season on 23 August 1986 against Wigan Athletic, Jimmy Sirrel laid out some of the challenges facing the club.

He referred to changes in the Leagues voting system and decisions taken at the annual meeting in relation to the share-out of Pools and sponsorship money etc. explaining how this would affect the finances of Notts County. "… it means that the likes of ourselves will find our income drop by more than £50,000 this season." He goes on to state, "I am bound to say that it won't surprise me in the slightest if a number of clubs go out of business during the next nine months or so."

Obviously upset by the situation he went on, "For someone like myself, who has been involved in professional football virtually all my life, it's a very sad state of affairs. But we have to be realistic enough to accept the situation as it is and do our utmost to overcome the problems which have been presented to us."

Later in the piece, he appears optimistic about the team's ability to do well with the players they had, but realistic enough to understand that the club's fortunes depended largely on what their young players (brought into the first team set up from the club's Player Academy) can achieve.

Not long afterwards, the full state of the club's finances would be out in the open.

On the 15 September 1986, a crisis meeting was called. This drew 1,500 supporters to the Astoria Night Club in Nottingham. Many more were locked outside.

Supporters were told the club had been leaking money for several seasons and debts totalled around £2million. The Directors had considered bringing in the liquidators but thanks to offers of help from sponsors, and financial support offered by the fan base, it was agreed they would carry on.

Several key decisions were made because of the meeting. Key amongst them was the formation of "Notts County Lifeline." The project entailed a scheme to encourage supporters to pay £2 each week to enter a prize draw.

To jumpstart the scheme, Jimmy Sirrel enlisted the support of his friend and rival across the River Trent, Brian Clough. A friendly match was swiftly organised between Notts County and Nottingham Forest with all funds raised going into the "Lifeline" scheme.

The match was sponsored jointly by Wrangler and Nottingham Forest club sponsor, Home Ales. It took place on the evening of Tuesday 14 October 1986.

Our public relations team organised a competition in the specially produced Match Magazine. Highlighting our unique status, as current sponsors of the Magpies and previous sponsors of Nottingham Forest, the Anagram Competition encouraged both sets of fans to enter to win one of 25 pairs of Wrangler Jeans.

In addition, we specially commissioned a "Lifeline Trophy" to be presented to the winning team at the end of the game. It was hoped to organise the "Lifeline Trophy" match on an annual basis to feature Notts County and first-class opposition.

The match was won by Nottingham Forest in front of an enthusiastic crowd of 3,299 people. I presented the trophy to Ian Bowyer, captain of the winners.

A total of over £14,000 was raised and all of it went into the survival fund. I remember being disappointed with the low turnout especially as so much effort had been put in by everyone involved.

Looking back at Notts County match statistics, revealed that attendances at the first six home matches during the 1986/7 season had only averaged around 3,500. Even so, I would have thought that a crowd of 10,000 should easily have been achievable. The fact that it was not, only served to emphasise the situation the club found itself in at that time.

Thankfully, "The Lifeline Prize Draw" was particularly successful raising over £100,000 for club funds, during the first season.

The Astoria meeting also provided the catalyst for a change of ownership. Chairman, and former Nottingham MP, Jack Dunnett announced he would be retiring at the end of the 1986/7 season after 19 years at the helm. In a TV interview following the meeting at the Astoria, he explained how promotion to the First Division had, ironically, been responsible for the decline in the club's finances.

Notts County had a reputation for being prudent with their spending and had diligently ensured that their books were always in balance making sure income always exceeded expenditure. As a result, they had built up a healthy surplus when the club had been promoted.

From the 1981/2 season, their first year back in the top league, they had budgeted for home gates of 15,000. This figure was small for a first division team playing all their games against the major clubs. Actual attendances averaged less than 10,000 during their three years in the top league of English football. Successive relegations, and even smaller average gates, had only made the situation worse.

When asked why he had announced he was leaving with the club in such a plight, he responded, "The club is not in a plight. It would be next season without the "Lifeline" scheme. I was worried about leaving with no one or nothing (like Lifeline) to sustain the club's future finances."

He pledged to continue to support the club financially until the end of the 1986/7 season, whilst the Board looked for a successor. Jack was happy in the knowledge that the "Lifeline" scheme would ensure Notts County's survival, at least in the short term.

Following Jack Dunnett's shock announcement the Board had begun a search for a new benefactor. Director, John Mounteney, had held informal talks with former Nottingham Forest Director, Derek Pavis. Eventually, he persuaded Derek to take a major financial stake in the club and to take over as Chairman at the end of the season.

With the help of Commercial Manager, Elaine Howes and her team, our guests enjoyed fantastic hospitality at all the remaining home games.

Despite finding himself operating between administrations, Jimmy Sirrel had continued to work miracles on the pitch, without the funds necessary to invest in new players. It was a testament to his man management skills that the club remained within touching distance of a play-off place throughout the season.

He had tearfully confided with me that he would be standing down at the end of the season. "This time retirement will really mean retirement," I was assured.

Football had been his life, and it was difficult to believe he would be able to just walk away from a club that he had served with distinction for so many years.

I had already decided, we would not be renewing our contract as club sponsor at the end of the season and had informed the club of my decision. The notice period allowed plenty of time for the new management team to find someone else.

By the close of the season, County had accumulated 76 points in the league scoring 77 goals and conceding 56. In the end, their 7th place was only 2 points off a playoff position.

Jimmy Sirrel was true to his word and retired after eighteen years at the club. As I had suspected, it was not the end of his connection with football. Shortly after, he joined Derby County as chief coach.

In 1993 the newly redeveloped County Road Stand at Notts County's stadium in Meadow Lane was renamed the Jimmy Sirrel Stand in his honour.

The Clough and Sirrel Legacy

Over time, football fans in Nottingham have come to realise how fortunate the city was to have two real legends of the game managing their football clubs, during the same period.

As custodian of the Wrangler brand during the time that we sponsored both clubs, I have often been asked "who was the best manager?"

It is almost impossible to answer. Both became managers of unfashionable clubs and took them to their respective pinnacles of success.

Brian Clough would probably be acknowledged as the greatest in most people's eyes. This is because the achievements of Derby County and Nottingham Forest, during the time he was manager, were tangibly better. Clough also enjoyed a greater profile in the media mainly because he was no shrinking violet and enjoyed being at the centre of controversy.

Throughout his career, there was plenty of that!

On the other hand, Jimmy Sirrel and his assistant Jimmy Wheeler took Notts County from the bottom of the Forth Division of English football to the very top tier of the game. During a very productive partnership, the club won the Division Four title in 1971 and finished runners-up in Division Three in 1973 and Division Two in 1981.

All this was achieved on a very limited budget!

Jimmy was a much more private man but, in my opinion, a much better man-manager than his good friend across the Trent. He was particularly adept at spotting talented youngsters and nurturing their potential through the Academy system at the club.

Both men were passionate about football. I am sure, that Jimmy would have been able to achieve, at least as many honours in the game, if he had received the same level of transfer money for players, that Brian had enjoyed.

They were both legends in their own lifetimes and both left behind a legacy that transcends football. Both had stands named after them, Brain Clough at the City Ground, and Jimmy Sirrel at Meadow Lane.

In the memorial stakes, Brian Clough still outshines his great friend and rival.

In August 2005, a stretch of the A52 linking Nottingham and Derby was renamed Brian Clough Way.

After a long process of fund-raising, Middlesbrough his birthplace, commissioned a statue of him which was unveiled on 16 May 2007 in the town's Albert Park. Another statue of Clough was erected in Nottingham on 6 November 2008 at the junction of King Street and Queen Street in the centre of the city.

In April 2009, Derby County announced that they would erect a statue of the former Rams' managers Clough and Peter Taylor, at Pride Park, The Brian Clough and Peter Taylor Monument was officially unveiled in a family service on 27 August 2010 and publicly on 28 August 2010.

It was not until May 2016 that Jimmy Sirrel received similar recognition when hundreds of fans gathered to see a statue of him, and his former assistant, Jack Wheeler, unveiled at the club's Meadow Lane ground. The memorial is situated between the Derek Pavis Stand and Trent Navigation Inn pub.

Chapter Thirteen

Stella Artois Tennis Tournament 1981/1990

The Wrangler advertising account had been moved to Collett Dickenson Pearce at the end of 1979. One of the agencies main accounts at that time was Whitbread's, who marketed and produced the premium beer, Stella Artois, under licence in the UK.

CDP Chairman, Frank Lowe was a keen tennis player and a member of the Queens Tennis Club situated at West Kensington in London. Queens had a long tradition as a bastion of amateur sport. Established in 1886, it was the first multipurpose sports complex ever to be built, anywhere in the world. It was named after Queen Victoria, its first patron, and is still widely renowned as one of the world's premier Lawn Tennis and Racquets clubs.

Since 1887, it had organised its own Club Tennis Championship with past winners drawn from a who's who of the sport. With the advent of the open era of tennis, Queens Club had found it increasingly difficult to attract the top players.

Step forward Frank Lowe!

In 1979, he persuaded Whitbread to sponsor the Queens Club Championship under the Stella Artois brand name. Changing the name to the "Stella Artois Tournament" had been hard for some of the more conservative club members to swallow. It proved to be an inspired move, heralding the start of an association that was to last for nearly 30 years. The injection of sponsorship money began to draw in all the top names in men's tennis.

Ian Schoolar, Wrangler Account Director at CDP, was also a Queens Club member and one of the tournament management team. They were keen to exploit other possible sponsorship opportunities.

"Might Wrangler be interested in becoming involved with the 1980 Stella Artois Tennis Tournament?" he enquired after one of our meetings. "What kind of involvement had you in mind?" I countered.

It turned out they were looking for an official clothing sponsor for the ball girls and match officials. Ian felt that a clothing brand like Wrangler would sit well with the younger, more forward-looking image that tennis, in the Open Era, was trying to project to the world.

At that time, the Grand Slam tournaments at Wimbledon and the French, Australia and USA Open events all received national media coverage, including television. Other tournaments received minimal exposure.

Ian explained that an agreement was in the process of being reached to televise the Stella Artois event final in 1980. There were several issues that had to be overcome in evaluating what a Wrangler involvement would cost.

Firstly, all the tops for the ball girls had to be printed with the Stella Artois logo. Because of this requirement, the existing Wrangler branding would be totally overshadowed.

Secondly, all the stewards, line judges and umpires required matching casual shirts, chinos, and a jacket.

Last, but not least, Wrangler would be required to provide something in the region of 150 outfits in total.

Even at wholesale prices, this was a large commitment for very little obvious return!

The figure required by the Queens Tournament team included full corporate facility for 20 people for each day of the tournament. This was made up of two corporate boxes, lunch and afternoon tea, coffee, alcoholic and soft drinks.

I spoke to Dick Webzell about the opportunity and my reservations. To my surprise, he was enthusiastic about the prospect of giving customers across the country an opportunity to see some top-class tennis action, just weeks before the start of Wimbledon.

We agreed a top line figure beyond which we were not prepared to negotiate.

I met up with Ian to see if we could reach an amicable agreement.

"We are interested," I told him. "Our problem is that what you are asking us to support, is an unknown quantity. It is difficult to determine the value of the clothing sponsorship element or indeed the added value of the corporate package."

"I understand your reticence," replied Ian. "I feel that the clothing sponsorship will be rewarded by members keen to purchase the 'uniforms.' I can guarantee that our corporate package is the best in the business. You and your guests will be well fed and watered," he concluded.

We finally agreed to a lower fee based on my assurance that we would renew the package for a second year if everything went to plan.

Wrangler in-house and external PR teams worked with the tournament team to provide measurements of all the stewards, line judges and umpires. In parallel with this, the Wrangler merchandising team presented some alternative ideas for the 'uniform' that would satisfy both the commercial needs of Wrangler and remain within the tournament dress code.

In the end, a compromise was reached that both parties were happy with.

Dick Webzell and the sales team worked on the retailer invitations to ensure that the 'mix' of independent and group buyers from across the UK, was representative of the market.

It was also agreed that the finals day would be reserved for members of the Wrangler senior management team and their partners.

Sponsorship of this kind was relatively new to the conservative world of tennis. Corporate boxes were situated at the top of the main stand opposite the member's clubhouse.

The stand on left was for the exclusive use of Whitbread. Their guests included the drinks retail and wholesale trade, and publicans from across the UK. They had their own, "exclusive," corporate hospitality facility situated directly behind their stand area.

Other hospitality facilities were shared by the corporate box holders. Within this area we had our own section, complete with catering staff, who looked after the specific needs of Wrangler staff and our guests.

It became obvious during the week of the tournament that it was necessary to ensure this facility was not abused.

We appointed senior sales managers to look after the guests in each of our two boxes. Portion control of the food on offer was not an issue but with alcoholic drink on tap, all day long, it was very easy to forget that the main purpose of the day was to watch world-class tennis.

Our sales managers did very well in controlling the alcoholic intake. This ensured that none of our guests over-indulged and embarrassed themselves or spoilt the experience for others.

Whitbread had many times the number of guests that we had. They also encouraged everyone to have a good time without spoiling the spectacle for those who had come just to watch the tennis. With one or two exceptions, this was achieved.

In 1979, Queens had given a wildcard entry to a brash, young American called John McEnroe who was beginning to make waves in the men's game. An unconventional approach to officialdom quickly made him a favourite of the crowds. His very presence encouraged fellow professionals to make Queens the essential pre-Wimbledon tournament to enter.

In 1980, he had progressed quickly through the rounds playing exceptional tennis. In the final, we watched him beat Kim Warwick.

Feedback from guests had been very positive and it was clear that a long-term relationship with the Stella Artois tournament would be beneficial.

True to our word, we made it clear that we would continue as official clothing sponsors in 1981. The deal was agreed at a slightly higher fee.

Early in 1981, two events occurred that could have easily torpedoed our relations with the Stella Artois Tournament. First, Ian Schoolar left CDP to return to

Scotland. Then Geoff Howard-Spink and Frank Lowe left the agency to form Lowe Howard-Spink. They took with them the Whitbread account.

I had realised that our initial arrangement with Queens Club and the Stella Artois Tournament was a result of our CDP connection. We were committed to a sponsorship deal we had struck following the previous year's tournament. At the same time, these defections had, in my eyes, caused the ground rules to change.

Wrangler did not want to embarrass CDP nor at the same time, did we wish to renege on our agreement with Queens Club.

I met with the agency and explained the situation. "Wrangler will not be following Whitbread to Lowe Howard-Spink," I assured them. "We have a commitment to the Stella Artois Tennis but will try and pull out if it creates a problem for CDP," I continued.

CDP assured me that they had no problems with the arrangement and were happy that we had shared our concerns with them.

I had a similar conversation with Geoff Howard-Spink. "I appreciate your frankness," he said. "The change of circumstances will have no effect on your relationship with Queens."

The tournament offered another glut of world-class tennis. Once more John McEnroe reached the final beating Brian Gottfried in an excellent match.

The 1981 event was our last as official clothing sponsors. As the Stella Artois Tournament grew more prestigious, more and more people were jostling each other to be associated with its success.

We were unwilling to enter a bidding war. Wrangler had blazed the trail and the brand had undoubtedly benefited from being involved very early on.

This was not the end of our association. We retained our options on the two corporate boxes with full hospitality facilities all through the 1980's.

During that period, we witnessed John McEnroe lose two consecutive finals to Jimmy Connors and win another against Leif Shiras. We marvelled at the skill of the

17-year-old Boris Becker who won in 1985 and became Wimbledon Champion a week or so later.

In 1986 Jimmy Connors lost to Tim Mayotte. Boris Becker triumphed again in 1987 and 1988 against Jimmy Connors and Stefan Edberg respectively. Ivan Lendl won 1989 beating Christo van Rensburg. He beat Boris Becker in the 1990 final.

The 1980's was a great time for men's tennis. Before our involvement in the Stella Artois Tournament, it was not really a sport that interested me.

Today, I am still a great fan!

Chapter Fourteen

Other Sponsorship Activity

During my time at Wrangler, we were involved in several sponsorship deals that were not sports related.

Some were localised activities that we undertook in conjunction with Wrangler retailers. Others involved fund raising events for local schools or for national charities with affiliations in Nottinghamshire.

The majority were headline making activities that helped the Wrangler brand to increase its awareness and credibility amongst its core markets.

Ideal Home Exhibition, Olympia Exhibition Centre, 13 March -3 April 1976

Towards the end of 1975, my newly appointed PR agency, Joan Chaumeton Public Relations, came to me with a proposition they felt might be of interest. They had been approached by the organisers of the Ideal Home Exhibition that was due to commence in London, in March 1976.

It was planned to create a Fashion Theatre at the Exhibition. The organisers were keen to break away from the traditional catwalk show and to create something that would have wider appeal to the younger market they were now targeting. They felt that jeans and jeans related clothing would be just right and that, "as a leading brand in this area, Wrangler would make the perfect partner."

The agency had already produced a strategic plan that involved careful placement of the Wrangler product in popular television programmes.

"The Ideal Home Exhibition takes place over a four-week period. The theatre will hold around 250 people with four, 45 minute shows a day, seven days a week. Tremendous exposure and great potential for extensive media coverage," they argued.

I was not convinced!

"It is headlined as the Daily Mail Ideal Home Exhibition. Daily Mail readers are not our target market," I argued. "How much coverage will the other national press titles give to an event promoted by a major rival? "I enquired.

I was assured, by the agency, that they were confident my fears would prove unfounded.

The exhibition organisers wanted Wrangler and they were prepared to reduce the cost considerably to get us. They were also prepared to create a shop area connected to the theatre where the merchandise featured in the show could be sold.

I discussed the proposition with Dick Webzell and Kevin Black. We agreed to give the idea some consideration.

Chaumeton's were given permission to investigate the cost of producing the show and developing a comprehensive plan for maximising the outlay.

We did set up some ground rules!

The show needed to be slick and, whilst the Wrangler merchandise needed to look good, the overall presentation would be key to its success in helping to enhance the image of the brand. Any selling area needed to be large enough to enable enough stock to be displayed and sold.

A few weeks later, the PR agency came back to us.

They believed that the fashion show should be treated as 45 minutes of light entertainment during which Wrangler branded product had a starring role. Each segment needed to be dedicated to a specific part of the Wrangler range.

To achieve this, the participating "models" needed to be dancers who looked good in the merchandise rather than trained fashion models who thought that they could "move."

Joan Chaumeton had a lot of contacts in television. She had asked them to recommend names of choreographers who had the experience to cast the right team and put together a stunning show.

One name was mentioned time and time again – Malcolm Goddard!

Malcolm had a classical dance background. Over the years, he had become a renowned producer and choreographer with a far-ranging body of work from classical and modern dance to music hall and light entertainment shows on television.

"Can we afford him and is he prepared to take on the work?" I asked when the agency came back with their recommendations. They assured us "we could" and that "he was," before presenting us with a comprehensive plan that was fully costed.

We had also done some homework in respect of the level of turnover that could be expected from the selling area the exhibition organisers were offering. It was calculated, that when this was offset against the cost of staging the whole event, the actual sum involved was very reasonable. If the agency could deliver on their plan for spin off coverage, the effort involved would be very worthwhile.

Go-ahead was given, the necessary contracts were signed.

Kevin Black and I met up with Chaumeton's and Malcolm Goddard for a presentation of the ranges we wanted to be featured.

At the end of 1975, Malcolm Goddard was approaching his 50th birthday. He still had a dancer's physique. The only concession to his "advancing years" were the tell-tale flecks of grey in his hair. As I recollect, he had an easy-going manner, a wicked sense of humour and extreme confidence in his own ability.

He was somebody that we could do business with and rely on "to deliver the goods!"

During our presentation, he asked questions and participated fully in the discussions making positive contributions where he felt clarification was necessary.

He suggested that a cast of 10 dancers (5 men and 5 women) would be needed, and the selection process had already begun. "I will be working the cast hard," he explained. "Four shows a day, seven days a week over a period of four weeks, will be exacting. I need to be sure that the final selection is correct and that they are willing, and able, to give 100% at every performance." Malcolm continued.

We were very impressed by his self-assured manner and came away from the meeting convinced that he was the right man for the job!

Our PR team worked closely with Malcolm as he built up his team of performers, dressers, and backroom assistants. They also worked with Kevin Black and his team of merchandisers to put together the range of outfits required.

The exhibition organisers agreed to enlarge the selling area. In consultation, with our London Area Manager, it was decided to offer the "concession" to Selfridges of Oxford Street in London.

Blue Bell Area Sales Managers had organised a rota of senior members of the salesforce. It was important for us to have a member of the company at every show to act as our "authorised representative." Staff selected would be responsible for overseeing the sales area, answering any questions from the public and liaising with the exhibition management.

"Theatre managers" would coordinate the whole operation on their duty days, including all security arrangements. Other members of the sales and sales administration team were selected to man the ticket office and to show members of the public to their seats.

Security was a major concern of the organisers!

In 1976, "The Troubles" in Northern Ireland had escalated. The IRA had declared London as a legitimate target for a possible terror campaign.

A few days before the exhibition opened, we held our rehearsal in the Fashion Theatre. True to his word, Malcolm had produced a spectacular show. Far removed from the fashion show norm of the conventional catwalk, it was full of energy and fun.

Just the right image to promote the extensive Wrangler jeans and jeans related clothing line!

Whilst all this was going on "theatre managers" and "Selfridges concession staff" were being fully briefed on their responsibilities.

The exhibition organisers had devised a security message key that would be changed daily. If this seemingly innocuous message was relayed over the Tannoy system, the "Fashion Theatre" needed to be quickly evacuated, without causing panic. The occupants would be led, in an orderly manner, to a pre-designated holding area.

Security staff would carry out a thorough search. Only when the area was deemed safe, would the public be allowed to return. Anything suspicious that was left behind in the "Theatre area," was not to be touched or removed. Wrangler staff, including the backstage team, would have to be evacuated and security staff called to carry out "a sweep" to decide whether it was safe to remove the offending item.

Nobody would be allowed to return to the theatre area until this was done.

We all heeded the briefing, but none of us really felt that anything untoward was going to happen.

How wrong we all were!

It was clear from the onset, that the "Fashion Theatre" would be a magnet for media interest. Chaumeton's had sent out invitations to the media for a press preview show on the first day. Take up had been very high. It proved to be a great success and resulted in a great deal of positive press, radio, and television coverage.

Our PR agency was aware that some of the visual media might wish to take pictures or film during a show. This would need to be handled sympathetically so as not to spoil the enjoyment of the public who had come to watch the show.

It was also agreed, that should there be a need to film extra footage, this would be accommodated after a show had finished. A nominal additional fee was agreed, to compensate the performers.

Ridley Scott Associates (RSA) had been commissioned to produce a documentary about the exhibition on behalf of the BBC. They were keen to include some extensive coverage of the fashion show. I had a discussion with the producers, and our PR agency, to determine what they were seeking to achieve and what they were looking for over and above access to the theatre during a live show.

It was clear, some additional footage would be required. Chaumeton's agreed to clear this with Malcolm and his team, and to negotiate an additional clearance fee with the agents of each of the performer.

This was done, and a date and time agreed for the extra filming to take place.

A week or so later, I was sitting in my office when I received a call from our stand manager. "I have a problem, Robin," he said. "The RSA film crew have arrived and one of the performers is refusing to get involved unless they are all guaranteed an extra fee."

I was taken aback by the situation. We had a great relationship with everyone involved with the show. It seemed inconceivable to me that any one of them would jeopardise that relationship when the extra fee had already been negotiated, and agreed, beforehand.

This was during the days when there were no mobile phones or Skype. I could not just talk to the performers face-to-face via a conference call. The crew from RSA would not hang about whilst protracted discussions took place. I had to be decisive.

"Please tell the person concerned that a fee has been agreed with his agent and I expect him to be professional and fulfil his contract. If he has a problem, he should sort it out afterwards, with his people," I instructed. "If he still refuses to appear, I will have no hesitation in cancelling the remaining shows, making the general public aware of the reason why."

My hardball response produced the required result and filming proceeded as planned.

When. later in the week, I met up with the dancer concerned, he was full of remorse and apologised for the trouble he had caused. We had no further problems during the rest of the exhibition.

On Saturday 20 March, I took my wife to see the show. Security was very tight, and bags were being examined at all the entrances. There were thousands of people in and around Olympia and we were aware of a large security presence. As a result, the Ideal Home Exhibition had been running, without major incident for well over a week. Everyone was confident that it was as safe as it could possibly be.

We went to the fashion theatre to see the show. I was pleased that it was as slick and professional as it had been on all the previous occasions, I had watched it. The reaction from the audience, and particularly my wife, was very positive.

The audience left the theatre, and I was chatting with the stand manager when one of the Wrangler personnel on duty came up. She told us that a plastic bag had been left under one of the seats. "Don't touch it until it had been cleared by security," I advised.

The stand manager brought in the security people, and they ushered us all out to what they considered a safe distance.

One of the security staff carefully lifted the bag, and was about to look inside, when it slipped out of his hands and dropped to the floor. There was an audible gasp and we all dropped to the floor. After what seemed like many minutes, a voice broke the silence. "Nothing to worry about. We will take the bag to lost property. If anyone comes back to collect it, tell them where it is," we were told.

On Saturday, 27 March 1976, all our worst fears were realised!

The Wrangler Fashion Theatre was located at the top of the escalator on the second floor of Olympia. Our "theatre manager" had been for a look around the exhibition in between fashion shows. On a busy Saturday, all the halls were extremely crowded, especially the first-floor area.

He was returning to the "Fashion Theatre" when he noticed several people pointing at a plastic dustbin next to the escalator, close to the Guinness Stand. It began smoking and, realising what it could be, he started to run up the moving stairs. Before he had reached the top, there was a loud explosion followed by a searing pain in the back of his legs.

Our sales manager was lucky that his injuries were relatively superficial. Others were not so fortunate! The explosion had left the hall below filled with smoke and screams of people caught up in the mayhem, many badly injured.

It was later established the smoke our manager had seen in the rubbish bin, was coming from a two-pound bomb that had been placed there to cause maximum injuries. No warning had been given. In the event, miraculously nobody had been killed, but four people had lost limbs and the total injured numbered 70.

It was later confirmed by the police that a man had telephoned the newsroom of BBC Television, after the explosion had occurred, claiming the bomb was the work of the Irish Volunteer Force, a militant breakaway organisation of the IRA.

During the last week of the show security became even tighter. Nevertheless, the bombing had not prevented large numbers of people from attending during those last few days.

Thankfully, no other incidents took place!

Despite the horror of the bombing, we concluded that our involvement with the show had been money well spent.

After a slow start, the Wrangler selling area, manned by Selfridges, had proved a great success. This had encouraged the menswear buyer to stock an even larger range of Wrangler merchandise in their flagship Oxford Street store.

When the organisers of the Ideal Home Exhibition advised us that they would be bringing a version of the show to the Forest Showground in Nottingham, in the October of 1976, we were happy to reprise our successful Fashion Theatre show.

Apart from one dancer who was ill, we succeeded in bringing back to our home city, everyone who had made the show in London such a success.

We were also able to negotiate a favourable deal, which included an allocation of tickets. This enabled all the staff at Calverton, along with their families, to attend the show that they had heard so much about.

Women's World Balloon Record in 1977

Early in 1977, I was made aware of the fact that a Wrangler branded hot air balloon was being constructed in Bristol by Cameron Balloons. As far as I can recollect, it had been commissioned by Blue Bell Inc. and would be used in the USA for promotional purposes.

At that time, hot air balloons were used primarily by enthusiasts who competed in events around the world. Very few organisations had taken advantage of potential commercial possibilities.

Don Cameron, the founder of Cameron Balloons, was a Glaswegian who had studied aeronautical engineering at the University of Glasgow in 1961. He obtained a master's degree at Cornell, in the USA, in 1963. Returning to the UK to take up a job with the Bristol Engineering Company, and had developed the "Bristo" the first British made, modern hot air balloon.

In 1968 Cameron had formed a company, Omega Balloons, with Leslie Goldsmith and they constructed 10 balloons before parting company.

Cameron Balloons was founded in 1971. His company quickly built up a reputation as one of the world's leading hot air balloon manufacturing companies. Almost single-handedly, he had opened a new world of commercial possibilities for the new hot air balloon technology.

Don flight tested all his new balloons in the UK often acting as flight director and consultant.

I believe, he had introduced my colleagues in America to the commercial possibilities of a Wrangler branded balloon. He had then put them in touch with Anneke Sandel, a young but experienced balloon pilot. 29 years old at the time, she hailed from Rotterdam in Holland but saw a move to the USA, where the sport was more entrenched, as good for her career.

Don Cameron, never a man to miss out on an opportunity to promote his products, had suggested that, as part of the testing programme, Anneke and the Wrangler branded balloon, should attempt to break the world altitude record for women.

I was contacted and asked, or more probably instructed, to coordinate all promotional activity through Blue Bell Apparel Limited, in Calverton.

The attempt was planned to take place in Cambridgeshire, just 80 miles down the road from our head office. It was felt that our in-house and external public relations resource would enable the company to maximise exposure for the Wrangler brand, both in the USA, and across Europe.

I met up with Anneke and the Wrangler PR team to discuss the possibilities. Being Dutch, she spoke several languages. She also came across as extremely self-assured and articulate.

"How confident of success are you?" I asked during the meeting.

"100%, we are going to smash the record," was her reply.

I was impressed. The PR team was impressed. Together we moved forward to develop a plan of action.

Radio, TV, magazine, and press interviews were carried out in the weeks prior to the attempt. These resulted in a lot of extremely positive pre-publicity in the UK, Europe, and the USA.

A "first day cover" was produced to commemorate the attempt and a limited edition of 250 was printed. The copy read, "World Balloon Record. This envelope, one of only 250, was carried in the gondola of the Wrangler Balloon during the attempt on the women's world altitude record for hot air balloons and was posted on landing."

The cover also featured the date of the attempt, the previous record and the altitude achieved during the flight. There was also an illustration of the Wrangler Balloon, a Wrangler logo, and a photograph of Anneke herself. Each cover was individually signed by Anneke. A mailing list was compiled of the great and the good who had been selected as recipients.

On Tuesday 2 July 1977, Anneke made the final checks of her equipment before stepping into her gondola, firing up and casting off. Several hours later, and 50 miles away from her starting point, she and her balloon landed safely. During her flight, the Wrangler balloon soared to a height of 27,036 feet, breaking the existing record by 3048 feet. The number of miles covered during the flight also set a Dutch hot air balloon distance record. The success generated world-wide media coverage and fully justified the expense incurred.

The "first day covers" became much sought after at the time. For some reason, I received two although I must admit that both were addressed my attention at Blue

Bell Apparel Ltd and not to me personally. I still have them in my collection of Wrangler memorabilia.

However, the record achieved by Anneke Sandel did not stand for long. In October 1977, another Cameron produced prototype, piloted by Sue Hazlett, increased it by another 3,000 feet.

Chapter Fifteen

Cinema and Television Product Placement

Today, placing products in popular television programmes and in films has become a perfectly normal and extremely lucrative business. In the 1970's and 1980's, there was very little activity in this area.

Props and wardrobe departments in television production companies were only too happy to use their trade contacts to obtain merchandise. These enabled them to purchase what they needed, for the best price they could negotiate.

The idea that the company's might pay them, to feature their products, was little more than a pipe dream!

In the UK, our public relation agency had developed good contacts in the wardrobe departments of many top UK programme production companies. They were all very happy to pay heavily discounted prices for products that were highly regarded by the consumer market.

Resulting from this activity, Wrangler merchandise was worn by the stars of many of the top television drama series of the day. The more our product appeared on the small screen, the more requests we received.

Whenever jeans or jeans related clothing was worn on screen by actors or programme presenters, it was nearly always, Wrangler branded. Many of the stars from these shows were only too happy to visit our London showroom to view, and buy, the latest items from our ranges for their own use, at discounted prices.

For me and my colleagues in Calverton, this was a win, win situation.

Film companies in the UK were very slow to pick up on the product placement phenomenon. This was perhaps because, in the 1970's most of the "youth culture" productions were being filmed in the USA.

American based production companies had recognised that they could reduce spiralling production costs by judicious product placement featuring mainly car, soft drink and fast-food manufacturers. By creating a cost bidding war between competing brands, the programme makers had turned what had been an expense into a revenue stream.

Suddenly, in the late 1970's and through the 1980's, film production companies began to contact me to discuss possible commercial tie-ups and collaborations.

Grease the Movie – 1978

Early in 1978, our public relations company was approached by the Robert Stigwood Organisation (RSO) to sound out whether Wrangler might be interested in some form of commercial involvement with their latest movie. At the time, it was in the final stages of post-production.

RSO had been founded by Australian born, Robert Stigwood. He managed music stars such as the Bee Gees and Eric Clapton. RSO had many other mega music stars signed to their record labels.

Stigwood had expanded into film production in 1973 with "Jesus Christ Superstar." In 1975, he had followed this up with "Tommy" by The Who.

In 1977, he produced "Saturday Night Fever." The movie had not only popularised "disco music" it had also catapulted the Bee Gees, an act he managed, to superstardom on the back of the soundtrack they had written, which Robert Stigwood had then released on his own label.

The film also launched the film career of John Travolta and propelled him to international stardom. Made on a shoestring budget of $3.5 million, "Saturday Night Fever" had taken $237.1 million at the box office. In addition, the album of the soundtrack had become one of the biggest selling albums of all time. 35 million copies were sold worldwide.

Was I interested in getting involved with Stigwood's next production? You bet I was!

A meeting was arranged by the RSA commercial team to view an early cut of the movie – "Grease." The film, a High School love story, featured John Travolta, Olivia Newton-John, Jeff Conaway and Stockard Channing. It had been conceived as an adaption of the smash hit, stage production that had broken records wherever it appeared.

The cast members were all playing young people of High School age. This stretched credibility a little when you consider that at the time the film was released, John Travolta was 24, Olivia Newton-John 29, Jeff Conaway 28 and Stockard Channing 34.

Nevertheless, "Grease the movie" was vibrant, the acting credible and the music tremendous. There was no doubt in my mind that it would be just as big a success as "Saturday Night Fever" – if not bigger!

It was clear why RSO felt that a tie up with a major jeans and jeans related clothing brand was a good idea. In the UK, Wrangler was right up there with Levi's as THE biggest jeans brand. We were by far the biggest name in jeans related clothing.

The only problem was that the film had been shot and there was no Wrangler merchandise featured in it. If we were to profit from the association, we would have to be creative in the way both RSO, and Wrangler, merchandised the link-up.

As custodian of a brand name that the film's producers wanted to be associated with, it was my view, our involvement with "Grease," would enhance the overall image of Wrangler product ranges in the UK market.

Key cinema audiences at the time consisted of mainly 16-24-year-olds. This was the same demographic as our core target market.

The film was due to be released in UK cinemas in the middle of September 1978. Through our advertising agency Wasey's, we had already booked a TV and radio campaign that was scheduled to start around the same time.

The TV advertisements, featuring the Mr Wrangler and Rickenbacker characters had already been shot. There was nothing we could do to create a link there.

Radio was another story. It would be possible to produce several radio commercials that made a direct reference to the Wrangler connection to "Grease the movie" and use them as part of our campaign.

In addition, through our Field Promotion Representatives and national salesforce, we had the ability to create "Wrangler/Grease'" instore and window displays on nearly every major high street across the country.

Our FPR's had close associations with night clubs and dance venues across the UK. They would be able to work with them to develop "Wrangler/Grease" nights in key venues.

We wanted approval to feature the "Grease" logo on Wrangler point of sale material and to pre-select music tracks from the soundtrack to be interspersed on a tape featuring the Wrangler radio advertisements. The tapes could then be use as background music in retail stores and dance venues with a small number offered as "Grease" dance competition prizes along with posters and Wrangler merchandise.

Initially, RSO had wanted us to pay money for the privilege of being involved with the film. When we presented our ideas, they realised that we were serious in our determination to ensure that the association worked for both parties. They understood that we were prepared spend both time and money to do so.

For this reason, they accepted a "quid pro quo" arrangement.

RSO agreed to provide a tape master of five of the tracks from the soundtrack. Wrangler was granted permission to produce a small number of "Wrangler/Grease" cassettes to be used for promotional purposes only. They also agreed to the use of the "Grease" logo on four specially produced Wrangler posters and to provide "Grease movie posters" for use in retail stores.

We undertook to supply a quantity of "Wrangler/Grease" posters for cross-merchandising in cinemas showing the film.

No money would change hands but "A Terms of Agreement" document was drawn up to ratify the "Gentleman's Agreement" we had shaken hands on.

I was keen that the "Wrangler/Grease" posters should feature the latest Wrangler ranges. The outfits would be transposed into an authentic American environment that could be readily identified as being in the 1950's. In this way, we would create a direct link between the Wrangler product ranges of 1978 and the era represented by "Grease the movie."

I searched around my photographer directories and asked for recommendations from my PR and advertising agencies. In the end, we came across an American photographer who specialised in what I later described as "time-based, clutter set-ups." He had little or no experience of fashion photography but his portfolio of still life sets told their own story.

What we needed were 1950's set-ups into which models wearing the latest Wrangler fashions could be placed. His style of work matched our requirements perfectly.

I made contact, and a meeting was arranged at his studio in London. The photographer had seen the stage version of "Grease" and therefore understood immediately what era we were asking him to re-create. Briefing him on our requirements, I also presented samples of the four sets of Jeans and jeans related merchandise we were looking to feature.

A few weeks later, we met up again and he presented his suggestions for several scenarios. The final four were agreed and approval to go ahead was given.

The first set-up, "Sleepover," featured two young women relaxing in a bedroom fitted out in the décor of the period. It was cluttered with 1950's magazines, clothes, and cosmetics. A large poster of Elvis adorned the wall.

Second was "Pin Ball." This featured a young man and two young women playing on a 1950's style pin ball machine in an American coffee bar setting.

The third, "Bumper Cars," featured two young men and two young women standing at the side of a fifties style American Bumper Car ride. The photographer had tracked one down to a site close to his studio, on the outskirts of London.

The final set-up, "Chevrolet," featured a group of three young women in a fairground setting. They were admiring a 1950's red, open top "Chevrolet," under the watchful of an American police officer. The shoot was scheduled to take place at the same location as "Bumper Cars."

A single day was allocated for each set-up. The finished photographs were extraordinary! No by-line was necessary. Each picture told a story. All that was required was the addition of a Wrangler and "Grease" logo at the bottom of each poster.

The association with Wrangler and the film was clear for all to see.

The finished posters went down very well with the trade. They quickly became much sought after by both fans of the movie and the Wrangler product lines.

Wasey's created three "Grease" related 30 second radio commercials "Greece," "Drive in' and "Drainpipes." All three commercials featured the Mr Wrangler and Rickenbacker characters who were appearing in our advertising campaigns at that time.

The "Greece" radio commercial went as follows: -

Rickenbacker: "Mr. Wrangler, here in Athens we are about to bring the glory that was Greece back to life. We have clothed the acropolis……. Mr. Wrangler, you look puzzled?"

Mr. Wrangler: "Rickenbacker, why all this Greece nonsense?"

Rickenbacker: "Because you told me to produce an advertisement about Greece."

Mr. Wrangler: "Grease the Movie, Rickenbacker. G-R-E-A-S-E!"

Rickenbacker: "Sorry Mr. Wrangler. S-O-R-R-Y!"

Mr. Wrangler: "Good grief!"

Voice over: "Wrangler, the very best because Mr. Wrangler said so."

In the "Drive in" commercial there was a similar scenario. This time Rickenbacker has hired a limousine to drive Mr Wrangler to the premiere of the film "Grease." Mr. Wrangler feels that the car is driving too fast and will miss the cinema. There is a sound of a crash as the car ends up in the cinema lobby.

The 'Drainpipes' commercial features Rickenbacker telling Mr. Wrangler that, for once, he has anticipated what Mr. Wrangler will want him to do. There is a heavy clunking sound and Rickenbacker explains that Mr. Wrangler had told him that, after the film "Grease" is released, the demand for drainpipes would be large. That is why he has brought along the biggest "drainpipes for buildings" that he could find.

Naturally, Mr. Wrangler was not impressed!

With the approval of RSO, I had selected the five tracks that I like most from the soundtrack, "Grease" (Frankie Valli), "Summer Nights" (John Travolta and Olivia Newton-John), "Hopelessly Devoted to You" (Olivia Newton-John), "Sandy" (John Travolta) and "You're the one that I want" (John Travolta and Olivia Newton-John).

A master tape of the tracks chosen, was supplied by RSO, and a "Wrangler/Grease" cassette was produced. The featured tracks selected, were interspersed between the three "Wrangler/Grease" commercials plus two others "Boob" and "Good Idea," that were also used in the Wrangler radio campaign. RSO loved the concept. With their approval, 1000 copies were produced for the agreed promotional purposes!

By this time, the UK release of the film had been announced as 14 September 1978. A Gala Premiere had been confirmed for the day before, on the evening of Wednesday 13 September. Dick Webzell, me, and our spouses, had been invited to attend the film premiere at the Empire, Leicester Square. We were also sent tickets for the after-show party at the Lyceum in the Strand. Both Olivia Newton-John and John Travolta had confirmed they would be attending both events.

The Wrangler salesforce and our Field Promotion Representatives had ensured that the additional supporting product and window displays were booked with major retailers. In addition, a series of "Wrangler/Grease" promotion nights had been planned in dance halls and nightclubs throughout the UK.

Immediately prior to the film premiere, Dick Webzell and I were in Dublin for the Futura Fair Trade Show. It ran from Sunday 10 September to Tuesday 12 September 1978. On the day of the London premiere, we flew from Dublin to London. Our wives had driven down from Nottinghamshire and met up with us at the Wrangler company flat in St Anne's Mews, just behind Harley Street. Because we had important business in Calverton the following morning, the plan was to drive back when the after-show party finished.

In retrospect, this was not the best of ideas!

On our invitations, the dress code was stated to be informal. In 1978 this meant a suit and tie for the men. New dresses for our wives were an essential prerequisite of course!

We had been warned beforehand that it would not be a good idea to try and enter the theatre from the front entrance. We had been allocated a side entrance that was closest to our seats. Several of the premieres around the world had already taken place. Large crowds had been attracted to all of them. In all the excitement, there had been several unruly incidents.

It was anticipated that the London premiere would probably draw larger crowds and more over the top reactions, especially when the film's two stars made their appearance.

Even when we made our way to the entrance that we had been allocated, the noise was mind blowing and we had to struggle past hordes of fans. One female enthusiast even proffered an autograph book for me to sign, but not before asking who I was. When she realised that I was not associated with the entertainment business, she quickly lost interest.

We settled into our seats at the allotted time of 7.45pm. This was a good 45 minutes before the published start time of the film. There was a long delay because the show biz guests, and the stars of the movie, had experienced great difficulty getting into the Empire via the red-carpet entrance.

A crowd, estimated at around 5,000 people, many dressed in 50's outfits, had crammed into the small square outside the Empire. They cheered and surged forward every time a guest arrived. A police presence, of about 200 officers, had just about managed to keep control.

Olivia Newton-John arrived in a limousine with co-star John Travolta and his then girlfriend, Marilu Heener. As their car came to a stop in front of the theatre, all hell broke loose, and a frenzied crowd surged forward.

They quickly breached the police lines and swarmed all over the limo!

Both the stars were later to relate how frightening this was and how they feared for their lives when two hooligans climbed on top of the vehicle and started jumping up and down. The police struggled to bring matters under control. Eventually, they managed to hustle Olivia, John, and Marilu into the theatre lobby.

All three were badly shaken, especially John!

In the theatre, we, and the rest of the audience, were unaware what was going on outside. Everyone assumed, when the lights were finally dimmed, that the two stars had taken their seats. It was only when we arrived at the Lyceum, for the after-show party, that we realised what had happened. John had taken the decision to leave the theatre by a side door and missed both the film showing and the Lyceum event.

Olivia had taken the experience in her stride seeing the film and attending the party.

At the Lyceum, the great and the good were shown to their tables. There were copious quantities of alcoholic drink available and a veritable emperors feast of a buffet.

Glenys, my wife, turned me when we sat down to devour our food (we had only had a light snack all day and were starving). "George Chakiris is sitting next to me," she whispered. "George who? "I whispered back. "George Chakiris the film star," she repeated. "He is probably telling his partner that the women next to him is sitting next to Robin Dilley of Wrangler Jeans," I joked, receiving an elbow in the ribs for my remark.

George Chakiris had played Bernardo Nunez, leader of the Sharks and brother of Maria in the classic movie of the musical "West Side Story." It was Glenys's all-time favourite film. Being in the company of George Chakiris had been one of her teenage fantasy's - now fulfilled!

Dick Webzell was driving us back to Nottinghamshire. Because of this, he had very little to drink. I was tired, because of all the travelling and the late hour. Like Dick, I had drunk very little in case I was required to take a stint on the drive back home.

The combination of excitement and alcoholic beverage had taken its toll. Glenys and Carole were merry and perhaps a little boisterous. We looked around for a taxi to take us from the Lyceum to the Wrangler flat about a mile away, where our car was parked. There were none outside the Lyceum. We tried to hail a cab in the street, but they all seemed to be reluctant to pick up four people who, for a variety of different reason, looked slightly the worse for wear.

We spotted Olivia Newton-John sitting alone in her Limousine returning to her hotel. It didn't stop and give us a lift either!

Eventually, we arrived back at the flat and everyone piled into the car. Before we had reached the motorway, both Carole and Glenys had fallen asleep. I managed to keep up a conversation with Dick but, must have fallen asleep shortly after we passed Newport Pagnell.

The next thing I remember was waking up when we arrived back at his house. I had left in my car there before we left for Ireland. Glenys and I then had to drive, the short distance home.

The take up for the campaign was excellent and the "Wrangler/Grease" dance nights proved very popular.

Our relationship with RSO had worked very well, with one notable exception.

Near the end of the "Grease" campaign, the Wrangler receptionist rang through to my office to say that Robert Stigwood was on the telephone and wanted to speak to me. To this day, I cannot be sure that the person I spoke to really was Stigwood himself. The "great man" had acquired the reputation for being "hands-on."

Anyway, a man with an Australian twang was on the other end of the phone. "It's come to my attention that you have been offering counterfeit tapes of the "Grease" soundtrack at a night club in the Newcastle area," he said.

"I don't know what you are talking about," I responded.

"I have the information from (name of DJ) that he was working at the nightclub. During the evening, someone from Wrangler was giving the tapes away," he continued.

It then twigged that the tapes he was referring to, were the promotional tapes with the five tracks interspersed with the Wrangler advertisements.

"I think that you will find that the tapes referred to were produced from a master tape provided by RSO and that the content of cassettes concerned was signed off by your marketing people," I advised. "We also have a 'Terms of Agreement,' signed by a representative of RSO, to use the tapes in the way we have done."

"I will investigate this and get back to you," the "Australian voice" assured me.

I did not receive another phone call from him but did receive a letter of apology from my contacts at RSO.

I have not named the DJ concerned, even though I know who he was. He was well known in the industry for creating problems for others, in numerous attempts to further his own ambitions. I can only assume that the "Australian voice" came down on him hard!

The "Grease" tie up was the first of its kind and had broken new ground in film and product endorsement. Was the tie-up beneficial for both parties concerned?

I would say that the answer was a resounding YES!

All the activity stimulated by our team, increased the amount of Wrangler jeans and jeans related clothing sold through the retail trade. This clearly impacted on our market share, particularly in jeans. In this part of the market, our share closed in on the brand leader, Levi's.

"Grease the movie" performed exceedingly well at the UK box office. The initial $6 million investment in its production resulted in worldwide box office receipts of $395 million.

The album of the soundtrack was number one in the UK for around 13 weeks.

All five of the tracks I had selected for the "Wrangler/Grease" cassette, entered the charts with "You're the One That I Want" and "Summer Nights" reaching the top spot. They also appeared in the "UK top 100 records sold during 1978." The two number ones were second and third respectively. "Sandy" was 23rd, "Hopelessly Devoted to you" came in at 34th and "Grease" achieved 35th place.

The "Wrangler/Grease" posters became much sought after and still sell well when they occasionally come onto the market.

I am proud that we achieved so much for a relatively small investment.

Breaking Glass 1980

The success of the "Wrangler/Grease" collaboration was noted with envy by the film production community. This resulted in film producers beating a path to my door.

Our research of our core market of 16-24-year-olds revealed that there were many different sub-cultures.

"Grease" had been a success because it relived a period that spawned the success of rock music. All subsequent 'pop' music owed its origins to this music base. Because of this, "Grease the movie" had appealed to a wide segment all of music lovers.

By the 1980's a more anarchic trend was developing. Young people have always tried to rebel against the values of their parents. Music had been a way they could achieve this. Parents of the teens of the 80's were the teens of the 50's and early 60's. They had been responsible for the rise of a more open society dominated by loud rock music. When their children played loud music at home, they were dismayed that their parents loved it.

Rebelling had become much more difficult!

This had resulted in music lyrics becoming more and more anarchic. In the early 1970's a new kind of rock music evolved. It was fast, heavy and its lyrics were initially dark and full of death and gore. This "heavy metal music" ran in tandem with, the even darker, "punk rock" revolution.

This morphed into "garage music" that expressed a punk attitude but was not as fast and furious. Its lyrics were not as violent as "heavy metal" or "punk." The so called "new wave" would become pre-eminent as the 1980's progressed.

In 1980, the 'heavy metal sound" and a "punk attitude" were much to the fore. When the producers of a new movie, "Breaking Glass," made contact, I was interested to see whether it would appeal to any segment of the Wrangler jeans market.

The film itself revolved around the rise and fall of Kate (Hazel O'Conner) a singer songwriter struggling to achieve success with her new band called Breaking Glass.

It opened the lid on the sometimes-seedy world of the pop industry. Kate met Danny (Phil Daniels) who, recognising her talent wanted to promote her. He was working for an unscrupulous agent buying up hundreds of copies of records made by one of their artists, to manipulate the charts.

Kate and Danny finally fell in love and started a relationship. He helped to develop her career without any attempt to influence her creative output. For her career to reach the next stage, it was necessary to introduce her to a famous music manager, Woods (Jon Finch).

Unfortunately, Woods had designs on her. He became involved in sanitising her lyrics to ensure they received airplay. This caused Danny to be first side-lined and then abandoned. The band broke-up and Kate, by this time Woods lover, started a downward cycle of drugs that led to a total breakdown and hospitalisation.

It was clear Hazel O'Conner was the real star of the show. She epitomised the cross-over from "punk" to "new wave." All the songs in the film were written and performed by her.

For this reason alone, I agreed we would get involved!

It was almost impossible to create a meaningful link between the film's content and the Wrangler product. This said, jeans were worn in the movie and the producers agreed to include Wrangler on the films credit list.

We did organise some "Wrangler/Breaking Glass" dance nights, in clubs involved in the "new wave scene." Our Field Promotion Representatives also created in-store and window displays featuring "Breaking Glass" film posters. All this activity was timed to coincide with the release of the film in September 1980.

The aim of our involvement was to begin a process of "hardening up" the Wrangler image and to keep it relevant for an ever-changing, core market.

For her performance in the film, Hazel O'Conner won the Variety Club of Great Britain Award for Best Film Actor. She was also nominated for a BAFTA for both Best Newcomer and Best Film Score.

The films soundtrack spent 36 weeks in the album chart, reaching number 5 and being certified Gold. Several tracks were released as singles with the two of the most successful, "Eighth Day" and "Will You," entering the top ten in the singles chart.

When Hazel toured the UK to promote the film, her selected opening act was a then unknown group called Duran Duran. The tour attracted large audiences and was instrumental in them securing a recording contract.

It is difficult to measure the success of our association. Did it help to give Wrangler "street cred" with the large fan based who followed Hazel O'Conner?

It probably did!

Moonlighting - 1982

After "Breaking Glass," discussions with our public relations agency had led to the decision that we would no longer consider joint promotional activity with the film industry.

Our previous experience with "Grease" and "Breaking Glass" had confirmed to us that, like any other form of sponsorship, success could only be guaranteed if 100% commitment was made to merchandising the involvement through the point of sale, public relations, and promotional expenditure through the media.

Film production companies had become aware of what we had previously achieved. Because of this, I was bombarded with propositions to repeat our success. Unfortunately, they were now requesting large financial contributions for the privilege of our getting involved with them.

Towards the end of 1981, I received an approach from the office of the stage and film producer, Michael White.

He had acquired the reputation of picking winners. His C/V included stage shows such as "Oh! Calcutta," "The Rocky Horror Show," and "Annie". Film credits were equally impressive with "Monty Python and the Holy Grail," and "The Rocky Horror Picture Show."

What set this request apart, from the many that I had rejected, was that the film, "Moonlighting," had not yet been shot. The producers had sent a scenario of the whole film and the script from one specific scene for me to look at. This involved the films hero in a jeans shop trying to acquire a pair of Wrangler Jeans.

The man they had signed up to play the lead role was Jeremy Irons. He had appeared, in the recently released film, "The French Lieutenant's Woman," starring opposite Meryl Streep.

Jeremy was also starring, as Charles Ryder, in a blockbuster TV adaption of novel "Brideshead Revisited" by Evelyn Waugh. At the time of the initial contact, it was just coming to the end of an 11-episode run on the ITV channel. It had drawn in huge audiences and tremendous popular acclaim.

Jeremy Irons was big box office!

His high profile, and Michael White's reputation, caused me to reconsider the urge to send back a rejection latter. Instead, I discussed the concept with my in-house and external public relations people who, in turn, contacted the production company.

These talks established that the film had been written, and was to be directed by, the acclaimed Polish film director, screenwriter, dramatist and actor, Jerzy Skolimowski.

Jerzy had effectively been expelled by the communist regime in Poland because they had taken exception to the anti-Stalinist theme of his film "Hands Up." The film, produced in 1967, had been banned and was not released until 1981. Resettling in London, he had written and directed several films including "The Shout." It had enjoyed critical success when it was released in 1978.

The new script was the basis for the fifth of a series six semi-autobiographical feature films. It had been written following the declaration of Marshall Law in Poland in December 1981. This had resulted in the crushing of the Solidarity movement and imprisonment of its leaders.

The storyline of "Moonlighting" was set during the weeks before and after the banning of the Solidarity movement.

A team of Polish builders led by Novak (Jeremy Irons) had been hired to remodel a house in London that had been purchased by a Polish government official. By bringing them into the UK on tourist visas, he had calculated that he would be able to get the work done at a fraction of the cost that would be charged by British builders.

The proposition appeared to be too good to be true for the builders. Led to believe that they would be receiving good wages, and aiming to live cheaply, would enable them to take most of what they earned back to Poland at the end of the contract.

Nobody had counted upon the upheaval that took place after the crushing of Solidarity and the imposition of strict regulations on travel to and from Poland!

Novak was the only one who spoke any English. As the foreman, he guided his team through London to the house where they have been contracted to work. Once there, he advised them that they must keep a low profile. Only he went outside the house to buy food and therefore was able to keep up to date with the news from his homeland. It was on one of these expeditions that he found out about the crisis occurring back home and the difficulties this might create for him and his team.

He decided to keep this from his work colleagues!

With money becoming tight, he began to steal things and concocted an elaborate scheme to defraud the local supermarket.

An hilarious episode involved his interaction with a salesgirl in a blue jeans store where he was intent on acquiring a pair of Wrangler Jeans.

In the end, the illegal builders made their way, on foot, to Heathrow Airport to return to Poland. It is only when they arrived at the airport that Novak told his comrades about what has happened in their homeland. Incensed, at what they saw as an act of treachery, they exacted a vicious revenge leaving him bloodied and unconscious in a car park.

The producers were open with us. Skolimowski wanted to produce the film quickly and on a low budget. No financial contribution was required from Wrangler.

They simply wanted us to help them trim their production costs by providing Wrangler branded instore equipment and stock. This would enable them to create the jeans shop set for very little expenditure on their part. I received a promise that everything would be returned after the shoot. It was agreed that any stock not returned would be charged to them at wholesale price.

This was not the sort of film that could be cross marketed. Its subject matter was just too political for that. Never-the-less we concluded that any film starring Jeremy Irons extolling the virtues Wrangler Jeans would do us no harm!

It was agreed that a couple of our Field Promotion Representative would erect the instore units in a warehouse hired by the producers and merchandise it with Wrangler product and point of sale material.

The film was shot over a two-month period with Jeremy Irons speaking Polish (with an English accent) to his team of builders and English (with a Polish accent) when out and about in London. The narrative throughout the film was also provided by Irons.

Most of the film was shot in Jerzy Skolimowski's own house in London which was in the process of renovation at the time. It was later claimed, that three of the Polish builders working on the project, were also recruited to Novak's fictional team, and appeared in the film. Skolimowski himself made a brief appearance as the diplomat who had hired them, on what turned out to be starvation wages.

The biggest investment was the casting of Jeremy Irons. This turned out to be an inspired choice. He was a revelation in the role.

The film was previewed, to critical acclaim at the 1982 Cannes Film Festival where it won the "Best Screenplay Award." It went out on full release on 26 September 1982. Whilst not setting the box office alight, like our previous movie associations had, "Moonlighting" was both a critical and commercial success and generally agreed to have been Skolimowski's most influential film.

Today, it is acknowledged to be one of the best of its genre ever made!

It was difficult to evaluate whether the Wrangler association with "Moonlighting" produced any meaningful additional sales in the UK. The film had not been merchandised at the point of sale and I would guess that many retailers were not aware that it was appearing in their local cinema.

Marshall law was not ended in Poland until 1983 but the situation was not "normalised" until three years later.

After this, Wrangler was one of the first western brands to be invited to sell our products in several Polish cities. Our agreement involved developing concessions within a state-owned department store chain. The then manager of our UK retail concessions department in Calverton, was seconded to Poland for several weeks to help with store merchandising and staff sales training.

The experiment was very successful. In a relatively short space of time, Wrangler became a leading jeans brand in Poland.

Perhaps our involvement in Skolimowski's film might have had some influence on Wrangler sales after all?

Freddie Mercury at the Live Aid Concert 1985

Not all the celebrity product endorsements were the direct result of the activities of the Wrangler PR teams. On the 13 March 1985 the Live Aid Concert took place at the Wembley Stadium in London in front of 72,000 people. It had been organised by Bob Geldof and Midge Ure to raise funds for relief of the ongoing Ethiopian famine.

The event was held simultaneously in London and at the John F. Kennedy Stadium in Philadelphia, Pennsylvania, United States where a further 100,000 people watched the show live. An estimated global audience of 1.9 billion, across 150 nations, watched the live broadcast.

All the major pop artists of the time performed at one or other of the venues. Phil Collins performed at both by travelling by helicopters and Concorde.

In London, during a twenty minute performance by Queen, lead singer Freddie Mercury stole the show whilst at times leading the crowd in unison refrains. The band's six song set opened with a shortened version of "Bohemian Rhapsody" and closed with "We Are the Champions."

It has been voted – by many artists, journalists, and music industry executives – the greatest live performance in the history of rock.

The iconic and lasting image of the performance features Freddie Mercury, mike in hand working the crowd, wearing a plain white cutaway vest and a pair of Wrangler stonewashed jeans.

This priceless piece of exposure was not contrived by the Wrangler marketing team but remains a lasting piece of brand imagery even to this day!

In October 2018, "Bohemian Rhapsody," a biographical film about British rock band Queen, focusing on their music and the life of lead singer Freddie Mercury, was released to much acclaim. Featuring Rami Malek as Freddie, Gwilym Lee as Bryan May, Ben Hardy as Roger Taylor, and Joseph Mazzello as John Deacon, it covers the period from the band's inception to their Live Aid performance in 1985.

During the Live Aid sequences every detail had been meticulously replicated including the clothes that Freddie Mercury was wearing, a plain white cutaway vest and his stonewashed Wrangler Jeans. The branding on the back pocket was even more prominent than it was on day of the original broadcast.

The film undoubtably brought about a renaissance of the music of Queen. It probably did the same for Wrangler Stonewashed Jeans!

Chapter Sixteen

Student design and Photographic competitions – 1982/1986

During meetings with some of the top creative minds in advertising and working with some of the top photographers, I was struck by their comments about the way that universities and colleges prepared their students for life in the commercial world.

Many described their personal experience of trying to secure a job armed with a portfolio of their student work. Nearly always, they were asked to show the interviewer examples of any commercial work done by them. This proved impossible because they didn't have any!

The main criticism of academics, by professional photographers, was that their focus "was getting students a work qualification and not helping them to achieve a qualification for work."

During my time at Wrangler, I was asked to visit local Colleges and Universities to talk to them about the advertising campaigns we had developed through our agencies. During conversations with design students, many expressed the view that finishing the course with a good grade was the end of their learning process, not the beginning.

Every year thousands of students were entering the job market intent on securing a high paid job with a top agency, design house or photographer. Sadly, the majority would have their hopes dashed at the first hurdle.

In my job, it was important to develop measurable objectives and a clear brief for the communications agencies, which would enable them to develop creative outputs that achieved the results we wanted.

Fancy creative work was no good to anyone, us least of all, particularly if the work failed to increase sales of the Wrangler product being featured!

Involving College Students and their Tutors

I had friends who were college and university lecturers in both product design, creative design, and photography.

One of them, working in the fashion department of what was then Nottingham Trent College, now Nottingham Trent University, was interested in incorporating an actual commercial brief into the course structure. This would enable "commercial concepts" to be included in the student's work portfolio and at their final year show.

We offered a small prize for the best concept, that in the judgement of the Wrangler Merchandise Team, offered the greatest commercial potential. This led to friends in the creative design and photographic design departments of the same college, asking me to offer something similar for their students.

It occurred to me, that what we were doing might have wider appeal. It was time consuming, but if a concept could be developed to include more colleges, on a national basis, all the effort might be worthwhile.

We sat down with our public relations agency to discuss how this might be achieved.

They reported back that there were several national student fashion design awards but there was very little for students on graphic design or photographic courses. It was recommended that we look at these two areas to investigate the best way forward.

At around this time, Lindah Kiddey had joined my in-house team at Calverton as Public Relation Co-ordinator. Her husband, Paul, was a senior college lecturer at the South Nottinghamshire College of Further Education. It was regarded as one of the leading learning centres for graphic design and photography in the country. He explained some of the problems of incorporating an award brief into a national teaching programme that was rigidly set. "Difficult but not impossible," summed up his view.

Using Pauls contacts, Lindah began to canvas the views of other senior lecturers at other colleges throughout the UK.

CDP, our advertising agency at the time, handled the Olympus camera account. They had associations with some of the top fashion photographers in the world.

Wrangler/Olympus Student Photographic Competition

I felt Olympus might prove and excellent partner in a national student photographic competition. The Wrangler account director at CDP, approached his colleague who handled Olympus and explained what we were considering. He agreed to run the idea past his client.

The Olympus response was very positive. Not only did they want to be actively involved, but they also agreed to provide photographic equipment as part of the prize fund.

In addition, they also offered the services of one of their contracted star photographers to be part of the judging panel, and to present the awards to the student whose entry was judged to be the winner.

The involvement of Olympus, alongside Wrangler, put the whole concept of a national student photographic competition into a different league!

Lindah found previously insurmountable obstacles, that had been in place during her first round of talks, had suddenly disappeared. Nearly every college lecturer on our list wanted to be involved. To have one of their students declared the competition winner would give them, and their college, tremendous kudos.

In the first year of our association with Olympus, we were both finding our way. As far as I can recollect, the entry levels were relatively small and the whole operation was coordinated by our respective public relations companies.

In year two, we benefitted from that experience. The brief that we delivered to the various participating colleges was far more precise and more commercial in its approach.

Both Wrangler and Olympus were anxious that the process would not favour students with the greatest technical ability. We were both keen to reward those students most capable of interpreting the brief and producing creative work that fulfilled its requirements.

This time, the judging panel comprised of me, the Marketing Director of Olympus, and the renowned photographer Terence Donovan.

Having Terence as a member of the judging panel was a major coup!

Along with his great friends and rival photographers David Bailey and Brian Duffy, he had played a major part in developing the culture of high fashion, and celebrity chic, in the 1960's. This period became known as the "Swinging Sixties." London became its epicentre.

The trio, dubbed "The Black Trinity," by society photographer Norman Parkinson, socialised with, and photographed everybody who was anybody during this period. This included actors, musicians and even royalty. They found themselves elevated to celebrity status and were well known by just their surnames.

Donovan had branched out into film production during the 1970's moving his studio to the lofty atmosphere of 30 Bourdon Street in London's Mayfair. Throughout this most productive period in his career, he had continued to work with all the major fashion magazines at the time, including "Harper's Bazaar" and "Vogue."

Judging took place at the offices of the Wrangler public relations agency in central London.

Donovan was a larger-than-life character in every respect. It came as no surprise to learn that he had a passion for judo and held a black belt in the sport. He was passionate about discovering and promoting the work of a "new wave" of photographic talent. His experience proved invaluable as we sifted through the many entries we had received, before agreeing on our winners.

When we were relaxing after the first stage of our judging ordeal, he also proved to be an excellent raconteur.

One of the stories he told us on that day has stuck in my mind.

He was in the middle of a location shoot in the Yorkshire Dales, an area I know very well. It had been a very hot day and they had been carrying their equipment "over hill and down dale."

At the end of the day, he and his crew had reached their overnight destination, a hotel in the tourist haven of Knaresborough, near Harrogate. Emptying their Land Rover of all the expensive photographic equipment, the party of six people had presented themselves at the check-in desk.

The woman at the front desk was confronted by the imposing frame of Donovan and his party. They were literally steaming from their exertions and badly in need of a shower and refreshment.

"What can I do for you?" she enquired. "We have come to check in, party of six in the name of Donovan," she was told.

The name, and the photographic equipment should have been a dead giveaway as to the identity of her guests. Unfortunately, the hotel owner, acting as receptionist, had no idea who Donovan was. Celebrity photographers, with international reputations, did not check into her hotel on a regular basis.

She looked through her register, found the details for each member of the group and asked them to sign the documents. When all this had been completed, she handed over their keys.

Whist this protracted process was going on, Donovan engaged the hotel owner in conversation. "We are very hungry and would like to book a table in your restaurant when we have had time to clean ourselves up, say 9 o'clock?" he suggested.

The woman was taken aback. "Last orders in the restaurant are at 9.30pm," she advised, "I'm sorry but you have no reservation, so it will not be possible to provide you, and your party with, a table," she continued.

This did not phase Donovan at all. "Do you mind if I make a call on your phone," he asked. "I want to contact my friend, Egon Ronay."

The hotel owner knew who Egon Ronay was!

Threatening to call the most famous restaurant reviewer in the land, publisher of the renowned "Egon Ronay Restaurant Guides," was something that might be a cause for concern for hotel owners across the country. No doubt many people had tried to pull that sort of stunt before

Trying not to look phased by the request, she called his bluff. "You give me the number and I will make the call for you," she offered.

Donovan pulled out his black book of contacts, found the number required, and gave it to his adversary.

She started to dial the number. "When the phone is answered, ask for Egon and tell him that Donovan would like a quick word," he suggested.

The phone was answered. The hotel owner posed the question and then handed the phone over to Donovan. She was visibly shaken.

"Hello Egon," Donovan said. "We have just arrived at the hotel you recommend in Knaresborough. We are really looking forward to eating here. I will let you know how we get on." After exchanging a few more pleasantries with his friend, Donovan handed the phone back to the hotel owner.

"Mr Donovan, I have been in touch with the chef and the maître de and we have managed to sort something out for you and your friends. A table is booked for 9 o'clock, as requested," she informed him.

Donovan told us, with a grin on his face, that "the hospitality and the food, during the rest their short stay, was worthy of its Egon Ronay rating."

During my recent research, I established that Donovan and Egon Ronay were well known to each other and had met on many occasions. Whilst the story may have been embellished by frequent telling, I have no doubt that it had more than an element of truth behind it!

During the hectic judging process, there had been no real problems in coming up with a shortlist of what we all considered to be the most memorable. We all had our own favourites and deciding on the three prize winners, and in their final order of precedence, was no mean feat.

In the end, we all agreed with Donovan's choice! Several weeks later, he presented the prizes at the Olympus offices in London.

Both Wrangler, and our co-sponsors, were very happy with the tremendous amount of media coverage our involvement had received. We were also very pleased that we had succeeded in positively changing attitudes within the participating colleges.

Because of this, we agreed to run the competition again the following year.

Olympus announced that the celebrity judge for the next competition would be none other than Patrick Lichfield. Like Bailey, Donovan, and Duffy he had been influential in the events of the "swinging sixties" and social scene in London.

His upbringing was altogether different!

Born Thomas Patrick John Anson, he was son of Viscount Anson and Anne Bowes Lyon. Through his mother, he was also first cousin, once removed, to the Queen.

In 1950, two years after his parents divorced, his mother married Prince George of Denmark. His father died in 1956 and, when his grandfather died in 1960, Patrick succeeded him as 5th Earl of Lichfield.

Conventionally educated at Harrow and then Sandhurst, he had served in the Grenadier Guards. In 1962, to the consternation of his mother, he gave up his commission to become a photographer's trainee.

Initially, he tried to keep his privileged background out of the public eye by "bedding down in the studio and then sharing a condemned flat in central London."

In the 60's, it seemed to him that only photographers with working class backgrounds could achieve cult status.

Despite his apparently lowly lifestyle, Lichfield could always fall back on a 35-room apartment in the family home of Shugborough Hall, Staffordshire. He maintained this as part of a deal made with The National Trust, to whom he had handed over the family estate in lieu of death duties.

The "swinging sixties" had opened a whole new world to him. He could meet new people and do things that had previously seemed unthinkable to him. Eventually, he became accepted by his industry colleagues as the professional photographer he had elected to become, rather than the peer of the realm that he was.

Whist his royal connections had undoubtedly helped, hard work, dedication and flair had enabled him to acquire a reputation for studio portraits of beautiful women for glossy magazines, calendars, and advertisements, as well as regular royal and celebrity commissions.

Like Bailey, Donovan, and Duffy, he was instantly recognised as just Lichfield, his photographer's name, and for his very public associations with the "new wave" of models, movie stars and debutants that he was paid to photograph.

When our third photographic competition was launched, the Lichfield name worked its magic. More colleges than ever wanted to take part and the number of students participating reached an all-time high.

To enable us to accommodate those chosen to be part of the final judging process, Olympus made available the gallery space at their London headquarters.

In addition to Patrick Lichfield, the judging panel comprised the marketing director of Olympus, the editor of a leading professional photographic magazine and me.

When I look back at the photographs of the group that were taken on the day, it seemed a very relaxed affair.

In one of the shots, Lichfield is sitting in one chair talking to the man from Olympus. I appear to be reclining in another. The magazine editor is sitting between us on a third. Lindah Kiddey is sorting papers on a table adjacent to where we are all seated. Several other public relations people are either shuffling papers in their hands or peering at the photographic entries that are mounted on the walls around the room.

Appearances, as we all know, can be deceptive. Whittling out a short list proved to be a very exacting process. Picking the winners even more so?

In the end, we got there - without too much blood being spilt!

During the after-judging buffet and drinks, Lichfield proved to have as many anecdotal tales to tell as Terry Donovan had the year before. It was clear that all of them were great friends who respected each other's talent and spent a lot of time in each other's company.

Lichfield had just returned from exotic climes where he had been shooting an array of beautiful women for a Unipart calendar. He was suntanned and relaxed.

We all agreed that being involved in advertising, marketing and photography was very boring and extremely arduous!

This proved to be the final "Olympus/Wrangler photographic competition." I would like to believe that all the students who entered the photographic competitions, during the three years of our involvement, benefitted from the process.

We moved our advertising account out of CDP later the same year. The Blue Bell company was taken over by the VF Corporation and my marketing budget was cut.

This resulted in a change in my marketing communication priorities!

Student Poster Design Competition

In 1986, we organised a competition for students on graphic design courses at colleges of further education.

Using the contact list from the colleges who had participated in the photographic competitions, Lindah Kiddey lobbied hard for graphic design tutors to include our "commercial brief" within their course module.

This proved difficult because we did not have the support of a sponsorship partner like Olympus. Instead, we were offering a brief which involved the design of a poster for Wrangler jeans that would have specific relevance to the prime 16-24-year-old consumers.

The judging panel would include our advertising agency's creative chief and the editor of one of the leading "image" magazines.

Lindah convinced me that it would be a good idea if the main prize involved a pledge to print the winning poster and display it in retail outlets around the country.

"I think that this will encourage students to enter and will give kudos to the winning student, the participating college and their tutor," she advised.

I must have had a rush of blood to the head. I found myself agreeing with her. "OK, we will go ahead as you have suggested," I replied.

As Lindah had predicted, the idea seemed to break down many of the obstacles that had previously inhibited design colleges from participating. From memory, I believe that 20 or so colleges around the country entered and hundreds of submissions were received by the closing date.

Many of the entries had been heavily influenced by the Wrangler advertising that was running at the time, but there were some that stood out as both original in concept and pertinent to the brief.

Coming up to the closing date, I had suffered from a recurring nightmare that none of the entries would meet the criteria we had laid down. Furthermore, I was concerned I would have to print and display a winning poster that did not meet the creative standards we demanded from our professional designers.

I was too close to the brand. For this reason, I had chosen not to be part of the judging panel.

In the end, my fears proved unfounded!

The quality of the shortlisted entries was incredibly high. As I recall, "the winning entry had based a design around a British telephone box that had been customised in the Wrangler brand colours of blue and yellow." It had been submitted by a student from one of East Midlands based Colleges of Further Education, Derby from memory. A student from West Nottinghamshire College in Mansfield was also one of the prize winners.

Our public relations team generated a lot of media interest locally and nationally.

And YES, the poster was printed and distributed in retail outlets around the UK, as I had promised!

The winning student had the opportunity to include something into his college work portfolio that demonstrated his ability to interpret a commercial brief. I am sure it will have helped him to secure a successful career as a commercial artist.

Chapter Seventeen

Charity Events

Like all major multi-national organisations, we received countless requests for donations from charities. It was impossible to help them all, but we did encourage staff to support collections for good causes and actively participate in national events such as "Red Nose Day."

A decision was made by the Management Team that we would select a major charitable cause every year and then throw our weight behind activities designed to raise as much money as possible. It was felt that this was far more meaningful and effective than "just providing a one-off donation."

Many of the charities had been national or international bodies but as we started our marketing planning for 1986, we decided to focus on the local community in Nottingham building on the special relationships we had developed by our sponsorship of both the local football teams and our support of schools and colleges throughout the county.

Healthcare was a major issue at the time, just as it is today. We had been approached individually by both the Nottingham Hospitals Scanner Appeal and the Nottinghamshire office of the British Heart Foundation. Both were worthy causes and after many internal conversations we had found it impossible to choose between the two.

Dick Webzell was keen to help both by pulling together other local clothing manufacturers, fashion retailers and the local community, and underwriting a "special fashion show event," to raise a significant amount of money. This would then to be split between the charities.

The baton was passed to our in-house and external PR teams who went away to put on their collective "thinking caps."

Fashion for Life – Charity Fashion & Dance Show 17th April 1986

Towards the end of 1985, the team reported back with their recommendations.

"To maximise the audience potential, we need to hold the event in a large venue such as the Royal Centre Concert Hall in Nottingham," the PR team recommended. "We will need a team of about 10 models taking part in a dance show extravaganza lasting about 90 minutes. Other clothing manufacturers in the area will have to be recruited so that we can demonstrate the depth of fashion manufacturing in Nottinghamshire, whilst making the content relevant to the audience," they continued.

What had started out as a good idea was now in danger of becoming a major logistical operation involving a lot of time and effort from the whole Wrangler marketing team.

An outline budget was agreed with the rest of senior management team. The two potential recipients of the money raised from ticket sales were approached. Both were naturally delighted to be selected and a small group of volunteers from each charity were seconded to our organising group.

Clear lines of responsibility were drawn up. The charities would provide "bodies" on the night to supplement the small team of box office and bar staff provided by the venue, and to act as dressers backstage. They would also supply volunteers to check tickets and show people to their seats. Both organisations agreed to sell tickets through their own contact lists.

The Wrangler team agreed to fund the cost of the venue, the models and technical support staff, recruit other participating companies, promote the event in conjunction with retailers throughout Nottinghamshire, and by of direct advertising and PR in the local media.

Pat Keeling, the proprietor of a model agency based in nearby Leicester was approached. She had worked for Wrangler as a photographic model in the past. Pat quickly realised that participation in our event would be an excellent way to promote her portfolio of models and her skill as a fashion show choreographer. Despite the high workload required of her, and 10 of her models, before the event, at a rehearsal, matinee show and evening show on the day, she took on the role at a fraction of the normal fee.

The Royal Centre Concert Hall provided the venue at a discounted price and acted as joint ticket office with the Wrangler Head Office team. Ticket costs ranged from VIP seats at £7, Stalls and 1st tier £4 and all remaining seats £3. At the Matinee only, schools, students and senior citizens were able to purchase seats for only £1.

In addition to Wrangler, many big-name local clothing companies agreed to provide merchandise. The list included Jacques Vert, Speedo, Gossard, Charnos, Guy Birkin, Aristoc and a group of young designers from the Nottingham Fashion Centre. The Wrangler shoe licensee provided all the footwear and Keith Hall provided a team of hair and makeup professionals. The manufacturers of Flotex Carpets provided floor covering for the stage area.

The show was marketed as Fashion for Life Charity Fashion & Dance Show and, on 17th April 1986, the people of Nottinghamshire rewarded us with sell out audiences for each performance.

Thanks to hard work of everyone associated with the event, it proved to be a great success. When all the receipts came in, Wrangler was able to hand over a substantial four figure cheque to each of the charities.

PART FOUR

THE EFFECTIVENESS OF SALES PROMOTION ACTIVITY

Chapter Eighteen

A Sales Promotion Strategy

In the 1970's, the term, sales promotion, referred primarily to "the process by which a manufacturer or wholesaler incentivises a retail buyer to purchase their products."

In the fashion trade, this was traditionally achieved by reducing the wholesale price to increase the sellers' margin.

Buyers had always purchased in multiples of a dozen (12 units) up to a gross (144 units) which equalled 12 dozen. A popular method of buyer incentive was to offer "a baker's dozen," 13 units for every multiple of one dozen purchased. Once the retailer had purchased the product it was left to them to promote them, direct to their consumers.

Food retailers were already well versed in the practice of asking their suppliers to share some of the responsibility for merchandising their products at the point of sale and offering promotions to encourage customers to buy more.

Early in the 1970's, companies such as ASDA and the CWS Ltd, had opened superstores where non-food products were offered for sale in stores which had previously only sold food items.

In my capacity of Sales Promotions Co-ordinator of the CWS Ltd, Menswear Division, I had been directly involved in the opening of four Co-op superstores in the Midlands and North of England.

I had also helped to launch a new concept, called "Tailor Mates," in fifty or so stores throughout the UK. This new sales promotion approach enabled consumers to purchase a suit "off-the- peg" by selecting the trousers and the jacket separately to ensure a much better fit.

It was clear, to ensure unit sales could be optimised, stock that had been sold needed to be replaced as quickly as possible.

There were no powerful portable computers around into which store staff could enter sales data, and transmit it to another computer at their suppliers, which in turn would initiate the stock replenishment. We had to develop simple paper processes to accomplish the same results.

Not only were we expected to provide enough of the product, but also to ensure it was properly merchandised and replenished.

When I joined Blue Bell Apparel in 1976, I was surprised that they were not employing similar techniques to sell Wrangler products.

It became clear, that the market dynamics in the jeans and jeans related product area were totally different.

The consumer wanted to buy the product. The retail trade wanted to stock it. As manufacturing wholesalers, we were struggling to manufacture enough to satisfy the need.

The task that confronted me was to continue to maintain demand for the Wrangler product by developing strong brand values through above-the-line advertising.

Through our Field Promotion Representatives, merchandising assistance was provided along with supplies of quality point of sale material. This approach enabled us to reinforce our marketing message at the point of purchase.

The strategy worked very well through to the beginning of the 1980's. Then, the market expansion that we had all ridden on the back of, began to falter.

As a Management Group, we had to decide how we proposed to react to the slowdown in market growth. There were different alternatives available to us. These included supplying the discount retailers or, lowering our wholesale prices by reducing the quality of our core jeans product.

After a lot of discussion, we decided against either of these alternatives!

We had invested heavily in the Wrangler name and built up a reputation for producing a quality product line. This approach had allowed us to increase our distribution and achieve brand leadership in both the jeans and jeans related clothing markets. It was decided that we would continue "to invest in adding value to the

Wrangler name and supporting the trade to merchandise both our advertising and our product lines at the point of purchase."

In 1984, we had carried out intensive research as well as an in-depth analysis of our marketing effort. It showed that we had retained our market share in a static market but that we needed to increase distribution through retail outlets where it was poor.

A promotional package was produced that we were confident would encourage retail outlets to stock more Wrangler Jeans. Retailers were incentivised to "Turn to the Wrangler Blue Denim Bonus" and make more money from the sales of Wrangler jeans. The proposition was geared to sales of a limited number of core denim and stretch denim jean styles available in washed and stonewashed finishes.

The concept was simple, "Buy more Wrangler jeans – make more margin!" A specific and detailed breakdown of the promotion is outlined elsewhere.

It succeeded in its initial sell-in objectives, but highlighted that sales promotion needed to be regarded as a true partner in the marketing mix. We needed the input of a professional sales promotion agency to maximise all the promotional benefits available to us.

In Nottingham, a company called Counterpunch was making waves in the industry and earning itself a national reputation. I knew the Managing Director, Alistair Archer, through my involvement in the Nottingham branch of the Chartered Institute of Marketing.

I telephoned him. "I am looking to appoint a Sales Promotion Agency," I advised. "Are you interested in having in having a chat?" "Interested! Of course, I am interested!" he responded.

Through the years, I had worked with several London based promotional agencies. This experience had illustrated that tactical sales promotional activities needed a much quicker reaction time than top line activity. It also needed to be totally integrated as part of the overall marketing plan.

I had talked over my thoughts with Dick Webzell and the rest of the team. They were all in agreement that if the talks with Counterpunch went well, Wrangler would benefit from input from a company located just 8 miles down the road who would be able react quickly to our needs, "at the drop of a hat!"

The talks with Alistair and his team went well. They had fully researched the market and provided examples of work that they had developed, for several "'blue chip" companies. These were not only creative in their approach but also delivered the required outputs.

Counterpunch was appointed in the Summer of 1984.

Wrangler Denim Bonus promotions

Counterpunch was tasked, "to build on the denim bonus promotion in a way that would encourage the retailer to maximise its benefits whilst creating an incentive to consumers to buy Wrangler Jeans instead of another brand."

We also set up a meeting between them and our advertising and public relations agencies. In this meeting, I explained our overall strategy for developing the sales of our core product and encouraged all parties to liaise directly with each other so that the overall impact could be maximised.

This approach paid dividends!

Collette Dickenson Pearce had good contacts in the music industry. They suggested that a "Wrangler – That's What's Going On" cassette compilation would not only link with the music and special interest press campaign that would be running at the end of the year, it would also prove an excellent incentive to purchase for the core adult jeans market.

Working with Counterpunch and a record company, they came up with an exclusive collection of 12 "hot hits"' including tracks by "Kajagoogoo" and "Thompson Twins." These two groups also featured in the press campaign and related in-store promotional posters that we had produced. Other artists included on the cassette were, "Nick Hayward," "KC & The Sunshine Band," "Paul Young," "The Stranglers," "Cyndy Lauper," "Wham," "SOS Bank," "Art Company," "Marvin Gaye" and "Herbie Hancock."

Counterpunch then set about to enhance the initial concept into a fully blown sales promotional campaign.

The promotion concept they developed, provided positive benefits for the retailer and their customers through the provision of "an exclusive, 12 hits cassette, worth £3.99, to be offered free against sales of Wrangler Jeans."

One side of the sell in leaflet invited the retailer to "Make Wrangler Denim Top of Your Charts." For every extra pair of Wrangler Jeans ordered through the Denim Bonus offer they would be able to purchase the cassettes for only 70p each. If they required additional cassettes, these could be purchased for only £1 each. Full point of sale support was offered.

The reverse of the leaflet proclaimed how the promotion "Sounds Great for your customers." Not only would Wrangler purchasers receive "12 Hot hits" on one exclusive Wrangler cassette, but they would also be able to enter a special pop competition to win a trip to the CBS Studios in Los Angeles.

In addition, the first 1000 all correct entries would receive a "£5 voucher against their next purchase of Wrangler denim jeans," provided they were bought from the retailer where they had originally entered the competition.

In the mid 1980's, the "Parker Ad-Pen" was the "must have" writing tool for young people.

I had a long-standing relationship with Parker. When they contacted us with "an offer you can't refuse," to purchase a large quantity of Ad-Pen's at a very favourable price, I contacted Counterpunch to see whether they felt it might be the perfect incentive against sales of Wrangler Children's jeans.

They responded quickly. "We think it will make an excellent motivation to buy, especially if they can be supplied in an individually printed blister pack," I was advised.

I went back to my Parker contact, and we agreed a favourable volume price, including the preferred method of packaging.

The agency quickly responded with another fully integrated concept.

A two-sided leaflet offered the retailer, "the ability to offer a free Ad-Pen with every pair Wrangler Children's Jeans sold during the promotional period." For every pair of Children's jeans ordered under "the Denim Bonus offer," Wrangler would "supply one Parker Ad-Pen (retail price around £1.50) for only 50p." The retailer could then offer an "Ad-Pen for Free with every pair of Wrangler Children's jeans purchased."

A specially devised "Wrangler Slogan" competition had been organised in conjunction with the home computer company, Atari. Three winners would each receive the very latest Atari Home Computer. The competition was promoted, in full colour, on the front of the special Parker Ad-Pen blister pack. The competition entry form was printed in one colour on the reverse.

Both competitions were enthusiastically supported by the trade and helped to increase unit sales into those retailers participating.

After all this time, it is difficult to remember the precise numbers. I believe that around 100,000 of the "What's Going On" cassettes and 20,000 "Ad-Pens" were distributed into the trade.

Our salesforce reported that "the Wrangler brand share through participating retailers had measurably increased." The success of sales of the cassette resulted in Wrangler being presented with a mock "gold disc" by the record company.

Both competitions were well subscribed, and the prize presentations enabled us to maximise public relations opportunities to generate excellent press coverage.

1986 was a year that proved to be very difficult on several different fronts!

My marketing budget had been cut back as a direct result of the Management Buyout of Blue Bell, at the end of 1984, and all the uncertainty that this had caused.

Levi's had launched their campaign for 501's at the end of 1986 and had upped their planned advertising spend considerably for 1987.

I had been forced to use all my available budget to try and counter their TV advertising spend to protect the Wrangler brand share.

The plan to extend our sales promotion programme with Counterpunch was an early casualty.

By the middle of 1986, Blue Bell had been taken over by the VF Corporation and staff changes at CDP had resulted in a move to a new advertising agency, BBDO.

Thankfully, our marketing budget for 1987 had been increased and I began talks with Counterpunch, and others, to develop several major, national sales promotion packages.

Wrangler 40th Anniversary Promotions

The Wrangler brand had been purchased by Blue Bell in 1947 as a vehicle for the company to enter the jeans market.

A change in ownership, resulting from our takeover, had brought about a change of name for the UK organisation. Blue Bell Apparel Ltd had been become Wrangler Limited.

It seemed appropriate that we should use the "40th Anniversary of the Wrangler Jeans brand" as a peg for our sales development activity into the trade.

By chance, I received a mailshot from the Birmingham Mint. Since 1850, it had been producing metal tokens and coins, as a private enterprise, in cooperation with the Royal Mint. Having been heavily involved in a consortium with the Royal Mint in the 1960's and 1970's, it was now looking to expand its activities through private sector organisations.

I was intrigue by the possibilities and called in their representative to talk over what they might be able to offer.

One of the items in his sample case was a promotional coin holder measuring approximately 15 cm square. A coin was encapsulated between two plasticised sheets showing the "obverse" and "Reverse" sides. A further four sheets made up a six-page brochure that could be fully customised to meet our specific requirements.

Birmingham Mint was offering a full design and production service for both the coin and the promotional coin holder. The all-in price was in line with sums we had paid for "give-away" incentive items in the past. Their Wrangler coin idea offered something totally unique to promote the brand in its anniversary year.

Working with the Mint's design team, I produced some copy for the Wrangler story and supplied illustrations of some milestones during the brands 40-year life.

Levi's were promoting the American heritage of the 501 jeans in its advertising. The modern five-pocket western jean had been developed by Wrangler in 1947. We were keen to emphasise this American heritage in a very modern way. Our designers came up with the simple message – "Born in the USA 1947."

The outside pages told the Wrangler brand story up to 1987. This was achieved by highlighting all key moments, using illustrations from the archive of material I had provided.

A Wrangler "anniversary dollar" was encased between an "American Eagle" and a scroll with the words "One Wrangler Dollar."

The obverse design showed a montage of iconic American attractions such as "Capitol Hill" and the "Statue of Liberty" with the words "ONE WRANGLER DOLLAR" and "BORN IN THE USA. "The reverse featured a montage of working American cowboys. One of the figures was wielding a lasso that formed the words "Wrangler Heritage."

A limited run of around 1500 was produced. It was used by our salesforce as part of their sell in of Spring 1987 product ranges, to key buyers in the UK and Ireland.

The "Wrangler Dollar" proved very popular. The exclusive nature of its distribution resulted in a sales return that far exceeded face value!

Our public relations agency had talked to Lindah Kiddey about the possible development of the student design competition that had just come to an end. "It has gone down very well. We feel that there is mileage in carrying it on for another year," they enthused.

I was not convinced. A lot of time and effort had been required for a very small measurable return. "Every pound of our budget needs to be thrown behind increasing sales of the Wrangler product," I advised Lindah. "I understand what you are saying, but I believe that a regional competition across the Midlands can be run from in-house using the good contacts we have made," she argued.

In the end, we agreed to develop a special competition brief to produce a "Wrangler 40th Anniversary poster" design.' Once Lindah had produced it, with some input from our London based PR agency, college coordination was organised, and it was distributed to all those participating. The competition was launched in September 1986 with 10 colleges, and several hundred students were actively involved.

Judging took place early in 1987. The standard of design work submitted, was of the highest order. After heated discussion by the judging panel, a design produced by a student from West Nottinghamshire College of Further Education, in Mansfield, was declared the winner.

The design cleverly incorporated the Wrangler rope logo with the end of the rope constructing the '0' of the number 40. The '4' was made by arranging the legs of a stylised drawing of a pair of jeans.

Wrangler Jeans of course!

A shadow of the 40 gave the design perspective and depth. Simple, and yet effective, the work was fully deserving of the recognition it received. I went along to the college to present the prizes to the winning designer in front of his tutor and fellow students.

In the middle of 1986, I had briefed Counterpunch to develop a theme for a national promotion that would be run through the 40th Anniversary year of the birth of the Wrangler brand.

At around the same time, I had received a call from Noelle Campbell-Sharp who was a major magazine publisher in Ireland. In 1986, she owned around 11 titles including "Irish Tatler" that she had rebranded as "IT Magazine."

"I have great idea to help the promotion of Wrangler in the UK and Ireland," she enthused. "Tell me more," I replied.

I had met Noelle during my first trip to Ireland as Advertising Manager for Wrangler in the UK and Ireland. We were both born in the same year, and we had quickly developed a mutual respect for each other's professional ability.

If Noelle had an idea that might help Wrangler promotional activity, it was worth listening to!

"I have a contact with a company in Wexford who are manufacturing an all-Irish sports car designed by Frank Costin," she explained. "I believe it is possible to do a deal that might be great for you and for them," she continued. Noelle was a great car enthusiast. At the time, she owned a vintage Bentley that was driven to business meetings by her chauffeur, and a Lotus Seven she drove for her own pleasure.

"I'll send you over some additional details, some pictures of the car and will set up an early meeting in Dublin, if you are interested," she promised. "I'm seriously thinking of buying one myself."

The TMC Costin had been designed by Frank Costin, of Marcos fame, as a serious potential rival to the Lotus Seven. It was built in Wexford by the Thompson Motor Company (TMC) a small family-owned business run by four brothers, Val, Peter, Sean and Anthony Thompson. It had a fibreglass body, a unique Costin designed chassis and was available in a choice of four Ford engine sizes. The brothers claimed that the TMC Costin performed just as well as the Lotus Seven but had a larger boot space and an option to add two rear facing child seats.

The car had proved its credentials on the racetrack but efforts to sell it to the consumer market had been less successful.

After discussions with my colleagues in the UK and Ireland, it was decided to invest in two vehicles that we would use for promotional purposes. Thompson Motors Company agreed that both cars would be fully customised in Wrangler blue and yellow livery. I agreed to promote the TMC connection using our PR operations in both the UK and Ireland.

The Wrangler TMC Costin cars were ready in the early part of 1987. A decision was made to launch them in Ireland. Press interest had been high. The idea of a major brand like Wrangler investing in an Irish built sports car had proved exceptionally newsworthy.

What we really needed was a high-profile person to "do the honours."

Noelle Campbell Sharp used her connections and announced that Charles Haughey would be happy to preside over the launch. He had just been elected to a third term as Taoiseach, (Prime Minister of Ireland). Having the head of government endorsing the launch was as good as it gets.

Unfortunately, I was not able to attend as I had business elsewhere in Europe.

Our PR people wanted to take advantage of all photo opportunities. They required a senior representative of Wrangler to present the cheque to TMC. Charles Haughey would then be asked to symbolically hand over the car keys. It was decided that the Financial Controller for Wrangler in Ireland would represent the company. Barry Hillier was English, his wife Helen was Irish. He had previously worked in financial control in the UK.

One of the cars was driven to the Irish Parliament Building on a trailer and unloaded at a side entrance. The plan was that Barry would wait in the car, the Taoiseach would get in. Barry would then drive the TMC Costin a short distance to the front of the building where the press would be waiting.

Barry sat in the car with the engine running. After what seemed an age, the door was flung open, and a man jumped into the passenger seat. "Who the hell are you?" the man asked.

"I'm Barry Hillier of Wrangler Jeans," Barry replied. He told me afterwards that he almost responded, "Who the hell are you?"

"Pleased to meet you, I'm Charlie Haughey," his passenger said, extending his hand and shaking Barry's.

Seemingly, none of Taoiseach's entourage had explained what exactly was going on. Barry was quite taken aback by the informality of it all.

The rest of the presentation went perfectly to plan. Media response was excellent, resulting in positive coverage across Ireland and the UK.

The Wrangler Factor Promotion

Around July of 1986, Alistair Archer of Counterpunch, came back to me with his "big idea" for the major promotion that was scheduled to take place during the Wrangler Anniversary year.

Since 1977, a television programme called "The Krypton Factor" had captured the hearts and minds of ITV viewers. A mixture of brainpower and physical prowess, it put contestants through a series of tests that included studio based cryptic, brain-teasing puzzles followed by outdoor physical pursuits against the clock. Points were awarded for each element and the leading points scorer, at the end of all the tests, was declared overall prize-winner.

The programme was hosted by former sports journalist and Granada Television news anchor, Gordon Burns.

"Our idea is called the "Wrangler Factor," explained Alistair. "The competition will involve an instore competition run right across the UK and Ireland. Entry will be open to all customers who purchase a pair of Wrangler jeans during the promotion period. They will be required to answer a series of questions about the Wrangler brand and then complete a tie-break question 'I like Wrangler Jeans because…………?"

"Is that all?" I queried.

"No. There is more," replied Alistair warming to his task. "The competition is designed to produce regional winners. The prize for each regional winner will be an all-expenses paid weekend away for them and a guest. During the weekend, they will compete in several sports-based activities. The overall winner will be the person accumulating most points across all activities. That person will be the sole recipient of the "Wrangler Factor Award" and will receive an exclusive, big value prize," he concluded.

I liked the concept!

Not only was it linked to a Wrangler jeans purchase, but the format also ensured that the final prize would be contested by a person from every region across the UK and that we could also include the Republic of Ireland.

Public relations possibilities were endless!

We decided to develop the idea with a view to launching it at the trade shows, for the Spring 1987 ranges. These were taking place in September 1986.

The competition would run across the key selling period from the beginning of April to the end of June 1987.

Alistair went away to "put some flesh on the concept."

I talked to our area sales managers to determine how we would formulate competition regions that would incorporate all the existing Wrangler sales areas. After a lot of heated discussion, agreement was finally reached. The regions were designated as Scotland, Northern Ireland, Wales and the South West of England, North West, North East, East Midlands, West Midlands, London & South East, of England and The Republic of Ireland.

A few weeks later, I met up with Alistair to finalise the details.

He had some unexpected, good news. Gordon Burns, the presenter of "The Krypton Factor" had agreed to host the weekend final.

Counterpunch had contacted his agent as a long shot not really expecting a positive response. In 1986, Gordon had just joined a light entertainment programme on ITV called "Surprise, Surprise," as a roving reporter. Developed in around 1984 as a vehicle for Cilla Black, the show involved delivering surprises for the public and members of the audience.

After a slow start, it had become extremely popular.

When Gordon Burns joined, it occupied a prime-time slot on a Sunday evening and was one of the top-rated programmes across the networks. His regular appearances had increased his profile considerably.

Alistair had been looking for a venue for the final.

By chance, he had come across a company called Mithril Racing who had their headquarters at the former Goodwood Motor Circuit. The company had been formed around three years earlier and provided series of track-based activities for motor sport enthusiasts.

Through their Sales Director, Gavin Watson, they were keen to expand their activities to attract corporate organisations.

We arranged to go down to Goodwood and see exactly what their extended corporate offering included. It also provided us with an opportunity to look at hotels in the area that we might use as a base for the weekend. Three weeks later, Alistair drove me down to the venue to meet up with Gavin.

Arrangements had been made for us to stay overnight at a country house hotel near Bognor Regis, about 12 miles from Goodwood. With a limited number of bedrooms and a reputation for excellent service and food, Gavin felt that it would be prove an ideal base for the competition winners.

"I am sure that we can come up with a great package for you," Gavin explained when we met up with him. "I will be honest with you both, the corporate market is an area we want to engage more with. The endorsement of a brand name like Wrangler will help to considerably boost our marketing efforts." he continued.

Mithril had many event options available to us. A 'Wings and Wheels" package included driving 'classic' cars, Kart Racing and what was described as a "hands-on flying lesson in a Tiger Moth." These events were centred on the Goodwood Motor Circuit.

The nearby Goodwood Park, owned by the Earl of March, was the venue for off-track activities such as 'Clay Pigeon Shooting Competitions,' 'Archery,' 'Quad Bike time trials and manoeuvring contests' and 'Mad Moke' racing over a specially designed course.

We were "blown away" by the range of experiences that Mithril could provide. During lunch at their on-site facility, we also met other members of the team and were very impressed with the level of catering services available. There was no doubt in our minds, whatever the final package of events we decided on, our prize winners would be treated to "an experience of a lifetime!"

I was clear, in selecting the final mix, we should ensure that there must be a way of determining how a sliding scale of points could be allocated to each contestant based on their competitive ability over each event.

The winner of the "Grand Prize" would be the contestant who accumulated the highest number of points at the end of the weekend.

Gavin had given us a ballpark price covering the nine finalists and their partners. Subject to time constraints, their partners should be able to try out most of the activities but on a non-competitive basis.

Back in the office, I met up with Alistair to finalise the promotion package. We were agreed that the Mithril weekend was an excellent prize to reward the regional winners. A Wrangler outfit would also be also provided for each of them.

"How are we going to top that for the overall winner?" Alistair queried.

I suddenly had a flash of inspiration. "What about a hand-built sports car?" I suggested.

For some time, I had been wondering how we might maximise the promotional possibilities of the two TMC Costin cars being customised in the Thompson Motors Company workshop in Ireland.

It occurred to me that one could be used as the main prize in the "Wrangler Factor" promotion. The other could then be used for Wrangler promotional events across the UK and Ireland.

Alistair agreed this was a great idea.

We determined that the reward for the final challenge would not be revealed before an overall winner had been announced. Publicity would be maximised if the nature of the main prize remained a secret until the award presentations at Goodwood.

The point-of-sale material and public relations activity would concentrate on the "Wrangler Factor" regional competitions and the Gordon Burns hosted, competition final weekend where the "mystery prize" would be awarded.

From the list provided by Mithril, we chose the activities we considered best represented the combination of skill sets required of our "Wrangler Factor" finalists. These included 'Archery,' 'Clay Pigeon Shooting,' 'Kart Racing', 'Quad Bike time trial contest,' 'Mad Moke' racing, and, as a fitting finale, a 'Tiger Moth "hands on" Trial Lesson.'

Counterpunch designed a special "Wrangler Factor" logo that was used on a promotion leaflet to sell the competition to the trade and point of sale material to promote it to their customers. The Wrangler salesforce reported it had been well received and that entries far exceeded expectations.

Our public relations machine swung into action when the regional winners were finally announced at the end of July 1987. Press photo calls were set up at retailers where the winning entries had originated. Local personalities were recruited to make award presentations to the winners. Media interest was high and resulted in considerable coverage on regional television news programmes, local radio, and the press.

The "Grand Prize" they would be competing for during the Mithril weekend remained a closely guarded secret!

A meeting was set up with Gordon Burns to enable us to brief him about the winners and their partners who would be coming with them to the finals weekend.

Alistair and the Counterpunch team had worked closely with Gavin Watson of Mithril to determine how a points system would be applied to each of the competitive events, based on the level of competence displayed.

Gordon Burns was asked to brief competitors after dinner at the hotel on the night before competition started. He would also help to officiate at the start of each task and remind competitors how the points system would be determined.

Presentation of medals, to the winners of each competitive element, would made by Gordon after lunch on the last day. He would then announce the name of the overall winner and the "Grand Prize" would be revealed and presented.

Early in September 1987, Alistair and I made the trip to the country house hotel near Bognor Regis we had chosen as our base for the "Wrangler Factor" weekend.

Arrangements had been made to transport all the finalists and their guests from their homes to the closest airport or train station. Cars were on hand at their arrival point to complete the onward transfer to the hotel.

Despite the complexities involved, thankfully everything ran like clockwork!

By the middle of the first afternoon, all our finalists, and Gordon Burns, had arrived safely, booked into their rooms, and received their welcome packs. These contained a full programme itinerary for the following two days of competition.

A pre-dinner welcome drinks reception kicked off proceedings. This enabled Gordon, Alistair, and me, to circulate and introduce ourselves to the finalists and their guests.

It also created an opportunity for everyone to relax and to get to know each other before the real competition began.

The age spread of the regional winners was a close reflexion of the demographics of the Wrangler brand across the UK and Ireland. The youngest competitor was in their early 20's the oldest in their late forties. Of the nine regional winners there were six men and three women.

After dinner, Gordon Burns briefed the guests about what would be happening over the following two days. He referred to the judging process and how the points would be allocated over each event.

The highest points scorer over the six events would be awarded the "Wrangler Factor" mystery prize.

Even he was not privy to exactly what the overall winner's prize would be!

His easy manner captivated his audience. During his briefing, he provided many anecdotes about his time on the "Krypton Factor" and about his working relationship with Cilla Black on "Surprise, Surprise."

At the end of dinner, we handed out two specially designed "Wrangler Factor" t-shirts to every competitor and guest. These were to be worn throughout the competition.

Any specialised event clothing was being supplied by Mithril.

Guests were briefed that they would be picked up by coach at 8.30am next morning and transported to Goodwood for the first element of the competitive weekend.

An early night, followed by an early breakfast was recommended, but not obligatory. Despite the obvious attraction of the hotel bar, everyone took the advice offered. Next morning, they were all ready and waiting, "bright eyed and bushy tailed," when the coach arrived.

Everyone was dressed in their Wrangler jeans, and the t-shirts we had provided, including Gordon Burns. Admittedly, the pair worn by our host had not been purchased by him, they had been supplied by us.

Before lunch, on the first day of competition, activities comprised the more leisurely country pursuits of 'Clay Pigeon Shooting' and 'Archery.' It was clear from the onset that competition was going to be fierce. Despite any firm evidence, I had a distinct feeling that some of our finalists had been practicing beforehand.

Mithril had organised a separate Archery competition for guests of the finalists. This enabled Alistair Archer, Gordon Burns and me to also join in the fun. I can't remember who came out on top, but I have a photograph of me pulling my arrows out of the middle of the target.

Even if I say so myself, I seemed to have achieved a reasonably high score!

After a buffet lunch, in our marquee erected on the Goodwood Estate, the competition really went up several notches.

The 'Quad bike time trial' required a combination of driving skill and balance, over a specially designed uphill obstacle course, against the clock.

Our Mithril expert made it look easy when he demonstrated what our contestants were expected to do to achieve top marks. The reality proved to very different. The uphill, muddy course literally separated "the men and women from the boys and girls."

By contrast, the final event of the day, 'Mad Moke' racing, involved speed, skill, and ultra-competitiveness.

All the finalists were involved in a race around a specially laid down course that included road humps. These had been designed to be driven over at top speed causing the 'Mokes' to become airborne.

Unlike the Quad bike course, the track was extremely dry. An ensuing dust cloud made visibility difficult for every driver, except the leader. Key to success, involved getting into an early lead on the first of the multiple lap race. Each 'Moke' was fitted with balance bars. These made them very stable and perfectly safe for the drivers should they fail to negotiate a road hump cleanly.

Once more, the non-competitors were given an opportunity to "enjoy the thrill and spills" during their own race after the main event. Alistair Archer showed his true competitiveness by surging into the lead during the first lap. He then held on until the finishing line. I was just behind him after driving 'blind' for much of the race because of the dust cloud thrown up by Alistair's vehicle in front.

Dinner that evening was a very different affair from the more formal proceedings of the first evening. Everyone was "buzzing from the excitement of a very competitive day." Whilst none of the finalists had any idea of how they were placed in the overall competition, they all had a story to tell about their performances during the activities they had participated in.

It was clear that they all felt they were in with a chance of carrying off the "Wrangler Factor" title and, with it, the mystery prize. With seemingly everything the play for, they needed no encouragement to retire early and prepare for the "all or nothing final day sessions."

Following breakfast on the Sunday morning, we all checked out of the hotel and boarded our coach for the Goodwood Motor Circuit. Here we were greeted by Gavin Watson and the Mithril team.

The final two events in the "Wrangler Factor" involved 'Kart racing' and a 'Tiger Moth 'hands-on' Trial.'

The first event was hotly contested by all the finalists. The nature of the Tiger Moth challenge remained something of a mystery for everyone concerned!

After a refreshing break for non-alcoholic drinks, we led the competitors into a "flight briefing room." This was a small conference facility with chairs laid out in theatre style in front of a 'white board.' On the wall was a large photograph of a Tiger Moth Biplane.

If they were expecting to be tested in some sort of flight simulator, they were now beginning to realise that they would be taking a flight in the real aircraft!

After we had all taken our seats, one of the Mithril instructors started the briefing. "You will each be taking a 15-minute flight in a real plane," he explained. "Our pilot is very experienced but is required to fully brief you in all aspects of health and safety before take-off," he continued.

As if on cue, the door to the room was theatrically thrown open and in burst the pilot!

Dressed in World War 1 flying gear complete with flying jacket, leather helmet and goggles, he was also sporting a long, knitted scarf that flowed behind him. He looked like the embodiment of James Bigglesworth ("Biggles") the fictional pilot hero of the adventure books written by W.E. Johns.

Our "Biggles" was no character from fiction. He was the real deal!

Using his white board, he explained that the flight path for each of our finalists would take them over the sea. "Everything is perfectly safe," he assured them. "If you feel ill during the flight, please use the sick bag under your seat. If you feel you can't reach it in time, please ensure you are ill over the left-hand side of the cabin so that the prevailing wind will blow it away from the aircraft," he continued.

When the safety check was completed, he called out the name of the first finalist who was handed their own flying gear and then led out to the aircraft.

Whilst the first flight was underway, the remaining finalist changed into their flying gear ready for their turn to arrive.

None of our finalists were aware exactly how a skill factor would be introduced and how the points would be determined. To ensure that this remained a secret until they were in the air, none of the returning pilots would be allowed to return to the holding area where their fellow finalists were awaiting their turn.

When they were in the air, "Biggles" told them that once they were over the sea, they would be carrying out a "few aerobatic moves." He also advised that the Tiger Moth, they were flying in, was a dual control trainer and explained to them what to do in the "unlikely event that they would have to take control of the aircraft." The aerobatic moves included a few tight turns and banking procedures followed by a full loop the loop.

On the way back to Goodwood, contestants were advised by "Biggles" that they were now "in control of the aircraft." How each reacted to the instruction and how well they performed for the few minutes they were "flying the plane," was the basis of the skills-based points allocated.

Without exception, all our contestants thoroughly enjoyed the experience!

When the finalists had changed out of their flying kit and had regained their composure, we all boarded our coach for the short drive to our marquee in Goodwood Park.

Nobody present, except Alistair and me, had any idea what the mystery prize was. We wanted to keep this quiet until the very last moment for maximum impact.

I had organised for one of our Field Promotion Representatives, to bring the car down on a trailer from Calverton. He had stayed in another hotel locally that had an overnight garage facility. In the morning he had parked his car, and covered trailer, in a car park close to where our marquee was located.

Our PR people had driven up from London. They had organised a press photo opportunity and were liaising with Alistair and the Wrangler FPR, to ensure that the TMC Costin car would be unveiled at just the right moment.

Lunch was a very relaxed affair. Contestants, their guests and invited media, were taking full advantage of the excellent food and drink provided.

Whilst this was going on, the Mithril team were determining the winners of the individual tasks and totting up the cumulative scores of every contestant to determine the overall "Wrangler Factor" competition winner.

Before the presentations took place, we had briefed Gordon Burns with names of the winners of each individual event. He was also advised who was winner of the overall prize. Apart from knowing that the person concerned would win a trophy, he was not told about the TMC Costin car that he would also be handing over as the "mystery prize."

Whilst the prize presentation was underway, the Wrangler PR team was busy priming the press and ensuring the TMC car was being unloaded from the trailer and positioned close to the marquee for its grand entrance.

Gordon handed the individual event winners with their trophies and medals to all the competing finalists.

At last, the winner of the "Wrangler Factor" was revealed!

Much to the dismay of the younger contestants, he turned out to be one of the oldest. From memory, I believe he came from the Solihull area of the West Midlands and was in his late 40's. He had managed to accumulate good scores in all the events but had particularly distinguished himself in events where skill, and not raw speed, was required.

Just before Gordon presented him with the winner's trophy, I handed over a note giving details of the mystery prize.

"Now you may all be wondering exactly what the mystery prize is that our winner will be taking away with his trophy," Gordon said after the presentation of the

"Wrangler Factor" trophy had taken place. "We were going to have a 'drum roll' but I have something more dramatic in mind," he continued.

This was the cue to the Wrangler FPR, to switch the ignition and loudly rev the engine of the TMC. The entrance to the marquee was held open and the car roared into view.

To say that our winner was speechless was something of an understatement. He could scarcely believe his eyes!

Gordon handed him the keys whilst explaining that the vehicle he had won was one of only two, especially hand-built for Wrangler. Not only had he won the car, but Wrangler would also tax and insure it for one year.

At this point he was congratulated by all the other competitors and their guests including his wife. Our PR people organised the press photographs along with several radio interviews. Organised mayhem ensued for the next half hour whilst all this was taking place.

I remember thinking that it was just as well that the winner had turned out to be a mature driver with a clean license and no pending endorsements. As it was, the cost of insuring the car for a year was more than £1750. This was a very high figure for car insurance back in 1987.

Unfortunately, our winner was unable to drive the vehicle home on the day. All formalities of taxing, and insuring the vehicle, had to be taken care of first.

It provided another opportunity for our PR agency to obtain even more press and TV coverage when the car was finally handed over to our winner. This took place at a retail outlet in the West Midlands where he had entered the "Wrangler Factor" competition all those months earlier.

Whilst the TMC Costin provided high profile publicity for Wrangler, the same cannot be said for its manufacturers, Thompson Motor Company of Wexford in Ireland. Their UK distribution arm was unable to capitalise on the free publicity that the Wrangler promotion had generated. The company ceased production and filed for bankruptcy at the end of 1987.

Figures vary as to exactly how many of the cars were finally manufactured. One source quotes a total of 26. Another suggests it was 39. Today they are rare and much sought after by collectors.

I hope our competition winner had many happy hours driving it and would like to think that someone, somewhere, is still its proud owner. It would be safe to assume that its value today will be many times the figure that Wrangler paid for it in 1987.

The "Wrangler Factor" competition proved the be last major national consumer sales promotion that I instigated during my time with the company!

This had been the impact of several different factors. These included a change in the marketing direction of the Wrangler brand, resulting from our takeover by the VF Corporation, and pressure to increase our top line advertising spend.

Our emphasis changed from a policy of incentivising the consumer to purchase from our retailer customers. In a more competitive environment, it had become more important to encourage retail staff to merchandise and sell the Wrangler brand at the point of purchase over that of our many competitors.

Chapter Nineteen

Product Merchandising at the point of purchase

Around 1978, Wrangler became the first company to introduce the food concept of instore merchandising to the clothing industry. When I had first floated the concept in 1975, it was met with much scepticism. This was not surprising. At that time, demand for the Wrangler product far exceeded the ability of Blue Bell Apparel to supply.

As the supply chain improved and the market continued to grow, increasing Wrangler market share became a prime motivator.

I was given the green light to hire a team of instore merchandisers that I named Field Promotion Representatives.

Field Promotion Representation

The original four FPR's had a wide range of differing backgrounds that included window dressing, sales promotion, exhibitions, and advertising experience.

Initially, their responsibilities covered three different functions: -

To merchandise the Wrangler brand at the point of sale.

To merchandise the Wrangler Advertising instore.

To devise, sell in and implement a programme of sales promotion activity within their area of responsibility.

Working together as a close-knit team, with support from our in-house and external advertising, marketing, and public relations personnel, they quickly established a highly visible presence within key retailers.

Our main competitors were all playing catch-up whilst we continued to innovate and expand the service.

During the early 1980's, the emphasis of our marketing effort changed from brand to product promotion.

Our FPR's were concentrating their activity on co-ordination of the Wrangler product to ensure that advertised merchandise was highlighted at the point of sale. The Wrangler brand was still being strongly featured using cosmetic branding, permanent, branded point of sale units, promotional back up in shop windows and at the point of sale.

In 1981, we had developed an in-store merchandising system. The use of Wrangler colours, blue for the units and yellow for the Wrangler branding on them, made them highly visible in retail stores.

By 1983 the system had undergone several changes, but we were concerned that the heavy Wrangler brand projection had left the system looking somewhat dated. Retail merchandising was becoming more sophisticated and there was a requirement for greater flexibility in the method of garment presentation with more emphasis on product colour coordination.

Following discussions with our existing manufacturer, they had come up with an updated design which met all the new criteria and was more aesthetically pleasing than the existing units.

A new team of young designers had come up with a totally different creative design. After discussions with the FPR's, and through them, key retailers, it was decided to remain with our existing supplier.

More pressing was a need to look at the way that garments were presented on the shelf. Initially, we had taken on board the presentation that had been developed in the USA. This was fine when brand marketing was our key objective and "American" imagery on the garments was a major benefit.

Following the change to product promotion in our advertising, our research indicated that the image of the Wrangler product lagged some way behind that of the Wrangler brand.

CDP, our advertising agency, felt the garment ticketing presentation could be a contributory factor. They recommended that we speak to the Whitmore Thomas Design Group.

Whitmore Thomas Design Group

The company had been formed by Steve Thomas and Tim Whitmore. Both were graduates of the Chelsea School of Art and their collaboration had produced a fine portfolio of work that included everything from iconic fashion brands to blue chip organisations.

My first meeting with Steve Thomas took place in Calverton around September 1983.

Design companies of that period kept their designers away from potential clients. Perhaps they feared that creative people were too volatile to attend client meetings, because they might express controversial opinions that might jeopardise the client pitch.

Smart suited, hot shot sales professionals were employed to seal the deal.

I was not looking to employ a sales professional. Opinionated creatives prepared to challenge the status quo and back up their opinions with cutting edge design to achieve, even exceed expectations, was what Wrangler needed.

Steve arrived complete with shoulder length hair, designer stubble (decades ahead of its time), open-necked designer shirt, jeans (not Wrangler jeans, I noted at the time) and an expensive tailored jacket. Sitting down opposite me, he crossed his jeans clad legs to expose pointed "winkle picker" shoes. They could have been cowboy boots.

Clearly, Steve was a man full of fashion contradictions about himself and his work experience!

In the mid-seventies, he had helped to create Biba, one of the unique lifestyle brands in fashion retailing. He had spent five years working with Paul McCartney designing his recording studios, offices, farms, and various homesteads.

The Whitmore Thomas portfolio was full of cutting-edge design work.

Steve was somewhat self-depreciating. His lack of ego, in a world full of inflated egos, was a breath of fresh air!

It is difficult to describe an individual's personality, especially after so many years. On his website, the man himself had done this for me in a profile that read: -

"Having acquired a full house of utterly useless science A's, he managed to further upset an already confused family by insisting on attending Chelsea School of Art as a painter. Thus grantless & homeless, but free & still clueless, the King's Road was his patch in the early '60s – working as a fashion model for the education, and as a waiter for the food.

Mid-sixties, the rock'n'roll years, working with a highly successful American record producer who possessed a wicked array of personal hang-ups - his age, his height, being American & being successful. Fortunately, being out of his depth, Thomas paid little attention & just did the clubs, the drugs & the groupies, picking up all sorts including some design work.

Having done the music biz, by unexpected popular demand he formed the original Whitmore-Thomas design group with Tim Whitmore, another ex-Chelsea painter.

From the Rolling Stones to the Blue Chips, they managed by luck, pleading & bribery to work on some truly iconic projects around the world & have a thoroughly wondrous time. Spoilt jammy b*****d."

I was convinced Whitmore Thomas was the company to deliver the creative goods but needed to be sure they would be able to develop a fully integrated design concept.

Two weeks later, Dick Webzell, Kevin Black and I met up with Steve and Tim at our London showroom.

Having visited a cross section of retailers, examined the presentation of fashion jeans brands, including all our competitors, they presented their findings.

Some Wrangler garments had as many as 5 different tickets.

Size and style details were difficult to find.

The overprinting on information tickets was not up to the quality standards expected of a quality garment.

Positioning of the ticket on the garment was especially important.

We were astonished. It is said that familiarity breeds contempt. Having invested so much time on marketing the brand, it was clear that we had been "unable to see the wood for the trees" when it came to the presentation on the product.

In November 1983, Whitmore Thomas was contracted to provide a new design concept.

Steve Thomas and his team had a reputation for delivering creative design solutions. It quickly became clear to us, that they were also very adept at developing a strategic approach that was far more inclusive than just ticketing and labelling design.

Working closely with the Wrangler factory in Falkirk, they established a rapport with the engineers who were always sceptical about "the marketing people in Calverton getting involved in the production process."

Whitmore Thomas identified that fine tweaking of the existing label printing machinery would dramatically improve the print quality.

A lead time for implementation was proposed, it enabled buyers at the factory to run down their ticketing stocks. The proposal to reduce the overall number of tickets on each garment would reduce the cost per jean. This was something engineers in the factory were always keen to support. With the factory on board, Steve produced his design concept proposals and implementation recommendations.

New ticketing would go into production at the end of September 1984. It would be launched to the menswear trade as part of the sell-in of Spring 1985 ranges.

All informative ticketing details would be confined to the waistband of the jeans. Research undertaken by Whitmore Thomas, had determined that this is where the consumer looked first.

The design of waistband labels was more relevant than the labels they were replacing. More attention had been focused on the readability of information that the consumer wanted (waist size, leg length and style information) than projection of fashion imagery.

A second image ticket had been designed for each of the jeans, cords, chino products. Care had been taken to ensure it was positioned on the product in a way that made it visible, without being unsightly, irrespective of the method of merchandising employed by individual retailers.

On the denim jeans product line, Steve and his design team had retained those elements of the original American western theme that were integral to the established strength of the Wrangler brand. At the same time, they had made the whole range of tickets relevant to the more fashion orientated market.

The concept was well received by the Wrangler salesforce, retail trade and customers.

It says a lot for the vision of Whitmore Thomas that the system remained in place throughout most of the 1980's.

I kept in touch with Steve Thomas throughout this period. In my collection of Wrangler memorabilia, I came across a box containing a "Whitmore Thomas 21st Anniversary tile." Steve and his team sent to me as a Christmas greeting in December 1989.

Finding this prompted me to see what Steve Thomas had been up to in the intervening years. I tracked him down on LinkedIn. Having spent some time away from the design scene he had now returned as a freelance operator.

Older and wiser, he retained his sardonic, self-depreciating sense of humour although, like me, he now sported considerably less facial hair.

Addison Design Consultants

During the latter part of the 1980's, Wrangler Limited went through a traumatic period. After the stability of many years with Dick Webzell at the reigns, the company had experienced a management buy-out followed by a merger with the VF Corporation.

By the middle of 1988, we had waved goodbye to two Managing Directors and were in the process of welcoming on board a third. There had also been changes in the management of the product development process.

As always with new brooms, there is also an inevitable fine-tuning of direction. As the 1980's had progressed, the jeans market had matured from a commodity to a fashion staple. Our new men had a lot of ideas for "breathing new life" into the Wrangler product ranges.

Whitmore Thomas' design philosophy had been as much about where the ticket was placed on product, as the image portrayed.

The Wrangler product development team were proposing the denim jeans range for Autumn 1989, should be expanded from "authentic originals" to include "fashion classics" and "more leading- edge" jeans designs.

As the women's range had grown, it was also felt that classic male imagery on our ticketing required toning down and made more feminine. These were fundamental changes that would require a review of the way Wrangler ranges should be presented at the point of sale.

I was in favour of calling back Whitmore Thomas to carry out a re-design.

My new colleagues felt that a new look would only be achieved if the existing presentation was viewed through a different set of eyes.

Our advertising agency, BBDO had made several recommendations.

After meetings, and in-depth discussions, with a short list of potential candidates, Addison Design Consultants was appointed in the summer of 1988.

We all were impressed by their portfolio of work but what really clinched their appointment was their philosophy. "We at Addison Design Consultants believe our role is to enable our clients to identify their vision and express it effectively in everything they do. We have a strong belief in breaking new creative ground for clear-cut marketing reasons."

I was happy Addison were on our wavelength and would be able build on the strong Wrangler image we had created, and invested so heavily in.

We had not just appointed them to produce a new set of designs for our garment ticketing. Their brief was to create a different look. At the same time, we didn't want to lose any of the strengths of the existing Wrangler imagery.

At the first meeting after their appointment, the Addison team presented several "styling boards" to reflect the main jeans ranges. As well as helping to crystallise the image of each one, they demonstrated the way the word Wrangler had been presented in different forms, as new products had been added to the line.

This piece meal approach had defeated the aim of linking new product additions with our "authentic jeans" base.

Addison recommended that the design exercise needed to be split. The first stage would address how to tie in the Wrangler identity across the proposed product ranges.

The second stage would address the ticketing designs.

We were worried about any heavy-handed use of obvious cowboy associations but were keen to hold on to the brands strong American western traditions.

At our second meeting, Addison presented their design ideas for the use of the Wrangler logo across all product ranges.

We were advised that they had treated this task as a corporate branding exercise by "tying into the products." They had ended up basing everything around the familiar rope logo that had first being used when the Wrangler jean had been launched in 1947.

For the "Men's Authentic Western jeans range" they recommended it should be used in conjunction with the slogan "BORN IN THE USA."

On the "Men's Classic range," the Wrangler rope logo had the word "CLASSICS" incorporated underneath it.

For the "Men's fashion jeans" the "rope W'" was used behind a typeset version of the Wrangler logo with the word "PLUS" alongside.

The "Men's range of Chino's" also used the "rope W" behind the typeset Wrangler logo.

There was one other jeans style in our new Menswear range that did not fall under any of the categories. Until the mid-1980's, all Wrangler Jeans had been produced using a 14¾ oz. left hand, broken twill (LHT). This had many unique characteristics that set it apart from the 14¾ oz. right hand twill (RHT) used by every other manufacturer.

Cost constraints had forced the company to move over to RHT.

Our new product development team had introduced a single garment in 14¾ oz. broken twill denim for the Autumn 1989 range. It was not designed in the authentic Wrangler western jeans style. In fact, it was something of a hybrid. The Addison team recommended that this stand-alone product should be named "Wrangler Promos." This logo was used alongside the slogan "A new experience in jeans." The leather-look waistband patch featured the new logo and slogan. It also emphasised the broken twill denim credentials and style qualities with the words, "A promise of something else…smooth, durable and comfortable."

For the women's jeans ranges, the rope idea had been feminised by incorporating a "red ribbon W" behind the word Wrangler with the wording "UNIQUE STYLING FEATURES" underneath.

The Wrangler marketing team approved logo recommendations. Addison's team went away to work up the designs for the tickets.

When the final designs were submitted, we were pleased they had come up with a Western landscape solution for all the western jeans ranges. The design concept incorporated different photographic images from mid-west America that were relevant to a specific product range.

For instance, the image recommended for the "Authentic Denim Jeans'" featured a rustic boundary fence with the desert and bluffs beyond. It was an iconic, timeless American cowboy country image!

Their idea of using photography in this way, was new to the jeans market. The consistent wedge shape of the tickets helped to tie together individual product ranges and enhanced overall product identity.

The ticket for the "Chino" range projected the product as "a quality, superior Chino Pant." This reinforced all the traditional Wrangler product values.

We were very happy with the clear identity that Addison had developed. They had been asked to differentiate Wrangler product ranges and to build on the strengths of the Wrangler image at the point of purchase.

When the new concept was launched to the trade in February 1989, as part of the sell in of Autumn 1989 range, I was quoted as saying, "Ours is a fast-moving business but one where clear identity is vital. What Addison did was to inject lots of creative input but also help control and discipline it all."

When I uttered those words, I did so on the assumption that the new look would have enough longevity to establish itself in the market.

This did not turn out to be the case!

Design Associates

John Hart, Marketing Director of Levi's, had been appointed by Ralph Huschle to the position of Managing Director of Wrangler UK. He had brought in Robin Hollick to run the product development team and Kelvin Vidler as National Sales Manager.

Both had worked with John at Levi's!

Simons Palmer had been appointed as our new Advertising Agency at the end of 1989 and their recommendation to change the image of the Wrangler product away from its mid-western American heritage to a more American urban imagery, had led to the development of the "Crosstown Traffic" advertising campaign.

The campaign had polarised opinion, as the agency had promised it would!

Once again, there was a disparity between the recently introduced image of our product at the point of sale, and that being projected through our advertising.

When Ralph Huschle left the company, John Hart took his place as VF Vice President for the Wrangler brand in Europe. He appointed Alf Evans as Managing Director of Wrangler UK.

It was "all change" at the top once more!

The VF company had been busy negotiating with Wrangler licensees in Europe to end their agreements and bring the brand back under the company's control.

International brand development research I had undertaken, had shown that the image of the Wrangler brand had been diluted across most of the main markets across Europe.

The UK and northern Europe, who had remained wholly owned subsidiaries, continued to present a consistent brand image and had maintained their brand share.

John Hart felt it was necessary to begin the development of a European product line. Once this had been achieved, thought could be given to rolling out a Pan-European advertising campaign. He was convinced this would bring economies of scale and help to relaunch Wrangler, across all markets.

I was aware how difficult this had proved in the past, when all the major countries in Europe had been operated by separate, wholly owned subsidiaries.

Both John Hart and Robin Hollick were unencumbered by the problems of the past. I realised that I had to step back and go with the flow, otherwise my comments might be construed as obstructive. Having said that, I had considered myself guardian of the brand values that had enabled Wrangler to become a major player in the UK market.

Simons Palmer felt the ticketing on the product should reflect the new rugged urban American image projected by the "Crosstown Traffic" advertising.

The Wrangler team, quite rightly, did not want to lose the heritage of the brand.

Robin and John were aware that the success of the Levi's jeans brand, developed in 1873 by Levi Strauss and Jacob Davis, was based on its longevity. This enabled the company, as the main player across Europe, to lay claim to have been the creators of "the first pair of blue jeans."

This message had been consistent on its product ticketing over all the intervening years!

The Blue Bell company traced its origins back to 1904, but only purchased the Wrangler brand from the Casey Jones Workwear Company in 1943. In 1947, Blue Bell designed and developed the first five-pocket Western jean style and introduced it to the market under the Wrangler brand name.

To celebrate the brands 40th birthday in 1987, I had commissioned the production, by Birmingham Mint, of a unique "Wrangler Dollar." The Obverse design celebrated the birth of the brand with the words, "Born in the USA 1947." "Wrangler Heritage" using the rope logo, reinforced by cowboy imagery, appeared on the reverse.

It was packaged in a specially designed, six paged coin holder that told the Wrangler story. The back page brought that story up to date.

"In 1986 fashion has gone full circle yet again. The "classic" look is back along with the excitement of the 50's and 60's, blue denim, and the retro look, is high on the shopping list of young fashion leaders. Wrangler have all the permutations, washed, stonewashed, bleached, stonebleached. But it's the Western theme that's important. Cult figures of the fifties are being given the star treatment – and Wrangler is up there with the big names – as a leader in branded fashion leisurewear."

In PR terms, Levi's had been able to lay claim to the origins of the denim jean. Nobody could take that away from them. Similarly, Wrangler had ownership of the origin of the design for five-pocket Western jeans that, despite any claims to the contrary, was still the predominant style of jeans in the early 1990's.

The Wrangler brand had entered the VF Corporation stable of brands when it acquired Blue Bell in 1986. H D Lee had been similarly acquired in 1969.

VF corporation was established as the Reading Glove and Mitten Manufacturing Company in 1899. When it began manufacturing undergarments in 1919, it changed its name to Vanity Fair Mills. In 1969, it changed its name again, to the VF Corporation.

Lee Jeans, our sister brand in the VF stable, was established as a wholesale grocery distributor in 1889. The company entered the clothing manufacturing industry in 1912 because it was unhappy with the quality and inconsistent delivery of workwear from its suppliers.

John Hart, Robin Hollick, and I had been working, together with Design Associates, to develop the product range imagery in a way that would reflect the changes taking place in the market. Our aim was to build on the heritage of the Wrangler brand in the UK. This needed to be achieved in a way that could later be rolled out across all international markets outside the USA.

Design Associates looked at the existing ranges.

"Wrangler Authentic Jeans" was changed to "Authentic Wrangler." This range retained the Wrangler stitched 'W' and leather patch on the back pocket.

"Wrangler Classics" became "Classic Wrangler." It retained the 'W' stitching on the back pockets but included a leather waistband patch featuring the Wrangler rope logo with the word "Classic" above and the line "built strength and endurance" underneath.

The Wrangler designed jeans range was replaced by a more generic term "Wrangler Quality Clothing." 'W' stitching was retained on the back pocket with the rope Wrangler logo, the words "Quality Clothing" and the line "built strength and endurance."

I liked these new concepts and the way that the labelling featured a consistent approach for tops and bottoms.

My only problem was the use of the wording "Established USA 1889." Looking back over time, I assume it referred to the earliest origins of the brands of jeans owned by the VF Corporation. Having spent many years promoting 1947 as the birthdate of the Wrangler Jeans brand, I would have preferred to have retained this date on the new design concepts.

I probably made a case for this to happen at the time but lost out in the discussion.

For the tickets on our jeans, the design company used the "Urban American" imagery from the shoots I had Art Directed in New York and Las Vegas. In addition to image and range logo, the ticket designs also included the product name and style information.

A range logo, size, style name, range name and finish information appeared on the waistband ticket.

Labels for Wrangler tops in the "Authentic Wrangler" and "Wrangler Quality Clothing" ranges featured the range logo on one side and logo and fit guide on the reverse.

It was decided that all the initial orders for the jeans waistband and back pocket tickets would initially be produced under my direct control.

Unlike previous labels, the new designs were intended not only to provide consumer size and range information, but also to reflect the new imagery that had been decided on for the Wrangler brand moving forward.

It was felt necessary for me to work with the print suppliers to set up the initial quality control standards required. The Falkirk factory could then use their local print supplier once the quantities required for the Spring/Summer 1991 had been produced and the delivered.

This ruffled some feathers at the factory. They looked upon the labelling as a cost item that needed to be purchased at the lowest possible price.

General Manager, Frank Dimech, had moved to Calverton to enable him to be closer to the other members of the Wrangler UK Management Team. He understood what we were seeking to achieve with the new product imagery and assured us that the factory would be fully cooperative in the important development stage.

The new back pocket designs also included fit and style name information.

In the "Authentic Wrangler" range, there were 20 different men's, women's, and youth wear style/fit combinations. "Classic Wrangler" featured a further 4 and "Wrangler Quality Clothing" 4 more.

Today, with digital printing processes, this would present no significant production problems Unfortunately, in 1990 the process was in its infancy.

Working closely with our printer in Nottingham, we came up with a cost-effective solution to provide top quality print utilising their 4-colour high speed printing presses.

The waistband tickets were more problematic!

The existing overprinting machine at the Falkirk factory was now "past its sell by date." We convinced Frank Dimech, and his engineers, that a new machine would have to be purchased.

After looking around the market, I found a supplier who manufactured a machine that was capable of not only over-printing the new designs but also providing the required print quality on reel fed labels. The machine was purchased, and the supplier's product engineers visited the factory to demonstrate its capabilities and to train the operators in its use.

The deadline for supply of initial quantities of the new ticketing, for trade show samples, were required by early September 1990. First bulk supplies would be phased into the production line shortly afterwards.

Our printer of the new back pocket tickets was based in Nottingham. They provided proof sample quantities, for the product sales samples and the initial bulk supplies on schedule. It was agreed that the printer would hold the bulk supplies in his warehouse in Nottingham. These would be called off against a schedule, agreed between him and the engineers in Falkirk.

Once again, supply of the waistband tickets proved more problematic.

Proofs for the tickets had arrived on time. They had been signed off by Robin Hollick and me. The new machine had been delivered to Falkirk. An initial supply of blank tickets was being tested by the suppliers working with the factory. Once everyone was happy, the factory engineers would be calling off the quantities required, direct from the suppliers.

I was assured by the manufacturer that everything was running to plan.

Suddenly all hell broke loose!

My internal phone rang, and Frank Dimech asked me to join him in his office. I got on well with Frank. I had known him for years and we had never uttered a cross word between us.

When I entered his office, he was obviously agitated. "YOUR waistband label manufacturers have let us down," he remonstrated. "MY engineers tell me that unless the labels arrive in the next two days, they will have to stop production."

I was surprised. Suddenly the labels were MY labels, not OUR labels. The threat that production would grind to a halt because the tickets had not arrived, was not something to be taken lightly. If it was to happen, it could prove very costly.

"YOUR engineers were working closely with the suppliers. What has gone wrong?" I enquired.

Frank blew his top. It was MY fault apparently. HIS engineers were totally blameless.

Faced by the verbal onslaught I overreacted. "I am not prepared to take this s**t," I shouted, before storming out of his office.

Back in my own office, I took a deep breath. I then picked up the phone and rang my contact at the suppliers. "Apparently, there is a problem with the delivery of the bulk supplies of tickets to Falkirk," I advised him.

He was very surprised to hear this. "I have just had a phone conversation with one of the engineers at the factory," he told me. "They are happy with the test results and the initial quantities they have called off will be delivered tomorrow, as requested," he continued.

I went back to Franks office. He was still seething. I apologised for my outburst and passed on the good news. "I assume there has been a misunderstanding," I suggested.

Frank mumbled under his breath and that, so I thought, was that!

In retrospect, it was not a good move on my part. Within a few months Alf Evans had departed. In his place, Frank Dimech was appointed Managing Director of Wrangler Ltd.

I consoled myself with the thought that Maltese men never bear grudges!

The launch of the new ranges was well received by the trade. How well the consumers reacted, I was never to find out!

PART FIVE

MEETINGS, CONFERENCES AND EXHIBITIONS

Chapter Twenty

Meetings Policy

Throughout a long career, I have spent a lot of time either preparing for or attending meetings of all shapes and sizes.

A lot of these meetings have been interesting, stimulating, and educational. Others however, have been endless exercises in "navel gazing" that served no real purpose and provided no positive end outcomes.

During my time at the CWS Limited, meetings tended to have no plan or direction. They were similar, in many respects, to parliamentary sub-committees. At these, attendees try to win points, by endlessly putting down other attendees, in an on-going attempt to make themselves seem superior to their peers.

Perhaps this was not surprising. The Co-op movement was, and I presume still is, a very politically motivated organisation!

Around 1973, an attempt was made to drag to CWS into the 20th century by getting the senior management to adopt a more modern approach to running the organisation.

Apart from introducing a state-of-the-art job evaluation system, the HR Department introduced an "Overhead Value Analysis" process. This required all senior managers, including myself, to fill in a daily breakdown of what they had done during their working hours. Headings covered included: - telephone calls, meetings with customers, meetings with each other, travelling, writing reports, thinking about writing reports etc. etc.

Much to everyone's surprise, an average of around 60% of time was spent in some sort of meeting, 20% on the telephone and writing reports. This left only 20% to interact with customers and suppliers to develop the business.

At Blue Bell, it was clear from the first day, that the customer was king!

The whole organisation was geared to improving and maintaining the interaction between the company's manufacturing, buying, and selling functions of the Wrangler product ranges.

If the senior management team held an in-house meeting, the receptionists were instructed to put through all calls that required the personal attention of any one of the managers attending. The words "I'm sorry he, or she, is in a meeting," were banned.

Because of this approach, in-house meetings tended to be well planned, very focussed, and very short!

Meetings away from the office were formally structured, requiring clear inputs from all the presenters and specific outputs from the group of people attending.

In my 16 years with the company, I travelled around the UK and across the globe. I can honestly say that most of these "out of the office" meetings were necessary and well planned. I met a lot of interesting people and by interacting with them, both formally and informally, I not only learned a lot, I also had a lot of fun!

Chapter Twenty-One

Sales Meetings

When I joined Blue Bell Apparel, the sales managers reported direct to Dick Webzell. An ex-salesman himself, Dick liked to keep a "hands-on" approach. He realised that, in difficult times, a professional, well-motivated salesforce would pay dividends.

In those early days, head office staff had regular interaction with every salesperson. Potential sales personnel had to endure a form of "Spanish Inquisition" from the whole senior management group, as part of their final interview process. Those who were successful spent a week in head office participating in a well-structured induction process.

Our objective was to ensure that not only was the Wrangler salesforce THE best in the industry, but also to make them all aware that EVERYONE in the company was working to support them, throughout the sell-in and selling-out processes.

The senior management team also attended the two major trade shows, and Spring and Autumn range pre-trade shows, for major customers. These were held in London, Glasgow Birmingham, Newcastle, and Manchester.

A major sales conference was held once a year, normally in June or November. The purpose of this was to keep the salesforce up to date with the organisation's performance against sales and brand share targets, brief them on new product development and expose them to the marketing support ideas being created for the following year.

These meetings were held around the UK in four-star city centre or country house hotels.

In the period 1975-1978, the jeans and jeans related clothing market had grown organically. Motivating the salesforce was not a problem in an environment where unit sales and brand share was booming.

The senior management team in Calverton was aware that the good times would not last forever. Our market data pointed to a slow-down in growth during the early part of the 1980's. If, or rather when this happened, we would rely very heavily on the investment made in the Wrangler sales team. They would become key to maintaining the brand leadership position we had all contributed towards achieving.

In August 1978, we held a sales conference in Nottingham, to introduce the Spring 1979 product ranges and the marketing support programme I had developed with our advertising agency. At the close of this conference, Dick Webzell announced that, providing the salesforce was successful in meeting, or preferably exceeding, their sales targets, the next sales conference would be held in the USA.

The announcement was enthusiastically received, and the salesforce went away fired up to deliver.

We were confident that the additional incentive would have the desired result and the planning process began.

Williamsburg, Virginia and Greensboro, North Carolina in 1979

Dick decided that the promised overseas sales conference would be held in Williamsburg, Virginia. This would be followed up with a trip to the Blue Bell Inc. headquarters in Greensboro, North Carolina.

The logistics were made more difficult because of Blue Bell company rules on air travel. These stipulated that no more than two senior managers could travel on the same flight. It was also felt imprudent for the whole of the salesforce and all the sales managers to travel together. The purpose of these rules made perfect sense. If there was a fatal accident, then a large majority of the management team and salesforce would not be involved. The company would be able to continue its operations, albeit with some major disruption.

For the conference in the USA, direct flights from the UK, to and from either of the chosen destinations, was not an option. Clearly, we needed the assistance of a specialist company who could be briefed on the full requirements and would be responsible for all travel arrangements.

A major travel company, based in nearby Leicester, was recruited.

In the end, the attendees were booked on four different routes from London. Each of the four parties would eventually arrive in Washington DC for a short stay (to recover from jet lag) before continuing the journey to Williamsburg.

Two of the parties took, less stressful, direct flights into Washington. The other two parties had "drawn a short straw." They had to fly to Kennedy Airport, New York and, after going through American immigration, change terminals to board internal flights to Washington.

Kevin Black and I were recipients of a "short straw" and travelled together with 10 members of the Wrangler salesforce. Our flight to New York was scheduled for an early morning take-off from Heathrow. Normally, we would have travelled down in the early hours but opted instead to travel down the night before and stayed over at one of the airport hotels.

This meant a less stressful travel schedule than would have otherwise been the case. It also enabled us to leave our car in the hotel car park, free of charge, whilst we were away.

At around 10am. On the 1 June 1979, our plane took off for the 8-hour flight to Kennedy Airport in New York. On landing, we had to collect our luggage, navigate immigration, and then take a short walk to the nearby domestic terminal. There we checked in for our internal flight to Washington.

After a wait of a couple of hours we boarded our shuttle aircraft for the ongoing journey. By this time, we were extremely tired, but the adrenalin was kicking in making it difficult to relax. For many of us, this was our first visit to the USA. We were keen to ensure that we did not miss any part of the 90-minute internal flight.

Everything appeared to be running smoothly as we began our descent over the Potomac River and approached the runway. As a frequent flyer, I had been through such procedures many times before. It seemed to me that we were travelling too quickly, and that the aircraft was too far down the runway.

"Surely the pilot will abort and try again?" I thought to myself.

At that moment, the wheels slammed down onto the tarmac. The overhead luggage compartments all opened spilling their contents on to our heads. The brakes of the aircraft were engaged, and the engines thrust into reverse. This was followed by a screeching noise and smoke entering the passenger compartment.

This seemed to go on for several minutes. The reality was that it was probably no more than a few seconds before our aircraft came to a halt, at the very end of the runway.

It was eerily quiet. Even the most experienced flyers had been rendered speechless!

The silence was broken by an announcement from the pilot. "Sorry for the heavy landing," he said. "Welcome to Washington. Will passengers leaving the flight here please remain seated until the plane comes to a complete halt? On-going passengers are requested to observe the no smoking signs until after take-off."

Our party of 12, were glad to be leaving the plane. Some of those remaining would have to endure two more take-offs and landings before arriving at their ultimate destination of Miami in Florida.

Our arrival to Washington had been full of drama!

I had heard stories of the "gung-ho" approach of pilots on internal flights in America. Many had returned from war service in Vietnam and, it was said, "liked to spice-up their journeys from time to time." Whatever the reason for our heavy landing, all thought of jet lag had disappeared. For the time being at least!

We collected our luggage and made our way through to the departure lounge. A driver was waiting for us, and we boarded our coach for the short journey to the Washington Hilton Hotel.

By the time we checked into our rooms, we had been travelling more than 14 hours. The late afternoon sun was beating down in Washington but, in our heads, it was midnight UK time and jet lag was beginning to set in.

Nevertheless, Kevin Black and I decided to look around the hotel's facilities before dinner, followed by an early night. We found our colleagues, who had been "forced to endure a direct flight," sunning themselves by the hotel pool. Having arrived over four hours before us, they had taken the opportunity to have a late lunch and to look round some of the sites.

In our rooms, was an itinerary for the next 24 hours. This included a group dinner at the Hilton (so much for our early night). The next morning would include a sightseeing tour of Washington before embarking on the 167-mile drive to our conference venue in Williamsburg, Virginia.

Despite making my excuses, and retiring to my room immediately after dinner, I did not get to bed until the equivalent of 3am, UK time. I was asleep the moment my head hit the pillow.

My alarm call roused me from my slumber for what would prove to be another eventful day!

Immediately after breakfast, we boarded a coach for a guided tour of the sights of Washington. This included the White House, Capitol Building and the Lincoln Memorial. Following a light lunch at the hotel, we checked out of our rooms and, complete with our luggage, met up in the hotels covered car park facility. Our travel agency representative had organised 12 white Cadillac's, with sequential number plates, for the onward journey to Williamsburg.

I was one of the nominated drivers and my allocated passengers were three "lucky" members of the Wrangler salesforce.

Our "man from the travel agency" briefed us before we started our journey. The instructions were somewhat rudimentary to say the least. He concentrated his attentions on reminding us about the speed limit on all major highways.

"All the cars are automatics and are fitted with air-conditioning and cruise control," we were told. "If you have driven in mainland Europe, the same road safety rules apply here," he continued. "Once you reach the major highway to the south, I suggest you set the cruise control to 54 mph. This will ensure you will not exceed the 55 mph. speed limit."

He stressed the importance of this by adding, "Law enforcement officers, in the southern states of America, operate a no tolerance attitude to speeding. If you are pulled over, they will either issue you with a fixed penalty ticket for on-the-spot payment or, in extreme cases, escort you into the nearest town for summary court justice to take its course."

Luckily, I was used to driving an automatic car and, although this was my first trip to the USA, I had a lot of experience of driving in Europe. In my mind, nothing could possibly go wrong!

One of my salesforce colleagues, and a fellow Yorkshireman, was handed the map, the printed route instructions to Williamsburg, and the responsibility for ensuring that I had timely information on the way.

With two members of "God's Own County" in charge, our fellow passengers were in good hands!

We were sixth in the convoy. Luckily, for a city the size of Washington, the Sunday afternoon traffic was not particularly heavy. I followed the cars in front until we came to the first set of traffic lights. These turned to red just as I drove up to them. The cars I had been following sped off into the distance and out of sight. From being the sixth car in a convoy, I was suddenly the driver of the lead vehicle for the rest of my colleagues to follow.

More by good luck than good management, we succeeded in navigating our way to the highway south. After all these years, I cannot precisely remember the route we took. I do recall that it was very scenic and full of historic references to the American Civil War and the War of Independence. There was not much traffic. The journey to Williamsburg was 167 miles and took nearly four hours.

90 minutes into our journey, having crossed the State line into Virginia, I noticed that we had been joined by a police highway patrol vehicle. It drove up fast behind us, then slowed and kept in close formation for several miles. My salesforce colleagues, sitting on the back seat, thought that the idea of a police escort was very amusing and were taking pictures of the vehicle out of the back window.

I was not amused and glanced anxiously at the speedometer. Having engaged cruise control as soon as I had reached the main highway, just as our travel representative had recommended, I was relieved to note that our car was travelling at just below the speed limit.

"Why are we attracting the attention of the police patrol?" I remember wondering. Everything would become clear when we finally reached our destination!

Thankfully, at the next junction, my unwanted follower pulled off the highway never to be seen again.

At roughly 5.30pm, we pulled into the car park of the Hospitality House Hotel in Williamsburg. This was our conference venue for the next three days. The hotel had opened in 1972 and was in the historic area of Williamsburg, about 10 minutes walking distance from the town centre and all its facilities. Close by was the historic Jamestown Settlement, Colonial Williamsburg and William and Mary College.

Dick Webzell had arranged a reception meeting in our main conference room, for 6.30pm. Here, he briefed all the participants. Conference packs and social itineraries were handed out covering activities planned over the following three days.

Whilst talking to Kevin Black after this meeting, I was finally able to solve the mystery of our highway patrol encounter during the journey. Kevin was driving the Cadillac directly behind mine in the convoy. Because of a traffic hold-up he had experienced coming out of Washington, he was some miles behind me and travelling above the speed limit in the hope of catching me up.

Suddenly, out of nowhere, a highway patrol vehicle had appeared and pulled him over. "Do you know what the speed limit is on this road is?" the officer had demanded. Kevin feigned innocence and replied. "I have just arrived in the USA from Scotland. This is my first visit to your country. In my country, the speed limit on major highways is 70 mph. Isn't it the same here?"

The officer had believed the story and, instead of issuing an on-the-spot fine, he sent Kevin on his way with a caution and a warning. "I will let you off this time. You are now aware that the speed limit on this highway is 55mph. I will radio your car details to my colleagues down the road. If you are found exceeding the limit again, you will be pulled over and fined," he advised. "Have a nice day and enjoy your stay," he concluded.

Because of the enforced delay, Kevin's car was now about 9 miles behind my identical white Cadillac. Our number plate details were the same as those that the officer had radioed ahead except for the final number, 6 on mine and 7 on Kevin's.

When my car had passed the parked patrol vehicle, it had been assumed that this was the speeding vehicle he had been warned about. To have arrived where he was since being stopped, the officer on board clearly felt that the speed limit warning given to Kevin, had been ignored.

This was the reason he had followed close behind me. When he realised my car was not the one that he had been warned about, and that no law had been broken, he had pulled off at the next junction.

It transpired two other members of our convoy had also been pulled over. Only one driver had been issued with a fixed penalty fine. He was the travel agency representative who had briefed us prior to setting off from Washington!

A clear case of do as I say, not as I do!

Despite the "story" that he had told the patrolman, Kevin was a seasoned traveller in the USA and had travelled the same highway on several occasions. He also, been to Williamsburg before with Dick Webzell. They knew all the best eating places.

Dick invited us both, with four other members of the senior management group, to join him, and his wife, for dinner at his favourite restaurant in the area. "Nick's Seafood Pavilion" was situated at 324 Water Street at nearby Yorktown. It had been founded in 1944 by Greek immigrants Nick and Mary Matthews. They were still very much involved.

It had developed an enviable reputation for serving up great seafood and it was not unknown for diners to travel many miles for the experience. The restaurant also had become the "in" place to eat for celebrities and politicians visiting the area. All guests, whether rich and famous, tourists, foodies, or trainees from the nearby US Coast Guard Reserve Training Centre, received the same fantastic welcome.

You could not book a table at "Nick's." You simply turned up, joined the queue, and waited for a table to become available. When we arrived, we became aware that there were two queues. One catered for up to four people and the other for large parties, like our own, of five or over.

Before a table finally became available, we had made many new friends with fellow potential diners. All of them were impressed that we had "travelled all the way from the UK" to sample the food in their favourite restaurant.

The meal was superb, service impeccable, the atmosphere electric and, before we left, Nick and Mary came over to our table to shake everyone's hand and thank us for coming.

Nothing happened in "Nick's Seafood Pavilion" without them knowing!

The following day was spent within the confines of our conference room. Even with air conditioning and plenty of iced water, regular coffee, and refreshment breaks, this had proved an exhausting experience.

That evening, four of us decided we would walk into the centre of Williamsburg do a little sightseeing and find a small restaurant for dinner. We found a small bistro that was run by a very affable American/Greek restaurateur. He greeted us like long lost friends, took us to our table and introduced us to our waitress.

I quite like Greek food and the atmosphere in the restaurant was vibrant, as all good Greek restaurants tend to be.

The owner came over to our table with the wine list. We ordered a bottle of Chablis. Our host suggested that we should also have a bottle of his best house wine, "a fine Retsina all the way from Greece," he explained.

Our meal was excellent. The "Californian Chablis" had gone down very well. The bottle of Retsina was uncorked and ready to go but remained untouched.

For those who know nothing about wine, Retsina is a white "resinated" wine whose origins go back at least 2000 years. Its flavour is "unique." One of those "Marmite" experiences, you either love it or hate it!

Perhaps, if we had poured and drunk the Retsina before the Chablis everything would have been OK. Drinking it after, would not have been a pleasant experience.

Our host was beaming at us from across the room.

I asked the waitress to bring us another glass so that we could share our untouched bottle with the owner. The glass arrived. "Can we have a bigger glass," I enquired. "The biggest glass you have," I suggested. She came back with a huge wine glass that I filled to the brim with the Retsina.

I then asked her if she would invite the owner to have a drink with us. He smiled at us across the room, gave a "thumbs-up" and came bounding over. At this point, he spied his large glass, laughed, and observed, "I guess you guys did not like my wine?"

We assured him that his food had been great but, his insistence that we try his recommend wine had not been one of his better ideas. "Don't worry," he assured us. He went away and returned with another bottle of Chablis. "Enjoy, with my compliments," he said.

We left the restaurant well fed and well-watered ready to face another arduous day!

The conference continued the next morning finishing with a buffet lunch. Afterwards, we boarded a coach for the short journey to Colonial Williamsburg.

This was, for most of us, the first opportunity to visit what would now be described as a "living history experience." Today, such concepts are more commonplace but back in the late 1970's it broke new grounds in presenting a vision of how people actually lived centuries before.

Part of the historic district of the city of Williamsburg, Colonial Williamsburg featured a range of 16th, 17th and 19th century buildings, some restored, others reconstructed from the original plans. Covering a large area, the trustees had been determined to re-create and interpret life in a "Colonial American city," during different periods of its turbulent history.

Modern vehicles were not allowed onsite, and the "inhabitants" wore outfits of the period and spoke a version of "Colonial American English."

Back home, cultural heritage tourism was very much in its infancy. We had an abundance of historic sites but, in Williamsburg, our American cousins, with a much smaller pool of historical resources, were showing us what could be done to bring mere bricks and mortar to life.

The motto of Colonial Williamsburg was "That the future may learn from the past."

Everybody in our party agreed that the offering they had put together delivered everything they had set out to do. We were all very impressed!

That evening, we returned once more to "Nick's Seafood Pavilion" for another memorable meal.

After breakfast the next morning, we checked out of the hotel, loaded our luggage into our Cadillac's and set off for Greensboro, North Carolina.

On paper, the journey south to Greensboro appeared straightforward!

By now, I was more confident in my own driving ability. After all, I now had over 200 miles under my belt. During that time, I had managed to negotiate myself out of Washington to Williamsburg and into Yorktown. My navigator was also confident in his ability to ensure that we would easily find our way to our next destination. The city of Greensboro was home to the corporate headquarters of our parent company, Blue Bell Inc.

We set off in good spirits on our journey of around 250 miles.

Our travel agency representative had advised us that he had chosen a more scenic route. This would take us through several small towns rather than skirt around them.

"I thought that you might appreciate a seeing a slice of real America on your journey south," he had informed us during a briefing before we set off. "You will be able to stop at a roadside diner around the halfway point of your journey and should arrive in plenty of time to check in, and get ready for dinner, when you reach Greensboro." He continued.

He was true to his word. The journey was indeed scenic. Some of the homesteads we passed through could have been straight out of one of the "Deep South movies" that we had seen back in the UK.

After about 2 hours, I noticed that the petrol gauge reading was suggesting that I needed to stop and put in some fuel. "I think I will pull over at the next diner that has petrol pumps," I announced to my fellow travellers. "We can fill up the car and have a quick snack, if you all agree?"

Everyone thought this was a great idea.

On the outskirts of the next small town, we saw a sign for a diner and turned off on to the forecourt. When we pulled up at the pumps, I realised it was self-service. This was common practice in America at that time but a relatively novel experience for a vehicle full of Brits.

I jumped out of the car and walked round to where I thought the patrol cap would be situated. It was not there. I walked round to the other side of the car. It was not there either. By this time, all my passengers had joined me and were offering their own ideas of where the petrol cap might be. After several minutes, we were still no nearer solving our dilemma.

Throughout the whole this period, the attendant waiting to take our money, had been watching our antics with ever increasing amusement.

Eventually, he left the safety of his pay desk and proceeded to "mosey on over" in our direction. "You guys seem to have a problem" he drawled. "Is there anything I can do to help?"

I explained that we seemed to have lost the petrol cap in our car and that we wanted to fill up and then eat.

I followed him to the back of the car. Once there, he kicked aside the number plate revealing the missing petrol cap that was behind it. "Don't worry, it happens all the time," he explained.

I thanked him for his patience, filled up the car and paid him.

We then parked in front of the diner and went inside. To all intents and purposes, we could have easily entered the set of an American movie. Completing the picture were a "motley crew of curious locals" and the archetypal diner waitress.

She showed us to a table, handed out the menus and explained what the dish of the day consisted of. Once we had ordered, the dishes quickly followed. The food and the service were excellent. Half an hour later, we were back in the car and ready to continue our journey.

The rest of the drive was completed without incident. Finally, we arrived at our accommodation at the Sedgefield Country Club. The Club was a multi-sport complex and boasted several tennis courts, a championship golf course, and an Olympic size outdoor swimming pool. Our accommodation was relatively basic but entirely adequate for our two-night stay.

A group dinner at a nearby restaurant had been organised and, after the meal, we were happy to have an early night ahead of our visit to Blue Bell Inc.

After breakfast the next day, we boarded our coach for the short journey to the head office complex. Here we were greeted by members of the corporate board. Afterwards, we received several presentations from the corporate officers responsible for sales, marketing, product development, manufacturing and research and development.

One that particularly stands out in my memory, was the one facilitated by Fred Birdsong, Vice President of Research and Development.

It was generally excepted, throughout the garment manufacturing industry, that Blue Bell led the world in technological development. As a result, the manufacturing and warehousing facilities were state of the art. Many of the manufacturing processes used "Blue Bell Technology" specially developed to streamline manufacturing efficiency. This ensured that all Blue Bell brands, especially those that were Wrangler branded, were cost-effectively produced to the highest standards.

Fred had joined the company in 1937, 10 years before the introduction of the Wrangler jeans product. He had been part of the team who introduced, and continued to develop, a "quality blueprint." This was designed to ensure that the company's manufacturing and warehousing operations maintained their lead over all competitors.

He explained some of the measures used to assess the quality of fabric and findings, and quality control techniques that were applied during manufacturing. Every supplier, factory and warehouse used the same engineering standards in all locations used by Blue Bell around the world.

In rounding off his presentation, Fred announced that he would be retiring from the company at the end of the year. "I will be sorry to leave but I do so in the knowledge that my team will continue to develop new manufacturing processes," he said. "We already have in the pipeline laser cutting technologies and advanced sewing machines that will allow us to bulk manufacture to the exact specifications provided by the product development teams. When the machinery is introduced to our plants around the world it will spell an end to production tolerances," he continued.

Turning to Kevin Black, and the other members of the Blue Bell Apparel product development team, with a smile he raised the question, "When that happens, who will you blame then?"

In 1979, product development teams operated on a size tolerance of plus or minus half an inch. Any product falling outside these measures could be legitimately rejected.

Before we left the Blue Bell offices, each member of the party was presented with a designer key ring specially engraved with the words "BLUE BELL INC G'BORO NC JUNE 1979."

Our programme included a visit to a department store in downtown Greensboro. This offered an opportunity to see how the Wrangler USA product lines were displayed in this type of outlet. It also provided a stark contrast between the leafy green suburbs and the, far grittier, down-town urban American scene.

We then moved on to Municipal Office Building for a Civic Reception hosted by the Mayor of Greensboro. The arrival in the city of a large group of visitors from Britain, had come to the notice of the local media and politicians.

After the formal proceedings and press photographs, each member of our party was presented with a book entitled "Spirit up the People.' Written by Joanne Young and illustrated by Taylor Lewis Jr. It celebrates of the story of North Carolina from the time of its discovery in 1524 until the ratification of the United States Constitution by the State Assembly in 1789.

The narrative depicts the history of the State from the arrival of the first settlers, through the turbulent times of the War of independence and its aftermath. It is a wonderful and evocative volume that I still treasure today.

We were also given a small box containing a gold colour key inscribed with the words "City of Greensboro North Carolina 1979."

That evening the Board of Blue Bell Inc. had organised a formal dinner at the Country Club. This event proved to be an introduction to the cultural divisions that still abounded in the deep south at that time.

There were only two women in our party. One was Dick Webzell's wife, Carole, the other his secretary, Brenda. The ladies joined the wives of the Blue Bell management Only the male members of our group sat down in the main dining room. Apparently, this part of the Country Club was strictly men only. We were served wine with our meal, but for the women the choice was water or soft drinks.

The State of North Carolina had applied rigid controls on the sale of alcoholic beverages and whilst the rules had been loosened, the city of Greensboro had voted "to maintain where, and how, alcoholic drinks were to be sold and where, and how, it was to be consumed."

In the private member's clubs, wines and spirits could not be purchased at the bar. Members brought in their own spirits which they poured into club glasses. Mixers could be purchased and added by the bar staff.

For the night of the formal dinner the male members of our party were admitted as "guests of members." This privilege did not apply to the women.

The only member of the Blue Bell Inc Management team that I knew well was Norbert A. Considine Jr., (Norb). As a Vice President and Principal Advertising Executive for the company since 1955, he had moulded the image of the Wrangler brand in the USA and oversaw the advertising output in all other markets. I had met him, formally and socially, during several meetings of European advertising managers I had attended since joining the company.

Born in Philadelphia, he had spent most of his working life in New York during which time he had lived in Princeton, New Jersey. He moved to Greensboro in 1975.

Norb could be abrasive and did not suffer fools gladly. He had no time for college graduates and MBA's whose whole experience of marketing and advertising "came from textbooks written by academics." Our career backgrounds were very similar. I found myself on the same wavelength.

Norb had a passion for drinking good wine and spirits and wearing made to measure clothes. In Greensboro, formalwear constituted of blazer and casual trousers. Norb was used to wearing suits that were made in Saville Row in London.

His lifestyle was not going to change simply because he had moved, I suspect under duress, to the deep south. It was rumoured that his wine cellar was the finest in North Carolina.

In the offices at Blue Bell Inc, he had acquired the title "The Squire of Greensboro."

I was sitting next to him at the dinner table. It soon became clear that the wine supply had been exhausted and no more was forthcoming. Norb liked a nice brandy after dinner. "I'm fed up with sitting here without a drink," he whispered. "Would you care to join me in the bar?"

I didn't need any persuading!

We moved into the next room and walked up to the bar. Instead of the usual selection of bottles behind it, there were several rows of safety deposit boxes. Each had a different number on the front of them.

Norb presented his numbered key to the barman. He opened the box with the corresponding number on it and pulled out a small leather case. This was handed to Norb for him to open. Inside the case were three small cut-glass decanters. One contained a fine brandy, another a top of the range gin and the final one a 12-year-old malt whisky.

"What would you like, Robin?" asked Norb. "A gin and tonic would go down nicely," I responded. The barman produced two glasses. Norb poured a large brandy into his and an equally large gin into mine. The barman poured some of the tonic mixer into mine until I asked him to stop. He seemed surprised and embarrassed that I had said "please" and "thank you."

We had enjoyed several fill ups before our "forced-abstainer colleagues" started to drift towards the foyer. I finished my glass, said my goodbyes to Norb and joined my colleagues for the short journey to our accommodation.

I only met Norb on one other occasion, at a European advertising managers conference in Brussels. In 1980, he retired "for reasons of health." He returned to his beloved Princeton to renew his pre-Greensboro lifestyle.

Next day after breakfast, we were taken to view one of the many shopping malls that surrounded the city. Here we visited a store that contained a shop in shop called a "Wrangler Wranch." Staffed by two Blue Bell Inc. staff members, it sold the whole range of Wrangler merchandise and was the blueprint for what was hoped, would be a national roll out.

The local Greensboro TV and radio stations covered our visit and interviewed several members of our party about their "Greensboro experience."

After lunch, we collected our luggage in preparation for the journey home. Split into the same travelling groups as on the incoming journey, we were all taking different internal flights from the airport that serviced Greensboro.

Two groups were travelling back to the UK via New York, a third via Washington and the fourth via Chicago. Surprisingly, the small regional airport at Greensboro had the facility to check our luggage all the way to Heathrow. This would enable us to go through immigration at our selected airport hub, when we landed there, without having to worry about our luggage.

Once more, the group led by Kevin Black and me had drawn the short straw. We were booked on the flight to O'Hare Airport in Chicago. Because we would be travelling West before our flight home, we had the longest flight time back to the UK, of any of the four groups.

Mid-afternoon on Friday 8 June 1979, we boarded our internal flight. Providing everything went to plan, we were scheduled to arrive at Heathrow on Saturday 9th June, at around 10am.

The flight was smooth until we were within 40 minutes of our estimated time of arrival in Chicago. Then we ran into turbulence. This was followed by heavy rain and finally a full-blown thunderstorm. After ten minutes or so, the pilot announced over the intercom that we would be taking up a holding pattern above Chicago Heights.

Another fifty minutes passed. We were still circling. The pilot came on the intercom again to advise that nothing was taking off or landing because of the thunderstorm. As soon as we were given clearance we would land. Passengers, like our party, scheduled to transfer to other flights, were assured that the same delay applied to outgoing flights.

The person sitting next to me turned out to be a very nervous flyer. Like all such people, they tend to install their fear into their fellow passengers. He reminded me that the deadliest aviation accident in the United States had taken place on 25th May (only a couple of weeks earlier). American Airlines Flight 191 had taken off from O'Hare on a scheduled flight to Los Angeles. The McDonnell Douglas DC-10-10, with 258 passengers and 23 crew, had crashed shortly after take-off killing everyone on board and two people on the ground.

This is something that you do not want to be reminded about. Especially after you have been circling, in exceptionally bad weather, for well over an hour!

When we eventually started our descent, my new-found friend was focused on the view out of his window. "Look there," he almost screamed. "You can clearly see the crash site." I am not a nervous flyer, but seeds of doubt began to creep in. When coming in to land I like to concentrate my attention on doing so safely. The antics of my fellow passenger was beginning to get under my skin.

Thankfully, soon afterwards, we landed without incident. It was then it became clear why there had been on such a long hold. We were in a queue of aircraft nose to tail from the runway all the way to the terminal building.

It would take us another forty minutes to arrive at a clear gate and disembark. Once inside the airport departure lounge, we received the news that we would have a two hour wait before our flight for London would be taking off.

After an uneventful flight, we eventually touched down at Heathrow at about 11am.

Red eyed and weary, we were delighted that our misgivings about our luggage going astray had proved unfounded. The baggage handlers in the USA had done their job.

Our luggage was amongst the first to appear on the carousel. Within an hour, we were through the airport and picking up our car from the hotel we had stayed in the night before our American adventure had begun.

A further 3 hours later, we were back home!

Looking back on the experience of my first ever visit to the USA, and our experience of Greensboro NC, I was quite shocked at the high levels of racial and gender inequality that we had witnessed.

Before we had left the UK, we had been led to believe that segregation and racial intolerance were no longer major issues in the USA. The civil rights marches of the 1960's was supposed to have put an end to the human rights abuses that had been highlighted by them.

Our actual experience seemed to show that although human rights laws had been introduced, in several States, implementation seemed to be progressing very slowly.

The leafy suburbs of Greensboro were populated almost exclusively by white upper and managerial classes. The Country clubs that they frequented appeared to have no black members. The inner city was full of poorly maintained buildings and a large, mainly black, working-class population. The gulf between the "haves" and "have nots" appeared to be very wide.

My research in the UK after my return, indicated that the African America population were still suffering acts of prejudice in Greensboro and in other parts of North Carolina. It was clear to me that friction existed and unchecked, could easily lead to violent disorder.

Unfortunately, this proved to be the case!

On the 3rd November 1979, only five months after our visit, the Communist Workers Party held an anti-Ku Klux Klan rally in the predominately black Morningside Heights neighbourhood of Greensboro. Four local news stations covered the protest live.

Eventually, large numbers of KKK supporters arrived and violence ensued. Protesters beat the Klan vehicles with sticks, their occupants responded by firing guns into the crowd. This resulted in the deaths of five demonstrators and the wounding of several others.

"The Greensboro Massacre," as it became known, appeared on television news channels in the USA and around the world.

12 months later, at the subsequent state criminal trial, both sides blamed the other for starting the trouble. After a week of deliberations, an all-white jury acquitted the six KKK defendants.

I returned to the USA many times after my first visit but never visited Greensboro again.

Monte Carlo in 1981

The incentive of an offshore sales conference had motivated the salesforce at Blue Bell Apparel to achieve record sales figures. These had been achieved despite a general slow-down in the jeans and jeans related clothing markets. A precedent had been set. The incentive of an overseas sales conference, on alternate years, was to continue through to the middle of the 1980's.

In 1981, Monte Carlo was chosen as the destination and the Loews Monte Carlo (now the Fairmont Monte Carlo) selected as the venue. A four-star luxury hotel, Loews was ideally located above the tunnel of the Monaco Grand Prix racing circuit, just before the famous hairpin bend. It was also within easy walking distance of all the major tourist sites.

By all accounts, the conference went very well and achieved its objectives on every measure.

Unfortunately, I was taken ill 24 hours before I was due to fly out. Dick Webzell had seconded a replacement and our travel agent managed to adjust the ticketing and hotel arrangements, without incurring a penalty charge!

Whilst my colleagues were enjoying the winter sunshine in Monte Carlo, I was recuperating in bed in Southwell, only 8 miles away from the Blue Bell offices in Calverton. Organising a replacement had been accomplished with the utmost efficiency. Informing the staff in my office that I was still in England, had been overlooked.

At a time before mobile phones and laptop computers, they assumed that I was "holidaying" 1,000 miles away. To add insult to injury, I had fully recovered by the following weekend and returned to the office on the same day as my colleagues who had made the trip.

"How was the weather in Monaco?" my secretary asked. "You don't look as though you have enjoyed much sunshine," she continued. I explained why. The envy was replaced by sympathy.

Having never visited Monte Carlo before, I had been very disappointed not to have made the trip.

Munich, Germany, December 1983

Early in 1983, it was agreed that the next UK Sales Conference would again be held at an overseas location.

The two previous overseas events had been in the USA and Monte Carlo. These had been successful on many different levels.

Our dilemma was to find a destination that could compete with the previous choices.

I received an invitation from Hilton International to attend a conference at their affiliate hotel in Stratford-Upon-Avon. This event had been organised to celebrate their 10th Anniversary. The Anniversary date was 14th March 1983, and the conference was scheduled to take place over Saturday and Sunday of 12th & 13th March.

The format included an afternoon of formal presentations by the Group Marketing personnel on the Saturday. This was followed by a special Gala Dinner and an overnight stay. Next morning, the participating hotels would be promoting their facilities in an informal exhibition environment.

I mentioned this to Dick Webzell. He too had received an invitation. We both agreed that our participation would offer an opportunity to access several different destinations and hotel venues, in one place and at one time.

The conference proved a worthwhile exercise. Formal presentations gave us an insight into what was available across the Hilton International Group. The Gala dinner not only delivered excellent food and top-class entertainment, but it also enabled us to meet several venue representatives on an informal basis.

By the end of the evening, we had already narrowed down our search area to a shortlist of about seven destinations.

Next morning, we visited the stands of all venues on our list. Dick and I explained to each of them exactly what we were seeking to achieve from our next sales conference. Naturally, they all did their best to convince us that theirs was the ideal venue.

One of the stands had particularly caught our eye. It was manned by large gentleman wearing a very small, and extremely tight pair of lederhosen, as part of a genuine Bavarian outfit.

He was representing the Munich Hilton Hotel. His stand was very busy. This was due, in no small part, to the fact that he was handing out Bavarian steins, with Munich Hilton branding, as part of his promotional pitch.

We had tried to catch his attention on several occasions and had spoken to nearly all the competition before we were able get close to his stand.

He saw us coming and held out his hand. "I guess you two guys are interested in my steins?" he said, reaching down to the box beside him and taking out one for each of us.

"Thanks," said Dick. "We both have wives. What about another two so that they can have a stein as well?" he suggested.

Our friendly Bavarian roared with laughter and gave us each another stein. It turned out that he was the General Manager of the Munich Hilton.

We liked his boisterous approach and his efficient manner. His hotel met all our requirements, and we were impressed with what Munich had to offer. It was suggested that December was a good time to visit. Munich had a famous Christmas Market, plenty of cafes and restaurants and a huge Bier Keller. He assured us that after a busy day at the conference, there was plenty to do just a short walking distance from his hotel.

After some toing and froing, the contract was finally signed.

Our meetings were scheduled to take place in the conference and breakout rooms at the Munich Hilton. Our party would arrive on Saturday 10th of December and leave on Wednesday 14th.

Reaching Munich did not present the same logistical problems experienced with some of our other destinations. Flights were available from London and some regional airports.

Once more, Kevin Black and I led a party of 12 people. Our Swiss Air flight left from Manchester Airport.

I had never flown by Swiss Air before but had heard many good reports. There was only one problem. The airline did not have a license to fly direct from Manchester to Munich. Our flight would land in Zurich, and we would have to stay on the aircraft for an hour. After that it became a scheduled, and licensed, flight from Zurich to Munich.

On the morning of 10 December 1983, we boarded the first leg of our flight to Munich. The flying time to Zurich was just under 2 hours, during which we enjoyed free drinks, a hot lunch and coffee. I was amazed that all the cutlery was metal. The cups and plates were porcelain. Our "one class cabin" was closer to first class than tourist. Lunch was full of flavour and hot. Service from the cabin crew was second to none.

Bang on time our plane landed in Zurich.

We were not allowed to disembark and had to wait in our seats until our mandatory hour on the ground had come to an end. Kevin observed, with some amusement, that a tank had been positioned close to the foot of the steps. "I presume they have heard that some members of the Wrangler salesforce are on board. They are making sure none of them escape into Switzerland," he commented drily.

With typical Swiss efficiency, we were on the move again at exactly the allotted hour.

Over the intercom, we were advised that the flight time from Zurich to Munich would be just under an hour. During this time, we would be served more drinks, a second lunch and coffee. Keen to get our monies worth, we all duly obliged, even though we were not exactly starving.

After coffee had been served, a passenger across the aisle, not a member of our party, asked for another cup. As it was being served, the plane hit some turbulence and a little coffee fell on to the man's in-flight table and onto his packet of cigarettes. Even though it was no fault of the hostess, and only three cigarettes were left in the packet, the man flew into a rage and berated her for "her stupidity."

She apologised, wiped down the tray, took away the cup and saucer and came back with another fresh cup.

The man was still chuntering loudly about his coffee covered cigarettes, and the "shoddy service" he had received, when the air hostess returned. Giving him a new full packet of his brand of cigarettes, she said apologetically, but loud enough for those of us close by to hear, "I am very sorry to have inconvenienced you sir, please accept a full packet of cigarettes with our compliments and thank you for flying with Swiss Air."

The 'offended' passenger went very quiet. It took a lot of restraint from the rest of us to prevent a spontaneous round of applause erupting.

We had just witnessed a classic example of "how to deal with a difficult customer."

I became an even more ardent advocate for the airline because of that incident!

When we finally reached our hotel, the December night was drawing in and the temperature was beginning to drop. By contrast, the reception we enjoyed could not have been warmer.

I have always believed that an organisation takes on the persona, good or bad, of the person in charge. We had selected the hotel because of the warmth and personality exuding from the General Manager during our first meeting, in Stratford-Upon-Avon. Every member of staff at the Munich Hilton was equally welcoming.

Our large rooms were well equipped to make us feel at home during our extended stay.

We had decided that Senior Managers would have dinner together on the first night. This would enable us to fine-tune the programme and direction of the conference over the following days.

When such meetings had taken place in London, they were nearly always located at "Trader Vic's," a Polynesian styled restaurant franchise, situated in the basement of the London Hilton in Park Lane.

We knew there was a "Trader Vic's" in Munich and had booked a large table for 12 before we left the UK. This had been done directly with the restaurant, on the mistaken assumption that it too was at the Hilton. The rest of our party had been booked into the main restaurant at the hotel.

The Management team had to brave the winter cold for the short walk to our restaurant. In Munich, the "Trader Vic's" franchise was located a few streets away at the five-star Hotel Baverischer Hof.

When we arrived, we were greeted by the Maître de who took our coats and led us to a space that he had reserved specially for us in the bar area. "Hello Mr. Webzell, welcome to Munich and Trader Vic's," he enthused greeting us like long lost friends. It turned out that this was not so far from the truth. Our host had previously held the same post in the London restaurant and had looked after us on numerous occasions in the past.

What's more, he remembered most of us by name!

"Trader Vic's" restaurants around the world, were then and are now, renowned for providing an eclectic mixture of global cuisine using Chinese wood-fired ovens. We all were acquainted with what to expect and choosing our favourite dishes presented no difficulties.

The restaurant also offered the signature range of tropical cocktails, including the wonderful, and potentially lethal "Mai Tai," all served in glasses specially developed for Trader Vic's.

Walking into the exotic atmosphere of the main restaurant, we were taken to the best table in the house. Here we enjoyed excellent food and superb service. Liberally interspaced by rum-based cocktails.

When we left two or three hours later, having consumed several "Mai Tai" cocktails, we were ready for the bracing walk back to our hotel and the conference to follow over the next few days.

Next morning the conference began. Presentations were made by Dick Webzell and me. These covered the performance of the salesforce during the Spring/Summer sell in period. We also outlined how this had affected the positioning of the Wrangler brand against our main competitors, over the previous 12 months and our sales objectives for the coming year.

The salesforce was then split into five equal groups containing representatives from each of the sales areas. A sales manager was allocated to each to act as moderator for brainstorming sessions geared to developing sales objectives and strategies to meet company goals for 1984.

Two hours had been allocated. After the brainstorming, an early lunch would be taken. The management group was on call to assist the individual groups on an "as needed" basis.

A coach tour of the sites of Munich had been laid on for early afternoon. Our party would return to the hotel at around 17.00 hours, time had been allowed for each group to reconvene and to put together a formal presentation of their ideas. These were scheduled to take place the following morning in front of the whole conference.

After an early buffet lunch, we all boarded a coach to be greeted by our official guide.

The tour included both the historic and commercial areas of Munich and allowed us all to orientate ourselves with where all the "must-see" locations were situated, in relation to our hotel. It concluded with a stop off at the Olympic Park, site of the 1972 Summer Olympic games.

Our guide had explained that our coach would be parked right next to the museum and factory of Bayerische Motoren Werke AG. Free entry to the museum had been organised and was highly recommended.

"FREE" and the explanation that Bayerische Motoren Werke AG was better known in the UK by its initials, BMW, meant that no other incentive was required. No sooner had the coach stopped, everyone disembarked eager to see what was behind one of the world's most iconic, luxury vehicle marques.

The BMW experience did not disappoint. The site has been extended considerably since 1983, but even then, the journey through the history of the company, founded in Munich in 1916, was very evocative. It was particularly interesting to see, and hear, how the company had recovered from the heavy production restrictions, placed on it after World War Two, to retake its place as one of the world's great car manufacturers.

Exhibits included a priceless collection of automobiles, motorcycles, and engines with an ongoing background commentary available to us in English. All this was housed within an enclosed tower ramp that opened out into a theatre. Here, we could sit back in comfort and watch a highly professional audio-visual presentation.

Today, such presentations are commonplace. Back then it was truly state-of-the-art!

Somewhat reluctantly, we returned to our coach for the journey back to the hotel.

"What did you think of that?" asked Dick Webzell.

"Fantastic, when are we changing our fleet of Volvos to BMW's," responded one of the salesmen, to loud applause.

I leave you to try and imagine the reply he received!

Needless-to-say, the plea "fell on deaf ears," although I recall it appeared the following day, amongst the ideas for sales motivators, put forward by one of the groups.

That evening, we all ate at leisure in the hotel and retired early. I am sure some of the brainstorming groups worked on their presentations late into the night.

Next evening, after a busy day of conference meetings, a few of us decided to visit the famous Christmas Market on Marienplatz (Mary's Square) in the centre of the city. Occupying the city's main square since 1158, it was decorated in festive style with a giant, beautifully decorated Christmas tree, occupying pride of place outside the Neues Rathus (New City Hall). This had been built between 1867 and 1908 in a gothic revival style.

The world-famous Glockenspiel in its tower, chimed at set times during the day and re-enacted two stories from the 16th century history of the area. It has proved to be a magnet for tourists from all over the world.

Munich's, reconstructed, gothic Old City Hall (Altes Rathaus) was located at the east side of the square.

We joined the hundreds of locals and fellow tourists strolling amongst the many festive stalls selling, amongst other things, Christmas decorations, German food, and mulled wine. A choir singing Christmas carols added to the seasonal mood.

Feeling hungry, we followed the throng walking between Marienplatz and Karisplatz, which proved to be an area full of shops and restaurants. We wanted to sample genuine Bavarian food, so avoided the obvious tourist spots.

Eventually, we came upon a restaurant that seemed full of locals and was very atmospheric. The problem was that none of the staff spoke English and the menu was written in German. Choosing the meal was going to be an exercise in faith along with a tremendous dose of added luck.

One of our group advised us not to worry. "I took German at school," he told us. "I am sure I will be able to translate the menu and order for everyone," he continued reassuringly.

Two of us ordered, what we assumed was a tasting platter of various meats, for our main course. When the waiter came to take the order from our only "German speaker," he was perplexed when it came to the two requests for the meat platters.

Waving his hands about he seemed to be trying to communicate something that he felt was very important.

"What's he saying," I asked. "I haven't a clue," admitted our translator. "I think he is saying that you are lucky that there are only two portions left."

When the food eventually appeared, the two enormous platters were presented in front of me and my colleague. There was enough meat on each to feed an average English family for about a week.

It quickly became clear that the helpful waiter had been trying to explain the meat platter was to be shared by two people and was not intended to be eaten by one.

A lot of beer flowed, and all the food was eventually consumed, with a lot of help from the rest of the party. When he came to clear the table, the waiter appeared very impressed with our prowess. All in all, it was a very memorable night out!

The final full day of the conference started with a presentation by me, covering a series of marketing support programmes. These included the advertising creative and media package, that had been developed for 1984, by our advertising agency, CDP. I followed this by explaining the sales promotional and point of sale material support that we were offering through the Field Promotional Representatives.

Kevin Black and his product development team took up the whole of the afternoon session. They presented the product ranges for Autumn 1984. These would be sold into the trade at regional tradeshows in January and the IMBEX Exhibition in London in February 1984.

That evening, an unofficial group activity had been set up. Instead of going off in small groups, an invitation was extended to anyone interested in a night out at a typical Bavarian Beer Hall. Around thirty people, "signed up'" and a booking was made the Hofraeuhaus Beer Hall close to the city centre.

It was considered close enough for the party to stroll to, and easy enough to "crawl back to the hotel!"

Whilst generally considered the most touristy beer hall in Munich, Hofraeuhaus was also the oldest and most traditional. It had helped to shape the city's beer culture and encouraged people to just get on and enjoy themselves.

Just the sort of place that our salesforce loved to frequent!

We arrived at the venue at about 7.30 pm. The outside had the look of an alpine chalet of the 17th century.

Our party was seated in high-backed chairs placed around one of the long wooden tables in the Festival Hall. There were hundreds of other people already in their seats. It was claimed, 900 people could be seated in the Hall. The Christmas markets were in full swing throughout the city, the venue was full on the night we were there.

Beer in the Hofraeuhaus Beer Hall is served in a onehanded glass called a Maßkrug. Each glass contains a Maß, the Bavarian language word that describes a regulation mug of beer. In modern measures, this is the exact equivalent of 1 litre.

No sooner had we settled down, the Maßkrugs appeared. As soon as one was drunk it was quickly replaced with another full one. The beer well and truly flowed!

Between the alcohol copious amounts of food appeared. It might have been the tourist equivalent of what we had tasted the night before, but it went down very well with the drink.

All of this provided an impressive backdrop for the traditional Bavarian dance and folklore evening laid on by our hosts.

The musical programme comprised of dancers, alphorn players, yodellers, whip performers and cow bell players. Bavarian "Schuhplatter"dancers were also much in evidence. "Schuhplatter" is a traditional style of folk dance popular in the Alpine regions of Bavaria and Tyrol in southern Germany. The lederhosen clad dancers stomp, clap, and strike the soles of their shoes (Schuhe), thighs and knees with their hands held flat (platt).

The professionals made it look extremely easy. A couple of the members of our party were encouraged to participate. They found to their cost, that it was not as easy as it looked, especially after several beers and in front of hundreds of people!

Everyone in the hall joined in the fun and sang along with the songs, regardless of their lack of German or understanding of the meaning. By the end of the evening people of many nationalities were totally immersed in the atmosphere.

The Bavarians have a word for this, GEMÜTLICHKEIT. Apparently, it is one of the many German words for which there is no English equivalent. Definitions refer to it "as a feeling of cosiness, contentment, comfort a relaxation. The sort of 'glow' that we get when surrounded by good friends and simply enjoying yourselves."

That evening, we were at one with the rest of the people in the hall. Gemütlichkeit it certainly was!

In the morning, we held the final session of the conference followed by a buffet lunch. Our afternoon was free. This enabled delegates an opportunity for one last visit to the city centre. Some took in some additional sightseeing, others visited the shops and Christmas markets to buy souvenirs of their visit, or special last-minute Christmas presents.

That evening, we had organised a farewell dinner. Our host had come up with a German Christmas theme and the General Manager had organised a surprise gift for all the conference attendees.

Remembering our first meeting all those months before in Stratford-Upon-Avon, he had purchased a specially produced run of the Hilton Munich Bavarian steins. These were very similar to the ones he had handed out to Dick Webzell and me at the Hilton Anniversary event.

They had an additional promotional message. It read: - "Wrangler Sales Conference, Munich 10 -15 December 1983."

Our tables had been laid out with traditional Bavarian Christmas decorations and a stein was included as part of each individual place setting. The food was excellent, the service superb and the wine flowed. It was a fitting end to an excellent experience.

The next day we checked out of the hotel and boarded our coach for the airport and our respective flights back to the UK.

Monte Carlo, January 1985

In 1981, I had been disappointed when a last-minute illness had prevented me from attending the sales conference in Monte Carlo. In the middle of 1984, I was delighted that the decision had been made to return once again in January 1985.

Just a month before the IMBEX exhibition in London, this conference would enable our salesforce to be briefed on results of the previous year's trading and introduce them to the ranges for Autumn 1985. The expected mild weather would also enable everyone to recharge their batteries in preparation for what was forecast as a difficult trading year ahead.

There were a few logistical problems to overcome!

Monte Carlo does not have an airport. Flights to the Principality land in Nice, onward transfers are made by road, or helicopter. Out of season, direct flights from the UK to Nice were limited. Blue Bell travel restrictions still applied. The lucky ones would fly direct. Everyone else would have to fly first to Paris and then transfer to an internal flight for the remainder of the journey.

Once more, Kevin Black and I drew a "short straw!"

Our flight landed at Charles de Gaulle airport in Paris, and we transferred to an internal flight to Nice. By the time we boarded our aircraft was full, except for three seats right at the back of the plane.

The doors were closed, and the crew went through the flight procedures in preparation to for take-off.

With the third seat on our row unoccupied, we were just about to spread out when one of the air hostesses came over to us. "Excuse me gentleman, I wondered if I could ask a favour of you," she enquired.

Before we could reply, she continued, "I have a lady at the front of the plane who is feeling a little queasy. We think she will feel better if she is moved to the back. You don't have any objections to her taking the seat next to you, do you?" Anticipating a possible negative response, she added seductively, with a smile, "I will make it worth your while!"

What could we say, but OK?

We were not really prepared for the arrival of the fur clad French lady "of a certain age," who looked slightly the worse for wear and was carrying a small poodle in a dog carrier. With some difficulty, our new companions settled down and, within minutes of take-off, they were both asleep.

True to her word, our air hostess did take care of us. She plied us with a steady stream of free gin and tonics right up to the moment the plane started its descent into Nice airport. We were very mellow by this time. I think we might even have helped the French lady to disembark with her dog.

After collecting our luggage, we met up with our courier who led us to the coach for the onward journey to Monte Carlo. Some of the party who, like me, had not been to Nice and the French Riviera before, enjoyed the commentary as he pointed out some famous landmarks on the way.

Eventually, we arrive at our conference hotel. Situated on the famous Place de Casino, the Hôtel de Paris is one of the great French hotels. Beloved of the likes of Winston Churchill, it had hosted world leaders, film, and sports stars. It was now set to welcome the "Wrangler Sales Conference."

It was mid-afternoon when we finally checked into our rooms. The temperature outside in the sun, was very pleasant 17°C.

Kevin suggested that we go for a walk and take in the sights. He had attended the previous conference in Monte Carlo and knew that once the conference began, we would not have another opportunity to look around during daylight hours. We strolled along the Marina and climbed the steps to the Royal Place before the sun set and darkness descended.

Our hotel exuded a sort of faded grandeur, particularly in the bedrooms we had been allocated. On the other hand, the magnificent public rooms and superb views made us realise how lucky we were to be able to bask in its opulence.

For the next two days, the good weather continued. Unfortunately, we were only able to take advantage of this during the conference coffee and lunch breaks. The late January sunrise and early sunset meant that our free time was confined to evening jaunts to find restaurants and bars that fell within our "non-millionaire" budgets.

We did have an opportunity to rub shoulders with the "high rollers," As guests of the Hôtel de Paris, we were given gold passes to the famous Casino, located just across the road.

On the second night, a group of us took advantage of our Gold Pass status.

Back in the mid 1980's, it was not possible to even enter the Casino unless suitably and formally dressed. The "inner sanctum," was only accessible to Gold Pass holders like us.

Entering this "holy of holy's" was like stumbling onto the set of a James Bond movie. Many of the people were dressed for a black-tie event and, of course, champagne and cocktails were the drinks of choice.

At the time, the Euro was still a distant dream. The French Franc was the currency of the casino. The minimum bet in the "inner sanctum" was a 10,000-franc chip. At the going rate of 10 francs to the pound, each chip had a face value of £1,000. Well out of our league!

We could only watch in awe as thousands of pounds were bet, and mainly lost, at the tables. In the time that we were there, "nobody broke the bank in Monte Carlo." A few of our number did try their luck in the main casino. In these humbler surroundings, a minimum stake of 10 francs enabled them to play, and lose, on the slot machines.

On the third day of the conference, the weather took a turn for the worse. Looking out from my balcony window, all I could see was swirling snow. Our last conference session was due to finish after lunch, and we then had the whole afternoon free to take in the sights.

Clearly, our decision to do this on the first afternoon was fully justified!

The conference formalities over, we did not venture far from the hotel. Snowfalls in Monte Carlo are both infrequent and unwelcome. Green grass had turned white overnight. Orange trees in the streets were just beginning to bear fruit. These too were covered in "the white stuff."

Expecting moderate Mediterranean weather, none of our party was really equipped for the snow, or the change in temperature that had come with it.

The receptionist informed us this was the worst weather they had experienced in the Principality for about 25 years. This was the last thing we wanted to hear!

Our group farewell dinner had been arranged as part of a predetermined itinerary. This involved a journey into the hills requiring a coach trip out of the city, the Principality and over the border into France.

We had all seen the final stages of the Monte Carlo Rally on television. The winding route into the city involved tight hairpin bends and very steep gradients. This was a challenging drive for experienced drivers even in good weather.

In the early evening, the coach arrived at the hotel, and we took our seats. The formalities of the conference were over. We were all in good spirits. I looked at the driver and gauged that he was about 27 years old. A thought crossed my mind. "If this was the worst weather for 25 years, how much experience of driving on snow had he gathered?"

He must have been a mind reader. "Don't worry about the weather," he advised. "I have driven all over the Alpine region. Thick snow is not a problem for me."

As we started our climb out of Monte Carlo, the snow became heavier, the road became more treacherous, and we witnessed several minor accidents involving vehicles coming down the hill towards us.

At the halfway point our driver pulled into a layby. "The road is worse than I expected," he announced. "Before we continue, I am just going to fit some heavier snow chains."

Several the members of the salesforce decided they would sample the conditions for themselves. The icy slope proved treacherous in their inappropriate footwear. A couple fell over, another was unable to walk uphill without sliding backwards out of control. Discretion proved the better part of valour. Everyone returned to the comfort of the coach. No sooner had the chains had been fitted, we were on our way again.

Eventually, we reached our destination and enjoyed a fantastic, "rustic" French six course meal, washed down with copious amounts of wine.

The amount of alcohol consumed was probably directly related to the fact that it was still snowing heavily, and we were now facing the equally testing journey back down to Monte Carlo. Normally, we would have expected everyone to be in good spirits, but this time the atmosphere was subdued.

After what seemed an age, we eventually drew up outside the Hôtel de Paris. The collective sigh of relief was almost audible!

Next morning, it was still snowing. It was clear that there would be some delay at the airport in Nice before we would all be able to board our respective flights for the journey back home.

Once at the airport, we were surprised that everything was apparently running to schedule. The same amount of snow falling back home would have meant long delays and even cancellations. The ground crew in Nice, where such occurrences were the exception rather than the rule, seemed totally unfazed.

We were sitting in the bar drowning coffees when a woman came across to me.

"It is you," she exclaimed. "You look much better in the flesh than on the telly," she continued. I was both flattered and puzzled but decided to go with the flow. "I heard that you had been training in the area. My friend had said that Geoff Capes was by the bar and thought I would come over and asked for your autograph."

The penny dropped. It was a case of mistaken identity!

I was not quite sure how to react. Geoff Capes was the European shotput champion at the time. He was the same height as me, had a similar beard but was four or five stones heavier. In my teens, I had been a club athlete, although my discipline was the discus.

Not wishing to deflate my "fan" and spoil her day, I signed the piece of paper she proffered with a personal message from Geoff Capes. All this took place much to the amusement of all my colleagues. Thankfully, she was on a different flight to the UK, so the subterfuge did not have to bear further scrutiny.

When we boarded our plane, we noticed that there was a member of the ground crew on each wing with a broom. They were using them to dislodge and sweep away the snow and ice that had collected there overnight.

With all the health and safety regulations now in place, I cannot conceive such a practice being tolerated today. At the time, we just laughed it off and settled down for take-off.

As far as I can recall, the rest of the journey back home was uneventful.

Measuring the effectiveness of Overseas Sales Conferences

Anyone reading about the Wrangler overseas sales conferences might be forgiven for thinking that they were all play and no work.

This would be an incorrect assumption.

During the growth of the jeans and jeans related clothing markets from the mid 1970's and the early 1980's, the Wrangler brand became one of the major players.

The Wrangler salesforce was the most efficient and well paid in the industry. This was not because the Wrangler branded product was hard to sell, on the contrary demand regularly exceeded supply.

At Blue Bell Apparel Limited, The Management Group had recruited a team of sales professionals who we believed would be able to up their game when the market became more competitive.

In the late 1970's, we had brought in McKinsey, the American business consultants, to assess our readiness to maintain business growth when the market stopped expanding "organically." We were aware, that when this happened, we would have to fight to maintain, let alone grow, our brand share.

The assessment of the consultants was positive. The McKinsey team were complimentary about our product development, our marketing, and our internal support structure. They flagged up the difficulties of maintaining the enthusiasm of the salesforce when a harder selling approach was required.

We were reminded of the saying; - "When the going gets tough and the tough get going!"

McKinsey made it clear to us that continuing to motivate the salesforce during difficult times would be key to achieving our ambitious growth targets.

"But how do you increase performance of a salesforce that is already well remunerated?"

At the time, we still employed four of the original sales agents who had, along with Dick Webzell, been the people who had established product distribution before the Wrangler brand was a major force.

Informal interviews established that sales agents were not motivated by the value of sales they achieve year on year. Instead, they judged their performance on the number of extra unit sales they made over the previous sales period. "Sell more units, make more money," was their mantra.

The members of the Blue Bell sales team were rewarded by the achievement of value of sales targets. "Hit the sales value targets and make more money," was their alternative mantra.

The Management Group realised that in a tough market it might be possible for a salesperson to meet value targets whilst at the same time selling in a reduced volume of merchandise.

We concluded, we needed to evaluate the inclusion of unit-based rewards that took account of the requirement to increase unit sales. This approach would ensure the company would be able to maintain and/or increase brand market share.

Added value incentives were part of a series of marketing programmes that were developed. The overseas sales conferences were also a key motivator.

It had been decided these meetings would be held every other year, provided the salesforce not only achieved their sales value targets, but also produced increases in unit sales and that the company increased its overall brand share and profitability.

Salespeople talk to salespeople in other companies. Success is measured by many different means. This includes the marque of car they drive and how often it is replaced.

Conferences in first class hotels, and in desirable overseas venues, sends out a clear message to competitors. "If they can afford to do this, they must be performing much better than we are."

From the onset of the overseas sales conference programme, there was clear change in attitude of the salesforce, particularly in areas against which success had not previously been measured.

Market research information that I presented at sale meetings stopped being regarded as "Robin Dilley's research statistics" and became "our research." Interest in brand share position against their competitors was now regarded as a tool to increasing their sales volumes.

During the period from 1979 – 1985, Wrangler managed to maintain sales volumes and brand share despite being outspent by our major competitor. This was as much to do with our success in motivating our salesforce, as the innovative advertising, sales promotion and point of sale campaigns that we developed and implemented.

Dick Webzell was a great believer in working his staff hard. He was also aware that rewarding them by letting them play hard, after they had achieved his demanding targets, would always pay dividends.

The effectiveness of the four overseas sales conferences was clear proof of the validity of this strategy.

Chapter Twenty-Two

International Marketing Meetings

When I joined Blue Bell in 1975, the company operated wholly owned subsidiaries across North America and Europe. In the Middle and Far East and South America, the Wrangler brand was sold under licence.

Blue Bell Apparel Ltd was responsible for marketing and sales in the United Kingdom and the Republic of Ireland.

In terms of financial reporting, we were also part of Blue International, an operational structure that was responsible for all sales outside the USA.

Regular meetings were held between the marketing and product development teams across all the European markets. This ensured that initial concepts for product lines, advertising and point of sale material could be shared at an early stage. If for instance, I was particularly interested in a point-of-sale item being produced by my colleagues in Benelux, I could add my requirements to their order. This would increase the overall order volume and reduce the price for both parties.

Our product development team could do the same with merchandise concepts.

During my time with the company, I travelled to 15 different countries, many of them on multiple occasions. It is always stimulating when you have an opportunity to interact and share ideas with your peers. I met a lot of very talented people. Along the way, I also learned that, despite language and cultural differences, good creative ideas are capable of transcending borders.

It is interesting how a common cause can create some interesting alliances!

My first Wrangler international marketing meeting took place in London, several weeks before I formally joined the UK operation.

I was warmly welcomed by all my colleagues to be, but I found myself on the same wavelength with two of them. One was Peter Koch from Germany. The other was Henk van der Feest from the Netherlands. The alliance seemed like a prelude to a joke about an Englishman, German, and a Dutchman. We had a similar sense of humour and could laugh with each other as well as at ourselves.

Peter's father would have served in the army for Germany during its expansion across Europe. My father was in the British army that was fighting against Germany. Henk's father was in the Dutch resistance during the German occupation.

We never mentioned the war. At Wrangler, we were brothers in arms!

I can remember one meeting in London that was being held in a hotel in Kensington.

My friends wanted to eat out and I took them to one of my favourite restaurants in Central London. After a great meal, we stood at the roadside waiting to flag down a cab. It was late, and we were not having much success. Peter Koch was becoming impatient.

"Never mind the taxi. We will walk back to the hotel." He declared. Quick as a flash, Henk responded. "Walk! I thought Germans only marched?"

We all looked at each other and burst out laughing and started walking. The usual stereotypes didn't apply to us.

I have many happy memories of the many international marketing meetings that were held at different venues across Europe. Several of the meetings proved to be particularly memorable.

European Marketing meeting in Bruges early 1977

Most meetings of the international marketing communications managers took place in Brussels. This ensured that members of the VP's covering planning development and advertising could attend without too much disruption to their day-to-day responsibilities.

We are all surprised when our meeting at the beginning of 1977 had been scheduled to take place in historic city of Bruges, capital of West Flanders, 60 miles from

Brussels. It was widely referred to as the "Venice of the North" because of its system of canals and bridges.

The reason quickly became clear during the meeting. It was announced that Jack Hill a senior European VP would be leaving to set up a new, wholly owned Blue Bell subsidiary in Australia.

Jack was a larger-than-life character who had been involved at the forefront of the company's growth in Europe during which he had opened many of the operating companies, including the UK. It was he who had appointed Dick Webzell as a sales agent and had recommended that he become Managing Director of Blue Bell Apparel Ltd.

It was generally agreed that Europe's loss would certainly be Australia's gain. We all pledged to provide him with as much support as he needed during the important start-up phase.

Amongst his many pleasures, was a love of sailing. He had an ocean-going yacht based in the port of Zeebrugge close to Bruges. As part of his farewell, Jack expressed a wish to entertain everyone for drinks on his boat and then introduce them to the delights of his favourite fish restaurant close by.

"A coach has been arranged and will pick you up at the hotel at 6.00pm. Dinner is booked for 8.30pm," he announced.

It was clear that it was going to be a memorable night. I calculated that the journey time to Jack's mooring was around 30 minutes. This left an awful lot of drinking time before dinner!

When we disembarked from the coach, Jack was already there to welcome us aboard in the spacious reception area below deck. He had arranged help from the restaurant to serve drinks and canapés. When a drink was finished, our glasses were quickly refilled. A copious amount of alcohol was being consumed. I consoled myself with the thought that the restaurant was only a few hundred yards from Jack's boat and the coach would be taking us back to the hotel afterwards.

At around 8.15pm jack called a halt to proceedings, "Everyone on deck please, our tables are waiting. I will lead the way," he advised.

We had been totally unaware, that during the time we had been enjoying ourselves below desk, the tide and gone out. Instead of a small walk across the gangway, we were now faced with climb of about 20 feet up an extremely wet and oily metal ladder. When totally sober this might have proved a daunting task but in our semi-inebriated state, and in the twilight, the climb seemed akin to scaling the north face of the Eiger.

None of us were prepared for such an arduous climb. The task was made more difficult because we were also dressed for dinner in our best Wrangler casualwear. I eventually made it to the top without transferring any of dirt from the ladder on to my clothes. Others were not so lucky!

The meal was memorial for its excellence and our ladder ordeal was quickly forgotten. It was Jack's ambition to exit Brussels with a bang. He had certainly succeeded!

Marketing planning meeting – Madrid, Spain - October 1979

During planning for the Spring 1980 season, the Management Team at Blue Bell Apparel had identified several factors that, if no remedial action was taken, were likely to affect the UK market share. Conversations with our colleagues in the other key European markets established they had similar concerns.

At the time, all European markets were part of the Blue Bell International Division. In the years of almost unrestrictive growth, Europe had made a massive contribution to the profitability of the whole organisation.

Any significant reduction in performance could have a major impact on future market development!

It was agreed that it would be useful for a European marketing planning meeting to be convened. Each country would present their marketing and communications plans and advise on actions to be taken to ensure that market share would not be eroded.

The meeting was scheduled to take place from 11-13 October 1979. Blue Bell Spain agreed to host it. Managing Directors and Advertising Managers from all the European Divisions were invited to attend.

A four-star conference hotel on the outskirts of Madrid was chosen as the venue. This was ideal for such an important meeting. Madrid can be a very seductive city with so much to see and do. Being more than 10 miles from the centre, we were able to fully concentrate on the job in hand and not be distracted by outside influences.

Dick Webzell and I presented our plan and explained how we intended to build our share through the activity planned through our sales promotion, advertising, and public relations campaigns.

Our optimism was shared by our colleagues in Germany, Benelux and Scandinavia who all reported they were also planning to increase their market share. France and Spain were much more cautious in their approach. Both markets had proved difficult primarily because strong local fashion brands had achieved brand leadership and neither Wrangler nor Levi's had managed "to carve out" a significant share.

Nevertheless, both subsidiaries were planning to maintain their unit sales to increase market share in a static market.

Only Blue Bell Italy seemed to be planning to buck the trend. "We have found it difficult to achieve any real foothold in our market," their advertising manager reported. "Italians are very fashion conscious. Wrangler is perceived as a basic commodity as far as the jeans retailers and consumers are concerned," she continued. "Our tops line is seen as extremely fashionable. We have decided to put all our effort to promote these heavily as 'Jeans above the waist.' It is hoped that this will help to stimulate sales of Wrangler jeans."

"How will that affect your market share and profitability?" she was asked. Wrangler manufactured jeans in our own factories and the profit margin was high. Tops were produced by outside companies, to our specification. Profit margins were much less.

"As you know, we have struggled to be profitable," the Italian General Manager advised. "Our new strategy is planned to reduce our loss to $250,000 by the end of 1980."

His response was met at first by stunned silence. Every member of the audience was aware that 1980 would be difficult. Part of our bonus package was geared to the ability of the whole division to at least remain profitable. The Italians were advised, in no uncertain terms, to return to the drawing board and review their marketing objectives and strategies. Nothing less than "break even" was acceptable.

Every other market offered to assist the Italians in product development and marketing support. I remember thinking, "the writing might be on the wall for Blue Bell Italy if no action is taken to significantly improve their sales of Wrangler jeans."

For the first two days and nights, all our meals were taken at the hotel. This was good for a constructive conference environment and facilitated a lot of informal networking. As we moved into the last day, we were all beginning to feel somewhat "stir crazy."

Our hosts had a little surprise up their sleeves. After the formal activities on the Saturday morning, we enjoyed a buffet lunch. A coach then arrived and took us on a guided tour of Madrid. "Just as a reminder of what you have been missing whilst cooped up in the hotel," our hosts advised us. "Tonight, we have booked a table for the group at the famous Sobrino de Botin in the Centre of Madrid. We suggest you take a taxi from outside the hotel. We will meet up for drinks at around 8.30pm."

I checked out the restaurant in the guidebook in my hotel room. Founded in 1725, It was listed in the Guinness book of Records as the World's Oldest Restaurant. Universally known as El Botin, it had been located at Calla Cuchilleros 17 since it was first opened.

Ernest Hemingway regarded it as his favourite restaurant and referred to "Botin's, and his favourite suckling pig," in his books "The Sun Also Rises" and "Death in the Afternoon." Other authors had referred to the restaurant in their works. These included F. Scott Fitzgerald, Graham Green, and James A. Mitchener. Folklore also suggested that the artist Francisco Goya had worked as a dishwasher in the kitchen when he was a teenager.

We were clearly going to have a great gastronomic experience!

The dilemma facing Dick and myself was how to get to the restaurant without having to pay for our taxi.

Having had two days of discussion related to marketing planning we had no wish to lose out in the "Wrangler expenses game" by picking up a taxi bill.

"No problem, I have a plan," Dick advised when we met up in the hotel reception. "I have checked with the hotel concierge he told me that a bus runs from outside the hotel right into the Centre of Madrid. It only costs a small amount of money, and anyone can direct us to the restaurant once we reach the bus station."

The arrival of the next bus was imminent, so we walked out to the bus stop. Within minutes we were on board. There were just a couple of problems. Neither Dick nor I was fluent in Spanish. The bus driver and, seemingly, none of the other passengers spoke little, if any, English.

My limited Spanish came up with "Dos boletos centre Madrid, por favor." This produced two tickets and a smile from the driver. My piece of paper with the address of Sobrino de Botin produced a flicker of recognition. As the bus set off, he made an announcement to our fellow passengers. This produced a flurry of conversation and a tap on my shoulder.

The driver had asked if anyone spoke English and could help him the answer the query that I had raised with him. Eventually, with the help of our "interpreter," and the enthusiastic intervention of fellow passengers, it became clear that we would have to catch another bus from the bus station in the centre of Madrid, to our restaurant. Our bus driver agreed to show us where it left from. He would then arrange for the driver to drop us off outside the restaurant.

We left the bus with a little more Spanish in our vocabulary and a lot of Spanish friends!

True to his word, the bus driver did arrange for our successful transfer to our next bus. He did speak to the driver, and we were dropped off outside Botin's.

After a journey of just over 30 minutes, and a total expenditure in the region of around £1, we were the first of the Wrangler party to arrive at the restaurant. Our colleagues were all impressed with the enterprise we had shown.

Botin's more than lived up to its reputation. Following in Hemingway's footsteps, the star of our meal was the "famous suckling pig" washed down with copious amount of Rioja.

For our return journey, we took advantage of one of the taxi's booked by our hosts from Blue Bell Spain. The journey was shared by our colleagues from Holland, after negotiating beforehand, an agreement was made to share the cost.

The Madrid meeting had highlighted how unprepared some of our colleagues in Europe were for the challenges ahead. The 1980's would prove to be a very interesting time.

European Marketing Meeting – Berlin 1980

Another meeting stands out in my memory. This took place in Berlin at a time when part of the city was situated in communist East Germany. The Berlin Wall divided East from West.

At the beginning of 1980, Peter Koch had signed a deal to sponsor the German leg of the world tour of "Up with People." The group comprised of college students from the USA. They were brought together to harness the positive energy of young people, and to give them a voice in the world, through the medium of music and song.

Peter was convinced that their message of hope would have resonance with the young people of Germany, who were also the core market for Wrangler Jeans. What better place to host such an event than Berlin where the division of East and Western Europe and the effects of the Cold War were brought very much into focus?

The event was scheduled around June 1980.

I had never travelled behind the "Iron Curtain" and had no idea what to expect when I took my seat for the flight to Berlin. At the time, there was only one non-stop flight daily from Heathrow to Tegal airport. The British Airways flight was operated by one of their ageing fleet of BAC One-Eleven 500s.

After leaving West German airspace, our aircraft had to maintain a constant flight path along what was referred to as the "Berlin corridor." The weather was perfect. Every landmark was visible on the ground. As we passed over a heavily forested area, I could clearly make out many wide, clearly defined tracks. They ran parallel to each other through the trees and appeared to go on for miles.

"I bet you are wondering what they are?" said the person sitting next to me. "They look like unfinished roads to me." I replied. "In a way, they are. They are used by the Soviet Army during manoeuvres in East Germany," my new-found friend advised.

We struck up a conversation during which he updated me on the political situation and the effect on Berlin and its inhabitants.

Eventually, we made the steep descent into Tegal Airport. There I met up with some of my colleagues from across Europe. We boarded a coach for the short journey to our Schloss Hotel and conference venue.

I was surprised how beautiful the city was. All greenery, forested areas, and lakes. This seemed a far cry from the urban wasteland, divided by the wall, that was featured on news reports and in feature films. We could have been in any European capital enjoying great company, luxurious accommodation, good food and drink.

Peter Koch had organised a great itinerary during our three days stay.

On our second night, we travelled to the centre of West Berlin for a meal. This was followed by a visit to the theatre for the "Up with People" concert.

When this was over, we walked the short distance to the iconic Brandenburg Gate. One of the best-known landmarks in Germany, it was built in the 18th century on the site of a former city gate. It had served as the monumental entry to the renowned boulevard, Unter den Linden, the direct route to the Royal Palace of the Prussian monarchs.

The building of the Berlin Wall had cut it off from the citizens of both sides of the divided city.

It was still early enough for us for us to climb onto a viewing tower and gaze across the mined no-man's land into East Germany. I can still remember how unnerving it was to see that our every move was being followed by armed troops, just a few hundred yards away. Their sole objective was to keep the West Germans out and keep their own citizens in. This involved using intimidation, and deadly force if necessary.

We all returned to the luxury of our hotel much chastened by the experience!

The conference moderator, Robin Hunter-Coddington opened proceedings on the final morning of the conference by introducing Charles Yatman, Vice President, Licensees, Blue Bell Inc.

At that time, his area of activity was mainly confined to South America where much progress had been made in developing the Wrangler brand in countries such as Brazil and Argentina.

Charles thanked us for allowing him to attend our meeting and explained that plans were in place to grow the market in South Africa, India, and Japan.

He felt sure that the markets he looked after would be very interested in the marketing activities of all the wholly owned subsidiaries. He requested the attendees keep him personally updated on any new marketing and advertising developments.

I had met Charles previously and was aware that, beneath an apparently quirky exterior, lay an extremely shrewd operator. He was well known for his somewhat "off the wall" sense of humour.

Winding up the session on behalf of our hosts, Peter Koch explained that a coach tour had been organised to allow us to see some of the sights of Berlin. This would also involve a tour of the East of the city behind the infamous dividing wall. He would be with us for the first part of the tour. Unfortunately, both he and our tour guide would not be able to join us in East Berlin. As citizens of West Germany, they were banned from doing so.

After a buffet lunch, we boarded our bus and set off on our tour.

Checkpoint Charlie was located on the historic Friedrichstrasse in the American occupied zone of the city. At the time, it was the only gateway through the Berlin Wall where Allied diplomats, military personnel and foreign tourists could pass legally into East Germany.

On the Allied side, our group registration visa was verified, before the members of our party crossed over the border on foot, re-boarded our coach, and met our East German guide and driver. A couple of heavily armed East German border guards boarded the coach and checked out our documents. This included the scrutiny of all our individual passports.

I was a little concerned because I sported a beard. In my passport photograph I was clean shaven. The guard took my passport and looked at the photograph. He looked at me and then back at the picture. After what seemed like several minutes, he handed back my passport and moved on. Much to my relief!

Whilst all this was going on inside the coach, two other guards were looking at the underside of our vehicle using large portable mirrors. They were checking to see whether anyone was trying to enter illegally by clinging to bottom of the vehicle.

When all our documents had been verified, the coach moved off. Our guide explained that we would see all the important sights of the city. He advised us we would be able to get off the coach for a short time but must stay together as a group. On NO ACCOUNT, should we wonder off alone. If stopped by the police, a person carrying a foreign passport, without an individual and up to date visa, might be arrested.

We had been warned!

As we drove round, our guide kept up a running commentary. Occasionally, this would include oblique references to the GDR's relationship with the Soviet Union.

"The radio mast you see over there, is the second biggest in the world. The biggest is in Moscow," he announced on one occasion. "The workmen building that tower block are from Sweden. We have no unemployment amongst men, or women, in the

GDR. We must rely on foreign workers for such manual work," he explained on another.

East Berlin contained all the historic palaces which had been reconstructed, with the help of the Soviet Union. Unfortunately, we could only view them through the windows of our coach.

At last, we arrived at Treptower Park. A visit here was the obligatory stop-off point for all Westerners on officially organised sightseeing tours into East Berlin.

Our guide explained that many of the smaller monuments in the memorial cemetery park to Soviet Army members who died in the battle for Berlin, contained marble recycled from the demolished New Chancellery.

The largest, and most dominant, of the monuments in the complex, was at the far end of the park. To reach it, required a long walk right through the war cemetery. It was several hundred metres from the viewing platform where we were standing.

A huge bronze statue, over 12 metres tall stood atop a large mound. Its pedestal contained a small memorial hall. The statue was highly symbolic. It depicted a Soviet soldier with a sword trampling on a smashed-up swastika. In his free arm, he was carrying a small child.

"Can we walk down and take a closer look?" asked Charles Yatman. "I am afraid not," explained our guide. "The memorial hall is closed today. We have only a limited time before we must leave."

That would have been the end of the matter for most people but, as we were to learn, Charles was not most people!

Our guide gave us "a guided talk." This turned out to be a mixture of historical fact interspersed with a large amount of "Soviet Era" propaganda. Nevertheless, it provided a new perspective on the cold war. In this case, from the other side of the Berlin Wall.

Little did we know, that within 10 years, the Berlin Wall and the GDR would be swept away with both two sides of Germany reunited as one nation!

We had come into the Treptower Park from what we thought was the only entrance.

Our Guide led us out in the opposite direction. "We have a drop-off and a different pick-up point to ease congestion," he explained.

When we returned to the coach, the driver had laid out a display of brochures, postcards, books, and trinkets for us to purchase as souvenirs of our visit.

In a hard-line communist state, capitalism was very much alive and kicking!

Our willing guide was certain that we did not have any East German currency but was happy to take West German Marks on a "one for one" exchange rate basis. As an East German Mark was worth considerably less than its West German equivalent, he was making even more money. The bus driver and our guide were both a state employee, all their takings were handed back to the East German Government.

As we bought our souvenirs, we were making a positive contribution to the economy of East Germany.

With the money-making activity concluded, our guide announced, "The coach will now leave for Check Point Charlie." "We can't leave yet," piped a voice from the back of the coach. "Charles Yatman isn't here."

Robin Hunter-Coddington looked horrified. As the named party leader on the group visa, he was responsible for ensuring that all his party returned to West Berlin. Our guide turned a deathly shade of white. He was responsible for the ensuring the return of all the party to the crossing point to the West, on pain of who knows what!

Instead, he was now faced with the task of finding an eccentric American tourist, walking around without a visa, before he was picked up by the authorities.

Robin and the guide returned to the viewing platform in the park. There, learning casually against one of the memorials, was the missing Charles.

It transpired that he had decided not to heed the explicit instructions of the guide and walked through the park to the statue of the Soviet soldier.

Finding the memorial hall was indeed closed, he had returned to the viewing platform to find that none of the party was there. Returning to where he thought the coach would be, he was dismayed to discover it was nowhere to be seen. He was faced with a dilemma. Should he stop an official and explain the situation or should he return to the viewing platform in the hope that his absence had been discovered and someone would come looking for him?

Thankfully, he chose the latter, much to the relief of Robin and the East German guide!

We reached the West without further incident.

Reflecting on the tour afterwards, the consensus was that East Berlin was quite impressive compared to many cities in the West. It did not stand comparison with West Berlin which was much brasher and more upwardly mobile.

Both parts of the city were shop windows for their respective ideologies!

In the East, the elite rich drove around in East German made Trabant's or Soviet made limousines. In the West, BMW's or Mercedes were the order of the day.

The conference finished with dinner in the hotel. The next day we all went our respective ways, thankful to be going home but grateful for the experience.

Did Charles Yatman forgive us for almost leaving him behind in East Berlin?

Newton's third law of physics states "For every action, there is an equal and opposite reaction." Exactly how that related to Charles and me, will be revealed elsewhere!

International Licensees Meeting – Singapore March 1981

At the beginning of the 1980's the Wrangler brand, was in demand across the world.

Blue Bell Inc. had a well-established policy of developing wholly owned subsidiaries in every country where they wished to operate. These were staffed by nationals who were experts in their respective jeans and leisure markets.

The blueprint had been especially successful across Europe where the company had succeeded in developing a significant market and profit share.

At a time of global expansion, the Board in Greensboro had decided on a different strategy to enable them to rapidly gain a foothold in markets across South America, Asia, and the Indian sub-continent.

They would appoint a licensee to handle and roll out the brand. In some cases, this involved the manufacturing process as well as the marketing. To maintain quality control, production standards used in the Blue Bell manufacturing plants around the world, were also applied to companies licensed to manufacture in these new markets.

The quality control department in Greensboro, and company engineers on the ground, were responsible for ensuring that standards were maintained through a rigorous regime of testing and factory visits.

A department was set up at the corporate headquarters to monitor and assist licensees to market the Wrangler brand.

Potential licensees undertook to follow the guidelines laid down to protect the international Trademarks. Blue Bell Inc. offered marketing material, produced in the USA and across their wholly owned subsidiaries, for licensees to adapt for their own use. This included advertising, sales promotion and point of sale material.

Initially, a representative from Greensboro attended the European International Marketing meetings. They then passed the information they had obtained to each of the countries under their control.

This system proved far from satisfactory!

At the end of 1980, it was decided international licensees would have their own meetings at which product and marketing ideas from north America and Europe would be presented.

I was invited to attend the first conference and present all new marketing concepts, that had been developed across European markets, for use during 1981. The meeting was scheduled to take place in Singapore at the beginning of March 1981.

Singapore had been chosen because new agreements had recently been signed in India and Japan. Blue Bell also had a successful licensee production and marketing agreement with one of the biggest manufacturing companies in Hong Kong and Singapore.

The invitation was a double-edged sword as far as I was concerned!

It offered the opportunity to visit Asia, but also involved additional work, when my schedule was already very busy. I was required to put together a half day presentation covering the marketing activity across the whole of Europe.

Dick Webzell was very supportive. He felt the experience would be of benefit both to me and to Blue Bell Apparel Ltd.

He and Kevin Black visited Hong Kong on twice yearly buying trips. They took advantage of a special ticket deal offered by Singapore Airlines.

This allowed them to travel first-class to Hong Kong returning via the United States. The overall cost of the journey was only marginally more than the price of an Economy Class return to and from Hong Kong.

Dick asked our travel agency to investigate whether I could take advantage of a similar deal for my trip. As it turned out, I could fly first-class by Singapore Airlines to Singapore where I would stay for the duration of the conference. From there, a connecting flight by the airline would take me to Hong Kong for three days and then on to San Francisco for one night.

Singapore Airlines associate Pan Am, would transport me first-class to Los Angeles for a two-night stop-over before the onward flight back to the UK.

The round-the-world first class ticket was only £130 more than the economy return journey from London to Singapore. In addition to the conference, I would be able to visit our licensees and manufacturers in Hong Kong and the offices of Blue Bell Inc in Los Angeles.

There was only one problem. The ticket was non-transferable. If any leg of the flight was missed, the additional ticket fees would have to be met by the ticket holder, on the full flight cost basis.

Dick signed off on the deal. "It is a long and arduous trip. We expect you to be at your best when representing the Blue Bell company. The benefits well exceed the relatively small additional cost," he argued.

Who was I to disagree!

On the 28 February 1981, I set off by car for the 150-mile journey to London Heathrow Airport for the first leg of my trip around the world. It was snowing heavily. With more snow forecast, I had allowed myself plenty of time to reach the airport.

It was just as well that I had. Forty miles into my journey, I realised that I had forgotten to pick up my wallet. As this contained all my money and credit cards, I could not travel without it.

In the days before mobile phones, I could not contact my wife and ask her to pick up my wallet and meet me halfway. I had no alternative but to drive back home, collect the missing item, and then set off once more. My error had added 80 miles to my journey. I now was in danger of possibly missing my flight.

I was aware, that failure to arrive on time would invalidate my original ticket and incur substantial additional cost. My wife rang the airline to explain the situation whilst I drove to Heathrow, as quickly as I possibly could, in the appalling road conditions. Thankfully, the weather had delayed both incoming and outgoing flights. I arrived at the check in desk well before my flight to Singapore was called.

Not a good start, but a salutatory lesson learned!

For the rest of my journey, I was careful to leave plenty of time for my connecting flights and to check that everything was to hand before setting out for the airport.

Eventually, my flight was called and, for the first time I experienced the pleasure of turning left, instead of right, on entering the flight cabin. It was like walking into a different world!

I came face-to-face with my first-class passenger hostess. She was dressed in an haute couture version of the traditional "Sarong Kebaya" that had been specially designed by Pierre Balmain in 1972. "The Singapore Girl" became the descriptive term for these distinctively clad hostesses. They also represented the visual trademark of the airline. The term was claimed to engender Asian values and hospitality. These were described as "caring, warm, gentle, elegant and serene."

These values perfectly epitomised my own experience.

"Follow me, Mr. Dilley," my hostess politely invited. After settling me down in my seat, she continued. "Can I get you a cocktail before take-off." Two cocktails later, the trauma of the first part of my journey had been forgotten. I settled down for my long flight, in a totally relaxed state of mind.

During my flight, I witnessed sunset over the Acropolis as we landed in Athens to take passengers on board. After an excellent dinner, I grabbed a few hours' sleep on my "full-size bed" on the first-class upper deck. I woke up in time to witness dawn over the desert during a refuelling stop in Abu Dhabi.

After several more excellent meals, washed down copious amounts of alcoholic drink, we eventually landed at Changi Airport in Singapore. My overall flight time had been over 17 hours during which we had passed through several time zones.

Having left London at 3.00pm on Saturday 28th February 1981, it was 7.00pm on Sunday 1st March, when I eventually checked into my room at the Intercontinental Hotel.

The conference organisers had left an itinerary covering the next three days. In it, I found that all the other delegates had arrived the day before me. Whilst I was in the air, they had been on a trip on a sailing boat to visit one of the 63 islands that make up the Territory.

Singapore lies about one degree north of the Equator and the temperature during March averages around 31.6 degrees. To cool down, they had enjoyed a dip in sea, in a secluded bay, before an al fresco lunch in the sun.

A group dinner had been organised in the hotel for 8.30pm, to allow them to "recover from their ordeal." I, on the other hand, was suffering from the effects of jet lag and the high humidity.

Deciding to walk around the area surrounding the hotel, I was immediately pestered by individuals on foot or in slow moving vehicles offering to introduce me to "all manner of unwanted dubious activities."

Retreating to the air-conditioned security of the hotel, I read all the literature that had been provided in my conference pack. One which particularly caught my eye, was a small hard cover book entitled "A guide to shopping in Singapore." The foreword, by the local tourist board, explained the barter principle that applied in even the most exclusive shops. It listed the branded items such as jewellery, watches, cameras, and small electrical items, that tourist tended to purchase as souvenirs of their visit.

For each item shown, there were three prices printed. These were, the recommended retail price, a suggested starting price for negotiation and the final offer price that should never be exceeded.

I made a mental note, to have this with me during my planned shopping and sightseeing trip, on the free day I had organised before I moved on to Hong Kong.

Meeting up with my fellow delegates during the pre-dinner drinks, I was far from my best. Whilst they all appeared refreshed and ready for an extended evening of social activity, I was nearly out on my feet. After dinner, I made my excuses, went back to my room, and crashed out immediately to catch up on some much-needed sleep.

The clock recorded the local time at 10.30pm. My internal clock was still on UK time which was 8 hours earlier. When my alarm call went off at 6.30am local time my body was telling me it was the middle of the night before. Very confusing!

Thankfully, I had a day and a half to recover before my presentation.

Our conference host was the Yangtzekiang Garment Manufacturer Co. Ltd. The company was not only a major supplier of Wrangler jeans related clothing, but it was also the licensee for the Wrangler brand in Hong Kong and Singapore.

I had met Chan Suk Ling, "Shirley," at several meetings in Europe. At the time, she was responsible for marketing the Wrangler brand in Hong Kong and Singapore. Her brother, Chan Wing Ming, "Michael," was heavily involved in the manufacturing side of the company in Singapore. He also attended some of the sessions.

Our new licensees from India and Japan, as well as all the licensees from South America, were also in attendance.

Owing to the high humidity outside, we were all thankful that the conference was taking place inside the air-conditioned splendour of the Intercontinental Hotel.

Three days of intensive presentations, interspersed with multiple drink and food breaks, may not seem like hard work - but it certainly was!

Since the conference began, I had not left the confines of the hotel and was looking forward to our farewell dinner on the last evening and a few hours of sightseeing before catching my Thursday evening flight to Hong Kong.

I explained to "Shirley" that I would be spending Friday and Saturday in Hong before my onward flight to the USA. She had spoken to "Michael" and he had invited me to look round their Singapore factory on the Thursday morning. Shirley was also keen for me to meet her other brothers Chan Wing Fui, "Peter," who was Managing Director of the company and Chan Wing Sun, "Samuel," the Company Secretary.

She would also organise a tour of part of their Hong Kong operation. To facilitate this, "Shirley" had set up meetings on the Friday morning and arranged for a car to pick me up from my hotel in Kowloon. This change of plan meant that my sightseeing ambitions would be severely curtailed. Nevertheless, I was grateful for the opportunity the visits would afford me.

On our last night, a coach was laid on to take us to the best Chinese restaurant in Singapore. Our hosts laid on a multi-course banquet of excellent food and drink. Afterwards, the toasts seemed to go on for ever. By the time we re-boarded our coach, we were all very mellow. Most of us went straight to our beds leaving the "more hardy members of our party" to hit the Singapore night scene.

The next morning, after breakfast, we said our goodbyes and checked out of our rooms to go our separate ways.

A car arrived to take me to me to the Singapore factory of Yangtzekiang Garment Manufacturer Co. Ltd. The plan was for me to meet up with "Michael," for a tour of the factory and have a spot of lunch. The driver would then take me on a short tour of Singapore before driving me out to the airport to catch my early evening flight to Hong Kong.

"Michael" was the youngest of the children of the company's founder. He had joined Yangtzekiang after completing a bachelor's degree at Boston University, USA in 1977.

Greeting me warmly, he began by explaining the YGM philosophy to garment production and human resource management. "We believe in investing in the latest technology to ensure that we maintain a consistent high quality of production," he explained. "Our staff are very important to us," he continued. "We invest a lot of time in training, and we pay above the market hourly rate. We also reward long service. Anyone retiring, with an exemplary service record, will receive a pension and equity in the company," he concluded.

The factory in Singapore manufactured shirts and tee-shirts for many well- known international brands, including Wrangler. The production line was indeed state-of-the-art. It was clear that every member was proud to be part of the team producing quality garments for the worldwide market. I was very impressed!

On our way to lunch, we entered the lift. It was operated by an old gentleman dressed in traditional Chinese clothing and sporting a long white beard that nearly reached his waist. "Michael'" introduced him adding: - "(He) is our longest serving employee. He came over with my father from mainland China in the early 1950's."

When we were out of earshot, I posed the question, "When will he be retiring to take his pension and equity?" "Michael" smiled. He understood what I was getting at. "He is very loyal to my father and the company and does not want to stop working right now," he replied. "When he does, he will be well rewarded." It became clear that the family were already looking after his welfare. In addition to a salary, they were also providing rent-free accommodation.

As we sat on the open balcony of a nearby restaurant, the heavens opened. The rain was so heavy that it was hitting the road and pavement and bouncing several feet into the air.

"It often rains like this, especially during March. It won't last long," "Michael" assured me. "It will clear up before you start your tour." Sure enough, after less than an hour, the rain had stopped, the sun was out and, in no time at all, there was no trace that the "monsoon conditions" had ever happened.

I had a couple of hours before I needed to check in for my onward flight to Hong Kong. My driver guide took me past all the main tourist spots including Raffles Hotel and the Harbour area. There was no time to sample the famous "Singapore Sling" but I made a mental note to ask for one on the plane.

I checked in on time for my early evening Singapore Airlines flight for the four-hour journey to Hong Kong.

Relaxing in my seat in the first-class cabin, I did indeed sample one, or maybe several, "Singapore Slings." I also enjoyed an excellent meal. Time does indeed pass quickly when you are really enjoying yourself!

Nothing quite prepared me for our landing in Hong Kong!

The old airport, in operation at that time, jutted out into the harbour. To reach it, the flight path took the aircraft between high rise buildings before making a sharp right turn on to the runway.

The runway was quite short. There was no margin for error!

Out of the cabin window, I could see inhabitants of the surrounding high-rise buildings sitting on their balconies, bringing in the washing and going about their everyday lives. They all seemed totally oblivious to the fact that large aircraft were passing close by, on a very regular basis!

I was full of admiration for the pilots!

Within an hour of landing, I was checking into the Hong Kong Hotel in Kowloon. Once my luggage was unpacked, I decided to go for a walk around the surrounding area. My hotel was well placed. It was close to the centre of the main shopping area, countless eating places and just a short walk from the waterfront.

Even though it was now around 11.30pm, the weather was relatively warm and the humidity not too oppressive. Despite the late hour, I was amazed just how many people were about. The whole area was absolutely buzzing!

The iconic view across the harbour to Hong Kong Island, was spectacularly lit up by both heavy sea traffic and beating heart of the busy metropolis just a short ride away.

I made my way to the Star Ferry jetty only to find that the last ferry of the night had already departed. Returning to the hotel after midnight with a ferry timetable, I was determined to make the journey later.

After breakfast on Friday morning, my driver arrived to take me on a short journey to the offices of Yangtzekiang Garment Manufacturer Co. Ltd. in the nearby business district of Kowloon.

"Shirley" met me in reception and introduced me to her brothers Chan Wing Fui, "Peter" and Chan Wing Sun, "Samuel."

"Peter" had received a master's degree in Administration Science in 1969 at Yale in the USA. Later that year, he had joined the company, became a director in 1971 and was appointed Managing Director in 1980.

"Samuel," received his bachelor's degree in 1970 from the University of Manchester in the UK. After qualifying as a Chartered Accountant in 1973, he had been appointed Company Secretary the following year.

During our meeting, I was struck just how enthusiastic they all were to build on the legacy and business ideals of their father, who had founded the company from scratch some 30 or so years before.

I thanked them for their time. Just has I preparing to leave for the visit to the manufacturing unit, the phone rang. "Shirley" answered it, engaging in a short conversation before putting the phone down and turning to me. "That was my father," she said. "He has heard that you are in the building and would very much like to meet you."

I was honoured. Chan Sui Kau had founded the company in 1949 building it from a single production unit to a multi-national conglomerate. At the time, he was President of the Federation of Hong Kong Garment Manufacturers and served on several other industry bodies. Unofficially, his peers had given him the nickname "King of Hong Kong's Garment Industry."

He was a very busy man, yet he had made time welcome me to his organisation. This was akin to really being granted an audience with royalty. The difference was that Chan Sui Kau had built his empire through his own endeavours, a lot of hard work and a shrewd business sense.

I can remember very little about the content of the meeting other than he appeared genuinely interested in what I was doing. He was also quite prepared to answer any questions that I put to him. We said our goodbyes before I left with "Shirley" for the factory visit.

In the 1980's, the British Clothing industry was going through a difficult time. This was due, in no small part, to a lack of technological investment during the previous 10 years. More and more orders were being placed offshore. Hong Kong had benefited hugely from this trend. UK bosses blamed their inability to compete on "cheap labour and a sweat shop culture in the colony."

Like the YGM plant in Singapore, the factory in Hong Kong was state-of-the-art. The latest technology, modern production machinery and a well-paid, motivated workforce, produced a world beating, quality product.

In that instant, I realised that the clothing industry in the UK was doomed. With a relatively high paid workforce and a low investment in technology, it would be impossible, in my mind, for the industry to catch up and get ahead of the game once more.

Over a working lunch, I chatted to "Shirley" about the future of the industry as she saw it. "We are not complacent," she informed me. "Currently, we have an advantage over our competitors in the rest of Asia."

"Where do you see the threat to Hong Kong's dominance coming from?" I asked.

"Taiwan, mainland China and India offer an immediate threat. As technology becomes less expensive and more readily available, smaller Asian countries, with a lower wage base, will eat into the market share that Hong Kong currently holds," she predicted.

"What strategy will YGM be adopting to grow your business?" I queried.

"We will invest now in the emerging markets. We can offer technical, production and marketing expertise. We will use these skills to train the potential management and their workforce. This will ensure that our quality standards, and profit margins, are maintained, even in low-cost based economies," she answered.

It was clear to me then, that the development of YGM was secure well into the future.

After lunch, I said my goodbyes to "Shirley" and her driver took me back to the hotel.

My outbound flight to San Francisco was scheduled to leave at around 10.30pm on Saturday evening. For the rest of Friday, and the whole of Saturday, my time was my own. After writing and posting cards to family and friends, I browsed through some of the tourist guides and worked out a plan of action.

I looked around the tourist areas of Kowloon and honed my bargaining skills to secure the best deals possible for presents for my wife and children.

The Chinese shopkeepers proved to be very adept at this skill and were careful to ensure their body language gave nothing way. Even though I was initially very happy with the deals I had negotiated, I was left with a lingering doubt that the shopkeepers had come out on top. At the end of the process, they always seemed even happier than they were at the start of the negotiations!

That evening, I took the Star Ferry across to Hong Kong Island.

If I thought Kowloon was busy, the crowds across the water appeared to be of a different magnitude. Hong Kong is a small place with a very large population. Being on the streets at night, was probably infinitely more attractive than being cooped up in a small apartment in a large housing block.

Having walked around for a couple of hours, I found a small restaurant, just off the main tourist route. With a mixture of broken English, arm waving and pointing, I selected several dishes from the menu. When everything arrived, I enjoyed a fantastic feast, despite being unaware, in most cases, exactly I was eating.

The journey on the ferry back to Kowloon was as spectacular as I had anticipated it would be. Crossing the busy stretch of water was reminiscent of the 'SON ET LUMIÈRE displays" I had witnessed in other parts of the world.

This, however, was the real thing. The working harbour was a maelstrom of sound and light. The journey exceeded all my expectations. It also provided the best value-for-money experience I have enjoyed anywhere in the world, before or since!

Back at the Hong Kong Hotel, I ordered a night cap in the bar before taking the lift to my room. All the hotel restaurants were located on the second floor. My lift stopped there, and the doors opened. A couple were waiting to get in.

To my surprise, I knew the man. He was a buyer for one of the big store groups in the UK. I had met him, and his wife, on several occasions back in the UK. The attractive young lady on his arm was certainly not his wife.

The buyer did not look pleased to see me. "Robin, what on earth are you doing here?" he exclaimed. As he regained his composure, he introduced his companion, "This is Melanie, (name changed to protect the innocent) my buying assistant. Melanie, this is Robin Dilley of Wrangler."

We shook hands and I explained that I was passing through and would be leaving the next day. He told me he and his companion were on a buying trip and would be staying for another three days.

At that point, the lift arrived at my floor. We said our goodbyes and went our separate ways. I didn't see them at breakfast, so any further awkwardness was avoided.

Back in England, I met him many more times over the intervening years. We never mentioned our meeting in Hong Kong. Funnily enough, I never saw his buying assistant again either!

I had arranged for a late check out from the hotel, and they had organised a taxi to take me to the airport at around 8.30pm. This gave me ample time to visit some of the islands close to Hong Kong. These were part of the 1898 Second Convention of Peking which leased the New Territories to the United Kingdom for 99 years.

Sadly, there was insufficient time for a quick tour into mainland China. I would be unable, therefore, to add another name to the list of countries I had visited.

The tourist guide recommended a long harbour tour that included a short stop over at Cheung Chau Island. Here, the guidebook assured me, I would get a feel of "the real China." Over the years Cheung Chau had evolved from a fishing village into "a commercial hub and marketplace" for people living on nearby islands such as Lantau.

Our small boat was not built for tourist travel. Only limited refreshments were available on board. The tour guide, "our captain," kept up a running commentary pointing out landmarks and the geography whilst avoiding being mown down by heavy merchant shipping that included Junks from mainline China, commercial shipping, and cruise liners from all over the world.

The weather in Hong Kong can be somewhat changeable in March. Luckily, the sun was shining and, even accounting for the sea breeze, it was pleasantly warm. This was just as well because if it had rained, there was only minimal shelter on board the vessel. Eventually, we came to the highlight of the trip. Our two hours stop over on Cheung Chau Island included a short tour and lunch in a local restaurant.

Another boat had docked immediately before us. This, our captain explained, was a funeral boat and that the funeral party and the coffin, would disembark and walk in procession to a nearby temple. "We are very lucky to have arrived in time to witness this event," we were informed. "Stay where you are. We will disembark for our tour as soon as the precession is out of sight."

I glanced at our "authentic Chinese funeral party." Many were dressed in designer jeans and modern tops. It seemed likely that this was a staged event for tourists rather than a "real funeral."

Today, I understand that tourism is a major source of income for the island. The old buildings and temples have been fully restored and the cultural heritage of its people projected in a very professional way. In 1981, tourism was in its infancy. What it lacked in finesse was more than made up for by the enthusiasm of the people to make us welcome.

Our lunch was very acceptable and locally produced souvenirs of our visit to the island, were readily available to purchase.

I arrived back at the hotel at about 6.30pm. There was ample time to complete my packing and have a small snack in the restaurant and check out of the hotel, before my taxi arrived.

My flight to San Francisco was on time and I soon settled into my seat drinking cocktails and preparing for take-off.

This flight proved to be one of the most unusual I have ever undertaken!

The direct flying time is under 14½ hours but because Hong Kong is 16 hours ahead of San Francisco, travellers find themselves landing in the USA 1½ hours before they set off.

Our flight was scheduled to land at Honolulu in Hawaii. There we would disembark to go through immigration into the USA. Honolulu is 18 hours ahead of Hong Kong. This meant that we were scheduled to land there at around 4.00pm in the afternoon. This was six hours before we had left Hong Kong.

None of this is any good for the body clock or for eating patterns. At take-off, I set my watch to San Francisco time and just went with the flow. When food arrived, I just ate it, regardless of whether I felt hungry or not.

The first part of our journey, all 11½ hours of it, appeared to be over in no time. I cannot recall having slept, but I must have done. Whether this was before or after breakfast, somewhere over the Pacific, was a blur.

I remember looking out of the cabin window as Honolulu came into view and feeling the welcome warm sunshine as we disembarked for the long immigration process.

Because we were officially "in-transit," neither I nor my fellow passengers were able to leave the airport building. Instead, we were ushered into an unwelcoming transit lounge with no access to any refreshments. Out of the window, I could only catch a glimpse of the enticing cloud free blue skies and only dream about laying on a sun-drenched beach as the Pacific rollers crashed in.

An hour of waiting passed slowly before we eventually reboarded the aircraft and I continued my first-class odyssey. After an afternoon snack and then dinner, the final 4½ hour leg of my journey ended when the aircraft finally touched down at San Francisco airport. I had arrived at my next destination on the same day and at roughly the same time as I had left Hong Kong.

I said my goodbyes to the crew, and Singapore Airlines.

The next two legs of my journey would still involve travelling first-class, courtesy of their partner airline Pan Am.

My schedule allowed for an overnight stay in San Francisco and a day of sightseeing before my onward flight to Los Angeles.

Dick Webzell and Kevin Black, who had made the same journey only six months before, had given me some tips on what to see and do during my short stay.

My overnight stay was at the iconic St Francis Hotel. It was centrally located in Union Square and well placed for everything I planned to do.

The Landmark Building had been originally erected in 1904. It was partly destroyed in the earthquake and fire of 1906. It was rebuilt and reopened in 1907. The newest part of the hotel was the 32 storey, Tower Building that had opened in 1971.

On the advice of my colleagues, I had arranged that my room booking would be for a business double in the Tower Building. "The Landmark Building needs updating," they advised. "The Tower Building is modern and much more comfortable."

When I arrived at the check in desk, I was told that they had allocated me a room in the Landmark Building. I had been travelling for 16 hours. I was tired, and jet lagged. All I wanted was a quick shower and a good night's sleep!

Usually, the service in hotels in America is first-class. When it is good, it is very, very good but when it is bad it is awful. This was one of those awful occasions. The night staff at the St Francis were insistent that I had not been booked into the Tower Building even though I had documentation, from my travel agent, to show that I had.

Tired though I was, it became a matter of principal!

I asked to see a manager. A young man, obviously not a manager, was sent out to see me. "There is nothing I can do," he said. "The room that is waiting for you is one of the best we have." Too tired to argue further, I took the key offered and went up in the lift to my floor.

My room was large. The furniture was in keeping with the grandeur of the hotel's heritage. The bathroom, and its plumbing, was functional, but far from fulfilling my expectations of a five-star hotel.

Although I was far from happy, I decided to take up my complaint again, after I had enjoyed good night's sleep.

Next morning, after a hearty American breakfast, I managed to track down the hotel duty manager. He checked my documents, agreed that I had been given the wrong room, and apologised for what had happened at check-in.

He organised a discount on the price, extended my check-out time to late afternoon and organised for a cab to pick me up at the hotel and transfer me to the airport. This concession meant that I would have time to check out many the sights of San Francisco. I could then return to my room, to freshen up, before leaving for the airport. My flight to Los Angeles was due to take off at around 7.00pm.

Like thousands of other tourists, I took a trolley car from almost outside the hotel and enjoyed the ride all the way to Fisherman's Wharf. The sun was shining in a cloudless blue sky. I had not booked any of the available tours such as a visit to Alcatraz or a Bay Cruise to the Golden Gate Bridge. Instead, I was content to mingle with the crowds and take in the sights I had only previously seen in films and on television.

I tried to avoid the obvious "tourist traps" and found a small fish restaurant where I enjoyed an excellent lunch.

Time just flew by. It was time to say goodbye to the waterfront and board a trolley car back to the hotel. Once in my room I enjoyed a refreshing shower and then had a farewell drink in the bar. Bang on time, my taxi arrived to whisk me to the airport.

I had never flown Pan Am before and did not know what to expect.

Turning left into the first-class cabin was still an exhilarating experience but Pan Am was no Singapore Airlines. In place of the exotic "Singapore Girl's," were conventionally clad, super-efficient, somewhat intimidating, Pan Am air hostesses.

I was shown to my seat, given a drink and dinner menu, and informed that my order would be taken – "as soon as the aircraft is airborne."

The flight time from San Francisco to Los Angeles was about 1½ hours. During that time, the crew managed to serve pre-dinner drinks and a very palatable three-course dinner complete with wine. Before I knew it, we were beginning our descent into Los Angeles.

By 10pm, I was checking in at my hotel, The Beverley Hilton, on Wilshire Boulevard in Beverley Hills.

At breakfast the next morning, I enjoyed a selection of American favourites whilst scanning the room to see whether any famous Hollywood personalities were staying at the hotel. One or two "B" list celebrities were sitting in prominent places around the room along with the odd television series star.

The "A" listers were obviously enjoying the breakfast delights in the privacy of their own suites!

I had ordered a hire car before leaving the UK. The company arranged to drop it off at the hotel before 10am. When it did not arrive, I asked the concierge to telephone them and find where it was. There had been a mix up apparently. My car would not be dropped off at the hotel until 1.00pm.

After travelling around the world with no mishaps, the American leg of my tour was not going to plan!

At the front desk of the hotel, I obtained a map of the Hollywood area. Not very far away was Century City. Built on the former back lot of the Twentieth Century Fox studio it boasted hotels, a shopping mall and many independent shops, cafes, and restaurants. The concierge informed me that it was only minutes away. He gave me a leaflet containing a map showing how to get there. It extolled the virtues of the places describing it as the place to be seen and the haunt of the rich and famous.

It was obviously one of THE places to visit!

The weather was perfect. The sky was blue, the sun was shining. Having spent much of the previous 10 days either on an aircraft, in a hotel conference room, or visiting suppliers, I convinced myself that a gentle stroll would be very refreshing. I had never been to Los Angeles before. Within minutes of setting off, I became acutely aware that I was the only person on the sidewalk. Apart from one passing jogger, I was the only pedestrian to be seen.

Clearly, nobody in Beverly Hills walked anywhere!

After a brisk stroll lasting about 20 minutes, I finally arrived at Century City and went into the Westfield Century City shopping mall to look round. This was a Monday morning and yet the place was buzzing.

I felt that I had inadvertently wondered onto the set of "Stepford Wives." The Centre was full of beautiful people sporting perfect tans, perfectly coiffed hair, perfect white teeth shining out of permanently smiling mouths. And these were only the people serving in the stores and cafes and restaurants.

Their customers were even more striking!

The realisation struck home. Hollywood was full of beautiful people who had travelled from all over the globe in the hope of being discovered and becoming a star. Out of the thousands of hopefuls, only a handful made the big time. The rest took up jobs in restaurants and stores where they could see and be seen.

Feeling a little like a fish out of water, I found a small café where I fortified myself for the lonely walk back to the hotel. When I enquired at reception on my return, I was informed that my hire car had still not arrived.

I decided to order myself a light lunch by the pool. The receptionist said that she would send someone out to inform me as soon as the car materialised. About 30 minutes later, the message came through and I went to reception to complete all the paperwork.

The representative of the hire car company was full of apologies. "We have upgraded you to a top of the range Ford Mustang," he announced. "The delay has been caused by an administrative error on our part. By way of compensation, we will pick up the car at the hotel on your last day here. Our representative will then drive you over to the airport in time to catch your flight."

I was happy to accept their offer and we agreed a pick-up time. They assured me that they would be with me in plenty of time although, I don't think I was totally convinced.

Driving in the USA was something I had done before but driving solo would be a new experience. Previously, there had always been a navigator to read the map and follow directions. LA was not the ideal place to go it alone.

I decided to visit the Wrangler offices in the downtown area. On the map, it seemed straightforward. I simply had to follow Wilshire Boulevard straight into the centre of the city, find the nearest public carpark and walk a few blocks to my destination.

Driving my Mustang was easy enough. The controls seemed familiar, and the car handled well. After a trouble-free journey, I reached the city centre and found a large outdoor parking lot. I realised, that the downtown area I was in, was not as salubrious as Hollywood had appeared. On the other hand, the carpark was patrolled and looked reasonably secure.

I parked up and switched off the engine. To my horror, I could not remove or turn the ignition key. Panic almost set it. I did not know what to do. It would not be sensible to leave the car unattended whilst I tried to get help.

Scrabbling about in the glove compartment, I found a booklet that included driving instructions for the Ford Mustang. The dashboard illustration included an "ignition key release button" that was situated close to the steering wheel. I pressed the button, and the key was released. Panic over!

I made a mental note to acquaint myself with the whereabouts of all the vehicles dashboard controls, lights, wipers etc. before my next journey.

Then, locking the car and checking that it was secure, I set off for the Wrangler offices just a few blocks away.

Leaving the lift at the appropriate floor, I found a large glass door on which were graphics indicating that this was the West Coast office of Blue Bell Inc. and showing all the companies brand names including Wrangler.

I had obviously found the right place and, pressing the doorbell, I stood and waited for someone to let me in. After a short delay, a man came to the door. Over the intercom, I explained who I was and showed him my business card through the glass.

The door was opened and the man behind it introduced himself as the Divisional Manager. "I apologise for all the questions," he said. "We used to have an open house but after a spate of robbery's, we have had to increase security."

My host appeared pleased to see me. Much of his time was spent monitoring the performance of his sales force and answering telephone queries from customers. As he showed me round, it became clear that he received very few visitors from the Blue Bell headquarters in Greensboro, NC. This was nearly 3000miles away.

To have someone visiting all the way from Europe was unprecedented. I was made very welcome, plied with coffee and biscuits and we had a very useful chat.

My new-found friend was operating deep inside enemy territory. Levi's was the main competitor to Wrangler in North America as well as Europe. Levi Strauss had its corporate head office in San Francisco. California was very much their own turf.

He was astonished to learn we had overtaken them in the UK and that Wrangler was a strong number two in most other European countries. We exchanged cards and vowed to keep in touch. Saying our goodbyes, I left him to his relative solitude and returned to my car.

Dick Webzell and Kevin Black had suggested that I should visit Rodeo Drive. More precisely they were referring to a three-block stretch north of Wilshire Boulevard and south of Little Santa Monica Boulevard. It, and the larger business district surrounding it, had become known as 'The Golden Triangle.' The area was both a shopping area for luxury fashion goods and a major tourist attraction.

"We go there to see what the shops are selling and what their customers are wearing," Kevin had explained. "What is big in Rodeo Drive, when you visit, will be the next big thing in the UK 6 months later." I was intrigued and decided that I must visit the area and see for myself.

Rodeo Drive was not far from my hotel. It was mid-afternoon. I had plenty of time to combine a little bit of business with pleasure. Consulting my map, I headed out of the city and back in the direction of the Hollywood Hills.

During my morning visit to Century City, I had been blown away by the sight of beautiful people being attended by beautiful people.

Rodeo Drive was frequented by beautiful people who had really made the grade. These were the success stories in a town seemingly obsessed with wealth and looks. When I visited, there was plenty of that on show.

My father always told me, that if something I saw in a shop window that did not have a price on it, I could not afford it. Rodeo Drive took that philosophy to a whole new level. None of the items, in any of shop the windows, had a price on them.

Browsing inside was only possible if you were able convince the security guard on the door that you were affluent enough to be able to pay for any goods selected. Shop sales staff only appeared to lavish attention on customers they felt certain were going to buy.

Anyone who has ever seen the film "Pretty Woman" will remember that it contains a famous scene that perfectly illustrates the reality of buying, or trying to buy, at a shop in Rodeo Drive.

Having said that, I was glad that I had taken the trouble to visit.

The casual fashions on display were being worn by people who in the UK would be labelled "fashion innovators." Back home, this group represented less than 10% of the market. In Rodeo Drive, it was probably closer to 80%. I could understand why Kevin was keen to ensure that he, and other key members of his product development team, made regular visits.

After a couple of hours, I had grown tired of watching the "haves" flaunting their wealth.

This "have not enough" was beginning to feel weary, and hungry. It was time to find my car and locate my hotel. Within 10 minutes, I was back at the Beverly Hilton and taking advantage of the valet parking service.

One of my favourite eating places in London was "Trader Vic's" located at the London Hilton. The Polynesian themed restaurant chain was founded in St Francisco in the 1930's by Victor Jules Bergeron Jr (nicknamed Trader Vic). The first franchised "Trader Vic's" opened in 1940. During the 1960's, they rapidly expanded around the world.

Trader Vic and his friendly competitor, Don the Beachcomber, both laid claim to the invention of the "Mai Tai" cocktail that was to become one of the franchises signature drinks.

It is said, "When in Rome do as the Roman's do."

Here I was in California, the spiritual home of "Trader Vic's." The Beverly Hilton had one of its franchised restaurants on the premises. There was only one place that evening where I was going to eat, and only one drink I was going to drink.

Both the food and the "Mai Tai" cocktails lived up to my expectations!

After a great night's sleep, I awoke to bright sunlight and clear blue skies. I was determined to see as much as possible during my last full day in LA. Immediately after breakfast, I called up my car and set off to nearby Santa Monica. In its publicity, it cast itself as "the perfect beach town with a plethora of attractions."

Beachside, there was not a lot of difference between it, and the seaside resorts on the east coast of Yorkshire where I went on holiday as a child. Except for the fact that it was warmer, the beach was cleaner, the rolling waves breaking on the beach had travelled all the way across the Pacific and there was a bright yellow disc in the sky.

Despite of all these things going for it, it was still a seaside town. Unfortunately, they have never been my thing. Putting aside my prejudices, I set out to take a closer look.

I strolled along the beach, visited the famous Pier with its iconic red and yellow Ferris wheel and quickly took in the "delights of Pacific Park." A full-service amusement park, it offered arcade games, tourist restaurants, bars, souvenir shops, street performers and many requests to "snag a stick of puffy cotton candy" (candy floss in the UK).

My kids would have loved it, unfortunately, they were 5,600 miles away. The whole experience simply reminded me how much I was missing my family back home.

Just a few blocks away from the beach, I found an entirely different Santa Monica. Here was an example of coastal sophistication with outdoor cafés, inviting restaurants and fantastic shops. For a single traveller like me, this was a far better place to be.

Discovering a smart café, I enjoyed a coffee and cake whilst watching the world go by.

Kevin Black had suggested a ride north along the Pacific Highway towards Santa Barbara was a must. Not only was it a very scenic route, on the way there were a plethora of small restaurants jutting out from the beach into the ocean.

This route was indeed spectacular with the ocean to my left and the rolling hills on the right. The famous Malibu Pier, my first scheduled stop, was about 18 miles down the road.

Just before I reached my destination, I spotted a beach restaurant sticking out into the Pacific. It was lunchtime and I turned off the highway and into its carpark. I can't remember the name, but I have a feeling it could have been Dukes. Whatever it was called, the food offering was spectacular. A massive, help yourself seafood buffet offered the promise of "as much food as you can eat." The fixed price quoted was also very reasonable.

After I had had my fill, I relaxed with my iced "non-alcoholic" cocktail, and listened to the rhythmic beat of the Pacific waves below my feet.

I stayed longer than anticipated. Back at my car, I decided that there wasn't enough time to complete my journey all the way to Santa Barbara and then back to my hotel in Beverley Hills. Instead, I walked on the beach in Malibu before continuing to Point Mugu State Park, located just off the highway, in the Santa Monica Mountains National Recreation Area. After admiring the fantastic views of the Pacific, I returned to my car and headed back in the direction of Santa Monica and then on to the Beverley Hilton Hotel.

For the last night of my long trip, I decided to roll the boat out and eat in at the main restaurant at the hotel. Enjoying a great meal, washed down with a bottle of fine Californian wine, I eventually returned to my room and within minutes, was fast asleep.

My flight home was leaving LA at around 4.00pm and the car hire people were picking me up from the hotel at 1.30pm so that they could drop me off at the airport in good time.

With a free morning, and a late check out from my room, I decided to visit the "heart of Hollywood" and see for myself the most famous of its tourist attractions.

Collecting my Mustang for one last time, I drove the short distance to the intersection of Hollywood Boulevard and Highland. Parking up, I joined the throngs of tourists.

Like them, I sought out hand and footprints of the famous in the cement courtyard of the Chinese Theatre. Following the hordes down Hollywood Boulevard, I sought out the inlaid stars of some of my favourite artists on the Hollywood Walk of Fame. There was time to shop for some overpriced souvenirs of "tinsel town" before I drove back to the hotel.

After a snack by the pool, I checked out of my room and waited in the hotel lobby for the representative of the car hire company to collect me. I did not have to wait long. Bang on time, he arrived. The Mustang was retrieved from the valet parking area, and we were soon on our way.

The flight time from LA to London was nearly 10½ hours and the UK was 8 hours ahead of LA. We left on schedule, and I enjoyed the privileges of first-class travel for one last time.

We were due to land in London at 10.30am UK time (2.30am LA time). After an excellent meal, and having declined a nightcap, I set my watch to UK time, settled down in my comfortable seat and tried to get a much sleep as possible. The rest of my journey continued without incident.

After landing, I shrugged off the trials and tribulations of baggage hall, immigration, and the coach transfer to the long-term car park. Once I had collected my car, I then had a drive of around 3 hours before I eventually arrived home.

After being away for 12 nights and having travelled around 22,500 miles, it was great to be back with my family and to sleep in my own bed!

International Licensees Meeting – Frankfurt, May 1982

The meeting in Singapore had gone down very well with all the licensees who had attended. They were keen to ensure that the get-together became an annual event. Charles Yatman, and his team, began to look at possible destinations for another conference.

This was scheduled to take place in the early part of 1982.

Charles contacted Dick Webzell to ask whether Blue Bell Apparel would be willing to co-ordinate the event in London.

Costs of the conference would be borne by Blue Bell Inc., so there would be no financial burden. A lot of time and effort, by Kevin Black and myself, would be required to put together a presentation of the Spring/Summer and Fall product ranges and the marketing programmes developed to support them.

On one hand the timing was not good, for a whole host of reasons. On the positive side, a location in London would enable us to draw on the expertise of other members of our teams. Doing this would ensure that the preparation and presentation duties could be spread.

It was decided that we would take on the role. A date was agreed for 20-22 April 1982. This was a little later than the successful meeting in Singapore, but it avoided the busy Easter period and gave us a little more breathing space.

Everything was running to schedule. By the middle of March 1982, all our preparations had been finalised. We just needed to fine-tune all our presentations.

All our plans were then thrown into chaos because of events that were unfolding, over 8,000 miles away, in the South Atlantic.

On the 19 March 1982, a group of 50 Argentinians posing as scrap metal merchants landed at Leith, on South Georgia, in the Falkland Islands, where they hoisted the flag of Argentina.

The British Government responded by sending "a gunship," HMS Endurance, and 22 Royal marines to expel them. Not wishing to cause a diplomatic incident, they held off from direct confrontation whilst the politicians tried to decrease the tension. Sensing an opportunity to fulfil their claim of sovereignty over the region, Argentine troops landed on the island. Still, the British Government held back from expelling them by force from the British Overseas Territory.

The situation escalated quickly. On the 2 April, Argentine forces invaded the Falkland Islands followed by South Georgia and the South Sandwich Islands.

Outraged at the occupation of British territory, the Government finally acted. On the 5 April, a naval task force was despatched by Prime Minister, Margaret Thatcher, prior to an amphibious assault to retake the islands.

What had started out as a minor skirmish, thousands of miles away, was now all out war against Argentina!

Charles Yatman, Vice President of Licensing operations at Blue Bell Inc., was half Argentinian with dual USA and Argentine nationality.

The owner of the Wrangler License in Argentina was now unable to enter the UK. Many other Licensees in South America were showing solidarity with the Argentine cause. If their colleagues were prevented from attending the London Licensee Conference, then they would not attend either.

We had no idea how long the hostilities would last. Too much time and effort had been expended, by everyone involved, to just cancel the meeting. After some, frantic toing, and froing, it was decided to move the location from London to Frankfurt in Germany.

This presented some major problems to the team at Calverton. The dates chosen for the meeting was 26 & 27^h May 1982. This coincided with major buying trips for

Kevin Black and his product development team, and the marketing development programmes that my team was due to roll-out.

It was agreed I should undertake the trip on my own. I would be presenting the UK product line as well as the merchandising, sales promotions, and advertising initiatives. Instead of just a half day of presentations, I would now be on my feet for a good part of day two of the conference.

We had just developed an award-winning instore display concept that comprised of Wrangler branded units and clothes hangers. I organised to ship out two units, along with clothes hangers for all the ranges, to the Blue Bell Germany office headquartered in Frankfurt. They agreed to deliver these to the conference hotel the day before the conference started.

The range samples provided a greater challenge because of the customs arrangements that were in place at that time.

To ensure that the goods arrived at the allotted time would require me to take them with me by air or by car. Because of the amount of excess baggage involved, travelling by car was more practical.

It was over 600 miles from Calverton to Frankfurt. This involved a drive to Dover and a sea crossing from Dover to Calais. The journey would continue across France, Belgium, into Germany and on to Frankfurt.

Blue Bell Apparel rules allowed me to take my wife on overseas trips, providing I paid her travel expenses. She had never been to Frankfurt and was delighted to take the opportunity to travel with me. Apart from accruing lots of "brownie points," the presence of Glenys by my side, acting as navigator, would make the journey far less stressful for me.

The only difficulty was the documentation required to export, and then re-import, the product ranges in an out of the countries we would be passing through. We had a special import/export department at Calverton. They organised a carnet, a temporary export/import document. This enabled me to clear customs during both my outward and inward journeys without the need to pay duties and import taxes.

In simplistic terms, the carnet included counterfoils and vouchers for each of the countries I would be passing through. At each border, it was necessary to ensure counterfoils were stamped out of one country and into the next. At the end of the outgoing and incoming journey my copies of the stamped counterfoils would be returned to the Chamber of Commerce in Nottingham, our guaranteeing organisation. After a review, and assuming all the paperwork was in order, our hefty collateral bond would be returned.

No pressure then!

On Sunday 24 May 1982, Glenys and I started our journey. We had organised that we would stay over at an hotel in Dover and then catch the early morning hovercraft to Calais. From there we had the whole day to drive the 380 miles to Frankfurt.

I would have to have the carnet stamped out of the UK, in and out of France and Belgium and into Germany. Allowing time for this process, and breaks for refreshment on the way, I calculated that the journey time would be about 8 hours. Assuming everything ran to schedule, we would reach our destination at around 6.00pm.

We had to visit the customs office at Dover for our carnet to be stamped out of the UK.

Our hovercraft journey to France went without incident, largely because the sea was calm. After 45 minutes we were docking at Calais. I drove into the red channel at customs. My carnet was examined and stamped by one of the customs officers and we were waved on our way.

Before long we arrived at the French border with Belgium. I pulled over and went into the customs office with my carnet. Again, it was stamped by the officer who then gave me permission to continue into Belgium.

Using my schoolboy French, I asked him "where is the Belgium customs post.' He replied in French. I thought he said, "it is just down the road." It turned out, what he had actually said was, "it is down the road at the end of this building."

I jumped in the car and set off down the road expecting to come across the Belgium border and customs post. After several miles, it became clear there had been a mix up in communications. "Without a stamp into Belgium, how would I fare getting out of Belgium and into Germany?"

The answer to that would become clear a couple of hours later!

After a leisurely drive through Belgium, we arrived at the border with Germany. Presenting my carnet document for stamping, an officious customs officer refused to stamp it out of Belgium, because it had never been stamped in. I remonstrated but without effect. Whilst acknowledging that I was driving out of Belgium with my goods, I could not prove that I had driven in with them. As far as the official was concerned, that was that.

The German customs officer was far more sympathetic. Apparently, my experience at the hands of Belgium customs was not uncommon. Many others had been treated in a similar fashion. "Belgians, bloody Belgians," he muttered. Shrugging his shoulders, he took my carnet and stamped it into Germany.

For anyone who has never driven in Germany, the autobahn system provides an exhilarating experience. There are no speed limits. This means that even when travelling at over 100mph it is still possible to be passed, normally by a Mercedes, as though you are standing still.

Interestingly, when a speed reduction sign was flashing, all the cars slowed down to the imposed limit. Clearly, German drivers are much more disciplined than their UK counterparts!

It was not long before we were experiencing the joys of rush hour traffic into the centre of Frankfurt. Eventually, tired but relieved, we pulled up outside The Frankfurter Hof, a five- star hotel, built in 1876, it was then, and still is today, one of the top hotels in the city. Our personal luggage was whisked off to our room and the product samples to an anti-room outside the conference room.

They were locked away securely. I was given a key to gain access when needed.

Our hotel room was perfect in every detail right down to the fresh roses, replenished every day, in the bathroom. All the attendees had brought their partners and a "spouse activity programme" had been lined up during the conference sessions. Our partners would be joining us for lunches in the hotel.

There was one dark cloud hanging over the whole event!

We were in Frankfurt, not London because of the troubles between the UK and Argentina in the South Atlantic.

On the 2 May a British submarine had sunk the ARA General Belgrano, an Argentine Navy light cruiser, with the loss of 323 lives. On the 4 May, a British type 42 destroyer, HMS Sheffield was lost following an Exocet missile strike by the Argentine Airforce. Fighting had escalated dramatically with many other losses, particularly involving British support ships.

As the conference was starting, both sides were preparing for an assault by the British Task Force to retake the Falkland Islands. This was not the ideal background for our meeting!

On the first day of the conference, every delegate but one, had their national flag positioned on the table in front of them. The one notable exception was my place. There was no sign of the Union Jack.

As chair of the meeting, Charles Yatman, asked all the attendees to introduce themselves, their companies, and the country they represented. When my turn came, I made light of the fact that my place had no Union Jack, suggesting "there has obviously been some mistake made in not supplying my nations flag. I presume this will be remedied at the first refreshment break."

It was. Honour of the UK had been redeemed. The ice had also been broken. A distant war, and its ramifications, were forgotten. For the time being, at least.

Lunch on the first day of the conference was a formal sit-down affair. Delegates and partners were seated in tables of four. When I looked at the seating plan, I was amazed to find that Glenys and I had been paired with the licensee from Argentina and his wife.

Charles Yatman, who had organised the place settings, was known as a prankster but this was a little over the top even by his standards!

It passed through my mind, that the last time Charles and I had been at a conference together had been in Berlin. During an excursion to East Berlin, Charles had fleetingly been lost.

Perhaps, this might be payback time, I gave him the benefit of the doubt and decided that it was probably a clerical error?

We took our seats and engaged in a perfectly normal conversation, despite the extraordinary situation. Topics discussed was a mixture of family and business talk. The war, and its implications, was never even hinted at.

At the end of the meal, we left the table as friends and not adversaries!

That evening there was no conference dinner at the hotel. Glenys and I decided to explore the centre of Frankfurt. Looking at a selection of leaflets in the hotel, we found that the famous Fressgassfest, celebrating the arrival of Spring, had started the previous evening. The leaflets explained it was the first street festival of the year. The Great Bockenheimer Straße, between Börsenstraße and Overplants, was almost fully pedestrianised.

We were offered, "old established traditions and gastronomic offerings. Here you can stroll, taste the best sounds, taste a fine wine, and treat yourself to culinary delights with specialities and treats." Convinced this was just what we were looking for, we examined a map of the city centre. To our delight, the Fressgassfest was in full flow only 4 blocks or so away, just a short walk on what was a balmy night.

As we neared the location, we began to have our doubts that anything was happening. Suddenly, a formally attired businessman came into view. Staggering towards us, he held his briefcase in one hand and a half empty glass of wine in the other. Although he seemed well the worse for wear, he greeted us as if we were old friends. We did not speak any German but the inflection in his voice convinced us that he was wishing us well.

We turned the next corner into the Bockenheimer Straße and were hit by a wall of sound. As far as the eye could see, there were stalls laden with food and wine. Thousands of people were taking advantage of the special tasting offers. It became obvious that nearly every vineyard in Germany had a stall and were offering samples of their wares at very advantageous prices.

This was certainly the place to be!

After a few hours of sampling the wines on offer, we found a seat in one of the street cafes and had a wonderful meal. We returned to the hotel very mellow and ready to face the rigours of the last day of the conference.

Following a very good night's sleep, I was up nice and early enabling me to have plenty of time to check that all the a/v equipment was working and that slides were in the right order.

My session on marketing was scheduled to take place immediately after the first coffee break. The merchandise presentation was immediately after lunch and would last until the afternoon refreshment break. After this, Charles would chair a questions and answers session.

The merchandise units had been erected by my colleagues from the Frankfurt office. They had been delivered, with the hangers, and were under lock and key with my samples. I decided to take advantage of the long lunch break to unpack the samples, put them on the hangers, and fully merchandise the units.

For the afternoon session, our team in Calverton had produced a pack for all the delegates. This listed details of all the merchandise featured. It also contained a copy of Spring/Summer and Fall product merchandisers. A pack was placed in front of all the attendees.

The morning session went without a hitch as did my preparations during the lunch break.

I had plenty of slides of the merchandise ranges and these compensated for a lack of a fashion show that we had planned for the original London venue.

During the afternoon break, I stayed close to the samples and made individual presentations to some of the licensees. One or two also showed interest in the merchandising units and hangers.

Charles started the question and answers session by thanking me for my involvement adding in Spanish words to the effect, "Mr. Dilley would like to thank you for listening patiently, He has asked me to say that if anybody would like to take away any of the garment samples, he is very happy for you to do so."

Spanish is not a language that I am fluent in. I did know enough, however, to understand the gist of what he had said. I made it clear with my body language that this was not the case.

The delegates all spoke English and were all aware of the quirky sense of humour that Charles often exhibited.

"I have brought the samples into Germany using a carnet. As you are all aware, this means everything that has come in must arrive back in England," I explained. "On the other hand, this is not the case with the hangers or the two merchandising units. If anybody is interest in them, please ask Charles after the meeting," I continued.

I had plenty of experience of overseas meetings. Even multi-millionaire licensees cannot resist the opportunity of acquiring something for nothing!

Immediately the proceedings were over, I packed everything away in their appropriate cases and, with the help of the hotel staff, placed them once more under lock and key. The hangers and merchandise units were left behind.

When I peered into the conference room a little later, it was as if the locusts had descended. Absolutely nothing was left, everything had been removed by the delegates. I believe that the units ended up in South America and the hangers were distributed far and wide amongst the other delegates.

I was relieved not to have to take them back to the UK!

That evening, we had a final conference dinner in the sumptuous surroundings of one of the hotel's private dining rooms. Great food, fantastic company, and superb service.

Many of the other delegates were staying on for a further few days. Unfortunately, Glenys and I faced the long road journey back to the UK. Immediately after breakfast, I called for my car to be delivered in front of the hotel and, with the help of the hotel porters, loaded all our luggage. By 10.00am we were on our way.

Driving on a Friday in the UK can be an horrendous experience. Consequently, I had decided to drive the whole 608 miles home on the Thursday. It was 371 miles to the hovercraft port at Calais. We were booked on the last departure which was scheduled to leave at 7.30pm.

Allowing ample time for having our carnet stamped at each border, a break for lunch and several comfort breaks on the way, I calculated that we would comfortably reach Calais before boarding closed.

Our journey to the German border was trouble free and the carnet was stamped out of Germany by their customs officials. It was duly stamped into Belgium by customs officers at the Belgium border.

We had enjoyed a quick lunch and were ahead of schedule when we reached the customs post at the Belgium border with France. Here we encountered the full might of Belgium red tape!

The customs officer looked at our carnet and examined it minutely, shaking his head as he did so. "Your carnet was not stamped entering and leaving Belgium on your outbound journey," he finally announced.

I explained what had happened on the outbound journey and he seemed sympathetic. "We can rectify the problem. This will require us to check all the garments in your cases against the original manifest. Assuming, that everything is in order, I will stamp all the appropriate counterfoils and you can continue your journey," he explained.

There was no alternative but to do as he asked. Together we went through every page of the carnet.

I was thankful that I had taken such great care to ensure none of the garments had been appropriated by delegates at the conference. Any missing garments would have spelt trouble from an officer who was hellbent on dotting all the 'i's' and crossing all the 't's.'

An hour passed before the job was finished. The paperwork was updated, and we were once more on our way. Now we were in danger of arriving late in Calais and missing the hovercraft we had booked. If this happened, we would have to stay over and take the first sailing next morning.

Something to be avoided at all costs!

I had no choice but to put my foot down, drive as fast as the road conditions and speed limits allowed, in the hope that we would arrive in time for boarding.

Eventually, we entered the Hover port with only 30 minutes to spare. I still had to go to the customs office and present my carnet for stamping.

The officer on duty looked at me blankly. He was probably newly recruited. Whatever the reason, this was apparently the first time he had seen a carnet and did not appear to know what to do with it. As I tried to explain, in my schoolboy French, an announcement came over the public-address system. "Will Mr. and Mrs. Dilley please load their vehicle immediately. We will be sailing in 15 minutes."

Whilst the customs officer was on the phone to his superiors, I dashed outside to the car and asked Glenys to load the car on to the hovercraft. "I am having problems with the paperwork but don't worry, I will see you on board," I assured her.

Inside the paperwork was still causing problems.

Another announcement came over the PA. "Will Mr. Dilley the last passenger for the 19.30 sailing, please board NOW!"

Thankfully, another officer arrived, quickly glanced at the document, and provided the appropriate stamp on the carnet. I quickly ran to the hovercraft and boarded just before the ramp was lifted.

The car deck was situated between the two passenger hulls. I was located on one side of the craft, Glenys was on the other. She had no idea whether I had managed to board in time. I was not allowed to cross the vehicle deck until the craft had left the harbour.

Fifteen minutes passed before we were reunited. Glenys was very concerned I might not have made it. If that had been the case, she would have been unable to clear UK customs because I had all the paperwork with me.

I was mightily relieved. If I had been unable to convince the French customs to stamp my carnet or if they had insisted on seeing the goods, I might have been in big trouble.

Thankfully, things had worked out well and in less than an hour we would be back in the UK!

At the time, our minds were focused on the last leg of our long journey. After we had cleared customs, there was the small matter of the 237 miles drive back home.

When the hovercraft docked, we drove off and headed for the red channel in the customs area. Once there the final stamp could be applied to the carnet. There were no officials in the red channel. Apparently, they were short of staff, and we had to wait until everyone else had cleared the green channel before someone came to attend to us.

Forty-five minutes later, the last stamp was finally applied to our papers, and we began the long drive home. Arriving close to midnight, we went straight to bed. We were thankful for the experience that our time away had provided, but extremely happy to be back.

Next morning, news was beginning to filter through about events in the Falklands.

As we were driving home from Frankfurt, British troops had begun the repatriation of the islands. Whilst we were crossing the Channel, they were engaged in a full-scale attack on Argentine troops at Goose Green.

17 days later, the Argentine army surrendered. The Falklands War was over!

Chapter Twenty-Three

Trade Shows and Exhibitions

When I joined Blue Bell Apparel, there was already a set pattern of trade presentations. The Spring/Summer and Autumn ranges were sold to the trade six months prior to their arrival in the shops.

In the UK, there were two main Trade Exhibitions. the International Men's & Boy's Wear (IMBEX) and Menswear Association of Britain (MAB). IMBEX was held at the Earls Court Exhibition Centre in London in February each year. MAB was an altogether more gentile affair and took place in Harrogate every September.

The February show provided a platform for the sell in of Autumn/Winter ranges. In September, Spring/Summer ranges were highlighted.

Whilst the trade shows were important, Blue Bell Apparel also organised a series of presentations around the country to preview the ranges to key customers. These shows took place in London, Birmingham, Nottingham, Manchester, Newcastle, and Glasgow. The pre-show presentations enabled our merchandise team to fine-tune styles and colour options and, if necessary, revise production estimates before sales were open to the whole customer base.

In London, the Area Manager used the company flat and office just off Oxford Street for individual presentations. Alternatively, he would visit group buyers at their own offices. The showroom at our offices in Calverton was used for buyers from Yorkshire and the East Midlands.

Hotel suites were taken in Birmingham, Manchester, Newcastle, and Glasgow. In this way, all key buyers in the major sales regions were covered.

Buyers from Northern Ireland were either visited by our Agent in their own offices or were invited to attend the Birmingham, Manchester, or Glasgow shows.

Menswear Association Britain (MAB) Trade Show

Traditionally, exhibition organisers had always found it difficult to entice buyers, from London and the south of England, to travel north of the capital to attend trade shows.

This was particularly so in the fashion industry. In the 60's, swinging London had become the cultural and fashion centre of the world!

The Midlands and North of England was where the bulk of the merchandise, to be found in the shops, was designed, and manufactured. Despite this, London was still seen as the place where fashions were showcased.

Fashion journalists were also reluctant to stray too far into what they still considered to be "the hinterlands of fashion taste."

The MAB Trade show bucked the trend!

Despite being the show where the menswear trade presented its Spring/Summer ranges, it was held in Harrogate, 200 miles north of London.

The show was well attended because of the ambience of the destination. Harrogate enjoyed a reputation as a fashionable spa resort that the Victorians flocked to in their thousands. This legacy continued in the Montpellier Quarter with the Royal Pump Room and Moorish-style Turkish Baths.

In the mid 1970's, the fading affluence of its hotel stock was offset by first-class service and a friendly Yorkshire welcome that had endeared itself to all its visitors.

Harrogate remains famous for its flowers and green spaces with Valley Gardens and the Stray to the fore. Within walking distance, on the western edge of the town, RHS Harlow Carr Gardens are situated.

To the East is the Yorkshire Dales National Park and within easy travelling distance, several racecourses, numerous golf clubs and many other tourist attractions. The picturesque towns of Wetherby, Ripon and Knaresborough and the vibrant City of Leeds are also only a short drive away.

Because the MAB show was held in early September, school holidays were over, and the weather was invariably, still very pleasant. Retailers from all over the country saw a trip to the show, in Harrogate, as an opportunity to combine an extended holiday with an important buying trip.

Although the show ran from Monday to Wednesday, many buyers arrived after Saturday trading along with their wives. Sunday was spent playing golf or visiting the sights nearby. An awful lot of "brownie points" were on offer.

During the period of the show, MAB organised trips for spouses to indulge in tourist pursuits or engage in retail therapy whilst their other halves toiled.

The show itself was equally relaxed!

All major players took small shell scheme stands at the Harrogate Exhibition Centre.

In the 1970's this was much smaller than it is today. Manning the exhibition stand could be likened to "standing guard over a vehicle in a municipal car park." The Exhibition Hall had a low ceiling and there was little, if any, air conditioning. When it was full of people, the atmosphere was invariably hot and sticky.

Big brand names, like Wrangler, used the stand as "a teaser to the main event." The real buying took place in private rooms, in nearby hotels.

The bigger the supplier, the closer their hotel was located to the exhibition centre.

Dick Webzell particularly liked The Old Swan Hotel and regularly booked it during the show. It is perhaps one of the most famous hotels in Harrogate with a history going back nearly 200 years. A short stroll from the exhibition centre, it boasted picturesque lawns and gardens and, most importantly, plenty of onsite car parking.

The crime-writing author, Agatha Christie retreated there when she famously disappeared for 11 days in 1926!

MAB in September 1975 was the first trade show I attended on behalf of Wrangler.

I knew Harrogate well. I had spent nearly all my early life living and working within 15 miles of the town. You could say it was an old stomping ground. Glenys, my wife had worked at "The Swan" during her college days.

We had booked the largest conference room in the hotel. It opened out on to the front garden, offering plenty of light. It was ideally situated for the task. At the time,

"The Swan" was renowned for the quality of its food. Their kitchen staff provided a continuous buffet in the conference room.

The hotel's Wedgewood Restaurant, with its famous glass ceiling, was on hand for our end of show dinner where we entertained our major buyers.

I had booked two local female models to act as hostesses during the show. Dick Webzell had informed me that the company had a regular hostess called Jackie Simmonds. She was a good organiser, an especially hard worker and was liked by the customers. She was also his sister-in-law!

I met Jackie for the first time whilst setting up in the conference room at "The Swan." We both agreed that she was to be treated no differently from any of the other models I had booked. She did a great job, and I was very impressed.

After that first exhibition in Harrogate, Jackie worked with us at many more events over the years. Behind the scenes she made sure that our clients were well fed and well-watered and took that load off my shoulders.

Dick had established several Harrogate traditions in the short time the company had been exhibiting at MAB. After setting up on the Sunday, there was time for traditional afternoon tea at the iconic Betty's Tea Room, located a short walking distance from the hotel.

On the Tuesday evening, all the Wrangler crowd decamped to the original Harry Ramsden's fish shop in Guiseley. There, we would devour "arguably the best fish and chips in the world," in the chandeliered splendour of its glitzy restaurant. It had been built, "behind the shop," in the 1931 as "an unprecedented palace for the people's food."

Pre-booking, well in advance, was essential. Harry Ramsden's had become a tourist attraction as well as an emporium for fish and chips. People who had not booked, stood at the back of a long queue to buy them in the shop. They would then eat them outside from the paper wrapping.

The MAB "Harrogate model" provided a reasonably cost-effective way of providing a platform for retail customers to view and order the Wrangler Spring/Summer ranges.

Early in the 1980's, the Menswear Association of Britain decided to upgrade the exhibition. and relocate it to the National Exhibition Centre in Birmingham.

On the face of it, a move to Birmingham was a good idea. The facilities were state-of-the-art compared with the ageing edifices of Earls Court and Olympia Exhibition Centres in London. The NEC was closer to London than Harrogate. Birmingham International Airport was on the doorstep. There was "onsite parking" in abundance and access to the exhibition halls was very easy.

For Wrangler, the cost of exhibiting was suddenly much more expensive. We needed to accommodate selling areas for 30 representatives and their customers. Instead of a shell scheme, we would need to design and build a large exhibition stand.

Accommodation at the NEC was limited at that time, as a result, hotel prices were nearly as high as those in London.

In Harrogate, all the cafes and restaurants were within walking distance. The tradition of Betty's afternoon tea and fish and chips at Harry Ramsdens would disappear.

It was unclear whether the retail trade would support the change. MAB would be brought into the 20th century but "would the cultural change be a move too far?"

I raised these issues with MAB Chief Executive, Brian Wiseman. "I appreciate the points that you have made," he acknowledged. "The soundings from our members have been very positive. We are confident that we will receive their 100% support."

Faced with additional exhibition costs of around £50,000, I was apprehensive, as was Dick Webzell and the rest of our Management Team.

Realising that we may not support the move, Brian came up with a package that was intended to soften the blow. This included some flexibility on stand space price and "the premiere site" situated just inside the front door of the Exhibition Hall.

Brian Wiseman was a very shrewd operator. He needed the support of a major brand. If Wrangler could be persuaded to come on board, the other jeans brands would follow. This would create a "snowball effect."

After some further haggling, we agreed a deal!

For Brian and his sales team, the necessary momentum was created. All the key industry names did indeed follow.

I was left with a dilemma. A big idea was needed to create maximum impact, when trade visitors entered the exhibition hall, and then create a talking point both during and after the show.

At a meeting with our stand contractor, we began to brainstorm the possibilities. During the session, someone (I would like to think it might have been me), came up with the idea of an aircraft fuselage. This would provide the space for selling areas leaving additional space for a check-in desk and aircraft lounge.

The stand contractor went away to draw up some ideas and to examine the practicalities.

Our stand was big, "but would the fuselage be able to accommodate 30 selling areas, each with a garment rail, table and four chairs, and not be claustrophobic? Would it be spacious enough to allow free movement without being cramped?"

Two or three weeks later our contractor was back with all the answers. They were all positive!

He had managed to obtain real aircraft seats from one of the major airlines. The design accommodated these within the fuselage. They were arranged in sets of four seats back-to-back with a table in between.

A rail fitted neatly under the curve of the fuselage below the aircraft windows. Overhead luggage shelves held a briefcase, order pads and range leaflets for each salesperson and their customers.

At the back of the aircraft cabin, there was space for "a galley area" with coffee and teamaking facilities and a small bar.

The fuselage occupied around two thirds of the stand area. This left ample space for an "arrivals hall" complete with chairs and cloakroom and "a check-in desk" where customers could be greeted.

Everyone loved the idea. Even more so, when it was discovered that it could all be done within the budget that we had allocated!

With our stand manufacturer working on the logistics of the construction, I held discussions with my internal team and PR agency to work on ideas to maximise publicity and promotional benefits of the stands "ground-breaking" design concept. It quickly became clear following through the "flight on the plane" idea could work beneficially on many different levels.

I discussed the initial concepts with my colleagues on the Senior Management Team and they were equally enthusiastic. It was agreed that the salesforce would issue "free travel cards" to all their major customers, who would be asked to present them at the check in desk on the Wrangler stand. They would then receive a "priority boarding card," for the "earliest available flight on the Wrangler aircraft."

We had estimated it would take our representatives about two hours to show their customers the product range and to fill in the order forms. On this basis, flight times had been allocated at intervals of 2½ hours throughout the exhibition.

Potential buyers, without "travel cards," would have their details taken at the desk and be added to the "wait list," after being greeted by one of the Wrangler team in the "arrivals hall."

The Wrangler promotional team continued the aircraft travel theme. All customers would be given a "duty-free bag," containing a travel related gift, when they left the aircraft.

Our PR agency had a client who was marketing Liquore Galliano L'Autentico, an Italian sweet herbal liqueur, more commonly known as Galliano. They obtained from them, at no cost, several hundred miniature bottles along with printed recipes for the Harvey Wallbanger cocktail, for which Galliano was a key ingredient.

I had a contact who supplied promotional items to the travel trade. From him, we obtained a similar quantity of travel hot water bottles to which we added a Wrangler label with an appropriate message. The Wrangler brand colours were represented by the blue of the hot water bottles and the yellow of the Galliano.

Our duty-free bag was complete!

Ensuring that our product ranges were delivered safely to our exhibition stand and then collected, safely and efficiently after the exhibition closed, had proved a logistical challenge in the past.

Our Administration Manager assured us that one of his main contractors, with major distribution facilities not far from the NEC, had been entrusted with the task.

The easy access to the NEC Exhibition Hall would enable them to take their vehicle right up to our stand for both delivery and collection. They had been given a clear set of instructions and were aware that they needed to report to NEC staff well before lunchtime on the final day. Access to the halls for breakdown was allocated on "a first come first served" basis.

What could possibly go wrong?

When we brainstormed the stand operating concept, we never expected that our customers would also enter the spirit of the "experience" we had created.

The finished stand exceeded all our expectations!

Our business class aircraft seats offered plenty of leg room. The selling and galley areas were generously proportioned. Importantly, the air-conditioning unit was very quiet and yet incredibly efficient.

The Wrangler product ranges were delivered to the stand on time and without incident.

To our amazement, customers were also arriving on schedule for their "pre-arranged flights" and the "wait list service" went down well.

A major customer arrived slightly late for his appointment. "Sorry I'm late," he told our check in attendant. "Can you still fit me on to the flight?" One of the Wrangler "air hostesses" was happy to do so.

The Wrangler "aircraft stand" was one of the main talking points of the show. Our PR agency generated a lot of positive publicity around the whole concept.

Sadly, our withdrawal from the exhibition hall at the end of the show was not anything like as successful.

On the last day the show closed around 4.30pm.

Our transport contractors had been advised to ensure that their vehicle arrived at the NEC early in the day. This was necessary if they were to be guaranteed an allocation of a favourable position, close to the front of the queue, at the breakdown of the show.

The manager in charge was supposed to liaise with me on our exhibition stand by mid-afternoon. We could then sort out the logistics before the "manic breakdown period began."

He was late. Very late!

I phoned Calverton. Our Administration Manager assured me all was well, and that everything was under control.

A worried representative from the transport company arrived on the stand at about 3.30pm. Despite our instructions, he explained that their vehicle had not arrived at the NEC until early afternoon. Instead of being at the head of the queue, he was parked up in an overflow van park over a mile away.

It was not scheduled to be with us until 7.00 pm at the earliest. This was not what I wanted to hear!

Anyone who has experienced the break-up of a major exhibition will be aware, a stand that requires three days to set up, can be taken down in a matter of hours. Anything that is not nailed to the floor, and many items that are, tend to disappear into the ether. Contractors and hire company employees appear from all corners of the exhibition hall and, like a swarm of locusts, devour everything in their path.

We had to ensure that our 30 sets of Wrangler merchandise remained intact!

"Don't worry, I have a plan," the representative of our delivery contractor announced. "My car is parked nearby. I will bring it to the front of the building. We can fill it up and I will ferry the merchandise out to our trailer in the overflow carpark."

His cunning plan had several obvious flaws!

"What kind of car do you have?" I enquired. A large estate would need to make at least 6 journeys to carry all our gear. "Err, a Ford Fiesta," was his reply. The number of journeys had just risen to well over 12. As a last resort, we would have to go with his "cunning plan." Unless I could come up with a better one, we would be waiting, with the merchandise, until late into the evening.

I went to speak to MAB Chief Executive, Brian Wiseman. "Can you pull any strings to help us?" I asked him, explaining our predicament. "I'll see what I can do but I can't promise anything." Brian informed me.

It appeared his influence was enough for our contractor's vehicle to be moved up the pecking order. 1½ hours after the show closed, the ranges were safely collected. I could finally leave for home.

Not a very auspicious end to what had proved to be a very successful show!

Moving MAB from Harrogate to the NEC in Birmingham had proved controversial. Members of "the old school" within the menswear trade loved Harrogate. They did not like the reality of a more commercial trade show environment.

The die, once cast, could not be reversed!

This new venue was not to the liking of manufacturers and buyers from London and the South East. They preferred London to Birmingham. Their lobbying of the organisers finally paid off. The MAB Exhibition was eventually moved to the Capital.

Their wishes defied logic, given the modern facilities, ease of access and central position of the NEC in Birmingham!

Wrangler supported MAB in London for a few more years. Eventually, cost constraints made the large investment, of supporting two major trade shows, in one of the costliest cities in the world, totally unviable.

International Men's and Boy's Wear Exhibition (IMBEX)

IMBEX was one of the largest clothing trade fairs in Europe. I had attended the show many times whilst working for the CWS Ltd and had visited the Wrangler stand in March 1975, just weeks before joining Blue Bell Apparel Limited.

The first IMBEX had taken place between Monday 25 February and Thursday 1 March 1963 at the Earls Court Exhibition Centre, in London. That show played host to 159 exhibitors from 14 countries.

It was a complete contrast to the laid-back environment of MAB in Harrogate. Buyers went to buy, and exhibitors were there to sell.

The first exhibition during my time at Wrangler, also took place at Earls Court and ran from 1-4 March 1976. By then, IMBEX had grown considerably in size and importance. There were now over 400 exhibitors.

My predecessor had developed a good working relationship with a locally based exhibition stand contractor. They had developed a modular based unit for Wrangler which they had in storage for use at the 1976 show.

This was good news for me. My first 8 months with the company had been very hectic. Being able to take over an existing modular design, to fit a stand space that had been reserved before I joined the company, enabled me to be more objective in my outlook.

I planned to observe the strengths and weakness of the company's approach to selling in a more aggressive exhibition environment.

The exhibition, and its related costs, came out of my marketing and promotional budget.

Costs of a London based exhibition were considerable. The stand space at Earls Court was high. This was doubled by the expense of manufacturing a stand and erecting it before the show and dismantling and removing it afterwards. Added to that, was the price of accommodating the sales force and head office staff in a suitable London hotel, for four nights with all food and drink provided.

Clearly, a lot of merchandise would have to be sold to justify such a large outlay!

During this first show, it quickly became clear that the size of the stand was too small. Wrangler was in demand. It was one of the "in brands" and retail buyers were clamouring for a piece of the action.

Representatives were sharing selling areas. They were having great difficulty servicing their existing customers let alone dealing with enquiries from new ones. Sales managers were striving manfully to deal with the flow of new potential customers. There was just no free space on the stand for this to be done. Rather than develop a relationship, they were only able to take down contact details to be followed up after the exhibition.

A lot of opportunities were being lost!

Our modular stand had served its purpose. I estimated that we would require double the stand area for us to maximise the obvious sales development opportunities.

The exhibition itself was relatively quiet. Indeed, many exhibitors were complaining that many trade buyers were conspicuous by their absence.

"I think that it is now time to change the thinking about IMBEX show dates," one trade colleague confided in me. "We should start on a Sunday and finish on a Wednesday," he continued. "In a difficult marketplace, buyers are reducing the amount of time out of their shops. That is why exhibition numbers have fallen." There was a lot of sense in what he said. By Thursday, even the stands of the major brands of jeans were dealing with significantly reduced numbers of buyers.

It occurred to me, that this was a good time to talk to the exhibition organisers about our requirements for 1977. I spoke to Dick Webzell, and we agreed our plan of action. When I tracked down the IMBEX sales director, an excellent deal was done!

The Wrangler exhibition team proved efficient during the set-up, performed manfully during the show but were totally disorganised during the breakdown. Our salesforce was quick to disappear. It was left to the Senior Management Team to ensure that nothing important was left behind.

Back at Calverton, we analysed the results and discussed my observations about the efficiency of our exhibition management.

It was agreed that the stand at IMBEX 1977 should be better planned, to enable the company to capitalise on the full potential of the Wrangler brand.

I explained that it was my intention to ensure every member of the salesforce would have an individual selling area. Whilst our stand should not be totally closed, a clear access should lead visitors to a "meet and greet area" where they could be "efficiently processed" by senior members of the Wrangler team.

Everyone agreed the existing modular system had outlived its usefulness and that the delivery and collection of the product ranges, to and from the stand, needed to be more efficient.

Six months before the 1977 exhibition, planning started.

I felt that we needed to recruit an exhibition stand design and construction company with whom we could build a long-term relationship. My criteria required they should have a strong creative bias and a developing reputation within the industry.

The IMBEX organisers were contacted to see if they could point us in the right direction. They gave me the names of several companies and one very firm recommendation.

A company they felt might work best for Wrangler was a new partnership that had just been set up and was working from a base in Milton Keynes. Its partners had worked with one of the biggest names in the exhibition design world. They had set up their own business to provide a service "that broke new ground in creative design and stand construction technology."

I picked up the phone and arranged an appointment to meet them at their premises.

Every new potential suppler will show you work that they have done for other customers. Whilst this reflects their capabilities, it does not demonstrate that they are able to connect to your wavelength and fully understand your requirements.

I had mentioned, during my initial telephone contact, that the selling areas on our stand needed to be functional and integral to any stand design. On arrival at their premises, I was whisked straight into their showroom. There, in the centre of the room, was to a hanging rail adjacent to a table with seating for four people.

"This is the optimum floor space to accommodate a Wrangler selling area," my host advised. "We understand that you need a maximum of 30 of these, one for each of your sales personnel," he continued. "We have checked the square yardage of the stand you have booked for 1977 and have drawn up an outline plan showing how the proposed selling areas will fit into the space."

I was impressed. The drawing incorporated all our additional requirements. Emphasis had been placed on the practicalities. "If we get those right, the creative design will follow. As you can see from the examples of our work for other people, our creative ability is second to none," the presenter concluded.

During our discussions, it became clear that having Wrangler on their client roster would be regarded a marketing coup. They assured me, as "a new kid on the block, we are price-competitive but will never sacrifice on quality."

They were my kind of company and a perfect fit for the Blue Bell philosophy of "determining the quality required and buying the specification agreed, at the most favourable price." That meeting heralded the start of a long-lasting business relationship.

With the stand design underway, the logistics of delivering 30 sets of garment ranges to our stand before the show and collecting them afterwards, needed to be resolved.

To reduce expenses, a car sharing plan had operated at previous shows. The car boots of our Volvo fleet were large, but not large enough to accommodate the luggage and product ranges for four members of the salesforce.

Representatives from Scotland and the agent from Northern Ireland flew into London for the show. It was impractical for them to take their range samples away with them.

The decision was made to use one of our transport suppliers to deliver the product ranges to our stand before the show, and to pick them up afterwards. This was a tricky process. Earls Court was not the easiest of places to access. Lorries were admitted on a first come, first served basis. Get the timing wrong and major problems would result.

Finding a hotel close to Earls Court able to accommodate up to 45 people and around 20 cars was another problem that had to be overcome. Whilst we enjoyed good relationships with our main competitors, we had no wish to share accommodation with them for a whole host of reasons.

For the 1977 exhibition, we settled on the Kensington Close Hotel which was ideally situated just off Kensington High Street. The venue had limited car parking and it was decided that once parked, the salesforce and head office staff would walk the 10 minutes to the Earls Court Exhibition Centre.

On the Sunday before the exhibition opened, I arrived early to check out the Wrangler stand and to ensure any last-minute, fine-tuning could take place.

Our new stand contractors had done an excellent job and the stand more that held its own in the exhibition hall. "If there are any problems during the exhibition call us on the emergency number and we will be with you within 2 hours to sort it out," I was assured.

By early afternoon, the ranges were delivered and, by the time the sales force arrived, each of the selling areas was fully merchandised and ready for action.

Dick Webzell welcomed everyone to the stand and outlined the show objectives.

Individual selling areas were allocated to each representative. Each of the area sales managers took on the role of stand manager for a day during the exhibition. Head Office staff were on hand to meet customers who required product clarification, details of the forthcoming television advertising and marketing support, or credit control issues. Jackie Simmonds and two other hostesses, dressed in Wrangler outfits, would be on hand to provide sustenance to customers during the show.

"Remember," advised Dick, "no alcoholic drink should be offered to customers until the purchase order has been signed." The instruction was delivered tongue in cheek.

At least I think it was!

With that, the meeting broke up and everyone returned to the hotel with the final words of Dick ringing in their ears. "Enjoy your evening. We will all meet on the stand at 9.00am (an hour before opening). I am confident that you will all deliver record sales!"

I handed over the stand to the security guard we had hired. It was his job to ensure nothing went missing during the night. That done, I left the exhibition hall and strolled back to the hotel for some well-earned relaxation. I had set off from home at 8.00am to drive down to London and it had already been a long day. An early dinner, and an early night was called for.

Over the next four days of the exhibition, the Wrangler team projected the sort of ultra-professional image that, sometimes, belied the reality of what was going on behind the scenes. These were the days before cell phones and laptops. Major decisions had to be made based on information derived from computer print outs, hasty calculations, and frantic telephone conversations to head office.

After dinner on each evening, the senior management team, excluding Dick Webzell, went back to the hotel room shared by Sales Administration Manager, John Gibson and Credit Controller, Tony Fleet.

Meticulously, the order forms handed in by each member of the salesforce, were added up by colour, size and the quantities deducted from the open to sell figures at the start of each day at the exhibition. This involved many hours of work to ensure that the salesforce had the most up to date information at the start of the next day.

In the 1970's, Blue Bell Apparel Ltd had an office and three-bedroom apartment in Queen Ann Mews, just behind Harley Street, in the centre of London.

During the trade show, Dick Webzell and his wife stayed there. They had several favourite restaurants and hosted dinners with different members of the "Wrangler Team" working at the show. Everyone on the stand, attended at least one of these, relatively formal affairs.

At other times, sales, and head office personnel split into smaller informal groups. There were plenty of good eating places in High Street Kensington to cater for all tastes.

1977, was the "30th Anniversary of the Wrangler brand." To commemorate the event, I had commissioned some small individual fruit cakes with icing bearing the anniversary message. Exhibition food was never the best. The cakes, baked in Lancashire by a company who supplied Marks & Spencer, went down particularly well after the relative bland fare that we were obliged to order through the exhibition organisers.

During my dealings with the cake company, I found out they also made the sandwiches that were a trademark speciality in M&S food outlets.

This information was to a change of food buying habits at future IMBEX shows!

The trouble with IMBEX 1977 was that it started on a Monday and finished on Thursday evening. Even though the show was held at the same time and place as the International Knitwear Fair, attendance was relatively sparse. This was particularly evident on the final day when the absence of trade buyers was clear to everyone.

It was a "shot over the bows" for the show organisers and a "shot in the arm" for those campaigning for a Sunday opening!

At around 3.00pm, Dick indicated that those salespeople travelling furthest could leave the exhibition. It was scheduled to close at around 4.00pm, but contractors were not allowed to enter the Hall until 5.00pm. Our London based salesforce had drifted away, even though they had been requested to stay on to help.

The senior managers from Calverton were left to guard our merchandise prior to time of the exhibition breakdown.

I was not best pleased!

My patience was further tested, when the van driver from our delivery contractors arrived on the stand. "We have secured a space close to the front entrance," he advised. "There are only two of us and one will have to stay with the vehicle."

He had brought two portable rails with him. It would require several journeys to transport all the ranges to the van. Thankfully, all the management team came to the rescue and within half an hour the task was completed.

By this time, I was furious!

I felt it was unedifying for members of the Wrangler senior management to be helping to load our van under the watchful, and judgemental eyes of our counterparts from the other major brands of jeans. The ultra-professionalism exhibited before and during the exhibition and been tainted by our amateurish departure at the end.

After the long drive home and a good night's sleep, I was still seething!

As soon as I arrived at the office, I dictated a short memo to Dick Webzell. In it, I expressed my displeasure in no uncertain terms. My secretary passed it over to his secretary for his immediate attention.

Within minutes my internal phone burst into life. Dick had received my missive. "Mr. Dilley come into my office NOW," he demanded.

The memo had the desired effect!

After a short, but heated discussion, he agreed steps should be taken to ensure that the exit from any exhibition should be as professional as our entrance.

In 1978, the organisers of IMBEX, succumbing to pressure from the trade, decided to start the exhibition on a Sunday and finish on Wednesday. The change was generally welcomed although, for exhibitors, it now meant that the stand dressing began one day earlier, on a Saturday.

We had rebooked The Kensington Close Hotel for the duration of our stay in London.

The exhibition organisers had made a concerted effort to beef up the attendance. Personalities from the world of entertainment and sport were invited to see what the world of men's and boy's fashion had to offer.

During the exhibition, many came on to our stand ever hopeful of being presented with a 'freebie.' Handing out free merchandise was not part of our PR policy, but we did make some useful contacts who were happy to receive Wrangler merchandise at wholesale instead of retail prices.

Our stand contractor had maintained the successful selling area concept that had gone down so well the year before. Creatively, they had managed to provide a totally different overall image. The new stand was equally as impressive as its predecessor.

Sunday opening seemed to be well received. Retail buyers used the non-trading day to bring along staff who would previously have been unable to attend. In this way, the first day numbers were boosted and, as a result, attendance was much bigger than in previous years.

Big buyers still came in on the Monday and Tuesday to do the real business.

The organisers were always keen to ensure the fashion, national and international media were well catered for. It appeared, at the time, the first day was when many of them attended. I was busy explaining how the growth in denim was undiminished and presenting items from our range that we were confident would be the big sellers over the next 6-9 months.

The IMBEX public relations team were keener on promoting the success of the show.

Some of the more traditional exhibitors were always happy to quote sales figures. Often these were exaggerated but the press like to quote statistics and the organisers used quoted sales figures as proof of the show's success.

I remember one well known manufacturer of formal knitwear telling the press that they had sold £125,000 worth of products in the first day. "This is a record for us on the first day of IMBEX," their sales director was quoted as saying.

This was widely quoted in the media as proof of success of the Sunday opening.

I had a wry smile to myself.

We never quoted sales figures, but I knew that our first day figures were well over 125,000 in unit volume and considerably more in value!

The final day was very quiet but, unlike the previous year, our London salesforce stayed behind and our final exit from the show was as professional as our entry.

I don't know what Dick Webzell had said to them. Whatever it was, it worked!

In 1979, IMBEX moved from Earls Court to Olympia. The new venue provided slightly better access for exhibitors and more exhibition space for the organisers.

Unfortunately, the date was slightly earlier, from Sunday 18th to Wednesday 22nd February. This meant that the set-up day was 17th February, my wedding anniversary.

The dates, over next 4 years, caused a lot of "aggro" in the Dilley household. February 14th, Valentine's Day, was followed by my wife's birthday, on the 15th and our wedding anniversary on the 17th. The exhibition clashed with some, sometimes all these dates.

A standing order with the local florist for each of these key days went some way to compensate for my being away. Unfortunately, it took me years to recover all the "brownie points" I had lost!

After making a deal with the exhibition organisers, we came to an agreement on the supply of refreshments. We would purchase all our coffee, tea, milk, alcoholic drinks from the exhibitions official catering supplier. In addition, we also agreed to purchase a limited number of sandwiches.

The bulk of our sandwiches were to be purchased direct from the M&S supplier we had tracked down in Lancashire. Our requirements were ordered prior to the exhibition and were delivered to the M&S branch in Oxford Street for us to pick up.

The first IMBEX at Olympia was well received by the trade.

One of the leading trade magazines opened its show report as follows, "Olympia surprised us all, not even the organisers expected IMBEX to be so successful."

Throughout the 1980's, Olympia became a permanent home for the exhibition.

During that time, we tried several hotels within walking distance. Our favourite was the Gloucester Hotel in Harrington Gardens, Kensington. It was close to some of our favourite restaurants and met all our requirements.

One occasion, we were shocked to find Levi's had also booked into the same hotel. We normally went to great lengths to avoid too much fraternisation. They were in what we considered to be "our hotel." What's more, they were also eating in "all our favourite restaurants."

One evening, I returned to the hotel after the show, with some of my colleagues. In the corner of the lift was a huge computer printout. Picking it up, I discovered it was a comprehensive account data listing, belonging to one of the senior representatives of Levi's.

It contained address and trading details for every customer in one of their key selling areas. I was tempted to spend the rest of the night evaluating the details it contained.

Instead, I wrote a note to the then Levi's Sales Director, Peter Abbiss, who was an old school friend. It read, "Peter, found this in the lift. Thought you might like it back. I haven't read it, honestly!" I signed the missive, attached it to the front of the printout and handed it into the reception desk of the hotel, asking them to hand it over to Peter.

He sought me out next day at the show. "Thanks for handing over the printout," he said. "I'm glad you found it and nobody else."

The dangers of being in too close a proximity to their major competitor had struck home. We never knowingly found ourselves sharing a hotel with Levi's again.

Throughout the 1980's our excellent working relationship with our stand contractor was maintained. The classic selling area was retained, but together we managed to produce a string of impressive stands, including the first "double-decker" at the show.

Despite the professionalism we exhibited before and during the show, we never seemed to totally master the breakdown.

The Wrangler salesforce were always quick to leave as soon as the last customers departed. This was often some time before the show officially ended. Those travelling some distance had some excuse. They had to catch a train, a plane or had a long car journey. This excuse could also have been used by all the Senior Management Team, but we never left the Exhibition Hall until the product ranges had been handed over to our nominated transport supplier.

On one occasion, our exhibition contractor had, through their trade contacts, tracked down some bone fide Directors chairs. These were in beautifully manufactured in wood with blue "denim" fabric. We had the chair back overprinted with a yellow Wrangler logo. During the show they had generated lots of positive comments from customers.

At lunchtime on the final day of the show, Dick Webzell made an announcement. "I know the Directors chairs have created a lot of comment," he said. "You have all worked hard during the show," he continued. "I have decided that you can all take the chairs, in your own selling area, home with you when the show has officially ended."

The selling area for each representative had four chairs. They were heavy, cumbersome and would be difficult to transport, particularly for those travelling by air, train or sharing a car with other colleagues.

At the end of the show, we were treated to a demonstration of just how resourceful the Wrangler salesforce could really be. As soon as the tannoy announcement signalled the end of the show, the chairs were swept up. We witnessed the sight of each Wrangler salesman leaving the exhibition hall balancing brief cases and suitcases precariously on top of four folded Directors chairs.

To this day, I still wonder how the four salesmen from the North of England, who were sharing a car, managed to fit themselves, their luggage and sixteen Directors chairs into one Volvo!

A brand like Wrangler did not need the selling platform that IMBEX provided. We had arguably the best salesforce in the business. Not attending the exhibition would not have impacted on our sales.

When our products first arrived at the show, much of merchandise on offer from other exhibitors was very formal. The mix reflected the products that were to be found in many high street retailers at that time.

Wrangler, and our major competitors, changed the dynamics of the trade show. Our dominant presence also changed the attitudes of major retail buyers both in the larger independents and high street chains. Suddenly, casual wear, in the form of jeans and jeans related clothing, became the dominant staple in every kind of menswear outlet.

Towards the end of the decade, IMBEX was becoming more and more relevant to the trade. In 1986, 512 exhibitors drew in a record attendance of 14,904. The exhibition organisers were jubilant. Dick Webzell served as a Director of IMBEX up to the time he left Wrangler. During the trade show, the Board held a dinner which was supported by the great and the good of the industry. These were always lavish affairs providing great food and first-class entertainment. In the mid 1980's, Dick always booked a table and invited members of the senior management team to attend. We had been spoilt by excellent interactive performances from the late, great Bob Monkhouse and the superb Lenny Henry.

1988 had marked the Silver Jubilee of IMBEX and the organisers had pulled out all the stops to make the occasion something special. What had become tradition continued, only this time Ralph Huschle was hosting our table at the dinner. Top double act Little and Large headed the bill for the cabaret. At the completion of their routine, they left the stage, there was a slight lull in proceedings because nobody knew if this was the end of the night's entertainment.

A buzz of conversation was interrupted, and then all conversations stopped, as the sound of military music filled the air and the Band of the Coldstream Guards marched into the room. We were now aware why each table setting had included a small Union Jack flag.

Ralph looked on in amazement at the reaction that the stirring music was having on the staid, seemingly conservative audience. To the strains of "Rule Britannia" they began to stand up, wave their flags and clap in time with the music.

Everything moved up a notch when the tune of "Land of Hope and Glory" filled the air. People who needed sticks to walk were marching on the spot in time with the music, sticks waving in the air in one hand and flag in the other.

Things really took off when the chorus began. Everyone in the room stood up, some on the chairs and several on their tables. The whole audience, except the bemused (American) Ralph, broke into song.

> "Land of Hope and Glory, Mother of the Free,
> How shall we extol thee, who are born of thee?

> Wider still, and wider, shall thy bounds be set;
> God, who made thee mighty, make thee mightier yet!"

After several more and more enthusiastic chorus renditions and number of encores, even Ralph was on his feet and waving the flag.

When the band departed to rapturous applause Ralph turned to me, "I had no idea how patriotic you Brits could be," he exclaimed. "We all stand together when the honour of our country is at stake," I replied.

At Wrangler, we were beginning to question the cost-effectiveness of our continuing support of trade shows. For us, the end, of what some considered a costly PR exercise, was fast approaching!

Futura Fair in Ireland

In 1975, the Wrangler operation in Ireland was run by General Manager, Bert Roddy. He had three salesmen and a small support team who operated from an office close to the Naas Road in Dublin. Bert reported directly to Dick Webzell. I was responsible for providing marketing and advertising support.

The showroom at the Dublin office was used to promote new ranges with representatives inviting and hosting their key customers.

Futura Fashion Fair, a new trade show for men's, women's and childrenswear, had been launched in 1974 by Gerry Murphy and Maureen Ledwith. It was run in conjunction with Futura, the fashion trade magazine that covered the whole of Ireland. The first event was a modest affair attracting 40 exhibitors to the exhibition hall at the Burlington Hotel in Dublin.

Bert Roddy had been invited to take a stand for Wrangler but had declined. At the time, he felt that the interest of Blue Bell Ireland would be best served by continuing with the existing in-house activity.

By 1977, Futura Fair had outgrown the Burlington and Gerry and Maureen took the courageous step to move to the Royal Dublin Society (RDS) showground, at Ballsbridge, in Dublin.

In the 1970's, the RDS was the home of the largest exhibition complex in Ireland. For the show to be successful, it would be necessary to bolster the number of exhibitors and significantly increase the foot fall.

To do this, they required the involvement of some major international brand names such as and Wrangler and Levi's. Through Bert, they pushed hard to secure our involvement. This would require a significant extra marketing investment to ensure that Wrangler had a meaningful presence.

The decision was made to go ahead.

Gerry and Maureen made it clear that buyers from Northern Ireland (the Six Counties) would be invited.

In 1978, "The Troubles" had been raging in Northern Ireland for around 10 years. At the heart of the violent conflict, was the constitutional status of Northern Ireland. The overwhelmingly Protestant majority wished to remain part of the United Kingdom. The, almost exclusively, Catholic minority wished to become part of the Republic of Ireland.

Despite the unrest, a continuance of cross border trade was essential to all parties. Controls at the border made this a little more difficult but Belfast and Dublin were well connected by road, air, and train and "all-Irish tradeshows" were not uncommon.

At the time, Stuart McVittie was our sales agent in Northern Ireland. Dick Webzell arranged with him that he would attend Futura and encourage his customers to attend, particularly those in towns close to the border.

Dick made it clear, from the start, that we would support the market in Ireland by making a strong brand statement at the first Futura Fair at the RDS. It was scheduled to take place during the 10-12 September 1978.

As part of the strategy, the decision was made that he and I would attend every day. This would enable us to meet key buyers, north and south of the border, as well as the Irish media.

Our stand at the first Futura Fair was a modest affair. Despite this, it created a high brand awareness in a market where Wrangler and Levi's were vying for sales supremacy.

We received a warm Irish welcome from Gerry Murphy, Maureen Ledwith, and their team. Nothing was too much trouble. Trade buyers throughout Ireland gave the show their full support and appreciated the fact that Wrangler and other UK based fashion brands had made the effort to be there.

I made excellent contacts with key members of the Irish fashion press including Noelle Campbell-Sharp and Terry Keane. These two ladies had a reputation as the "enfants terrible' of the Irish fashion scene." Between them, they knew everyone who was anyone!

Noelle was particularly helpful in subsequent years, helping to introduce Dick and I to the movers and shakers in Ireland. As one of the major "media moguls" in the Republic, she had the most influential fashion and business titles in her portfolio. We were the same age and hit it off immediately. In the future, if I needed a "sounding board," I only had to pick up the phone and call her. I knew the advice would be bang on the button.

Futura Fair was far more laid back than its UK counterparts. In Dublin, we found ourselves caught up in the informal atmosphere.

At a major trade show in the UK, there was no way that the Managing Directors of Levi's and Wrangler, and their senior executives, would meet for coffee and a chat on their respective stands.

At Futura Fair, this fraternisation not only took place, but nobody turned a hair!

The politics of "The Troubles" were also forgotten. Buyers, from both side of the divide, came to Futura Fair to see the latest fashion ranges, place their orders and enjoy the craic.

An extended stay in Ireland also helped us to develop a much better relationship with the staff at the Dublin office and the Irish salesforce.

Dublin is still one of my favourite cities in the world!

Our attendance at Futura Fair offered a unique opportunity to see more of what it had to offer. The show closed on the evening of Tuesday 12 September and Dick, and I stayed over. Next day we took a flight to London Heathrow to meet up with our wives and attend the gala premiere of "Grease the movie."

After analysing the sales data and reactions of the retail trade in Ireland, Bert Roddy advised that Futura had been a great success. A similar reaction was reported by Stuart McVittie. The show became a permanent fixture on our trade show calendar.

In 1979, the Fair had been scheduled to take place from 30 September to 2 October. We signalled to Maureen and her team that Wrangler would be attending, and we selected an excellent location for our stand.

Subsequently, we received the news that Pope John Paul II would be making an official visit to Ireland over the same weekend. The news caused a flurry of activity to book flights to Dublin and accommodation in the city. Irish people from around the country, and across the world, were signalling their intent to attend the historic event.

Thankfully, we had been quick off the mark!

Bert Roddy had reserved accommodation at the Shelbourne Hotel for Dick Webzell and me. Our travel agent had secured flights to Dublin to arrive on Saturday 29 September and back to the UK on the evening of Tuesday 2 October.

We were aware that the visit of the Pope to Ireland would be a major attraction. Quite how big we had not anticipated!

Pope John Paul II had arrived at around 10.00am on Saturday 29 September 1979. The Aer Lingus 747 that brought him to Ireland was appropriately named St Patrick. Dublin airport was festooned with the bunting in the papal colours of yellow and white. Thousands of people were on the viewing deck to welcome him. When he appeared at the door of the plane, descended the steps, and kissed the ground, the crowd erupted.

Apparently, I was told by an onlooker that, compared to that, "Beatlemania was small change!"

When our, much smaller, Aer Lingus flight landed several hours later, the crowds of people had left but the bunting and "electricity in the air" remained.

Bert Roddy picked us up at the airport. "It took me ages to get here," he told us. "Normally I cut through Phoenix Park but that is closed to through traffic."

Our journey of 6 miles to Central Dublin, took much longer than it would normally. The residue of the crowds who had welcomed the Pope were still to be seen. Papal bunting and flags were on display everywhere.

Whilst we were booking into our hotel, Pope John Paul II was celebrating Mass in Phoenix Park in front of 1.25 million people, a third of the then population of the Republic of Ireland. The whole exercise went like clockwork, although it had proved impossible to provide enough toilets for such a large gathering!

That evening, Dublin was still buzzing. Tens of thousands of visitors, far more than for any rugby international in the city, thronged the streets. In the bars and restaurants, the craic was all about the Pope and his visit.

The following day, when we arrived at the show, an ebullient Maureen Ledwith was still consumed with the excitement of the previous day.

Sadly, the absence of buyers created an almost funereal atmosphere in the exhibition Hall. At the time, Maureen played down the lack of buyers.

In an interview in 1999, she recalled it as a "major disaster." She was quoted as saying, "In 1979, the opening of Futura clashed with the arrival of the Pope in Ireland, and no one turned up at the fair,".

In fairness, my recollection was that the first day was very, very slow but trade picked up on the subsequent days.

I do remember that Maureen's PR people voted Pope John Paul II, "Best Dressed Man of the Month." It created a headline for journalist deflecting them away from the negative affect, that his presence in Ireland, had on visitor numbers at the exhibition.

Exhibitors held the faith!

Subsequently the show went from strength to strength.

Throughout the early 1980's we continued to support the Futura Fair. Our UK based stand manufacturer took over the design process maintaining the brand feel of our stands at the UK based exhibitions, albeit on a smaller scale. They worked directly with our office in Dublin, commissioned contractors based in Ireland to build the stand and liaised with them during the build-up period.

This meant Dick Webzell and I no longer needed to go out the day before to ensure that everything was in order. We quickly established a pattern. Arriving on a Sunday, we would enjoy an early Irish Brunch at the original Kitty O'Shea's before moving on to the RDS.

The Wrangler "aeroplane stand," that had gone down so well at the MAB show in Birmingham, had remained a talking point with buyers in the Republic of Ireland. "Can we do something similar at Futura?" Bert Roddy had enquired.

Our stand designer was up for the challenge. He came up with an adaptation that fitted into the much smaller stand space at the RDS. Bert was very happy with this and so were the Irish stand building contractors. They had used their contacts with Aer Lingus to loan from them enough First-Class aircraft seats for the four selling areas.

Somewhere, between the design and the build, there had been a lack of communication. It could have been a simple misunderstanding. Whatever the reason, the cylindrical aircraft fuselage had been built as a triangular shape.

I had never seen a triangular aircraft before. When our UK stand designer had arrived onsite earlier, he was faced with a "fait accompli." There was simply no time to build a new fuselage.

Everything else about it was superbly executed. The Wrangler stand was the talk of the show - for all the best reasons.

Fortunately, the "cock-up" had simply not been noticed!

As the years went on, Maureen Ledwith became the "face of Futura" but, as the show transformed into the premier trade fashion event in Ireland, Grainne Jordon became her "trouble-shooter." Between them they charmed exhibitors and visitors alike. If you had a problem, one or other would be quickly "on the case" to resolve the situation.

During the years Dick and I visited the show, Maureen was always quick to greet us. For some reason, I was always Robin (Raabin in her lilting Irish brogue) and Dick always Mr. Webzell. "Mr. Webzell, Raabin it's lovely to see you," she would say.

On one occasion we travelled from Birmingham on a new Aer Lingus flight. We had been booked into business class that was being introduced on the Dublin service for the first time. This elevation entitled us to breakfast and Bucks Fizz.

Apart from Dick and myself, there was only one other passenger in business class. Unlike us, he was not interested in having either food, or beverage.

Two hostesses had been allotted to "the business class cabin" for our flight of around 40 minutes. They were keen to impress on us the value of the new service.

Several glasses of Bucks Fizz arrived before a hearty breakfast. "Would you like a liqueur with your coffees?" they asked. We declined.

It was not yet 10.00am and we still had our Irish Brunch, at Kitty O'Shea's to come. An Irish Brunch is always accompanied by a pint of Guinness, we wanted to be sober when we arrived at the RDS. They pressed several miniatures into our duty-free bags as we left the aircraft and "clinked" down the steps and into the airport building.

We were very relaxed when we entered the exhibition hall. Maureen saw us and came across the hall towards us.

"Mr. Webzell, Raabin its lovely to see you," she exclaimed. Dick looked at her with a puzzled expression on his face. "Excuse me. Do I know you?" he asked. "It's me, Maureen," she replied in a surprised fashion.

Before she could say anything else, Dick smiled. At that point, Maureen realising that he was sending her up. We all laughed and exchanged pleasantries before going to the Wrangler stand and getting down to business.

In the summer of the 1983, our advertising agency in Dublin, in conjunction with Noelle Campbell-Sharp, came up with the idea for an attempt on the world record for the longest fashion show. As far as I can recall, the record was held by a team of four Australian models who spent 24 hours, covering nearly 42 miles, on a catwalk in Sydney.

The idea was that the attempt should take place in September during the period of Futura Fair.

"An Irish team attempting and beating the record, giving them recognition by the Guinness Book of records scrutineers, in the home of the Guinness brand, will generate a lot of media coverage across the world," they assured me.

I took some persuading. The logistics were formidable.

We needed a venue with a large catwalk, four models prepared to put their bodies on the line, a team of dressers to cover over two days of activity, staff to provide lighting, music and sustenance for the models, our support team and visiting media representatives.

Plus, an awful lot of Wrangler merchandise!

It was agreed that Young Advertising and our PR team would investigate the final cost of Wrangler involvement and how the benefits would be measured. The agency sourced an appropriate venue along with a team of volunteers to act as dressers. Our PR people persuaded four models to participate.

The Guinness Book of records people defined the criteria for the attempt. This included the minimum number of outfit changes, the number of comfort breaks allowed per hour and, critically, the measures that would determine the record had been broken.

A qualified team of auditors were also required to be present and to sign off that all the preconditions had been met before, during and after the attempt.

Any deviation from the agreed format would render the attempt null and void!

To beat the record each model would have to spend more than 24 hours on the catwalk (minus allowed comfort and sustenance breaks) and participants would need to cover more than 42 miles.

After consulting the management team in Ireland, we agreed to go ahead.

The attempt was timed to start on Sunday afternoon, the first day of the Futura show, and finish the following day. I was assured that everyone involved with the attempt would be fully briefed as to what exactly was expected of them.

Invitations would be issued to key retailers to attend the location of the record attempt after the show, to cheer on the contestants. They would be looked after by our Irish salesforce.

I would only be required to be there for the start and finish of the record attempt. Agency staff would monitor the proceedings during the whole of the two days.

The attempt was scheduled to take place at a nightclub venue on the outskirts of Dublin. The catwalk was built in the shape of an athletics track and measured precisely 220 yards, with 8 circuits equal to one mile in length. To beat the record, the models would need to cover more than 336 circuits in the 24 hours.

Once the event was underway, all Wrangler personnel moved on to the RDS to attend the Futura Fair.

Our advertising and public relations team remained to deal with the media. As predicted, a lot of interest had been generated.

The representatives, and some of their key customers, enjoyed a buffet as they watched the record attempt taking place. I joined them after dinner, later in the evening.

Everything appeared to be going to plan although I was a little concerned, that one of the male models was approaching the challenge more as a sprint, than the ultra-marathon it was. Despite my misgivings, I was advised everything was still going to plan and that the breaking of the record had become a distinct possibility. I had determined to support the models late into the night.

The energetic male model continued "to gallop through the circuits." One of the female models was struggling with an ankle injury. She appeared to be in danger of succumbing to her pain. If that were to happen, it would have been the end of the record attempt.

I walked round with her for more than 20 laps to give her the encouragement to continue. She seemed to overcome her discomfort and was re-motivated to complete the task.

At around 11.00pm the onlookers began to get more and more excited.

"It's great that you are cheering them on but there is still a long way to go before they finish," I observed. "Oh no!" came the reply. "One of the male models has nearly completed the 42miles on the catwalk. Another few laps and the record will be ours."

This was not my interpretation of what was required. The other models were well short of the mileage needed. Everyone had to continue for another 14 hours or so, before the time criteria could be met.

I needed to clarify the situation with Donald Helm from our advertising agency. I had his home number and called him. As I did this a roar went up from the crowd. They thought the record had been broken. Everyone, except me, was applauding and congratulating the models.

"You are right about the requirements for the record," Donald exclaimed. "Put our representative on the phone and I will give them the bad news." After the call, the agency representative hastily convened a meeting with the models and support staff.

Once the news had sunk in, thankfully, within the timescale allowed for the comfort breaks, the record attempt continued. There had obviously been a major breakdown of communications. I was thankful that I had stayed longer than originally anticipated.

Unfortunately, I was cast as the big, bad, interfering Englishman rather than the saviour of the day. As a pure-bred Yorkshireman, this was particularly hard to take!

My job done, I returned to my hotel room to enjoy a good night's sleep.

The following morning, I went straight to the nightclub. In the carpark, I met up with Donald Helme. "We have a problem," he advised. "The manager of the club has barred you because you did not applaud the models last night,"

"No, everyone else has a problem," I countered. "If I am unable to be present during the last hours of the attempt, I will pull the plug now! If I had not provided my support and counsel, the attempt would have been over last night."

Hurried consultations followed, and the "ban'" was lifted.

I was far from happy because no real apology had been forthcoming. I took the view that there are moments when you have just to bite your lip and carry on. This was one of them!

Noelle Campbell-Sharp arrived with one hour to go before the time limit expired. The models and support crew were very tired. One last push and the record would be theirs.

Noelle had a plan. "I will call Sabrina Guinness (one of the Guinness heiresses) and ask her to speak to each of the models individually. With her encouragement they will be motivated to ensure that the world record, and entry into the Guinness Book of Records, can be claimed for Ireland," she explained.

The call was made, and encouragement was given. An hour later the record was broken. Our earlier altercation was forgotten. The whole team and assembled media celebrated as one.

I made a mental note that, in future, I would not meddle in Irish affairs!

Dick Webzell was always on the lookout for good value options on air travel. It was still very expensive in the 1980's.

We had tried the private hire option of a small eight-seater Cessna turbo prop aircraft. Using the private plane, seven people were able travel for the price of six on a scheduled flight. There was no check in queue at the airport and you could choose when to leave and when to return. This was fine if seven people from the company needed to fly to the same destination, at the same time.

On one occasion. we took this option to fly to Dublin, it could have ended in tragedy. Our flight out went without incident. When we arrived at the airport for the return journey, we were met by our pilot. He had some disturbing news. The flight had been grounded by airport security and was being examined by bomb disposal experts who had been called in by the Garda (Irish Police).

We discovered later that a coded call had been received by the airport from a man purporting to represent the IRA. The message was very clear, "there is a bomb on the Wrangler plane." "The Troubles" in Northern Ireland were at their height. Such calls, especially one so specific, were taken very seriously. Nothing was found. After a long delay we were eventually given clearance to take off.

The Cessna option to Dublin was never taken up again!

In May 1986, an airline called Ryanair had obtained permission to challenge the high fares policy operated by British Airways and Aer Lingus on the Dublin to London route. The flight cost of £99 return was less than half the lowest return fare offered by their rivals.

In the September, Dick and I had planned to fly out to Dublin for the Futura Fair. By forward booking, we secured seats from Ryanair at the £99 return launch offer price.

We were apprehensive until our travel agent assured us that the airline used "real aircraft," albeit aging 46-seater BAE748 turbo props. He didn't tell us they only had two!

In those early days, the price included seat allocation and hold luggage. On the day, we checked in as normal. The flight was called on time and we took our seats. Dick had a small cool bag with him that he placed in the overhead locker.

"They serve some food and drink, but it is an extra cost," he advised me. "Don't worry I have everything under control."

After take-off, a hostess came around to take food and drink orders.

"Do you have soft drinks?" Dick enquired. "We serve bottled water and orange juice," she replied. "There is no charge for these items," she added. "Can I please have two orange juices and two extra plastic glasses," Dick requested.

Once the order was delivered, Dick retrieved his cool bag from the locker. Inside were two rounds of his favourite Marks and Spencer sandwiches and a small bottle of champagne. Using the free orange juice and his own champagne, he concocted a couple of Bucks Fizz which went down very well with our sandwiches.

Our hostess watched all this happening with some amusement. "To be sure, I've never seen anything like that before," she told us. I couldn't help feeling that our ruse would be passed down and enter the folklore within Ryanair.

It was not something that could be repeated. I am sure that the management of the airline will have concocted a new rule to prevent it from ever happening again!

My direct involvement with Futura Fair continued into the late 1980's.

Tragically, Bert Roddy died suddenly, Bluebell was taken over by the VF Corporation and Dick Webzell left the company. A new, younger management team was appointed. I was preoccupied elsewhere as the nature of my job changed.

Although I still visited Dublin, I was less hands on than I had been previously. The Irish sales and marketing team were more than capable of running their own affairs. I was available to provide my assistance at arm's length.

The continued involvement of the Wrangler brand in Futura Fair, was now in their hands.

PART SIX

PHOTOGRAPHERS AND PHOTOGRAPHIC SHOOTS

Chapter Twenty-Four

Using Photography to Market Fashion Products

Fashion photography in the 1960's and 1970's was dominated by a new breed of young mavericks that included the "Black Trinity" comprising David Bailey, Terence Donovan, and Brian Duffy.

Prior to their entry into the field, an old guard of studio photographers such as Cecil Beaton held sway until Norman Parkinson pioneered the use of outdoor location for his fashion shoots.

The "Black Trinity" expanded on what Parkinson had developed. They all used a hand-held camera and featured products from a new breed of fashion designers. All were also highly influential in the choice of models used on their shoots. They were continually on the lookout for men and women who could project their own "individual look."

The status of photographers was elevated to a whole new level. This "new wave" of photographers captured images in their lenses that brought about cultural changes in their audiences. They were at the forefront in the creation of a "new look" that epitomised, what is now known as, "the swinging 60's."

Trade and consumer fashion magazines editors liked to oversee their own photographic shoots. They chose the photographer, the models and the clothes that featured in them. For a brand to have its merchandise included, require participation in a three-way process.

Black and white shots were taken by Public Relations companies who represented clothing brands. By developing and maintaining close working relationships with fashion editors, PR companies would acquire advance knowledge of what was to be featured in forthcoming issues.

PR agencies would send a selection of photographs, from shoots they had supervised, of merchandise they felt might be of interest for these future editorial features. They would then follow up and arrange meetings with the editors to show the actual garments in which an interest had been expressed.

If the fashion editor liked the garments they were shown, they would include them in the feature.

Neither the fashion manufacturers nor their PR representatives had any input into the choice of photographer, or how the garments were presented during the actual photographic session.

Fashion editors were the sole arbiters of the products used and the fashion image that appeared in their magazines. They wielded considerable power!

The arrival into the UK market, of major American jeans companies, began to challenge these norms.

We were spending large amounts of money to create a unique image for our individual brands. As we grew our distribution and brand share, our impact on what was fashionable, or not, became considerable.

When I started work at Wrangler in the mid-seventies, fashion editors were asking our PR agency for denim products with "whistle and bells" that they felt were at the cutting edge of the market.

By the early eighties, they were contacting us direct to ask what the "hot" Wrangler products would be for the following season.

Our public relations activity had helped to achieve brand leadership. This had reaped the reward of extensive coverage in the fashion press.

Organic growth in the jeans market stalled at the beginning of the 1980's. As new entrants entered the fray, maintaining our share of voice in the fashion press was becoming more difficult.

Our advertising during the late 1970's, had focused on brand differentiation and the development of a set of Wrangler brand values.

In consultation with our PR agency, we sensed that the market was changing. We would now need to promote the fashion values of the Wrangler product ranges, both through the medium of the fashion press and at the point of sale.

We could not afford to enlist the services of the "big-name" photographers. Instead, we developed a strategy of seeking out the latest "new wave" of photographers and "fresh faced, untried models." It was agreed, that our "dual purpose photographic sessions" would all take place on location. This would enable us to mirror the images being projected through our advertising campaigns.

To ensure continuity, the sessions would be directed jointly by a representative of the PR agency and our own PR personnel. Initially, this worked very well. The pictures were accepted, and used by fashion editors, but their use as point-of-sale items was limited. The stills, taken during our advertising commercial shoots, were still doing a better job.

After discussions with Maggi Fox, our internal PR Coordinator, it was decided to approach the situation from a different angle. We would set up a shoot featuring products from the Wrangler product range for Fall 1982.

The objective would be to create a portfolio of pictures to be used in the product merchandisers for the Wrangler salesforce, posters at the point of sale and, where applicable, for PR purposes.

Maggi would act as stylist with responsibility for coordinating the ranges and putting together the outfits. I would take the role of Art Director selecting the locations and working with the chosen photographer to deliver the images required.

Together we would select the models, three males and one female. Our starting criteria was, that they should have never appeared in a shoot for any of our competitors.

Through our advertising agency in Ireland and, in conjunction with a couple of the key Irish fashion magazines, the name Ursula Steiger was mentioned as a possible choice as photographer. Swiss born Ursula, was setting the Irish fashion scene alight with her innovatory work. Maggi and I liked what we saw. The initial conversations with Ursula were encouraging. We wanted a new talent, she wanted to break into the UK market.

It seemed like a choice that could work for all the parties concerned!

The next idea was truly blue-sky thinking. "If we are using a photographer based in Ireland, why not use Irish models as well?"

Looking back, I can't remember who first voiced the notion, but it seemed like a good idea, and we went with it. I felt assured that the concept itself would generate a lot of press coverage both in the UK and Ireland.

Chapter Twenty-Five

Location shoot, the Cairngorms, Scotland, January 1982 - Ursula Steiger

Having decided on a photographer for our first PR and sales promotion shoot, the small matter of a location needed to be determined.

We would be promoting jeans and jeans related clothing for the Fall 1982 ranges. A full range of samples would not be available to us until the end of December 1981.

Finished product merchandisers were required in time for the IMBEX exhibition. This was taking place during the second week in February 1982.

The ideal location needed to have access to snow but also interesting indoor facilities. These would be useful in the event of the weather becoming too bad for shooting outdoors. It was also necessary that it enjoyed relatively easy access from Ireland, and the rest of the UK.

Only one location fitted the criteria, the Aviemore Centre in the Cairngorms in Scotland.

At the time, the 30-acre centre boasted three hotels, rows of chalets, a cinema, conference centre, swimming pool, ice rink and a dry ski slope. The promotional material offered us "a large number of bars, a choice of restaurants and an arcade of shops." Plus, it was only a short drive to the Cairngorm Chairlift. Using the ski slopes provided the probability of access to snow.

We booked the whole of our party of seven into the four-star hotel on the site. We also hired a small coach to ferry us, and the product ranges around during the 2 days of the shoot. The coach had toilet facilities and would be used as a changing room by the models and stylist.

Everyone was scheduled to arrive on the 4 January 1982.

Ursula and the four models had been booked on a flight into Glasgow and would be travelling up from there by minibus. Maggi and I planned to pick up the product ranges from Calverton early on the morning of 4th January and drive all the way to Aviemore in my car. This involved a journey of just over 400 miles. Allowing for refreshment breaks, we planned to arrive in time for dinner at the hotel.

We had to return to Nottingham on the 7 January because the ranges, that we were using on the shoot, were needed for a merchandising meeting in Brussels the following day.

Maggi had arranged to hand over the ranges to Alan Geddes, of the Wrangler merchandise team, at a hotel in Nottingham she would be staying in on the night of 7th January.

The journey to Aviemore was uneventful. We stopped off near Edinburgh for a bite to eat and then continued our journey via Perth on the scenic A9 road through the mountains.

As we neared our destination, it became increasingly obvious that the snow, we had travelled all that way to find, was only visible on the mountain tops. As we had not planned on scaling any peaks during our shoot, this was something of a disappointment.

Eventually, we arrived at our hotel taking the opportunity to look round the resort to pinpoint locations for the second day of our session. Later we met up with Ursula and the models for a briefing.

In January, the days are short in the north of Scotland. With just over 7 hours of daylight, we would have to be at the first location for a 9.00am start enabling us to maximise the light before darkness descended at about 3.45pm.

For the first day of the shoot, we had a twenty-minute journey to our chosen location alongside the Cairngorm Chairlift. The car park there would be our base for the day. Our plan was to use the chairlift to reach the available snowline for each different set up.

After an early breakfast, we arrived at the destination to find that the Scottish weather, in the form of high winds, had caused the service to be suspended.

Thankfully, about 100 metres above the carpark there was some snow. We would just have to work with what we had.

The sky was blue, and the sun was shining. Unfortunately, the gale force wind was bitterly cold. I discussed the situation with Ursula and the models. "I can understand if you feel that we should abandon this location but would appreciate if we could try to make the best of a bad job," I explained. Everyone involved was keen to give it a try. True to their word, during the rest of our time on the mountain, they worked exceptional hard in very trying circumstances.

Just before 3.00pm, the cloud descended forcing us to return to our minibus and drive back to the hotel. We were all very cold. A dip in the heated hotel pool followed by a sauna was the order of the day.

Maggi and I reviewed the day's shoot with Ursula. We had only missed a couple of set-ups and were all confident that we would be able make up for lost time, the next day.

We looked at alternative venues such as the dry ski slopes, ice rink, chalet, and shopping areas. These were all close to the hotel. If the weather was as bad as our first day, we had a "Plan B" to fall back on.

Perhaps we had been tempting fate?

After our group dinner, we all retired early. We would have to work hard on our last day to make up for lost time.

I woke at about 6.30am and looked out of my bedroom window. Nature had been busy. We had come to Aviemore for snow. Overnight, this had been provided in abundance. Driven by the wind, there was several feet on the ground outside. It was still snowing. Clearly, a return to the mountain was out of the question.

"Plan B," it was then!

Our final day of the shoot was not without incident.

Ursula had made provisions for two days of photography outdoors. Consequently, the lighting she had brought with her from Ireland was barely sufficient for the set-ups in the ice rink and other indoor locations. Using all her expertise, she did manage to complete all the indoor shots to everyone's satisfaction.

Thankfully, there was a break in the snowfall mid-morning. We were able to take advantage of the outdoor locations that were now visually enhanced by the snow that had fallen. Happily, at the end of the day, we had completed everything initially planned over the two days of the shoot.

Over our final group dinner, I thanked everyone for their hard work and wished them a safe journey home. Ursula and the models faced a relatively short journey by minibus to Glasgow airport. Maggi and I had a 400 miles car drive back to Nottingham.

Next morning it was snowing heavily. The weather forecast for the area between Aviemore and Edinburgh was not good. Snow would continue to fall all day. High winds threatened to cause drifting on the road through the Cairngorms to Perth. A weather warning advised against all unnecessary travel along our route.

The Edinburgh to Nottingham leg of our journey promised to be trouble free. There had been no snowfall there, and none was forecast.

As we set off, I was not too concerned. My car was a top of the range Volvo. Designed for the harsh winter climate of Sweden, I was confident that "a little bit of Scottish snow" would not present us with any difficulties.

Just 6 miles outside the village of Aviemore, the problems began!

First my windscreen wipers began to slow. Abruptly, they stopped altogether. Then the engine stopped and would not start. I had managed to pull off the road. In the blizzard conditions we faced a major problem. I had breakdown cover. We didn't have a mobile phone to call for help. They were still on the drawing board at that time.

We had not seen a telephone box that we might use.

"I am sure we passed a driveway, a few hundred yards down the road. There must be a house with a phone at the end of it," Maggi suggested. "You stay with the car, I will investigate and call for help," she offered.

With hindsight, perhaps I should have been the one to go for help. It made sense at the time, for me to stay with the car and the product samples. If I could get the car started, we could either sit tight in a warm vehicle until some intrepid traveller found us or drive back to Aviemore and find a garage.

In the end, we agreed that Maggi would try and find the house and I would try to start the car. All togged out in her winter coat, fur gloves, "Russian style hat," with her feet encased in extremely fashionable "Russell and Bromley" boots, Maggi disappeared into the swirling snow. The sight recalled the true story Captain Oakes of Antarctica.

On Captain Scott's ill-fated South Pole expedition, Oakes was suffering with gangrene and frostbite. He was slowing down his companions. In a supreme act of self-sacrifice, he walked out of the safety of the tent in which they had been sheltering. Uttering the words, "I am just going outside and may be some time." He was never seen again!

I was hopeful that our outcome would be far more satisfactory but consoled myself with the thought that, in the circumstances, extreme action was necessary.

After what seemed an age under the bonnet, cleaning spark plugs and drying off leads, the engine sputtered into life. Taking off my sodden jacket, I turned on the car heater and tried to coax some warmth back into my body.

Over 45 minutes had passed since Maggi had set off on her mission to find help. Just as I was becoming really concerned, two Land Rovers appeared simultaneously. Maggi was seated in the passenger seat of one. The other was a recovery vehicle sent by the RAC from a garage in Aviemore.

The driveway had led to a house, a fine country mansion to be precise. The owners had welcomed Maggi inside and she had phoned the RAC helpline. They had sent out the recovery vehicle. Whilst I was struggling under the bonnet of the car, Maggi was enjoying cake and coffee, and "a wee dram" of whisky, to ward off the cold. The housekeeper had dried off her wet clothes and boots before the chauffeur delivered her back to my car.

Despite my misgivings at the time, it was I who had apparently drawn the short straw!

The driver of the recovery vehicle took a superficial look at my car. He then requested me to follow him back to the garage in Aviemore. Once there, we were informed they would check that the car was safe to complete the rest of our journey. After an hour of tinkering, I was given the OK to continue.

Retracing our steps, we found that if anything, the weather had worsened. The road in front of us was mile upon mile of virgin snow. Until we neared the outskirts of Perth, we did not see any other vehicles. The journey of 84 miles should have taken around 2 hours. We had been on the road for nearly 5 hours. It was 1.00pm and we still had another 310 miles to go.

As we started the climb out of Perth, the windscreen wipers on my car slowed down and stopped. I managed to drive into a layby just before the engine cut out. This was a repeat of the problems we had encountered earlier on the journey. Although, as before, I managed to start the engine, there was no way I could risk the fault reoccurring. We had to find a garage. Perth seemed the best option. Turning the car round, I headed back down the hill.

Driving on to the forecourt of the first garage I came to, I was amazed to see that it was a Volvo main dealer. Luck appeared to be on our side. Putting the car straight into their workshop, they identified the culprit as a faulty alternator. They had the part and promised that "in less than two hours you will be on your way once more."

While we were waiting, I rang my wife and told her not to expect us back before midnight. She then rang Alan Geddes and advised him that Maggi would ring him when we reached Southwell. They would then meet up at the Nottingham hotel where she was staying. Maggi also rang the hotel to tell them her check-in would be very late. Nearer 1.00am than the expected 9.00pm.

Quicker than expected the engineer came out to advise that the car was ready. He expressed amazement it had been given clearance to continue by the mechanic in Aviemore. Thanking him for his excellent service, I paid the bill, and we were on our way.

Within 15 minutes we reached the M90 motorway. At the time, it was a new addition to the UK Motorway network. It is still the most northerly motorway in the UK, running from the suburbs of Perth passing Kinross, Dunfermline before crossing the Forth Road Bridge. That afternoon, every lane of the motorway was covered by several inches of snow. On our side of the road, the traffic was moving freely. By contrast, the north bound carriageway was a scene of carnage with multiple pile ups caused by the poor conditions.

We arrived in Edinburgh where we stopped for refreshments before completing our journey without further incident.

Maggi met up with Alan Geddes, albeit much later than originally intended. The range samples were handed over in time for his trip to Brussels the same day.

The photographic shoot had worked out well. Both the PR and sales promotional pictures were well received and fully utilised.

What did we learn from the experience?

Using a photographer keen to make an impression, and young relatively unknown models, "willing to go the extra mile," had proved a resounding success. The Wrangler commission had certainly helped to propel the skills of Ursula Steiger to a wider audience. Working on a Wrangler shoot had also proved a feather in the cap for the young Irish models.

I realised that an outdoor shoot in the UK, was a particularly risky exercise, at any time of the year!

An overseas shoot, at a venue where good weather was practically guaranteed, presented a greater logistical challenge. On the other hand, it represented a better option, and it would probably be not much more expensive. It would be some time before I was prepared to put the theory to the test.

In the intervening years, we continued to support up and coming photographers. We also provided a vehicle for many new faces in the modelling industry enabling them to break into the big time. Because of this approach, our PR and point of sale remained fresh and vibrant.

I remain convinced that this strategy helped Wrangler to remain a relevant brand in the eyes of the prime target group through the many difficult years ahead.

Chapter Twenty-Six

Location Shoot, Almeria, Spain, June 1988 - Martin Hooper

In the autumn of 1985, my long-time secretary, Janice announced her impending nuptials and resignation from the company. After the ceremony, and on returning from their honeymoon, the happy couple would be leaving the area.

My wife Glenys and I had been invited to the wedding. It took place at the Cathedral Church of St Barnabas, in the city of Nottingham.

During the reception, I was introduced to Janice's parents and several other members of her family. After all the formalities had concluded, and dancing had started, I was approached by a young man, who shook my hand vigorously.

"Hello Robin, you don't know me," he said. "I am Martin Hooper, a cousin of Janice's husband," he announced. "I am also a professional photographer and wondered if I can talk to you about the possibility of my doing some work for Wrangler?"

This sort of encounter happened frequently. I had made a point of never discussing business at a social event, especially with people that I had not met before. Not wishing to be rude, I exchanged cards with Martin. "Give me a call next week and we can set up a meeting," I suggested.

I thought nothing more of the encounter until, a week later, Martin did follow up our short conversation.

He explained that after completing his degree course he had set his own business, Martin Hooper Photography, in 1981. Having recently moved to London, he was keen to expand his portfolio to include work for some major fashion brands. "Perhaps we can meet up next time you are in town? I'd like you to look at some of the fashion photographic work I have already created," he concluded.

A few weeks later, along with my PR Co-ordinator, Lindah Kiddey, I had a meeting with our PR company in the capital. Lindah rang Martin and set up a meeting at our

London showroom later that same day. We were very impressed with what we saw and agreed to keep in touch.

Although he may have done some PR work for Wrangler in the interim period, nearly three years were to pass before we finally collaborated on a major shoot. Our first opportunity arose in in the middle of 1988.

A new Marketing Director had been appointed with a brief to invigorate the Wrangler product offering. With a new range to put together for Spring 1989, the new man was working under a major time constraint. The product line was scheduled for launch at the Men's and Boyswear (MAB) trade show in September 1988. A month before that, a series of regional shows were planned to take place.

We had talked amongst ourselves about the need to place more emphasis on product promotion at the point of sale.

The central theme of the new range revolved around a modern take on the Western jeans styling that had launched the Wrangler brand, over 40 years before. A portfolio of pictures was required to develop the theme, project the product, and help to make the concept desirable to buyers, and, through them, the prime target market.

The finished shots would be used as part of an extensive public relations campaign. They would also be featured in a range presentation brochure for our salesforce to use as a selling tool at the trade shows. Finally, they would also be integral to the creation of a range of material that would be developed for instore merchandising at the point of sale.

We needed a photographer who could instantly understand the concept, was creative and who would be able to work with me, under pressure. I picked up the phone and called Martin Hooper.

My experience, during the first outdoor shoot in Scotland, had convinced me that the location would have to be somewhere where the weather was more reliable. We also needed to be able to replicate the concept of the American wild west.

A location in Nevada, in the USA, was not feasible. Well, not on the budget that we were working with!

Our initial research convinced us that Spain was. The province of Almeria in Andalusia fitted the bill perfectly. The climate was classified between "hot semi-arid and hot desert." Areas such as Cabo de Gata-Nijar Natural Park, the Almanzora River and Tabernas Desert, were just a few of the places where we could find the type of locations we were looking for.

In late June, when we planned to shoot, we could expect to enjoy great light, more than 11 hours of sunshine each day and very little rain.

Martin was keen to show us what he was capable of. We agreed a very competitive total fee. This included a three-day reconnaissance of the area. He would select a base where we would stay during the shoot, and locations that would meet our requirements.

I would fly out the day before the models, hair and make-up artist and stylist. This would enable me to carry out site inspections of the locations Martin and his team had selected. We would sign these off and then agree the final shooting schedule.

On Saturday 25 June 1988, I flew out to Spain. At Almeria Airport, I was met by Martin, his photographic assistant Mark Adam, and his shoot administrator Sol. She was our fixer, and responsible for obtaining the necessary permissions for access to locations, organising refreshment during the shoot and, very importantly, holding the purse strings to ensure that everything came in on budget. The fact that she was fluent in Spanish would also prove to be very useful.

Martin's team had found an ideal base in a villa complex in the fertile valley of Cortijo Grande at the foot of the Sierra Cabrera Mountains. These soared to around 1,000 metres above sea level. Our location was about 4km from the small town of Turre and 8km from the larger resort of Mojacar, with its beaches and shops.

The complex of 6 villas, each with three/four bedrooms, were clustered around a swimming pool area that also boasted a bar and a small café/restaurant. It was owned by an English couple who had grand plans to turn the surrounding area into a sports complex complete with golf course, tennis courts and restaurants.

Sol had booked four villas. Martin, me, and Mark would share the biggest one. Sol, the hair and make-up lady and the stylist would share another. The two remaining villas were for the 3 male and two female models.

On the way to the villa, my colleagues talk animatedly about the locations they had selected. "I think you will find that all the bases have been covered," Martin explained.

Sol had organised the hire of two 13-seater minibuses to carry our crew of 6, 5 models and all the equipment and clothes for the shoot.

It was mid-afternoon when we arrived at the villa. After I had unpacked, Martin and Mark took me to see the nearest location.

To reach it, required a hair-raising drive from our villa in the valley up into the Sierra Cabrera mountains. It would be generous in the extreme to apply the description "road" to our route. It was simply a track that had been opened-up by a JCB, barely wide enough for our mini-bus, it followed the contours of the mountain.

Martin drove while Mark guided him so that we did not stray off the edge. I do not like heights. I try to assiduously avoid looking over deep ravines. The trip involved plenty of both!

Halfway up the mountain, we turned a corner to be faced with the David Bryant Bowling Centre. This comprised of two full-sized, crown green bowling courts that had literally been hewn out of the mountain side. When completed, these would represent the first stage of a grand plan for the sports complex. We did not stop to investigate. Our journey was far from over.

The view at the top, towards the mountains of Spain's Sierra Nevada, was worth "the hairy journey." The view down to the valley from where we had travelled, was equally breath-taking.

A short distance from where we had parked, was a partially deserted Moorish village. "I plan to use this location at about this time of day," Martin explained. "As you can see the light is fantastic and as the sun goes down it is very atmospheric." I nodded in agreement. My mind was already contemplating the journey back down the mountain.

Once back at our base, I was ready for a cold beer by the pool!

While we had been away, Sol had been organising dinner at a small Spanish restaurant in Turre. After a great meal, I was glad of an early night. It had been a long day. The next day was planned to be equally hectic.

After breakfast by the pool, Martin, Mark, and I headed off across the mountains towards the Almanzora River and Tabernas Desert.

Sol was meeting the rest of our party who were arriving at Almeria airport that afternoon. They were bringing the product ranges that we would be photographing during our time in Spain. On their arrival at Coptijo Grande, Sol and the stylist would be preparing the garments that were needed for the first day of the shoot.

In the full heat of the day, I quickly realised why this part of Spain was classified as a desert and why it was a perfect location for our shoot. The sky was blue, the sun was beating down, the light was fantastic and the scenery just stunning.

There were many dried out riverbeds in the area. Martin and Mark had found one that was perfect for our first set-up. In an easily accessible, off-road location, the riverbed was criss-crossed with cracks creating an artistic geometric pattern. This was just what I had visualised in our creative meeting back in the UK.

Within 100 metres of this site were other natural features suitable for all our other set-ups during the first day of the shoot. We moved further into the Tabernas Desert to an area that had been featured in some of the world's most famous films. The so called "spaghetti western" films, such as "The Good, The Bad and the Ugly" and "For a Few More Dollars," had been shot there. These movies had starred the likes of Clint Eastwood and Lee Van Clef.

At the time of our visit, many of the sets had been totally abandoned to the desert. Save for the occasional tourist and other photographic crews, they were seldom visited.

One site, was in the process of being developed into what is now marketed as the "film village of Fort Bravo." This is where we were headed. The location was situated in a canyon and accessible by via rough tracks through a dry valley.

Sol had obtained special passes allowing us to gain entrance.

The sets had changed little since the days that Sergio Leone had them commissioned and started rolling out his movie successes. Several were available for our use. These included an "authentic wild west town complete with saloon, a Mexican town and an army fort." They were well away from the main highway, and we were assured that we would have the location virtually to ourselves during the second day of our shoot schedule.

There was a small "cantina" close by where we could obtain drinks and refreshments. After lunch there, we retraced our steps passing through Turre before arriving in Mojacar. Back then, it was little changed from the picturesque hilltop village that had originally been built by the Moors in the 8th century. It overlooked the Mediterranean and the 17km of sandy beaches that would later become the resort of Mojacar Playa.

The revitalisation of the town from a back water without running water, electricity, and telephones, was started in the 1960's. Newcomers had been offered land provided they undertook to renovate the ruined houses. Encouraged and assisted to do this by an enlightened mayor, Mojacar became a haven of intellectuals, journalists, artists, and bohemians. They became captivated by the unique location, light and the proximity of the ocean.

In 1988, work was progressing at a pace to create the beach resort. The mountain village had been returned to its former glory and offered numerous locations for the last day of our shoot.

I was very happy with everything I had seen and confident that the choice of the Almeria region of Spain was the right one!

When we returned to Coptijo Grande, we were relieved that the rest of the crew and models had arrived safely. The outfits for all three days of the shoot had been placed on hangers and colour coded for each of the models who would be wearing them. I was very impressed with the efficiency of the process. It augured well for the activity ahead.

The models were relaxing in and out of the pool. It had been explained to them exactly how fierce the sun would be over the coming days. They had been asked to ensure they took all the necessary precautions against sunburn and sunstroke.

Over dinner, Martin and Mark started to wind up the models about the trip up the mountains we would be taking in the late afternoon, on the second day of the shot. "The road is too steep at the top of the mountain," Martin announced. "We will only be able to use the minibuses for part of the journey. Donkeys have been hired to take us, and the merchandise, to the location at the very top."

The models looked at each other not knowing whether to believe him or not!

I said nothing. Having undertaken the journey to the very top via minibus the day before, I knew that Martin must be joking.

During the first day on location in the Tabernas Desert, our shooting plan worked like clockwork. The models stayed in the shade when they were not working.

In those days, we relied heavily on Polaroids to determine whether a set-up was working or not. Martin was totally reliant on his own technical knowhow, and that of his assistant Mark, to determine that every shot he took would be reproduced on the film he was using. I had to maintain total faith in the professionals. Their practical and creative talent was what I had bought into.

The almost fool proof, digital cameras that photographers use today, were not commercially available in 1988. If there was a technical fault in any of the cameras Martin was using, we would not really know until the film had been processed when we arrived home. In the heat of the desert, the film had to be kept in a cool box to ensure that it did not deteriorate.

Shooting on location might have been fun, but it was not without risk!

During every break in shooting, Martin and Mark continued the banter about the ride up the mountain we would be taking in the late afternoon of the following day.

After the last shot of the day, and before the buses were loaded, he made a group announcement. "I understand that some of you are a little uneasy about the donkey ride up the mountain. Sol has contacted the 'donkey wrangler.' He will be coming to the villa before dinner at 7.00pm this evening. Anyone who has never ridden a donkey before will have a chance to practice. Miguel, the 'donkey wrangler,' will answer any questions you may have and set your minds at rest."

This was said with such a straight face that even I, who knew it was a send up, almost believed it.

Despite the warnings that had been issued, some of us had been caught out by the harsh conditions of the Tabernas Desert, even though we had taken precautions. After liberal applications of after sun lotion, I determined to cover up more for the remainder of the shoot. Whilst I had turned something approaching "lobster red," everyone else was turning a lovely shade of brown.

At 7.00pm, the rest of our party arrived at the villa that I shared with Martin and Mark. A few minutes later, there was a loud banging on the door. I opened it and in came Miguel wearing the same loose white outfit worn by all the locals. This look was completed by a sombrero and the Zapata moustache he was sporting.

"Hola everyone," he exclaimed in heavily, Spanish accented, English. "I have to allocate your donkeys and will then answer any questions you may have," he suggested. "Robin Dilley, as the head honcho, you will be riding the lead donkey Pedro."

He continued in this vein until every member of the party had been allocated a specific donkey to ride. The models were convinced it was all for real. None of them had noticed that Mark Adam, Martins assistant, was not in the room.

"Miguel," answered all the questions posed by his audience. He was just about to take a couple of the models out for their donkey trial when Martin signalled to him. Our 'donkey wrangler' whipped off his sombrero, ripped off his Zapata moustache to reveal his real self, Mark.

The whole room collapsed into laughter, a mixture of relief and the realisation that they had all been the butt of a cleverly contrived set-up. Drinks were then served. Normality was resumed.

On behalf of the whole party, I began to plan a set-up of my own. Sol had informed me it was Martins 30th birthday on the last night of our stay. He wanted to keep it quiet so as not to affect the shoot.

I decided that, with her help, we would make it a night to remember!

We had already selected the best restaurant in the area as the venue for the end of shoot dinner. Now we added to our initial list of requirements, a birthday cake, several bottles of Cava (a Spanish sparkling wine like champagne) and a "birthday surprise" for Martin.

Details of the birthday and the surprises we planned, were not revealed to anyone else.

The second day of shooting dawned to the same blue skies and blazing sun that had been a feature of or trip so far. After a hearty breakfast, we headed out to the "cowboy village sets" in the Tabernas Desert.

Utilising the facilities to the full, we were very happy with our more modern take on the Wrangler cowboy look. Unlike our first day, the film sets provided more cover from the elements, and we managed to avoid the consequences resulting from too much exposure to the unremitting sun.

We completed all the set-ups to everyone's satisfaction, arriving back at the villa, ahead of schedule, for mid-afternoon refreshments.

Sol had arranged for a late dinner, and everyone was in a boisterous mood as we made our way, in the minibuses, up the mountain for our final session. The mood changed, when it became obvious that the use of donkeys might not have been such a bad idea after all!

As we set up for the first shot, we had a glimpse of a sombrero clad individual, mounted on a donkey, making his way up from the valley floor by way of the track we had just navigated.

As the shoot continued, so did his slow progress. Two hours later, when we were well into our second set up, he appeared over the top of the steep incline. Stopping, to see what we were up to, he exchanged a few words with Sol.

She explained to us that he had asked what we were up to. Apparently, he and his family lived in the "deserted village" and he descended to the valley floor for provisions several times a week. The return journey, by donkey, took him just under 6 hours.

We all agreed, a hairy drive of 45 minutes in a minibus was perhaps the lesser of the two evils.

Our last set up, involved one of the male models, Joseph, in Wrangler jeans, tee-shirt and cowboy hat. Standing on the edge of the precipice, he would be looking out from the mountain top at the sun set over the valley below and the mountain range in the distance.

We needed as much light on Joseph as we could muster. Both Mark and I employed "fills" to bounce the light onto the model to Martin's satisfaction. I appear to have temporarily set aside my fear of heights, as I have a photograph showing me deploying the "fill" whilst standing on the edge of a long drop into the valley below.

After, Martin "wrapped up the session," we returned down the mountain. The deteriorating light made the descent even more difficult, and we were all thankful to arrive back at the villa complex without incident. In the on-site restaurant, normality resumed. We thoroughly enjoyed our meal and the well-deserved, accompanying drinks.

At around midnight, the area was hit by an electronic storm and heavy rainfall. As the lightening lit up the mountain where we had been only hours before, I breathed a sigh of relieve that the mountain element of our shoot had been completed.

Next morning, I looked out of the window. The blue sky and blazing sun had been replaced by thick clouds and a hint of rain. This was certainly not what we had come to Almeria to see! A quick check on the weather forecast revealed that it would remain overcast, with some rain, during the morning. It promised the afternoon would see "a return to business as usual."

After a short meeting with Martin and his team, the shooting schedule was altered to accommodate the changed circumstances. We were all thankful that we would be in the Mojacar for the whole of the day. Several of the set ups were indoors in one of the bar/ restaurants. At least, we could keep out of the worst of the mornings rain.

As promised, the sun and blue skies returned in the afternoon, and we quickly caught up with our original schedule. We even had time to sample the delights of the areas fine beaches and dip our toes in the inviting water of the Mediterranean Sea.

During a lull in proceedings, Sol and I had managed to finalise our plans for Martin's birthday treat. I wanted to hire a donkey, complete with an "authentic donkey wrangler," to arrive at the restaurant just after the cake and birthday greetings had been delivered to our table.

Martin would then be invited to take a ride down the main street of Turre where the restaurant was situated. This would provide payback for the donkey stunt that he and Mark had pulled prior to our trip up the mountain.

Unfortunately, the local donkey owner decided to play hardball. "For 6,000 pesetas, he will provide the donkey, dress up for the part of donkey wrangler and supervise Martins ride down the street," Sol advised me.

At the prevailing exchange rate 6,000 pesetas was the equivalent of £28.70. It seemed an awful lot of money at the time. "Are you sure he realises we only want to hire his services and not buy the donkey," I responded. Apparently, Sol had delivered a similar response. The donkey owner refused to negotiate.

It was one of those take it or leave it moments. We had no alternative but to take it. I was left with the dilemma of how to put through, the very expensive hire of a donkey, on my expenses!

We had also purchased a large birthday card. Sol was tasked with getting all the models and crew to sign it without Martin realising that we all knew his birthday secret. This was no mean feat!

That evening, we arrived at the restaurant in Turre. Martin remained blissfully unaware we were all involved in a conspiracy. We enjoyed an excellent meal washed down by liberal quantities of local wine.

As the coffee was delivered, Martin stood up to deliver a speech to thank the whole party for their hard worked during the shoot. This was the signal for the arrival of the birthday cake, card, and cava. The whole restaurant joined in the singing of "happy birthday to you."

For once, Martin was speechless!

I took advantage, to raise a toast in Cava and then deliver my own announcement. "I would like to thank you, Martin, on behalf of the whole crew, for your patience over the last few days," I said. "We could not let the occasion of your 30th birthday pass without giving you a very special present, from all of us." This was the cue for the appearance of the "real donkey wrangler."

Martin looked frantically around the room and quickly realised that Mark was still sitting at the table. "Happy birthday Meester Martin, please follow me, your surprise awaits you outside," requested the sombrero clad stranger. This time, the heavily accented English was obviously genuine.

They went outside, followed by everyone in the restaurant, including the staff. On the patio outside stood a large, not very placid looking donkey, in full harness, pawing the ground. "You please to climb on board, Meester Martin," the "donkey wrangler" suggested.

Once mounted, he was led down a few steps from the patio to the deserted road, accompanied by cheers from the crowd.

I gave the donkey a pat on the backside. To my horror, it leapt into action and shot off down the street amid much hilarity, with Martin clinging to the reins. Thankfully, the 'donkey wrangler" had not let go of the harness. He managed to keep pace with Martin and the careering beast.

After a journey of a few hundred yards, he eventually regained control. No damage was done.

At that point, that it was clear to me that the 6,000 pesetas outlay was exceedingly good value for money!

Martin was exhilarated and fully appreciated the joke at his expense. The birthday drinks kept coming and we had a great night.

Mark and Sol had agreed to be nominated drivers and to limit their intake of alcohol. I made sure that they each had a bottle of Cava, to take back to Cortijo Grande, as a reward for their temporary abstinence.

Next morning, everyone was very quiet a breakfast. I suspect that many of the party were suffering from the effects of the excesses of the previous evening.

The morning was free and after packing and loading the minibuses with our luggage, equipment and product lines, there was time to admire our surroundings or lie by the pool.

After a light lunch, we said farewell to our hosts and boarded the minibuses for the 80km journey across the mountain road to Almeria airport and the flight home.

The selection of shots, taken during the shoot, were exceptional.

Everyone was happy. Martin had captured the modern take of the cowboy imagery that the Wrangler product merchandisers were keen to project, to both the fashion trade and the consumer.

The pictures, used for PR, product merchandisers and point of sale material, enabled us to differentiate the Wrangler brand from the singular product 501 campaign that was being heavily marketed by Levi's.

A few weeks afterwards, I received some framed montage shots taken by Sol during the shoot.

There was one framed single picture of me holding the "fill" for the shot of the model Joseph standing near the top of the Sierra Cabrera Mountains.

Martin had signed this and added the hand-written message, "From all the crew for a very enjoyable holiday."

Chapter Twenty-Seven

Location shoot, Tenerife, Canary Islands, January 1989 - Martin Hooper

The experience during our shoot in Almeria had convinced me that an overseas shoot was viable. It reduced the risk of bad weather and increased the probability of good light.

There was no doubt in my mind, that a creative photographer and good support team was essential. Martin Hooper had established his credentials, not only with me, but also with the rest of the Wrangler team. It was decided that we would retain his services for the Autumn 1989 product shoot.

Final samples would not be available until the middle of December 1988 and a product merchandiser would have to be produced in time for the IMBEX trade show in London. This was scheduled to take place during the second week of February 1989. The shoot would have to take place during the second week in January. This date would avoid the New Year holiday period but leave us sufficient time to design and print the material required.

We did not have the funds to travel outside Europe but needed a venue that would provide a variety of locations. Tenerife in the Canary Islands was an option that I thought had possibilities.

Although January was the coldest month, the average daily temperature in the south of the island was over 18.4°C made up of highs of 22°C during the warmest part of the day and 15°C during the coldest part of the night. These temperatures made it one of the warmest destinations in Europe throughout the month.

In the North and East of the island the temperature was only slightly lower. Wintery conditions could be expected in the Teide National Park with snow on the peak of Mount Teide itself.

I bounced my idea off Martin and my marketing team. Martin did not know anything about Tenerife. He had never been there. Creatively, it was a blank canvas. It was agreed he would investigate what the location had to offer before getting back to me.

As usual, his research was very thorough. Within days, he was reporting back, buzzing with enthusiasm and full of ideas.

Tenerife, it was then!

Martin and his team had also identified that the second week in January was a good time to go. The New Year revellers would have departed. It had proved possible to obtain a great price for our group that included flights, minibus hire and accommodation in a small complex of apartments surrounding a private pool.

The location was within walking distance of the centre of Playa de las Americas, not far from the airport and close to all the main highways around the island.

Martin and his team planned to fly out two days before the main party to carry out a full reconnaissance. I was happy to leave the final location choices to Martin. We had discussed all the possibilities beforehand and drawn up an initial shoot plan. Following our experience in Almeria, I had complete faith in his ability to come up with places that would fulfil the requirements of the brief.

Stylist Jo Chapman, and hair and make-up artist Nikki Freeman, had attended one of our briefing sessions and the fitting session for the models. They would be responsible for the product line before, during and after the shoot.

On Sunday 8 January 1989, I met up with Jo, Nikki and models Kirstie, Eric, Vanessa, and Joseph for the flight from London to Tenerife. On arrival, we were met by Mark and Martin, each driving a minibus.

In no time at all, we were checking in to our accommodation. Whilst the models took advantage of the pool facilities, Martin briefed the rest of us on the locations he had chosen for the next three days.

On day one, the shoot would centre on the Corona Forestal Nature Park. Day two would take place in Santa Cruz in the East of the island and Puerto de la Cruz in the North. The third day of the shoot would take place in the Teide National Park.

During the location search in the Park, Martin had driven along Las Canadas, the only road across the crater. This led to a hotel, the Parador de Cañadas del Teide. Close by were some of the best rock formations in the whole of the craters surreal landscape. This was just what Martin was looking for. He had just purchased a new "panoramic" camera with a lens capable of taking in a vista of 180 degrees. This was the perfect place to use it for the first time!

A word with the hotel manager, resulted in a deal being done. Our party would be staying in the crater of Mount Teide on the second night of the trip. Martin assured me the extra cost involved would be met through the contingency he had allowed. "Robin, the experience is just too good to miss," Martin enthused. "It will allow us to maximise our time in the crater from sunrise until mid-afternoon," he continued.

I did not require much convincing!

People came to Mount Teide from all over the world to look at a night sky totally free of light pollution. We would be able to experience a "once in a lifetime look at the universe" from the relative comfort of our hotel.

In January, we were expecting around 10 hours of daylight. The sun was forecast to rise at about 8.00am and set around 6.30pm.

Our plan was to maximise the daylight hours to the full. Ample time had been allowed for travel to and from locations and fitting in all the set-ups that were required, without working the models and the crew too hard.

On day one, we set off to our first location, the Corona Forestal. This involved a drive of around 1 hour and 40 minutes up the twisting mountain road towards the summit of Mount Teide.

Whilst the weather in Playa de las Americas was a balmy 18.4°C, we entered heavy cloud as soon as we started our ascent. The temperature fell quickly. We had been warned to expect these conditions but, had been assured that no heavy rain or snow was forecast, and above the cloud, the sun would be shining.

The Corona Forestal Nature Park is the largest protected area in the Canary Islands. It is renowned for its pine forests and magnificent scenery. We had travelled up the mountain for the views of Mount Teide above the pine forests, the impressive ravines and large valleys that carve their way through the landscape.

During the first 45 minutes of our drive, visibility was down to no more than 25 metres.

Just as we were about to abandon our journey, we broke through the cloud. The sun was now shining, and the sky was blue. The scenery was everything we had hope for. As the morning progressed, the cloud gradually burned away and, by the early afternoon, the full glory of the Corona Forestal was revealed.

The morning shoot went according to plan. Once we had finished, we had time to enjoy a rustic lunch at a small restaurant in the Park. Martin and his team had discovered it during their reconnaissance trip earlier.

On our way up the mountain road, the only other vehicles we had come across was a convoy of six Mercedes 4 x 4 vehicles. They were full of earnest looking individuals uniformly kitted out for walking over the rough mountain terrain.

For the shoot in the afternoon, Mark had managed to "recruit" some local farm labourers as "background extras." Their inclusion gave the pictures a real rural feel. By about 4.00pm, we had completed all the required set-ups and climbed into our minibuses for the drive back to Playa de las Americas.

On our way down the twisting mountain road, we were passed by the same Mercedes convoy we had seen during our outbound journey.

When we arrived at our apartment complex, some of the hardy members of our team decided to explore the surrounding area. Those remaining chose to relax by the pool, with a welcome drink, before the sun went down.

Dinner had been booked at a local restaurant. After our meal, washed down with a liberal quantity of local wine, we all took an early night. We had a lot of travel planned for the following day.

Next morning, we had an early breakfast before preparing for the next two days of the shoot. Everyone in the party had been advised to take an overnight bag with them for our stay in the Teide National Park.

On the way to Santa Cruz, our first location of the day, we spied our Mercedes convoy driving in the opposite direction. "I wonder what they are up to?" Martin asked me. "They are probably asking the same questions about us, "I suggested.

In a game, resembling I-spy, everyone in our minibus began to speculate what our "friends in the convoy" were doing. Theories abounded. They included, "mad scientists building a mysterious facility close to the summit of Mount Teide" and "Mercedes 4 x 4 loving travellers, caught up in a continuous tourist loop." The consensus was, "they were German tourists keen to put down their towels first, at whatever part of the island they were travelling to."

After a journey of just over an hour we arrived at Santa Cruz de Tenerife (Santa Cruz). I was quite surprised how large the city appeared. Santa Cruz is the second largest city in the Island group. It shares the status of capital of the Canary Islands with Las Palmas in Gran Canaria. Since the 18th century, the port of Santa Cruz had steadily grown in importance as the communications hub between Europe, Africa, and the Americas.

In 1989, the cruise market was mushrooming. Increasing numbers of cruise ships were arriving bringing in more and more tourists.

The urban areas of Santa Cruz provided a complete contrast to the rural and conservation areas of the island that we had already visited.

After shooting a couple of set-ups in the port area, we moved a few streets away. Martin had been particularly taken by a rustic wall that was covered in Spanish graffiti.

He had taken a couple of rolls of film and was in the process of changing cameras, when we became aware that our activities had generated interest from a small crowd of people. This was not unusual. People seem drawn to the presence of photographic shoots and normally they just look on passively. There was something about this crowd that made me feel uneasy.

"I don't think we are welcome here." I advised Martin. "I think we should move on."

By this time, the murmur running through the crowd had grown in intensity. A couple of the onlookers began to shout and gesticulate in our direction. As we retreated down the street, bottles began to fly. The mood had become very ugly!

As we turned the corner, we were confronted by three or four policemen. "The following mob" came hurtling around the same corner. The sight of armed police halted their progress. It was now their turn to retreat!

We had a licence to shoot where we were and did not know what we had done to bring about such hostility.

One of the policemen explained that in that area of the city a Spanish nationalist faction had control. The wall we were using as a backdrop, was full of nationalist slogans that were particularly significant to them.

We were politely advised to continue our shoot closer to the city centre!

Following the incident, we were all shaken-up. Before continuing, we found a friendly restaurant for drinks and much needed refreshments.

After lunch, we completed our work in Santa Cruz and boarded our minibuses for Puerto de la Cruz, a 40minute drive away. I had stayed at the resort a few years before and knew that, despite it being the main tourist resort in the north of the island, it still retained many of its Canarian characteristics.

At the foot of the Valle de La Orotava, the area enjoys enough rain and sunshine to provide lush vegetation and an almost sub-tropical appearance. The views towards the summit of Mount Teide are magnificent.

When we arrived, we were greeted by clear blue skies and a winter sun generating a very pleasant temperature.

Our shoot went without a hitch and included shots from both a promontory overlooking the sea, and in the centre of the town.

Martin was using one of his extremely long lenses from an elevated position. I was placing the models, amongst the hustle and bustle of the crowds of shoppers, several hundred yards away from where he was standing. Our models were given free rein to express themselves to the utter bemusement of the crowds around them.

I still have a picture of me standing at the location amongst a crowd of Spanish tourists. I have one arm in the air, as I signalled to Martin that we were ready for him to start shooting the next set-up. From the expressions on their faces, you can tell that they had no idea what was going on or why this strange man was waving his arms about in the middle of their group.

Afterwards, we moved close to the banana plantations on the foothills rising behind the town. Here the brooding presence of Mount Teide provided a magnificent backdrop.

With all our set-ups completed, we set off once more for the 1-hour journey to Teide National Park. On the way up the twisting road, the familiar Mercedes convoy went by in the opposite direction.

We reached our destination, the Parador de Las Cañadas del Teide, just as the sun was setting over the craggy rim of the crater. Our hotel had the look and feel of a mountain lodge in the Swiss Alps. It was somewhat surreal to be sitting in front of a blazing log fire, at an altitude of well over 2000 metres, inside the crater of a dormant volcano.

In the cloudless, thin air, it was understandable why stargazing sessions were part of the programme of activities the hotel offered to its visitors.

After our traditional Canarian meal, Martin asked the hotel's manager what time the sun would rise the next morning. "The sun will rise at 8.00 am," he replied.

Martin was anxious to catch the sun as it rose over La Caldera de las Canadas, the rim of the crater. From the information he had been given, this required a 7 am breakfast for the whole team.

Outside in the clear night air, the temperature was plummeting. The night sky provided a spectacle that exceeded our expectations. Next morning, when we met for our early breakfast, it was still dark outside, and a thick frost covered the ground. The outdoor swimming pool had frozen over, and the temperature was well below freezing.

We had come to Tenerife equipped for more welcoming temperatures. When Martin and his team had visited the crater, it had been in the early afternoon. The sun was beating down in the thin air. "Don't worry, when the sun climbs over the rim of the volcano the temperature will rise very quickly," he assured everyone.

The crew set up for the first shot shivering in anticipation of the warmth to come. As it became lighter, the full beauty of our location was revealed.

During my research, I had read that Mount Teide was a volcano within a volcano. It was formed when a much larger volcano exploded leaving behind a 16km-wide crater, now the National Park. The smaller volcano, left behind on its northern edge, was Mount Teide. At 3,718 metres, it remains the highest point in Spain and the third highest volcano in the world.

The whole area of the Parque Nacional de las Cañadas has a weird volcanic landscape comprising lava rock, lava streams and ash beds. Apparently, it has similar geological and environmental conditions to the planet Mars. It is common for scientific expeditions to visit the area. It crossed my mind, that our "friends in the Mercedes convoy" were, perhaps, just such an expedition.

Close by the Parador, where we were waiting, we could see some of the famous eroded rock formations called the Roques de Garcia. Most famous of these, the Cinchado, is more eroded at its base giving the impression that it might topple over at any moment.

Rising, behind the Cinchado, was the summit of Mount Teide. I could now fully understand why Martin had chosen this spot as the starting point for our day in the crater.

At 8.30am, it was light but there was no sign of the sun. "Martin, are you sure that the sun rises above the rim at such an early hour?" I enquired, through chattering teeth.

Martin sent Mark to see the hotel manager to ask him the same question.

A few minutes later he returned. "I slight problem of misinterpretation," he advised somewhat sheepishly. "The manager thought we were asking what time the sun came up in Tenerife," he explained. "Down at sea level, the sun does come up at 8.00am. Up here, it will not be over the rim of the crater much before 10.15am."

A collective groan went up from the whole team!

Whilst the rest of the party went back into the Parador, for a warming coffee in front of the fire, Martin, Mark, and I were left outside to come up with a "plan B."

We could see a car that had been parked just down the road. In our props, we had a small petrol can.

A scenario was created using one of the male models.

In a series of quick set-ups, he was photographed leaving the car with his petrol can. He was then pictured walking along the road with the car in the distance. The last set up featured him, sitting on a stone mileage marker, trying to thumb a lift.

When we had finished this unscheduled series of shots, it was time for Martin to set up his new panoramic camera and position one of the models, for the arrival of the sun. On cue, or should I say, on second cue, the sun finally arrived. Almost immediately, the whole landscape took on a totally different appearance. The dull greys of the early morning light were replaced by greens, browns, multi shades of black and deep blues. The snow on the summit of Mount Teide, glistened in the sunlight.

Martin and his team set to work with a vengeance, like a well-oiled machine they soon made up for the time that had been lost. The sun would also be dropping behind the rim of the volcano 2 hours earlier in the afternoon, so time was of the essence.

We had intended to use the cable car to reach the station closest to the summit. Unfortunately, snow had fallen the previous night and it was closed. Instead, we parked in the car park at the base station and enjoyed a quick lunch snack in the small restaurant close by. Afterwards we completed our shoot schedule on the slopes behind.

At around 3.30 pm we packed the minibuses for the final time and began our descent towards Los Americas.

We decided to stop for drinks at a small bar in the village of Vilaflor. At an altitude of 1,400 metres, it is said to be the highest village in Tenerife. As we relaxed on the balcony with our drinks, watching the world go by, our "friends in the Mercedes convey" drove by. We all waved furiously but were unable to elicit any response from the occupants. They appeared intent on focusing their attention on the road ahead and seemed totally oblivious of everything else around them.

Back out our base in Los Americas, Martin announced that he had organised a special farewell meal at a fish restaurant he had come across during his location search. The restaurant was in a small fishing village close to Los Americas. Everything on the menu had been caught that morning. The food could not have been fresher.

To the sound of waves crashing on to the foreshore, we celebrated the end of a very productive shoot with fantastic fish dishes and plenty of alcoholic drinks. With no time pressure on us the following morning, the 'party' continued until our hosts politely suggested it was time for them to close and us to leave.

After a leisurely breakfast, there was an opportunity for us to visit the local shops for souvenirs of our time in Tenerife. After a light lunch, we then packed everything into the mini vans for the short journey to the airport and the flight back to a wintery UK.

The shoot provided a treasure trove of material that was used in the production of the Autumn/Winter 1989 range booklet, for point-of-sale support and public relations purposes.

The panoramic camera purchased by Martin had produced a dramatic series of shots that, when printed as posters, were well received, and widely distributed amongst our retail stockists.

Our investment in the "offshore shoots" had paid dividends. The quality of output had also laid down the benchmark for all future activity in support of the Wrangler brand.

Chapter Twenty-Eight

Location shoot, Miami, Florida, August 1989 - John Rutter

Early in 1989, a major restructuring of the Wrangler Management Team had taken place. This involved the appointment of several key members who had previously worked for Levi's. The marketing development team comprised of John Hart, Robin Hollick, and me. Both John and Robin had held key positions at Levi's, our main competitor.

An assessment was carried out and it was decided to review the image that the brand was projecting.

Despite the evident success of the creative work of our incumbent advertising agency, BBDO, it was felt that a change of direction was necessary. A new creative "hot shop," Simons Palmer was appointed.

They had secured the Wrangler account on the back of the extensive research they had carried out amongst the prime 16-24-year-olds. This concluded that "eighties design culture had passed its sell by date." The Wrangler target market apparently saw it as "clichéd and predictable."

Our new agency announced that, "it is no longer aspirational or believable."

The portrayal of contemporary America, projected by BBDO, was "too pristine." A "gritty reality of American youth culture was the way to connect with the consumer of the nineties and to differentiate the Wrangler jeans brand from all its competitors."

With Martin Hooper, we had pioneered the use of overseas locations for image photography for PR and point of sale use. My new colleagues agreed Martin's work had helped to move the Wrangler image forward. It was felt that a change was required. A new, "edgier photographer" was needed to pave the way for the "new look" that Simons Palmer was working on and that would be launched early in 1990.

The advertising agency recommended John Rutter. An American, he was working out of Milan and had amassed a catalogue of fashion work that the agency felt expressed the look they were searching for.

We agreed to arrange a meeting with John to look at his portfolio and to listen to his ideas. After speaking to his London agent, we were advised that he was happy to come over to the UK and meet us at our London showroom.

The meeting was very productive. Clearly, his style was just what Simons Palmer had recommended we should go with. It was also clear that he would need very careful direction to ensure the edgy style and earthy sexuality of his work was kept under control, without diminishing its effectiveness.

John was full of ideas. He was recommending Miami in Florida as the ideal venue, and August 1989 as the ideal date, to fit in with his existing work schedule.

I had my concerns!

In Martin Hooper, we had a known option who had proved his ability to interpret our brief and deliver the goods. He brought with him a complete team of assistants, stylist and hair and make-up. Importantly, he also took over the whole administration and day to day running of the shoot.

With John Rutter, we were simply buying the exceptional skills of a fashion photographer. He was only interested in providing the imagery that he believed we wanted. The day-to-day administration of the shoot would be the responsibility of the Wrangler team. It was a risk but, on balance, a risk that my colleagues and I felt was worth taking.

Lindah Kiddey worked with our public relations agency, Simons Palmer, and John Rutter to put together the team. This included a stylist, a hair and makeup artist and three male and two female models. She also coordinated the choice of outfits for each set up with the chosen stylist. The logistics of return travel and accommodation was put into the hands our travel agent.

Lindah was not able to attend the shoot. Charmaine, one of my marketing department coordinators, agreed to travel to Miami in her place. Her role involved taking responsibility for coordinating the outfits with the stylist.

The travel agent worked out a deal with Virgin Atlantic, who agreed to organise return flights for the whole party from London Gatwick to Miami, and to cover the cost of all our excess baggage. They also provided "suites" in a hotel with a pool and restaurant. It was situated right next to the beach and close to all the facilities and yet only a short taxi ride to the downtown area.

The inclusive package price that was negotiated also included travel insurance. In return, we agreed a special credit for the airline would appear on all Wrangler public relations material featuring pictures taken during the shoot.

At some point in the negotiations with the London model agencies, it was suggested that we should pay the models, in dollars, at the end of the session. The same arrangement was put in place for the stylist and hair and make-up artist.

John Rutter would invoice us direct, in the usual way.

Wrangler assumed responsibility for payment of model fees, all sustenance costs such as food and drink consumed during the shoot and providing every member of the team with an allowance for evening meals. From memory, this amounted to a figure of around $40,000 for the 7 days we were in the USA.

Obviously, I had no wish to carry such a large amount of cash around. Lindah Kiddey was tasked to research the options to provide a more secure method.

Wrangler Ltd had a corporate card arrangement with American Express. In conjunction with our travel agent, and after discussions with our credit card partner, it was agreed that I would take $6,000 in cash to cover expenses for the first three days and American Express dollar traveller's cheques, in $100 denominations, for the remainder. It seemed like the ideal arrangement.

On Saturday 12 August 1989, the whole party met up at London Gatwick airport. We all checked in together, at the group desk, for our flight to Miami.

Check-in went smoothly, and we were treated very well during our flight of nearly 10 hours. Once we had landed and passed through American Immigration, we boarded the Virgin transit bus and were soon checking in to the large and comfortable "suites" at our hotel.

The time in Miami is 5 hours behind that of the UK. This meant, although we had left the UK early on Saturday afternoon, it was only late afternoon of the same day when we began to settle into our accommodation.

A dinner had been organised at the hotel on the first night. Our party, except John and myself, had the whole of Sunday to relax and recover before the shoot began on the Monday.

Next morning after breakfast, a bearded, blonde, and athletic looking Swede, arrived outside the hotel at the wheel of an open top Wrangler Jeep. He was employed as a freelance location scout working on behalf of film companies and photographers coming into Miami.

John had hired him to not only find locations in the area that met the specific requirements of our brief, but also to ensure that all necessary photography permits had been acquired ahead of the shoot.

Before we left, he opened his map of the area and began to talk through his plan for the day.

It was clear that some of the locations John needed for his "gritty set-ups" were not on any of the normal tourist routes. Some of the districts of Miami that he had pinpointed were considered no go areas by the Swede.

"Why are we not going there." John demanded, stabbing his figure at a section of the map. "Not even the police go down there," the Swede replied. "If you turn up there with your models and crew, you are just asking for trouble," he continued.

"Well, can you take us down there to have a look," John persisted. "I'm sorry, but just driving through the area in our vehicle will attract unwelcome attention. If we get out to look around, I can guarantee there will be trouble," the Swede was adamant.

John finally agreed to drop his request and we drove off to look at the "less dangerous options" that our location scout had selected. This encounter had confirmed the nagging doubt in my mind. Keeping John Rutter under control was going to be a major feat.

The temperature in our vehicle was rising, actually and metaphorically! As we drove into downtown Miami, it had reached nearly 30°C. Humidity was pushing 83%.

During our site reconnaissance, we had many differences of opinion. John was anxious to include a "steamy bedroom scene." I was not convinced that this was necessary. "We have come to Miami to take advantage of the outdoor locations," I argued. "Surely, in this heat and humidity, even an outdoor interaction with male and female models will be 'steamy'."

In the end, we compromised!

John's preference, a "dodgy, downmarket hotel that charged by the hour, and offered grimy waterbeds in every room," was dropped in favour of a "boutique hotel with Art Deco styling that was located opposite Miami Beach."

We did agree, after driving well over an hour to get there, that there was nothing at Key Largo that could not be found closer to our hotel. Suitable, relatively safe locations were agreed in downtown Miami, close to Fort Lauderdale and at a nearby Seminole Indian Reservation.

We returned to our hotel tired but content that our locations, and the shooting schedule, had been agreed. Whilst John and I had been location hunting, Charmaine and the stylist had been finalising the outfits for each model and putting them into sets.

It was agreed that the first set-ups of the shoot would take place on the beach right next to the hotel and at another location close by.

Our large minibus was being delivered to the hotel the next morning and I was anxious to visit a nearby bank to cash in some of my Amex traveller's cheques. Each member of the party had been allocated a sum of money to cover evening meals for 2 days. It was my intention to supplement this, every two days, during the shoot.

I had a final briefing meeting at the hotel with John, Charmaine, the stylist and the hair and makeup artist. We agreed the outfits and model pairings for each set-up before eating at the restaurant in our hotel complex. The shoot was scheduled to start at 10.30am. This allowed plenty of time for John to sort out the hire vehicle and for me to collect some cash.

Or so we thought!

After a leisurely breakfast, I made my way on foot to the nearest bank. After waiting patiently to be seen, I asked to cash $1,000 of traveller's cheques in $50 denominations.

The bank teller looked alarmed. "I'm sorry Sir, but I am only allowed to cash $100 dollars at any one time," she informed me. "It is too dangerous for us to give out large amounts of cash." Sensing my puzzlement, she continued. "You could be attacked and robbed round here. The rule is for your safety."

This was a problem I had not been expecting!

"How many banks are there in Miami?" I asked her, as she handed over an envelope containing my $100 allocation. I had to cash in another $33,900 by Friday.

Rushing back to the hotel, I picked up the telephone and called Lindah Kiddey at the office in Calverton. It was turned 3.00pm in the UK. Lindah needed to work quickly to come up with a solution. She agreed to speak to the Amex office that had issued the cheques, and come up with a plan, before she called me back. I agreed to return to the hotel in 1½ hours.

Thankfully, the shoot was taking place only a few hundred yards from the hotel. Cell phones were almost non-existent in 1989. Communication with the UK would have been very problematic had we been at one of the other shoot locations.

At the appointed time, the telephone rang in my hotel suite. It was Lindah. "It's all a bit of a cock-up," she admitted. "Amex tell me you won't have any problems spending the cheques in shops or restaurants, but they should have made other arrangements for the big cash withdrawals they knew we needed."

"So, what's the solution?" I demanded, somewhat testily.

"I have organised for someone in Amex USA International office to sort out the problem. They are in Salt Lake City. It is 2 hours behind Miami. They will call you back at your hotel at 3.00pm Miami time," she advised. "Thanks for your help,

Lindah, "I replied. "If you don't hear anything else from me, you will know that the problem has been resolved,"

The shoot continued without incident.

Just before 3.00pm, I rushed back from the beach to my hotel room, just in time to pick up the ringing phone.

"There is a call for you from American Express in Salt Lake City," I was advised. "Thanks, please put it through," I replied. "Is that Mr. Robin Dilley of Wrangler Jeans?" the voice at the other end asked. I confirmed that he was through to the right person.

"I am the International Vice President of Travellers Cheque Services," the voice told me. "I'm sorry that you have experienced so much trouble. Let's first solve your immediate problem. We have a sub-branch just 5 minutes away by taxi from your hotel. They are expecting you at 10.00am tomorrow morning and will cash traveller's cheques to the value of $6000. Our biggest branch in downtown Miami will organise the cashing of the balance of $27,800 on Friday morning at 10.00am."

"Thanks, for sorting this out for me, I'm most grateful," I told him. "Thank you for being so understanding. We will of course get to the bottom of the problem and ensure that Wrangler UK is compensated for the inconvenience," he added.

I was relieved that everything was resolved even though the start of our second day of shooting would have to be delayed slightly.

Next morning, whilst everyone else set off in the minibus to Miami Beach, I called for a cab and arrived at the nearby office of American Express bang on time. The manager was expecting me and took me through to a small private office to countersign the $6,000 of traveller's cheques. "When you have finished, Mr. Dilley, I have arranged with the bank just up the road for you to go in. Make yourself known to them and they will issue the cash," he told me.

This was not what had been agreed!

"I was told that you would cash the cheques here. If it is too dangerous for a bank to hand over $100, there is no way that I am walking into a local bank, alone, to collect such a large amount of cash," I told him.

"But my branch only carries $10,000 in total," he protested." If I hand over what you want, I won't have sufficient cash for transactions for the rest of the day." "That is your problem. I am the customer. The International Vice President of Travellers Cheque Services has made the arrangements. I am sure that he will not be happy if he finds his instructions have not been carried out," I countered.

This did the trick, and the money was handed over. The branch manager also called for a taxi to take me back to the hotel. Once the bulk of the cash was tucked safely away in my room safe, I called another cab to take me to the spot at Miami Beach where the first set-ups had been planned.

I soon found John, the models, and the crew. Well, most of them!

Charmaine, and one of the male models, were missing.

"We've had a slight problem. Mark (the male model) got some sand in his eye during the first set-up. We couldn't get it out and have sent him with Charmaine to have it looked at the nearest hospital." John told me. "It's just down the road. We should be able to complete the rest this morning's shots without him."

This was at a time before mobile phones were readily available. The first one had been purchased for $3,995 only 5 years before. They were about half the width and about the same length as a standard UK building brick, and about as heavy.

John and his assistant had one each to cover just such emergencies. They were still very expensive to buy outright, so they had hired them for the duration of the shoot.

Suddenly the handset burst into life. The caller was the charge nurse in the emergency department of the Mount Sinai Medical Centre in Miami Beach. Mark was an American citizen and did not enjoy the reciprocal health care arrangements that applied to UK nationals. The nurse wanted to speak with his employer.

John handed over the "half brick" to me. "Are you Mark's employer?" she asked. "He is a model working on behalf of my company. Why do you want to know?" I replied. "Mark thinks he is covered by his parents Medicare Insurance, but we can't contact them. You need to come over and sign papers agreeing to cover the cost of his treatment before we can do anything," I was advised.

The day was going from bad to worse and it was not yet lunchtime!

I flagged yet another taxi. In five minutes, I was entering the multi-storey Mount Sinai Medical Centre complex. The taxi driver dropped me off outside the A&E entrance and I went inside in search of Charmaine and Mark.

Charmaine was sitting in a small waiting room containing about twenty chairs. She was the only person there. The wall in front of her contained one door, a sliding glass hatch, and a bell to ring for attention. Above it was a sign which advised that the initial consultation fee was $35. The wording that followed implied that if you didn't have the money, you wouldn't be seen.

"Welcome to heath care in America," I thought to myself as I rang the bell. The hatch opened. I introduced myself to the receptionist behind it. "Thanks for coming, Mr. Dilley. We have just made contact Mark's parents. He is insured and will now be treated. We don't need you to sign anything now," the receptionist advised me.

Apparently, there was a slight scratch on Mark's eyeball caused by the sand in his eye. There was no lasting damage. 10 minutes, and I don't know how many dollars later, we were travelling back to shoot location to join the rest of the crew.

After lunch, we had a couple more set-ups outside and the bedroom scene that John had been so insistent on including.

By this time, it was approaching 4.30pm and the whole crew settled down for a break for drinks in a nearby bar, before we returned to our hotel.

I was reluctant to leave our minibus unattended. The manager of the bar assured us that it was OK to leave it in the car park opposite. It was just 20 metres from where we were sitting and clearly visible. Whilst we were having our drinks a couple of locals engaged us in conversation. They had seen the "toing and froing" from the van during the day and were aware that a fashion shoot had been taking place.

After 15 minutes, we returned to the van. The door had been opened, without any damage to the vehicle. All the clothing used in the sessions that day had been stolen. Returning to the bar, we discovered our friendly inquisitors were no longer around. I had an uneasy feeling that they probably were involved in what had happened.

I was advised later, by the police, that distraction techniques were widely used by criminals operating in Miami Beach.

Using John's "half brick,'" I rang the number the bar manager had given me for the Miami Beach Police Department (MBPD).

"What is the nature of your problem," I was asked by the switchboard operator. "Our minivan has been broken into and some clothing stolen," I replied.

"Has anyone been injured or killed during the robbery?" the person continued. "No one has been hurt but the clothing stolen are valuable samples," I advised her. "You must come down to the station and complete a crime report. It will not take too long," I was assured.

I was aware that the crime rate in Miami was one of the highest of any city in the USA. In 1989, a crime took place nearly every minute in the city. Miami Beach had a high incidence of thefts and robberies. Many included violence. Minor thefts like ours did not warrant direct police intervention. Officers were struggling to contain much more serious crimes than the theft of a few garments from a vehicle.

I arrived at the MBPD headquarters at 1100 Washington Avenue and joined the long line of people queuing to report the "minor crimes" that had been committed against them.

The policeman who filled in my report was very sympathetic and interested that we had come all the way from the UK for our photographic shoot. When he had completed the form, he passed it over to me to read through the information, and then sign the document to confirm it was correct.

"I'm afraid you won't be seeing your merchandise again," he told me, somewhat apologetically. "If you come back in 5 days you will be able to collect the necessary paperwork you need to back up the claim to your insurance company."

"That's a problem because our flight for the UK leaves in 4 days' time," I advised. "Don't worry, I will give it a priority sticker. Come back at 2.00pm on Friday and we will have everything ready for you," he promised. With that, my interview was over. He gave me a crime number advice card and told me to present it to the duty officer when I came to collect my copy of the crime report.

Outside, I wasted no time in catching a cab back to the hotel.

In just one harrowing day, I had gained first-hand knowledge of the American Banking system, Healthcare and Policing services.

I vowed that I would never again complain about the inadequacies of these services in the UK!

During the rest of the shoot, the minibus was never left unattended!

The shoot went without any further problems, and we visited locations in downtown Miami Fort Lauderdale and one of the five Indian reservations owned by the, federally recognised, Seminole Tribe of Florida.

On the Thursday evening, John announced his intention to take a male and female model for a short, night shoot in downtown Miami. The Miami Tower, and several other high-rise buildings, had pioneered the use of lighting techniques to create a coloured light show during the hours of darkness. These "free shows" had quickly become a tourist attraction. By 1989, they had become synonymous with the cities total visitor offering.

Given our daytime experience on Miami Beach, I was somewhat reticent about putting John's crew, the models and myself at risk. To make the shoot less conspicuous, it was agreed that hair and make-up, dressing and styling would be done at our hotel.

John, his assistant, the two models and me, drove to the downtown area. Once there, we parked the minibus in a suitable location. Leaving John's assistant with the vehicle, we set off on foot until we found a spot where we could place the models in "an edgy inner-city situation" whilst, at the same time, maximising the background light show that John was so eager to capture on film.

The polaroid shots he took were spectacular. In the space of 30 minutes, John completed a series of set-ups that both he and I were totally satisfied with. We then walked back to our minibus and returned to the hotel for a welcome late dinner in the restaurant. Our mission had been accomplished without drawing any unwelcome attention to ourselves, our vehicle, or our equipment!

The shoot was now completed except for two or three set ups that had been organised for Friday morning in the area close to our hotel base.

Our flight back to the UK was scheduled to leave Miami International Airport at around 6.00pm on Saturday, arriving back in London Gatwick at around 8.00am on Sunday.

In the meantime, my own Friday schedule had been decided by situations outside my control. After breakfast, I took a leisurely walk to the main office of American Express. It was in the downtown area, close to the Cruise Boat Terminal.

I had time to sit and watch groups of tourists boarding and disembarking from their ships. Seeing these groups in holiday mode, simply served to remind me how much I was missing my own family. I was now intent on completing all the formalities that remained and then going back home to be with them again.

At 10.00am, I arrived at the American Express office. They were expecting me and took me into a private office to countersign my $27,800. This completed, I expected them to hand over the cash and organise a cab to take me back to the safety of my hotel. I pressed the button on the desk and the manager appeared with an athletic looking, gentleman standing around 6ft 10 inches tall.

"Earl will escort you down to our bank. They are expecting you and will hand over the money in a private room. He will then escort you back here and we will organise a car to take you back to your hotel," the manager announced.

After all my experiences during my time in Miami, I was just past the point of arguing!

"How far away is the bank, Earl," I asked my companion as we 'hit the streets.' "About 4 blocks," he replied.

At the time, the thought passed through my mind that a carefully place bullet would bring my companion down to earth - despite his height and build! Quickly discarding the thought, I determined to just go with the flow.

Earl told me that he had come to the USA from the West Indies on a sports scholarship. Basketball was his game and, after leaving college, he had joined the professional ranks.

It was clear that the manager at American Express was relying on his imposing presence to deter possible assailants. I was concerned that this was simply drawing attention to us.

In the end, we arrived safely at the bank. I collected my money and deposited it in my small holdall. Earl then escorted me back to the American Express office. Their driver took me back to the hotel.

The first of my two Friday missions was now completed!

After depositing the cash into the safe in my suite, I had just enough time for a relaxing lunch at the hotel pool restaurant before setting off for my 2.00pm appointment, at the MBPD headquarters at 1100 Washington Avenue.

On arrival, I joined the queue of people waiting to collect copies of crime reports. Once at the desk, the duty officer took my crime number advice card and disappeared into the next room. From where I was standing, I could see her flicking through a large pile of crime reports until she found the papers she was looking for.

This was in the days before computerisation. I would imagine that today the whole process is conducted online. Eventually, she emerged with my copy and charged me a small fee per page for the privilege.

It was nearly 3.30pm when I arrived back at the hotel.

John and I had arranged a group dinner for 8.00pm at a well-known Japanese restaurant near Miami Beach. Meanwhile, I had a few hours to finally relax, enjoy a refreshing dip in the pool to escape the high humidity and take some time to enjoy the Florida sunshine.

On the Saturday morning, Charmaine and I made up pay envelopes and release forms for all the models, the stylist and the hair and makeup artist. They were called in individually, the envelopes were handed over and the release forms signed. Once these formalities were concluded, everyone had the rest of the day to shop or to relax in the sun.

At around 3.30pm, we packed up the minibus for one last time, climbed aboard and set off for Miami International Airport. Check in went like a dream and, when the flight was called, we all made our way towards the departure gate.

There was to be one last twist in the Miami shoot story!

As we approached the jet bridge to board the aircraft, there was commotion just in front of us. A first-time flyer decided to freak out at the doors of the aircraft. No amount of cajoling from the ground crew could persuade him to board. The captain refused to allow him on the plane until he had calmed down.

His antics began to unnerve those around him who were waiting to board. Rumours spread, through to the passengers still in the departure lounge, that a potential terrorist had been prevented from boarding the aircraft.

The airport police were called.

The passenger would still not calm down and, in his hysterical state, lashed out at the officers. They had no alternative but to handcuff and forcibly remove him from the jet bridge. He was bundled away, via the holding lounges, to the airport police station.

It was some time before normality returned. By the time everyone had finally boarded the aircraft, we had missed our allotted take off slot. After waiting for about 45 minutes, we eventually took off for the flight back home.

The Virgin Atlantic crew handled the aftermath of the incident magnificently. Everyone on board had a free drink to ease the inconvenience of the delay and the in-flight food and service was of the highest quality.

At 9.00am on Sunday 20 August, the aircraft touched down at London Gatwick.

We all said our goodbyes and went our separate ways. I had organised a special transfer from the terminal to the long-term car park. This enabled Charmaine and I to transport our luggage, along with the product ranges, direct to my car.

Four hours later, after dropping Charmaine off in Calverton, I thankfully arrived back home!

The experience of the Miami shoot had not been a happy one. Nevertheless, a lesson had been learned. In future, I would ensure that we would not only plan for the expected but also do all in our power to build in contingency plans for the unexpected.

Better to be pessimistic than optimistic was the new mantra.

On the positive side, John Rutter's shots were well received. The pictures certainly projected the earthy reality of urban America.

In the advertising they were developing for the Wrangler marketing campaign in 1990, our new agency would take this imagery to another level entirely!

Chapter Twenty-Nine

Location shoot, New York, January 1990 - Norman Watson

In November 1989, I had been in New York with Simons Palmer, our new advertising agency. Under the direction of Roger Lyons, we had shot the "Crosstown Traffic" commercial that was scheduled to be aired in February 1990. The commercial was full of "real life, American imagery" but light on Wrangler product.

From the 11 -14 of February the Wrangler Autumn/Winter range was being launched at the IMBEX trade show in London.

It had been agreed that stills from the commercial would be used on our exhibition stand, to "project the strong image of the Wrangler brand of the 1990's."

We also needed "exciting product images." These would be included on our stand, in the 1990 Autumn/Winter product merchandiser and to promote the new product at point of sale, later in the year.

Simons Palmer felt that the link between the Wrangler product and their new advertising would be best achieved by photographing our product within the same gritty urban environment as the commercial.

That would require another trip to New York which, given my experience in Miami, I was reluctant to do. Apart from the logistics, a short time scale and the notoriously inclement New York weather in January, I would be spending even more time away from my family.

The agency recommended that we create our product related, urban imagery by acquiring the services of a "'new wave" photographer called Norman Watson. Norman was the eldest son of the world famous, New York based photographer, Albert Watson.

I was informed that he was already making a name for himself in his own right. "He is fascinated with the mechanics of photographic imagery. As a New Yorker, he knows where to find the right locations. He has already produced fashion work for some of the hard edged, UK fashion magazines that are read by our target market," they argued.

During a recent shoot in the UK, Norman had worked with David Bradshaw. an up- and- coming stylist with credits in magazines such as Arena. "David is available during the week that you have pencilled in for the shoot and will be happy to be involved. He has also suggested the names of some 'hot new models' that he feels are just right for the new Wrangler image," they continued.

My trepidation about the shoot logistics were finally overcome when Norman advised that he proposed using top, New York based, hair stylist Raymond Camacho and make-up artist Mark Hayles.

David had secured the services of male models Curt Buttrum and Mark Hester. The female model was an 18-year-old, native of Brooklyn, New York, called Lisa Barbacoa. She had arrived in Europe in 1989 and had made a big impact in the fashion world. Under the name of Lisa B, she turned, with some success, to her first love acting and singing. This happened not long after our shoot had been completed.

I agreed that we would be unable to control the weather in New York, but it was an Autumn/Winter shoot. A little cold and snow would not be inappropriate.

That left the not insurmountable problem of being away from my family!

Wrangler policy allowed me to take my wife with me, if I paid for the cost of her return airfare from the UK to New York. Glenys had never been to the USA. An opportunity to shop in one of the hottest shopping venues on the planet was irresistible. The suggestion that she came with me also earned me a lot of "brownie points."

One of the male models we had chosen, was visiting his parents just outside New York during the shoot dates.

This meant that money would be saved because only two of the models, our stylist, Glenys, and myself had to be flown out to New York. Norman and the rest of the crew were already based there.

Apart from Norman, everyone else would be paid in dollars at the end of the shoot. A "per dium" allowance was agreed to cover subsistence costs for all the models and crew. This would be paid out in cash before shooting started.

Our travel agency organised a good deal for the airfares which not only helped the final budget but also reduced my private expenditure on the seat for Glenys. The deal included rooms at an airline affiliated hotel in New York.

The only obstacles to overcome was the transportation of six bags of Wrangler product for the shoot and handling of the large amount of cash needed to cover fees and expenses.

Our transport manager at Calverton, insisted that we use a carnet. This required me to declare the goods in London, on arrival and departure in New York and on arrival back in the UK.

During the shoot In Miami, I had encountered problems in cashing my pre-ordered American Express Travellers Cheques. After discussions with Amex, they arranged for me to cash in some of the cheques at their New York head office on arrival. Collection of the balance would be organised for the last day of the shoot.

To ensure easy transit of our luggage to and from the airport, we had organised for a car hire company to supply a chauffeur driven stretch limo.

On Friday the 12 January 1990, I dropped my wife and our 8 bags of luggage outside the departure lounge at Heathrow Airport before parking in the long-term car park.

After the carnet documentation was signed and stamped by customs at Heathrow, we met up with David Bradshaw and the two models. We booked in as a group, at the check in gate. The TWA staff were very helpful and did not charge us for the excess baggage we were carrying. Once on board we were all able to spread out because the flight was not very full.

New York is 5 hours behind London. This meant that after 8 hours, we began our descent into John F Kennedy International Airport at around 4.15pm.

Whilst Glenys and I went through the red channel to present our carnet documentation, the rest of the party went straight to the hotel.

I had never travelled into the USA with a carnet before. I assumed the procedure would be straight forward. The officer in charge must have been coming to the end of a long shift and was most unhelpful. He looked through the documents that I presented and shook his head slowly.

"The documents are incorrect. No fabric contents have been listed," he informed me. "The documents do not require this information." I replied. "I am telling you, SIR, that unless you add this information to the documents, you are going nowhere," he threatened.

We had been travelling for over 14 hours and were very tired. My appointment at the Amex offices was for 5.30pm. There was no time to spare to argue the point. It took 30 minutes to add the information he was requesting and to have the corrected documents stamped.

After we had transferred all our luggage to our waiting limousine, our driver had only 25 minutes to cover the 19.6 miles to downtown Manhattan.

Thankfully, our luxury transportation carried an in-car telephone. I could speak to the member of the Amex team and explain that we were running late. "Don't worry, Mr. Dilley. We expected that you might be delayed and look forward to meeting you when you get here," I was assured.

Eventually, we arrived at the Amex offices. Glenys carried on to the hotel in the limousine. I had given her all the booking information so that she would be able to check into the large room, with extra clothes hanging space, that I had booked, and paid for, in advance.

The staff at the Amex office were extremely helpful. I had originally organised that I would be able to cash in $6,000 of the total of $40,000 of traveller's cheques we had ordered. I was not aware that Monday 15 January was the Martin Luther King Birthday Celebration and, therefore, a Bank Holiday.

I was advised to cash a further $4,000 to ensure that I did not run short of cash.

I signed the 400 traveller's cheques that I had pre-ordered in $100 denominations. After countersigning 100 of these the cash was handed over. An appointment was made for me to return to the office, on the following Tuesday afternoon, to countersign the rest and collect the $30,000 balance.

"It is too dangerous for you to carry $10,000 dollars around Manhattan," the office manager advised me. "I have arranged for a cab to pick you up from here and we will send one of our security people with you to your hotel," he continued. With that, he introduced me to a thick set individual with the obligatory broken nose, who would accompany me on the rest of my journey.

Once in the cab, I struck up a conversation with my new companion. It turned out he had been a member of NYPD until his retirement. He had then taken up the security position with AMEX.

"Forgive me for asking, if someone was to try and get into this cab and rob me at gunpoint, what would you do?" I enquired. My companion said nothing. He simply rolled up his trouser leg to reveal the large handgun that was strapped to his ankle. No words were necessary. From his body language, it was clear that he had used a gun before. I felt equally sure he would be prepared to use it again, to ensure my safe arrival at our destination.

Eventually we reached the New York Penta Hotel, situated right opposite Madison Square Gardens. This was to be our home for the next five nights. My "bodyguard" stayed with me until we were safely in the hotel lobby. I thanked him for all his help, and he disappeared into the night.

It had been well over an hour since I had parted company from Glenys. I expected that she would be settled into our room with a gin and tonic for company. Much to my surprise, I found her sitting in an armchair, in the lobby, next to a trolley containing our 8 bags of luggage.

To say that she did not look very pleased, would be an understatement!

The story tumbled out. On arrival at the hotel, the limo driver had arranged for a porter to collect the luggage. At the check in desk, she had presented all the documentation but had not been allowed to collect a key "because they needed to take an imprint of my credit card."

I was furious!

Our corporate booking had been paid for in advance and I felt that the hotel staff were being unnecessarily pedantic. The desk clerk was unrepentant but did give us a room key when they had swiped my card.

We went up to our room and opened the door. Far from being a large double, it was the size of a single room containing a double bed. There was only enough wardrobe space for my shirts. Nowhere near enough to accommodate all of Glenys's wardrobe and the garments for our photoshoot.

There was a knock on the door. Our luggage had arrived. The bellboy realised there was a problem and advised us to go back to the check in desk and ask for a larger room. Back at the desk, I explained, that the room they had given me was not what our travel agent had ordered and that we had paid for.

They gave me the key to another room.

Our bellboy arrived with our luggage and asked for the number of our new room. "I would not waste your time going up to it, it is the same size as the one we have just come from," he advised. "I would talk to the duty manager if I were you. "

Many of my American colleagues, had insisted that the sign of good hotel management was the disposition of the duty manager. In most large American hotels at that time, the duty manager could be found seated at a desk in the middle of the hotel lobby.

"If the duty manager is looking harassed, continually on the phone and faced with a queue of equally harassed hotel guests, don't even bother to check in," I had been advised. "If people feel the need for his services to that extent, the overall hotel service will be very poor,"

Looking at the desk in the lobby, all my worst fears were being realised!

I had almost lost the will to fight but joined "the queue of the disgruntled" and waited for my turn to pour out my grievances. Eventually, I reached the front of the queue and explained the situation. The duty manager agreed that there had been a mix-up and by way of compensation offered a Junior Suite for a heavily discounted, but additional premium.

The suggestion got the "thumbs up" from the bellboy.!

Nearly an hour after I had arrived at the hotel, we were safely ensconced in our suite with Queen size bed, large lounge area and, most importantly, a walk-in wardroom with more than enough hanging space for all the clothes.

The time was approaching 9.00pm, 2.00am in the UK. We were hungry, tired and it was freezing cold in the streets outside. More than 20 hours had passed since we had left home.

We booked a meal from the hotel room service menu, opened the mini bar, and drowned our sorrows. It was our hope that the worst that could happen, had already happened. Well-watered and well fed, we were soon fast asleep.

The next morning, jet lag ensured that we were awake early. After a relaxing breakfast in the hotel, I took Glenys for a leisurely walk around the area close by. She was pleased to note that the New York Penta Hotel was well situated to allow her to indulge in her favourite activity, shopping! Macy's and Fifth Avenue were just a short walk away and Glenys was keen to visit all the shops as soon as the opportunity arose.

The weather was bitterly cold, at minus 7°C, it felt considerably colder as the wind funnelled between the skyscrapers of Manhattan. We had come prepared for the winter weather and had ensured that we were well layered, from our thermal underwear to our heavy winter coats. The one thing we had forgotten to bring with us was something to cover our heads and ears.

This was soon remedied!

I had arranged to meet up with Norman Watson and David Bradshaw at a 24-hour eatery close by the hotel. After a quick meal, Glenys left us to tour the multifloored emporium that was Macy's.

The rest of us returned to my suite at the hotel. There we met up with the three models and discussed the shoot itinerary. I also took the opportunity to hand out the per diem envelopes to cover sustenance over the period of the shoot.

Norman advised us that he had hired a large Winnebago for the following three days. The company supplying it, were "one of the best in the business." They supplied similar vehicles, as luxurious, mobile dressing room facilities, for all the major film companies.

it was heated and fitted out with comfortable seating, a fully equipped kitchen and bathroom facilities. Clearly, it was going to be cold shooting on the streets, but between setups an oasis of warmth, with all home comforts, would be available to us.

"I assume that you have organised all the necessary filming permits?" I asked Norman. He looked at me in astonishment. "Permits. I'm a New Yorker. Dad and I have worked all over this city for years. Neither of us have ever bothered with permits!" he explained. "We are photographers not film makers," he added.

I wondered whether his supreme confidence might come back and bite him!

It was planned that the following day's shoot would take place at various locations in Manhattan. On the Bank Holiday Monday, we would be moving across the East River to Brooklyn and Coney Island. The last day of the shoot would take place in Central Park and at an old-fashioned barber's shop in Harlem.

David took away the garments that were required for the next day. Norman advised the Winnebago would pick us up outside our hotel at 8.00am. This would enable us to maximise the daylight hours before sunset, at around 4.45pm.

When I had been in the city the previous November, the advertising agency had taken me to French restaurant called Raoul's, situated in the Soho district.

Before I left the UK, I booked a table for Glenys and myself for the Sunday evening, and for a farewell dinner on the Tuesday evening for the whole crew. I had also booked a table, just for the two of us, at the Grand Central Oyster Bar restaurant for the Monday evening.

Glenys returned from her shopping trip sporting a large badge on her coat. It read 'Don't tell me what kind of day to have!'

She had gone into a major chain store to buy some small items that she had forgotten to pack. The woman at the checkout was not happy that she had handed over a $20 bill to pay for the low value items. "Is that the smallest change you have?" she was asked in the brusque manner that New Yorkers adopt when faced with visitors from elsewhere. "I'm afraid so," replied Glenys. "I have just arrived in the country, and this is all I have."

The women made a point of making sure that Glenys was aware she was not happy. She sorted out the change in $1 bills, dimes and quarters and then slammed them down on the counter. Forcing a smile, she handed over the goods with the words, "Have a nice day!"

Glenys had not experienced the best of American service since we had arrived in New York. When she saw the badge, in a tourist souvenir shop, containing the words "Don't tell me what kind of day to have!" she felt it provided a perfect riposte to a phrase uttered by rote, without feeling, by everyone she had encountered since she had arrived. "I have been treated much better since I put it on," Glenys assured me.

Back at the hotel, she had spoken to staff on the desk, and they suggested that she take a bus tour to see all the main sights of the city. Using their contacts, they made a booking on her behalf and organised for a taxi to pick her up from the hotel to take her to where the bus started and finished its journey. The fully guided tour lasted for about five hours. It included a lunch break and short stop offs at all the key attractions. It was a relatively safe, inexpensive way, for a person on their own to see everything that the Big Apple had to offer. Especially, on a cold January day.

That evening, we strolled up to Times Square. Despite the bitterly cold weather, the lights and the atmosphere improved our spirits. I had intended to try and book a table at Gallagher's Steakhouse, but it had slipped my mind. Normally, without a booking, it was almost impossible to find a seat in this New York institution. As we were close by, I decided to take potluck and call in anyway.

We were greeted warmly. I explained we had not booked a table but had just arrived from the UK. Their restaurant had been highly recommended by friends back home who were regular visitors.

The head waiter had heard all this sort of thing before. Whilst it was "like water off a duck's back," he took pity on us. "Why don't you have a drink in the bar," he suggested. "I will fit you in, but it might take 45 minutes or so," he explained. We were in no hurry and happy to soak in the atmosphere whilst doing some celebrity spotting.

The place was busy, as it always is. The cocktail list was extensive. We were encouraged, in the nicest possible way, to try one. Several classic martinis later, we were called to our table and enjoyed two of Gallagher's trademark, immaculately presented, prime dry aged steaks.

All in all, Gallagher's had served up the authentic New York dining experience that we had been promised it would.

Back at our hotel, we went straight to our suite. It was going to be very busy the next day and we were soon catching up on our lost sleep.

We were up bright and early and, after breakfast went our separate ways.

The Winnebago was just as luxurious as we had been led to believe it would be. We were introduced to the rest of the team, Raymond Camacho and Mark Hayles, hair stylist and make-up artist respectively.

As soon as our driver pulled out into the traffic, they immediately got to work preparing models Lisa and Mark for the first set up of the day at Battery Park. A 25-acre public park, it is located at the Battery on the southern tip of Manhattan Island, facing New York Harbour. The area and park were named after the artillery batteries that where strategically positioned there in the early years to protect the growing settlement behind.

Norman worked quickly, using black and white and colour film, to photograph three set ups. These included a double with Lisa and Mark and single shots featuring Curt and Lisa. Once these had been completed, we set off for our next location on New York's Lower East side.

This neighbourhood is in the south-eastern part of Manhattan between the Bowery and the East River, Canal Street and Houston Street. Traditionally an immigrant, working class area, in 1990, it still projected the gritty American urban imagery that we had travelled so far to find.

There is always something refreshingly familiar about locations in New York. This is probably because nearly every district has been featured in films, television shows or in news bulletins. As we shot our next two set-ups, I had an eerie feeling of "deja vu," even though I knew I had never been on the Lower East side before.

When it was time for a lunch break, Norman suggested that there was only one place to go, Katz's Delicatessen. It is situated at 205 East Houston Street on the corner of Ludlow Street. By chance, or maybe by design, it was just around the corner from where we had been shooting our last set up of the morning.

In 1888, a small deli was set up by the Iceland brothers. In 1903 Willy Katz joined them and the store became Iceland & Katz. Willy's cousin Benny joined in 1910 and bought out the Iceland brothers. Katz's Delicatessen was born. It moved across the street to its present location several years later and a New York institution was created.

Katz's pastrami, corned beef sandwiches and its other Jewish deli classics are legendary!

I have never seen or tasted anything quite as delicious as the corned beef sandwich that I ordered. Nor have I ever seen so much meat between two slices of bread before. Eating this speciality is an art form that, sadly, I was unable to master.

Full to overflowing, I wondered whether I would be able to eat anything else that day. I had to remind myself that Glenys and I had booked a French restaurant for a romantic candlelit meal, for that evening. Would I ever be able to eat again?

It was a struggle to walk back to our transport and to lever myself into my seat before we set off for our final location of the day, the Meat Packing District.

The area is in Manhattan and runs roughly from West 14th Street south to Horatio Street and from the Hudson River, east to Hudson Street.

In 1990, the Meat Packing District was the epitome of downmarket, urban America. Semi-abandoned, desolate warehouse buildings were covered in graffiti and an air of, almost terminal, decay permeated the area. The inhabitants represented a cross-section of American society from working butchers, "down and outs'" keeping warm by open fires, people of "ill repute" plying their dubious trades, nightclubbers, celebrities looking for the new "in" places to eat and film crews and photographers, using the area as a backdrop for their projects.

The commercial possibilities were first explored by Florent Morellet. He took over the rundown R & L Restaurant in 1985 and renamed it Florent. Within 6 months, purely through word of mouth, he had turned it into what the New York Magazine described as "the hottest downtown eating spot." A truly 24/7 eatery, it continued to cater for the needs of the local clientele whilst becoming the "place to go" for the downtown creatives and uptown yuppies.

Just 2 months before, I had enjoyed eggs benedict during an early morning breakfast at the restaurant with my advertising agency and the director of the commercial we were about to shoot. The food was great and the mix of clientele interesting!

This time, we were there to capture the true image of the area before it succumbed to the power of the developers who would change the character of the place for ever.

The planned sets-ups went without a hitch. We continued to shoot some additional atmospheric shots as the sun went down. An eerie silence descended across the area. This was punctuated by the sound of the butchers plying their trade in one of the buildings that was still occupied.

The side of another building, close to where we were working, was illuminated by the flickering light of a fire. Around it sat four vagrants. They were huddled together for warmth, in the freezing temperature, gazing into the flames oblivious of what was going on around them.

We retired to our warm Winnebago, and very welcomed hot coffees before returning to the hotel. The first day of our shoot and gone very well!

Glenys had also had a good day. Her bus tour and taken in some of the main sights of the city with a lunch stop off on the way. She was seated next to another "single" woman from Chicago. Glenys's new friend had never been to New York before either. They had a lot in common and got on well together during the five-hour tour.

The female tour guide, a hard-headed, New Yorker, had demanded total attention.

Glenys found her running commentary extremely interesting and informative. A party of Italian tourist at the rear of the coach were obviously less impressed. They were chatting away loudly to themselves and making it difficult for the rest of the passengers to follow the narrative.

The tour guide took no prisoners. She stopped in mid-sentence and glared at the offending group. "Italy," she announced over the radio, "Zip it!"

The intervention worked. The Italians became extremely attentive and absorbed every word thereafter. Much to everyone's relief and amusement!

Glenys had marked off several places of interest that she would be revisiting over the following two days.

After resting following our day's exertions, we took a cab to Raoul's and enjoyed an excellent meal with great service in a wonderfully relaxed atmosphere. All this, despite my earlier trepidation that I would be able to do it justice, following my overindulgence during lunch at Katz's Delicatessen.

On the second day of our shoot, we boarded the Winnebago for the trip across the East River to Brooklyn. Miraculously, the weather had taken a turn for the better. The January cold winds dropped in intensity, the sun had come out and the temperature was rising.

Norman was anxious to maximise the benefits of this good fortune. He had added the Old United States Navy Yard to our shoot itinerary.

The proposed venue had been closed for many years. In the late 1980's, the Brooklyn Navy Yard Development Corporation had taken over the whole site. They had been tasked with maximising the asset but failed in all their attempts to lease the six dry docks, and adjacent buildings, to private shipbuilding or ship repair companies. There were many old and historic buildings on the site which, although run down and deserted, offered countless photo opportunities.

We had just begun our first set-up, when we were approached by a uniformed individual. Attached to his belt was a large keyring. It contained an impressive array of keys.

"What do you think you are doing?" he enquired in a belligerent manner. It was blatantly obvious to anyone what was going on, but Norman responded politely to his enquiry. "We are taking some fashion pictures for a client in England," he said. "Unless you have a permit, you will have to leave immediately," the caretaker/security man warned us.

The keys on his waistband rattled ominously!

A friend back in the UK had a theory about such people. He surmised, the larger the number of keys carried, by such individuals, was directly related to the level of intransience they adopted when encountered.

There were an awful lot of keys on our man's keyring!

"We haven't got a permit, but we will not be long," I replied. "Perhaps, we can offer a donation to a good cause?" I suggested. This seemed to do the trick. A $20 donation to HIS good cause changed his attitude from aggression to compliance. "Have a nice day," he said, doffing his hat and rattling his keys. "Just call in at my office before you leave. Then I can sign you off the site," he requested. With that, he shuffled away in the direction of a small wooden building a short distance away.

"I'm saying nothing," I whispered to Norman. Instead, I gave him a knowing look to remind him of the conversation we had, before the shoot began, about the need for permits.

Meanwhile, the ambient temperature continued to rise.

Norman and I began to shed some of our thermal layers. The models were standing in the sun between shots. All the other crew members came out from the comfort of our Winnebago to take advantage of the unseasonable weather.

We quickly wrapped up our session at the Navy Yard and moved on to the area known as DUMBO neighbourhood. An acronym for Down Under the Manhattan Bridge Overpass, it includes the area between the Manhattan and Brooklyn Bridges.

Our destination was Washington Street. More precisely, at the end closest to the Manhattan Bridge and at the intersection of Water Street. This location provides access to some of the most iconic views in Brooklyn of the Manhattan Bridge and the famous Clocktower Building at 1 Main Street.

Because of the Martin Luther King Birthday Celebration Bank Holiday, we found ourselves vying with hordes of amateur, as well as fellow professional photographers. We finally took the shots we were after before moving on to the Brooklyn Heights Promenade.

The Promenade is known the world over for the cameo role it has played in many movies and TV shows. At one third of a mile long and lined with flower beds and trees, it is claimed to be a favourite destination for joggers, stroller's, lovers, and tourists alike. It also offers magnificent views of the Manhattan Skyline, the Brooklyn Bridge, and the Statue of Liberty.

If there was one backdrop that would place our shoot firmly in New York, this was it!

Unfortunately, for Norman it was a case of 'familiarity breeds contempt.' He was more interested in the close-up shots of the models. I wanted more of the background to appear in the shots. Eventually, we reached a compromise that went someway to meet the requirements of both parties.

After lunch in one of the waterfront eateries, we moved on to the Coney Island peninsula adjacent to the Atlantic Ocean. The site was once an outer barrier island but had become connected to the rest of Long Island due to landfill operations.

In 1990, the area was in dire need of redevelopment. It projected a distinctly run-down feeling. On the other hand, it was still a major leisure and entertainment destination with Sea Gate to the West and Brighton and Manhattan Beaches to the East.

The warm January weather and the Bank Holiday had drawn large crowds to the area but many of the main attractions were still closed for the winter period.

We set up shop on the Riegelmann Boardwalk. Named after Edward J Riegelmann, and more commonly known as the Coney Island Boardwalk, it stretches for 2.51 miles. It is reputed to be the second-longest boardwalk in the world.

Thankfully, cold winds off the Atlantic had quickly reduced the numbers of people braving the facility, to a few intrepid walkers, joggers and foolhardy photographic crews like us. Between takes, we took refuge in our motor home and indulged ourselves with endless warming cups of coffee to keep out the cold.

Shortly before sundown, we called it a wrap and headed back across the East River to our hotel.

During the day, Glenys had enjoyed visiting The Metropolitan Museum of Art and the Empire State Building. She had been amused by how the transformation in the weather had changed the attitude of nearly everyone in the city.

People had been shedding the layers of clothing but still carrying around heavy topcoats in case normality returned. "If it's as warm tomorrow, I will have to do some clothes shopping," she warned me. "I have only brought my winter wardrobe with me,"

That evening, I had booked a table for us at the Oyster Bar Restaurant. I had been before and knew that Glenys would love it.

The restaurant is situated on the Lower Level at the Grand Central Railway Station. It is an unlikely location for one of the world's great fish restaurants. The Old Oyster Bar had been launched in 1913 and for over 60 years had become a landmark. This was based more on its location at the hub of the USA's long-haul passenger train system than for the quality of its cuisine. The advent of air travel had signalled a significant reduction in the long-haul rail passenger numbers and with it a decline in the fortunes of the restaurant.

In 1972, the old Oyster Bar went bankrupt and remained closed for 2 years. The New York Metropolitan Transit Authority approached Jerome Brody. He owned several restaurants in the city, including the famous Gallagher's Steak restaurant. After touring fish restaurants in the area, he was convinced of the venue's viability. In 1974, Brody took over the lease and set about reviving the fortunes of the 440-seat capacity venue.

The Grand Central Oyster Bar and Restaurant was re-born!

Although the concourse of the Grand Central Station is well known, its Lower Level is seldom exposed to the scrutiny of the wider world.

On our way to the restaurant, Glenys and I found ourselves stepping over vagrants, settling down for a night's sleep. Once through the door of the restaurant, we entered a totally different world. I was reminded of the children in the book, 'The Lion, the Witch and the Wardrobe' by C S Lewis. In it, the main characters walk through the back of an old wardrobe and discover the magical land of Narnia.

Beneath the high vaulted ceiling, Jerome Brody, and his wife Marlene, had recreated the architectural grandeur and decor of a time gone by. A Narnia for fish eaters, no less!

The daily fish menu offered every conceivable variety of fish from every part of the world. I cannot think of another fish restaurant on the planet that offers as many as 25 varieties of oysters!

Glenys was very impressed with the menu and the total ambiance of the place. My "brownie point" total rose considerably.

The service was great, the food exceptional. It was easy to see why people returned again and again.

The next morning, our schedule included a couple of set ups in Central Park. We were then travelling on to Harlem. There we had booked a couple of hours in an old-fashioned barber's shop for our concluding session.

The Martin Luther King Birthday Celebration Bank Holiday in Harlem had been marred by a flare up of violence. With tensions still running high in the area, I questioned the wisdom of continuing with our original plan.

"I'm certain that everything will be OK," Norman assured me. "As a precaution, I suggest that we limit the number of people entering the barber's shop to you, me and the male models, everyone else will stay in the Winnebago." This seemed a sensible idea. If we were going ahead with the Harlem set-up, we needed to be aware of the tensions that might be aroused by our all-white team, in a predominately black area.

Central Park, our first location, is a large urban park in central Manhattan. It is also the most visited in the United States. Another iconic location for film companies and photographers, it provided a well-known backdrop ideal for any fashion shoot in New York.

The weather was even better than the previous day. The sun was shining, the sky was blue, it was more like a spring day than the middle of January. Because of this, the joggers were out in force. The heavy winter tracksuits had been discarded. There was not a topcoat in sight. I had come to New York well prepared for the cold. This unseasonable weather was welcomed, but totally unexpected.

Norman got to work. To take full advantage of the weather, he added several additional setups before finally preparing to leave for our final location. By the time we left the park, we were running behind schedule. I had to be at the Amex offices in downtown Manhattan for my 2.00pm appointment to cash in my remaining traveller's cheques.

When we arrived at the Harlem location, I went into the barber's shop, and we discussed with the owners exactly what set-ups were required. They were only too happy to oblige. I suppose business was always slow on a Tuesday and we had paid them handsomely for their time.

I looked at my watch. It was time for me leave. Our hosts suggested that it might be safer if the Winnebago took me to a place where cabs were more readily available. "It's not safe for you to be walking about on your own," the owner advised.

I had not considered my own safety and began to feel a little uneasy. When our Winnebago reached a major junction, I saw an empty cab queuing at the lights. "Let me off here and I will take that cab," I requested. With that, I jumped out of our vehicle and raced across the road. Out of the corner of my eye, the Winnebago was fast disappearing into the distance.

The cab driver looked up, somewhat alarmed as I waved my arms in his direction. "I need to go to the Amex office in Lower Manhattan," I shouted through the window.

Realising that I was a legitimate fare, and that he was not about to be the victim of a hijack, the cab driver opened the cab door and let me in. "You should not be walking about this area on your own," he advised me. "Normally, I do not pick up fares in this neighbourhood, but I realised that you were a stranger and took pity on you."

It was only then that the folly of what I had done hit home. If the cab driver had driven off without me, I could have been in deep trouble. As it was, I was safe, and the taxi driver had bagged probably his most lucrative fare of the day.

Eventually, he dropped me off outside the Amex office. It was absolutely heaving with people. This did not overly concern me. I fully expected that I would be taken to the same private office that I had used the previous Friday.

The person at the information desk was expecting me. He called over the manager who had been allocated to look after me. Instead of being led to the private office, I was taken to a desk, behind a screen, in the open office area. The manager produced the large pile of 300, $100 denomination, traveller cheques for me to countersign.

Several minutes later he returned. Leaning over the screen he enquired, "Mr. Dilley, how would you like your $30,000 broken down?" He probably whispered the words, but it did not seem like that to me at the time. Paranoia set in. The whole office appeared to have been plunged into silence. I felt that I, and my large pile of traveller's cheques, was the centre of everyone's attention.

Handing over the breakdown written on a sheet of paper, I waited for him to return with the cash. I was not unduly concerned. Amex had provided a cab and an armed guard to escort me to my hotel with the $10.000 I had collected on the first day. They would probably provide two armed guards for the same journey but with three times the amount of cash, I reasoned.

No such luck. The manager returned with the cash, counted it out for me to check and asked me for a signature. I packed the cash into the holdall I had brought with me. "Thanks for using American Express," the manager said, as we shook hands. "Have a nice day."

No armed guards, just me and a bag containing a large amount of cash, walking out into one of the world's most dangerous cities!

I crossed the office convinced that every eye was following my every move. The door closed behind me. Looking back, I checked that I was not being followed.

Thankfully I saw a cab, flagged it down and was soon on my way back to the hotel.

Glenys was waiting for me in our hotel suite. She had spent the morning shopping. We had not expected Spring weather and so neither of us had any suitable clothing. Glenys had remedied this problem by doing some clothes shopping for herself and splashing out on souvenirs of the visit and gifts for the family.

Her credit card was even warmer than the weather!

"I have been watching the TV. Apparently, today reached plus 16°C. That is the hottest ever recorded temperature in New York in January," she announced.

She helped me to sort out the money for the models and crew into envelopes and to prepare the release documents. I was palpably relieved to get the job out of the way and to put the money, that I had been carrying around the city, into the room safe.

It had been arranged that the whole crew would be coming back to my suite to collect their envelopes and complete the paperwork. With two hours to kill, Glenys and I found a nice coffee shop on nearby 5th Avenue and settled down to watch the world go by.

Back at the hotel, I thanked all the crew for their help and assistance, handed out the cash and received everyone's signature on their release documents.

The farewell dinner at Raoul's had been booked for 8.00pm. This gave everyone ample time to relax, spruce up and catch a cab to the restaurant.

I had provided open flight tickets for David Bradshaw and the two models who had flown with us on the outward journey. This gave them the opportunity to stay on in the city for a few days more if they so wished. The lure of being able to spend some of their newly acquired dollars had proved irresistible. They were all staying on. David's PR girlfriend was also working in New York, on a different shoot. She was joining our party for dinner in place of our make-up artist, who was working on another job that evening.

Only Glenys and I, with all the clothes from the shoot and the extra luggage she had purchased, would be travelling back to the UK next day.

The dinner was excellent, the wine flowed freely, and we all had a very enjoyable experience before saying our goodbyes. Norman was due in London the following week and we arranged to meet up to view the end results on our time together.

Next morning, I organised a late check out from the hotel. Our flight was due to take off at around 6.00pm and our limousine was collecting us at 3.00pm to take us to the airport.

The weather was still quite warm, so we decided to spend some time doing purely tourist things. We walked about Battery Park enjoying the scenery and took a return trip on the Staten Island Ferry.

The Ferry serves one main purpose, to transport Staten Islanders to and from Manhattan. The journey, of 5 miles, takes 25 minutes. It also provides the most majestic views of the New York Harbour. It has been described as "One of the world's greatest (and shortest) water voyages." From the deck, we had a perfect view of The Statue of Liberty and Ellis Island on the outboard journey and the skyscrapers and bridges of Lower Manhattan on our return.

All too soon, we had to return to the hotel, organise our luggage and to check out.

Once our limousine was loaded, we sat back in comfort as we sped, through the pre-rush hour traffic, to the John F Kennedy International Airport. At JFK, our chauffeur helped to load up two trollies with our luggage. I then had to locate the US customs office to have my documentation stamped before check in.

On arrival, this had proved a traumatic experience. This time the friendly officer went through my carnet, asked about the photoshoot, and stamped the documents without any problems.

At the TWA check in desk the staff were less helpful. The flight was full and the check in queue was long.

At Heathrow, the excess baggage charge was waived. Not so at JFK. "Your excess baggage is $179," the woman at the checkout barked. I had some excess dollars and handed her two, $100 notes. "We don't carry change, you will have to get the notes changed and come back with the correct amount," she responded, unhelpfully.

I had spent the past few days making excuses for the New York version of what constitutes good service. This woman's attitude was trying my patience just a step too far!

"You are charging me excess baggage. I have given you the money to pay for it. I am the customer. You go and find the change!" I exploded. The women realised the error of her ways and found the necessary $21, seemingly out of thin air.

Sadly, our last interaction in New York had not been a pleasant one. The flight home was not memorable either. TWA was on the brink of oblivion. They were doing everything they could to meet the challenge of a new breed of competitors such as Virgin Atlantic. They were failing!

Our flight out had been almost empty. Our flight back was jam packed with America tourist travelling by curtesy of a $99 return offer. After a noisy, bumpy, and uncomfortable journey we landed at Heathrow at around 8.30am. Leaving Glenys with our luggage in the arrivals lounge, I collected our car from the long-term carpark and returned to the terminal. At close to 10.00am, we were on our way home.

The journey had been fraught at times, but the results of the shoot made all the effort worthwhile. Glenys had enjoyed the trip and we were left with plenty of anecdotal stories to tell.

During my research, I came across an article about a New York crime peak that happened during 1990.

It read as follows, "It is still difficult to fathom the sheer volume of bloodshed and violence that plagued New York City in 1990. The carnage skewed toward senseless violence: children hit by stray bullets, drug killings at the peak of the crack epidemic and random robberies gone wrong. With 2,245 homicides that year - a record unsurpassed except by the Sept. 11 attacks - it averaged out to more than six killings a day."

Whilst we were in the city, there were 13 homicides. We had no concept at the time, that our search for "a gritty, USA, urban reality" could have put us in great danger.

Chapter Thirty

Location shoot, Las Vegas, July 1990 - John Rutter

The Norman Watson photoshoot in New York had produced a set of pictures that worked well in our Autumn/Winter product range sales merchandiser. They had also been enthusiastically received by our public relations agency and had gone down well with the fashion editors.

Whilst they projected the gritty, urban American feel we had sought to achieve, they were relatively tame by comparison to the image projected in the Wrangler "Crosstown Traffic" commercial that had been shot in New York in November 1989. This had been running on television and in cinemas throughout the UK and Ireland, in the Spring and Summer of 1990.

Our advertising agency was working on a sequel that would be aired during 1991. As we finalised the Wrangler Spring/Summer product ranges, no work had yet materialised. After several meetings with the agency, it was clear that the recommended work was likely to be heavy on image and light on Wrangler product.

During discussions internally, it was felt that we needed product related, image shots that could be used for the product merchandiser, public relations and point of sale material.

Two names were in the frame, Martin Hooper, and John Rutter.

Martin Hooper was my favourite. His work was excellent. He was also easier to work with. The photographic images produced by John Rutter, during our Spring/Summer 1990 range shoot in Miami, were undoubtedly grittier. On the other hand, the shoot had been a roller coaster ride for me.

John could be something of a loose cannon. He needed very tight control to ensure that he did not stray over, what some might consider to be, the boundaries of decency. Martin's pictures had worked at both image and public relations levels. The images produced by John had worked well at the point of sale but less so in support of our PR campaigns.

In the end, we compromised. It was agreed to organise two, separate shoots!

Martin Hooper was hired to produce controlled, studio image shots of the whole product line. These would be used in the product merchandiser and for public relations purposes.

John Rutter was tasked with building on "the gritty image work" that he had pioneered, during the Miami shoot. The work would be used for the product merchandiser and to develop a range of point-of-sale material.

Lindah Kiddey would work with Martin to art direct the studio-based PR shoot. This would take place at Martin's studio in London. I would art direct the John Rutter shoot, on location in the USA.

One of us had drawn the short straw, guess who?

Since the Miami shoot with John, he had moved back to the USA and was looking to base his activities in Los Angeles. In June 1990, he had just completed an assignment in London. This presented an opportunity to meet up with him, to discuss his thoughts for a shoot that was planned for the following month.

During the meeting, he presented his concept. His feeling was that Las Vegas would be an ideal location. It was full of iconic American imagery, perfect for a mixture of day and night sets-ups he was envisaging. The surrounding landscape of the Mojave Desert offered a complete contrast to the urban sprawl of the city itself.

John had been working with an up-and-coming British male model who was based in Paris. He was keen to use him as the lead male model for the Wrangler shoot. To protect his identity, I have called him "Jean Paul."

All the other models, one male and two females, plus John's assistant, a hair and make-up artist and a fashion stylist would be recruited in Los Angeles. John was confident that this approach would ensure we had a greater choice of talented people to select from. It would also save money in model fees. The cost of airfares would be minimised because only two people, me, and "Jean Paul" the male model from Paris, would be flying in from Europe.

The downside was that I would have to travel out early to attend model casting sessions, sort out the logistics of transporting garments to the USA, booking models and crew on return flights from LA to Las Vegas. I would also have to stay on in Los Angeles after the shoot, whilst the film was processed.

Once this had been done, John and I would work on the contact prints and transparencies to select our choice of the best pictures before I returned to the UK with them.

The green light was given. The shoot date planned from the 15-18 July 1990. Lindah Kiddey would be working with Martin Hooper on the UK product shoot at around the same time.

Previous shoots in the USA had turned out to be logistical nightmares. This time, I was determined that we would learn from all our earlier experiences.

By splitting the product and image shoots, we could limit the amount of merchandise that I would have to transport. Instead of having samples of the whole range, a selection of Wrangler jeans, jackets, shirts, and tee-shirts, for each of the models, would suffice. Where around eight large travel bags had to be carried out before, only two would be needed this time.

Our travel agent did a deal with TWA for the return flights from London and Paris and the room bookings for nine people at the Las Vegas Hilton, a TWA affiliated hotel. Return flights on Delta Airlines had also been booked from LA to Las Vegas for nine people. I would have to confirm the names and travel times after the casting sessions had taken place in LA. They also organised rooms for me, at a hotel in Los Angeles, for my pre and post shoot stays.

For the return flight from London, I was booked into business class on a special deal. It was agreed with the airline they would also waive the cost of the extra baggage that I would be carrying. This ensured there would be no excess baggage charge. The model from Paris was booked to fly direct, on a separate flight.

As documented earlier, cashing my American Express traveller's cheques had proved problematic during the Miami and New York trips. I was assured that no such problem would be experienced this time!

Las Vegas Hilton was used to providing cash for the high rollers using their casino. My requirements would be "small change" by comparison to theirs. What's more cashing in the cheques and carrying large amounts of money around the hotel afterwards would be totally safe. "The hotel goes to great lengths to protect their clients' money," I was advised. "They want to ensure that if anyone takes the money from you it will be the staff in their casino and nobody else." As it turned out, this latter statement was to prove prophetic.

On the 11 July 1990. I arrived at the airport for my late afternoon flight to Los Angeles. Leaving my car at the long-term carpark, I struggled with my three large suitcases to the TWA Business Class check in desk.

Checking in should have been straightforward but surprise, surprise, there was a problem!

The check in staff claimed to have no information regarding my pre-arranged excess baggage. They were prepared to accept two of the cases as part of my flight allowance but remained insistent that I pay excess baggage on the third.

This was not a good start to my adventure!

I decided not to cause a fuss at the check in desk. Instead, I registered my concern and told the staff to give me a receipt. I would claim back the excess cost on my return from the trip.

On board the plane, I enjoyed all the comfort, culinary delights, and free drinks that TWA bestowed on business class travellers. Eventually, after a flight of just under 11 hours, I arrived safely, but tired, at Los Angeles International Airport. After navigating immigration and baggage control without incident, and finding a cab, I arrived at my hotel, on Wilshire Boulevard, at around 9.00pm.

The next morning, I met up with John Rutter and stylist Tanya Gill at the offices of the model agency in downtown LA.

Tanya was a Brit and had studied fashion at Kingston University. Her CV was impressive. She had worked for Jean Paul Gaultier in Paris and had styled fashion shoots for many British based magazines including The Face, Arena, GQ. She had also worked with John Rutter before. Tanya knew the British fashion scene and was aware of the positioning of the Wrangler brand in the UK.

She was the ideal choice as stylist for our shoot!

During her discussions with John prior to the shoot, he had outlined what he was proposing to do during our time in Las Vegas. Tanya was anxious to get her hands on the merchandise so that she could "work her magic." The three of us, were joined by Johnny Hernandez who was John's choice for hair and makeup artist. He was generally regarded as one of the best in the business.

During the morning, I presented the merchandise that I had brought with me, and we discussed the logistics of the four days we would be spending in Las Vegas. In the afternoon, John and I held a casting session of models the agency had shortlisted for our shoot. A final selection was made, and the chosen models were recruited. John suggested we should take out an option on one additional male and female model "as insurance." This was not something that we would normally do.

With the benefit of hindsight, it was just as well that we did!

To minimise the amount of cash I would have to carry, it had been arranged that John's fee would include the cost of his assistant, and the fees for stylist, and hair and makeup artist. I had organised for a cheque to be written, and signed for the agreed amount, before I left Calverton. I would hand this over to John, when the film had been processed after the shoot and the transparencies, negatives and contact sheets had been passed over to me to take back to the UK.

We organised with the model agency that the chosen models would be paid in cash at the end of the shoot. They would be responsible for remunerating the agency with their proportion of the fee. The model agency welcomed this idea. It meant that there would be no lengthy delays before the model fees, and the agency commission, were finally paid.

The "per diem" payment system, I had tried out during New York shoot earlier in the year, had worked well. At the beginning of the shoot, every member of John's crew and all the models would be given a cash payment to cover lunches and dinners for the four days of photographic sessions.

My second day in LA was spent confirming the names of nine people for whom rooms had been reserved at the Las Vegas Hilton.

When this had been done, I contacted Delta Airlines with the passenger names and flight times for the return journeys from LA to Las Vegas. Our travel agent had booked and paid for these in advance.

John, his assistant, and I were booked to fly out early on the morning of 14 July. The Los Angeles based models would fly out later that afternoon.

The male model from Paris would not be arriving until early the same evening. We had organised that his return ticket to Las Vegas would be waiting at the Delta booking desk for him to collect once he had cleared the International Terminal. He just had to go to the desk, give his name and show them some identification and his ticket would be handed over.

No problem!

John was keen to hire a 1970's Oldsmobile Convertible. This would be used as a "moving prop" for several of the set-ups. Hiring one had proved problematic. These vehicles were highly sort after for weddings and special events. The price that the hire companies were asking, including insurance fees, was just too expensive. We did manage to find a garage who had one for sale. It needed work doing to it, but they claimed it was drivable. If we liked it, there was a deal to be done.

A 14-seater luxury minibus, to transport everyone to and from the different locations, had been hired by John. We would collect it at the airport when we arrived in Las Vegas.

On the morning of 14 July, the advance party comprising John, his assistant and I, took the early morning Delta airlines flight to Las Vegas. After a flight of around 1¼ hours, we touched down safely and, after picking up our minibus at the airport we made our way to the garage which had a 1970's Oldsmobile Convertible to sell.

At first glance, the vehicle, I think it was a 1970 Oldsmobile Cutlass Convertible, seemed in good condition. Mechanically, it left a lot to be desired. The engine started easily enough but it clearly needed a good overall. The throaty roar from its exhaust was more a sign of an engine on its "last legs," than that of a finely tuned "eye-turner."

John was quite keen to get his hands on it. As a photographic prop, it was just what he was looking for. "I know it sounds a bit rough, but we will only be driving a short distance in it. 100 miles at the most," he argued. "What about tax and insurance?" I asked. "My assistant will add it to his documentation," John replied.

The garage owner was keen to do a deal and haggling began. He wanted $1,000. We were not prepared to pay more than $500. In the end, we settled on $750 on the basis that he would "buy the car back," at the end of the shoot, for $250. He also agreed to have it valeted before we picked it up next morning. "If it claps out during the time you have it, just call us and we will send out our breakdown truck to collect it," he added, reassuringly.

Assuming the vehicle remained drivable over the next four days and stayed in one piece until we returned it to the garage, we would save ourselves a considerable amount of money against the hire rates we had been quoted. The deal was struck, the cash and documentation changed hands. We arranged to collect it next morning.

From the garage, we made our way out into the Mojave Desert and towards Red Rock Canyon State Park, the site for the first day of our shoot.

On our return journey, we called in at the Whistle Stop Bar and Silver Sands Motel in Las Vegas that John had chosen as additional venues. The site survey completed, we then made our way to the Las Vegas Hilton, our base for the next four nights.

At the desk, I was asked to produce my corporate Amex card so that it could be swiped. I was advised, "this is to cover the cost of any extras not included on the bill incurred during the time your party is here."

To my surprise, my room turned out to be a mini suite on the top floor. It featured a full-length picture window that offered panoramic views of Las Vegas and, in the distance, the mountains of Red Rock Canyon State Park.

Before leaving Los Angeles, I had been in touch with the Marketing Director of the Las Vegas Hilton and arranged a meeting with her to set the ground rules for any filming we undertook on hotel premises. "Thank you for your help in sorting out our accommodation. I am very happy with my room," I told her. "Glad you like it and welcome to the Las Vegas Hilton," she replied. "Would you like me to show you and the photographer around the hotel?"

I thought that this was an excellent idea and put a call though to John's room to pass on the invitation. A few minutes later, He joined us in the lobby and our host gave us a personalised tour. "The casino and the rooftop pool are out of bounds for commercial photography," she advised. "We have no problems with your using the hotel grounds, lobby or bedrooms."

John appeared very enthusiastic about the scope that the venue offered. He was particularly blown away be the rooftop pool. I knew I would have difficulty in controlling his requirement to satisfy his creative desire to use the pool area. Especially, as he had been advised that the prized location was out of bounds!

The rest of the Los Angeles based members of the party were arriving on the late afternoon flight. Whilst John and his assistant went to collect them in the minibus, I took the opportunity to walk along "The Strip" only a block away from the hotel. It was my first opportunity "to be a tourist" since arriving in the USA.

The temperature in the desert had exceeded 41°C. When I returned to the hotel, with the sun just about to set, it was still around 33°C and very humid. It felt as a though a storm was brewing.

The rest of the crew arrived from the airport. We assembled for a briefing after which, I handed out the "per diem" expenses.

"Jean Pauls" flight from Paris had been delayed and his connection would be arriving in Las Vegas at around 9.00pm. John's assistant would be picking him up from the airport and I would meet and greet him briefly, when he arrived at the hotel.

Before dinner, I watched the lightening show emanating from a violent electric storm that was raging in the distant mountains. I had read that Las Vegas was situated in a basin on the floor of the Mojave Desert and was surrounded by mountains on all sides. The area was susceptible to flash floods caused by mountain storms. To mitigate the potential for flooding, an intricate series of flood channels directed the water to the only outlet, the Las Vegas Wash. From there, it was collected and eventually deposited into Lake Mead.

I was glad to be in the safety of my air-conditioned suite watching from a distance, and not having to face the possible consequences of the rush of rainwater into the storm drains close to the city. A news item on my television announced that a car had indeed been swept away by a torrent. Its occupants had not survived.

After dinner in one of the hotels many restaurants, I was relaxing in the lounge bar waiting for "Jean Paul" to arrive from Paris. An attractive woman walked past me, smiled, and said hello. I smiled back and returned her greeting.

At that moment, a call went out over the hotel public address system. "Will hotel guest, Mr. Robin Dilley please go to the nearest telephone, there is a call for him," it announced.

I went to the bar, introduced myself to the bar manager and was handed the phone. It was John. "'Jean Paul' has had problems with the ticket for the flight from Los Angles," he said.

As he spoke, I felt a hand caressing the back of my neck. I turn around and saw the face of the women with whom I had exchanged pleasantries a few minutes earlier. In close-up, she was nothing like as attractive as she had seemed from a distance. It was clear to me that she was probably a 'hooker' who was working the hotel lobby seeking out business. Obviously, my response to her greeting had been misinterpreted.

Undeterred, I continued my conversation with John. "What do you want me to do?" I queried. "Can you come out with me to the airport to meet the flight and sort out the problem?" John continued. "No problem. Meet me in the bar in 5 minutes," I answered.

I put the phone down and looked my unwanted companion straight in the eye. "I am not looking for company and about to leave for a business meeting," I informed her somewhat brusquely. With that, she tottered off in the direction of the casino. A few minutes later, when I left for the car park with John, I saw her going through the same routine with another possible punter.

On the way to the airport, John filled me in about the problem. Apparently, "Jean Paul" had gone to the Delta booking desk at Los Angeles International Airport, as requested. He alleged he had been advised that his return ticket to Las Vegas was not there. He had no alternative but to purchase a one-way ticket to Las Vegas before he could board the flight.

I was not happy!

Either the airline had not carried out my clear instructions or the model had not gone to the correct desk. Either way, Wrangler had paid for a return ticket that had not been utilised and the cost of which might not be refunded.

When we arrived at the airport, and before "Jean Paul's" flight arrived, I went to the Delta information desk and explained what appeared to have happened. They rang the Delta desk at Los Angeles International who confirmed the ticket was still there and that the model had not been to the desk to collect it.

When the flight arrived, "Jean Paul" was adamant that he had gone to the correct desk. There the Delta staff told him there was no ticket waiting and insisted he bought another. "I have had to buy a one-way ticket with my own money. I want an immediate advance from my fee to pay for it," he demanded.

I was reluctant to do this until I had fully investigated the matter. I needed to be sure that the fault lay with the airline and Wrangler would be refunded with the return ticket that had already been paid for.

"Jean Paul" was quite aggressive, even though I explained that he would be receiving his per diem expenses in cash when we arrived back at the hotel.

He would not need to spend any more of his own money and by the end of the following day, I was sure that the matter would be resolved. His ticket money would be refunded and a return ticket, for his flight back to LA, would be delivered.

In all my days in advertising, I had never had a situation where anyone had displayed such a level of disrespect for the client, as this model had shown to me. I put it down to jet lag on his part and hoped that his attitude would mellow during the next few days of shooting.

Next morning, we had an early breakfast. The forecast for the Red Rock Canyon State Park was for unremitting sunshine and mid-day temperatures exceeding 41°C. John and I were keen to wrap-up all planned set-ups before the temperature became unbearable. Enroute to our first destination, we had to pick up the Oldsmobile. There was no time to waste.

When the models saw the car, they all wanted to ride in it. There was no doubt that it had "brushed up well." Despite, or maybe because of the throaty noise it was emitting, it was a head turner. Just the sort of vehicle for beautiful people to be driving and to be seen in.

They would have been much better riding in the air conditioned, relative comfort of the minibus, rather than being exposed, unnecessarily, to the elements and the unremitting sun. But the lure of being the centre of attention just proved too strong!

We were well prepared for the rigours of filming in the hostile desert. Tanya Gill ensured we had plenty of creams to protect us from the sun's harsh rays. There were plenty of cold drinks in our fridge in the minibus and we had a selection of large golf umbrellas to provide shade between takes.

Having said that, it was hot, VERY HOT!

John seemed impervious to the conditions. I had noticed, during our previous shoot in Miami, that once a set-up had been explained to the models, he entered an almost hypnotic state, during which he was seemingly oblivious to all outside influences. He centred all his thoughts and attention to the image captured through his lens. Instructions to the models were barked from behind the camera, in a seemingly unending commentary, until he was finally satisfied that the shot was "in the can."

Most models responded positively to John's cajoling. "John Paul" did not. "It's too hot and I need to rest," he moaned to me, after only a few minutes. "He's working us too hard!" he exclaimed petulantly.

I pointed out to him that a shoot in Nevada, in July, was always going to be difficult and he, and his colleagues were being paid handsomely for their services. "I know that it is not easy," I explained to him. "Everyone here is suffering from the heat, but we are just getting on with the job. The sooner we finish this difficult section of the shoot, the sooner we can move on to next location and less hostile conditions," I continued.

The models had the highest hourly rate of anyone on the shoot, including John and me. There was a temptation to tell him to "just get on with it and think about the money" but I adopted a less confrontational stance.

My concern was that "Jean Paul's" prima donna attitude was beginning to affect at least one of the other models on the shoot. I determined, "to pluck out the potential rotten apple" before others were "contaminated." Once models become unhappy, the unyielding eye of the camera picks this up. Very quickly the resultant pictures can be compromised.

Just before the heat of the midday sun, we wrapped up the Red Rock Canyon State Park section of the shoot. Before we set off for lunch at our next location, the Whistle Stop Bar in Las Vegas, I pulled John aside and explained the situation. I suggested that he had a quiet, private word with "Jean Paul" before the start of the next session.

Our shoot at the Whistle Stop went without incident. The air-conditioned interior of the bar offered a welcome respite from the blazing heat of the desert. The set-ups orchestrated by John had certainly turned the temperature up several notches. I had to be on my guard to ensure that the resultant pictures did not "overstep the mark,"

Before returning to the hotel, I thanked the whole crew for their patience during the shoot so far. "The heat in the desert made it difficult for everyone," I stated. "I would like to thank you for the professionalism you have all shown. If any of you have any problems that you would like to discuss privately, please let me know and we can meet up back at the hotel."

The last comment was aimed at "Jean Paul" and the female model who I had sensed was also aggrieved. Sure enough, back at the hotel they both asked to speak to me. In separate meetings, they told me they felt that they had been worked too hard in the difficult conditions. Neither was prepared to put up with the situation for the rest of the shoot.

All the models were being very well paid for their services. I felt it was necessary to take strong action. I could not change the weather. For the next few days, it would be equally as hot. John drove models hard, but his methodology provided the sort of results we had hired him to produce. I had no intention of asking him to change his ways.

There was no alternative, if the models were not prepared to continue to work in the prevailing conditions, they would have to leave the shoot. "I am sorry that things have turned out as they have. I will organise flights back to LA for you tomorrow and will pay you in cash for your fees for today's work," I advised them both.

It had been my intention to bring forward "Jean Paul's" return flight to Paris. He advised me that this would not be necessary. He had friends in LA and would be staying with them for a few days. I think the decision I made, took them a little by surprise. They were assured that my decision for them to leave the shoot, would not result in any further recriminations on the part of Wrangler.

Hence the reason that the models concerned are not identified in this narrative, even after all these years!

During the casting session, John and I had selected a male and female model as standbys. The wisdom, or luck, of that decision was now apparent. It was Sunday evening and not an ideal time to change our arrangements.

John had a home contact number for the head booker at the model agency. He contacted her to call in the standbys.

We would need to contact Delta to change the date of the female models return flight from Las Vegas to LA and book a one-way ticket to LA for "Jean Paul." Our travel agency in the UK was not open until the following morning. I would have to wait until early the early hours, Las Vegas time, to make the arrangements and to sort out two additional return flights for the standby models.

I spoke to John, and we decided to slightly re-arrange the shoot schedule for the next two days.

The evening shoot, around the hotspots of Las Vegas, would now be rescheduled for the Tuesday. Our full complement of models would be available by then. Monday would be a slightly less arduous shoot in and around the hotel.

John spoke to the two remaining models and explained what had happened. I am sure that the "Brit Art Director and client," would have had to bear the brunt of any blame. Thankfully, I have a very broad back!

In the early hours of the next morning, I spoke to Karen, my PA at Calverton. She sorted out all the flight arrangements with our travel agency.

"The tickets will be left at the Delta booking desk," she advised me when she phoned me back to confirm the arrangements. I groaned when she said this. The original problems with this arrangement for "Jean Paul" had probably sown the seeds of his discontent. "Some good news," she continued. "Delta have agreed to reimburse the return ticket "Jean Paul" had failed to collect. They have assured us all the new tickets will be at the respective booking desks and that there will be no problems."

The 8-hour time difference had compounded the difficulty of communicating with the UK. By the time, everything had been sorted, it was nearly breakfast time in Las Vegas. I had little or no sleep and I still had to organise the release forms and money for the two models who were leaving. This would take most of the morning.

In the meantime, John was on the loose with his camera, the remaining models and without my restraining hand.

Surely, I thought to myself, nothing could possibly go wrong?

The flights to LA had been booked for early afternoon. Once more, we would have to rely on "Jean Paul" picking up his ticket at the booking desk. His companion would have to hand in her original return ticket and collect her reissued one-way ticket at the same desk.

Hopefully the two of them, working in tandem, would be able to do that without any problems?

The two models were paid, less the "per diem advance" for two days. This gave them a generous return for their short time in Las Vegas. They were far more contrite during this farewell meeting. I think the enormity of being sent home from a shoot for a major worldwide fashion brand, had now struck home.

Not that this got in the way of their future success!

"Jean Paul" became a top model much sought after by leading brands and fashion magazines. The career of the female model also went from strength to strength. I believe she married a film star and started a new, successful enterprise on the other side of the camera.

A car had been organised to take them to the airport. When John and his assistant arrived later in the day, to pick up the two replacement models, neither "Jean Paul" nor his female companion were anywhere to be seen. They had obviously caught their flight without further incident.

It was late morning before I had finally concluded all the arrangements necessitated by the change in personnel. At last, I was free to go in search of the rest of the team who were working in and around the hotel complex.

When I could not find them, I decided to go up to the pool area.

During our briefing with the hotels Marketing Director, she had specifically advised us that the pool area was out of bounds to our shoot. "Our guests use the pool area to chill out," she had told us. "We do not want to distract them with a photographic shoot and all the disruption it brings with it."

A specific request not to do something, was, in my experience, a direct challenge to John. Living, and working, on the edge was very much a part of his psyche. Following my instinct, I went up to the rooftop. Sure enough, the whole team was there. Not only was a shoot in full swing, but the two models, wearing their Wrangler outfits, were up to their necks in the water.

"No problem," said John, sensing my displeasure. "There was nobody else here when we arrived. After this final shot, we will have finished all our set-ups around the hotel," he concluded. "Don't worry about the merchandise," Tanya Gill advised," I will send it down to the hotel laundry. It will be in pristine condition when you take it back to the UK."

We had a late lunch, in the poolside bar. I then returned to my room to catch up on some of the sleep I had lost during the previous night.

I advised John that the two replacement models were due to arrive at the airport at around 4.00pm. It was agreed that he and his assistant would go out to collect them. When he returned from the airport, I met up with him, Tanya Gill, and the new models for a shoot briefing. When this was over, I handed over the "per diem" cash to the new arrivals.

They were not needed for the evening element of the hotel set-ups. John had arranged to start immediately after dinner. "I will put a call out for you when we are ready and let you know exactly where we are," he told me.

Refreshed, after a few hours of much needed sleep, I made my way down to the hotels steak bar for a light dinner. Just as I finished, a call went out over the hotel tannoy system advising that there was a call for me. It was John. "We are just about to start shooting in room 380," he said.

Once again, my heart sank. John was obviously about to start one of his trademark bedroom set-ups.

When I arrived, the two models were just about "to get to grips" on the king size bed that dominated the relatively small double bedroom. With the lighting equipment, John, Tanya, Johnnie Hernandez, John's assistant and me, there was barely space "to swing a cat."

Twenty minutes into the action, there was a loud knocking on the door. "Hotel security. Open the door please," came the command.

I opened the door slightly. Standing there were two large, aggressive and, I presumed fully armed, uniformed security men.

"What's the problem?" I enquired. "We have had a report, from another guest, that a blue movie is being shot in this room," one of the men snarled. "I can assure you that we are not shooting anything untoward. We in the middle of a fashion shoot and have permission, from the hotels marketing team, to use one of the bedrooms," I advised him. "Come on in and see for yourselves," I suggested.

The security guards pushed passed me. The two models were hot and sweaty and entangled on the bed. It could well have been the prelude to something more erotic. John gave the security guard his card and explained that we would be wrapping up in a few minutes.

I am not sure that they were 100% convinced of the legitimacy of our claim, but they turned and made for the door. "Cut out the noise," one commanded. "If we have any more complaints, we will have to close you down." With that they left the room, closing the door behind them.

I was not happy! The next morning, I would have to apologise to the hotels Marketing Director for the unauthorised shoot around the pool and the intervention of security during the bedroom set-up.

Thankfully, the meeting went well. "I appreciate that you have let me know," the Marketing Director told me. "We had no complaints from our guests around the pool and the security issue has been logged as a misunderstanding," she continued. "I am sure you will give the Las Vegas Hilton the necessary credits, if the pictures are used."

Over breakfast, John met up with all the models. The two new arrivals and the two original models knew each other, they had worked together on previous shoots. "I have no worries and am positive that the remainder of the shoot will be trouble free and productive," he assured me.

The third day of our shoot had been scheduled to take in the iconic sites of Downtown Las Vegas, known locally by the abbreviation DTLV. As the historic centre of the city, it was the gambling district of Las Vegas prior to the development of the Strip. Located to the north of the Strip and is centred on Fremont Street.

In 1990, the area had a somewhat run-down look during the day. It came alive at night when the lights of its casinos, and adjacent buildings, completely transformed the whole area.

To capture the "open 24 hours a day," essence of DTLV, John had decided to split the shoot into two segments. In the morning, we would concentrate on the gritty reality. He planned to return in the evening to record the exciting night-time contrast.

The 1970 Oldsmobile Cutlass Convertible came into its own. It was used extensively as a prop featuring models standing beside it, standing on it and sitting inside it.

Tanya had organised for one of the men's Wrangler denim jackets to be studded with large diamante script that spelt out "Las Vegas." A cool "fifties hairstyle" and "aviator style shades" completed the perfect retro look that complemented the denim shorts, tight top, and shoulder length hair of his female companion.

Downtown Las Vegas had been featured in many Hollywood blockbusters and one iconic image epitomised everything that Las Vegas stood for, the waving Cowboy sign known as Vegas Vic. Originally, when it was erected outside the Pioneer club in 1951, the sign featured a waving arm, a moving cigarette, and a recording of the drawling greeting, "Howdy Partner," that was played every 15 minutes. When we visited in 1990, Vegas Vic had seen better days but, when lit up, it was still an impressive sight.

As part of our morning shoot, John took colour pictures of one of the female models standing on the back of the car across the road from the unlit sign.

That evening, we returned to the same location. This time, one of the male models was seated on the front of the car in a studded stonewashed denim outfit. The resulting moody black and white image emphasised the Wrangler product whilst demonstrating how the neon lights of Vegas Vic, and those on the surrounding buildings, totally lifted the image of the Downtown area.

Later in the evening we moved down the block to the entrance of the famous Golden Nugget Casino.

As we began to set up the shot, we were approach by a large, suited "bouncer." His broken nose and bulging jacket were the warning signs that this man was not to be trifled with. "Have you guys got permission to film here," the man growled. "We have a photographic permit to film around Las Vegas," I countered. "This is private property. If you have not received clearance, in writing from the owners, you will have to move on, NOW!" he growled back.

It fleetingly crossed my mind to offer him a cash incentive to allow us to continue. Looking at him at him again, I quickly decided that discretion was the better part of valour.

Whilst all this was going on, John had managed to take the shots he required. We duly packed up and moved on as we had been ordered.

The Oldsmobile Cutlass Convertible was parked just across the road from the Golden Nugget.

Under the ever-watchful eye of our "bouncer" acquaintance, we set up a single and then a group shot. John's camera was able to pick out the casino's iconic exterior, our classic car and our Wrangler attired models. The finished series of pictures exuded everything that Las Vegas is all about.

After we had finished, packed away the clothes and all our equipment, we waved goodbye in the direction of the "bouncer" in the entrance of the Golden Nugget, and then beat a hasty retreat to our hotel.

Despite the daytime temperature of 38°C and the evening 32°C heat, we had managed to complete our shooting schedule for the day, without any other major incidents. The models had worked well together as a team. They had clearly enjoyed the experience.

This was in complete contrast to the earlier part of the shoot.

At the beginning of the day, I had sent off an "I love Las Vegas" postcard to my wife. Its content clearly echoed my frustration during the first two days. "The going has been pretty tough, one way and another. Hot weather and problems, problems all the way. No, I don't really love Las Vegas. It's really New York with lights – if you know what I mean!"

With only one more day of shooting left, I was now in a much more positive state of mind.

The weather on our last day of the shoot was again very hot. In the morning, we headed out into the desert. The temperature was hovering at just over 40°C. An early start was intended to ensure that the remaining set-ups were completed before the midday sun made it unbearable. There were none of the tantrums that had caused so many problems during our trip to Red Rock Canyon. The models interacted well together, and we wrapped up at around 11.30am.

Our last location was the Silver Sands Motel. Situated on the outskirts of the city, it had numerous indoor and outdoor facilities. In the short term, it offered a respite from the heat of the sun and a welcome intake of food and liquid. Immediately after lunch, I took a cab to the Hilton. I had made an appointment to cash my traveller's cheques at the hotel and then sort out the individual payments and release fees for the models.

All the crew and models had worked very hard. By way of reward, I organised a farewell dinner at the Hilton followed by a cabaret.

Once everything had been sorted out, I returned to the Silver Sands Motel to catch up with the shoot. John had assured me beforehand that there would be no more antics in the pool!

We were leaving Las Vegas the following day. Tanya would have little time to ensure that the Wrangler merchandise was in pristine condition before our departure for the flight to Los Angeles.

When I arrived back at the Silver Sands, I could not find the crew and models anywhere. John had promised no pool shots. I figured there was only one place that they would be.

In and around the pool!

Sure enough, that's exactly where all the action was. Tanya was surrounded by a pile of soggy clothes. John was positioned on the poolside and a male and female model were frolicking in the water in their Wrangler outfits. It was the last set-up of the shoot, and I was not in the mood to kick up a fuss. There was a laundry back at our hotel and Tanya was confident that she would be able to sort out the merchandise overnight.

After our group dinner and cabaret, the younger, more energetic members of our party, went "out on the town" to sample everything that Las Vegas had to offer. Having received their cash payments from me, before the evening began, it was no doubt burning a hole in their collective pockets.

Our flights to Los Angeles had been booked for the following afternoon to ensure that everyone had time to recover from the exertions of a difficult but, hopefully, productive shoot.

I was happy to return to my suite for an early night.

When booking the hotel, I had organised a late check out. Our flight to LA was due for take-off at around 4.30pm. We would be leaving the hotel for the airport at around 2.30pm.

After breakfast, John and I returned the Oldsmobile Cutlass Convertible to the garage where we had purchased it five days before. The garage owner gave it the once over and paid the "buy back fee of $250 in cash" without any quibbles. He seemed surprised that it had survived the ordeal of been driven around the area for so long without the occurrence of any mechanical problems. It was my belief that the engine sounded much better, on its return, than it had when we first drove it away.

The deal had proved a winning situation for both of us! I had saved a lot of money that I would otherwise have had to pay out to hire a similar vehicle. The garage owner had pocketed $500 in cash and still had the vehicle to sell on.

John and his assistant dropped me off outside the hotel and I went out on my own to visit some of the big-name casinos on the Strip. I don't gamble, but it is always interesting to watch other people "trying to beat the house."

Earlier in my career, I had worked in the entertainment industry. My employers ran cinemas, night clubs and bingo halls. Gambling laws in the UK at that time only allowed them to have two slot machines in each establishment. Even with such a small number, I knew that the odds were firmly in favour of the house.

Casinos like Caesars Palace had thousands of slots from a dime to hundreds of dollars for a play. No wonder their premises were so opulent!

It was clear to me, that inside the casinos time stood still. People played the slots and the tables 24 hours a day, seven days a week. The weather outside was fantastic but many never saw the light of day in their endless pursuit of a jackpot win that was, for the majority, little more than a forlorn hope.

A lot of people were wandering around clutching polystyrene cups full of dimes. They would stop every now and then in front of a different row of slots. Playing several simultaneously, they would dip into their cups to feed the machines. Sometimes they collected winnings to refill the cups, mostly they lost. They continued to "play the game," always hoping that the BIG jackpot was only one more pull of the handle away.

It was very sad, and not at all glamourous!

Returning to the daylight of the Strip, I watched a volcano erupt to order several times an hour, musical water fountains shooting water high into the air. Each casino had their own gimmick to draw the punters into their premises to idle away their time and lose their money.

Las Vegas and its "superficial glamour," was not for me!

I bought some souvenirs of my visit for Glenys and my children and returned the hotel to pack and settled the bill for extras.

At the airport, there was some time to kill before our flight took off.

In the departure lounge, I was surprised to find that the ever-invasive slot machines, were to be found in abundance. There was nothing else to do. I had a few dimes in my pocket, so I decided to exercise my arm and chance my luck.

To my surprise, I won. I won again. I kept on winning!

By the time we were called to board, my pockets were bulging with dimes. Now I knew why the polystyrene cups were so popular in the casinos of Las Vegas!

I deposited my ill-gotten gains in my hand luggage. I would change the dimes into paper money when we arrived in Los Angeles. When I finally got around to doing this, I found that my winnings amounted to the princely sum of $12!

At the airport, my hire car was ready for collection, and I ferried Johnny Hernandez and Tanya Gill into the city centre before driving back with John to my hotel on Wilshire Boulevard. He asked if he could use the car the next day to enable him to take the film to the processing house. I had no plans to drive around Los Angeles. I was happy to hand over the keys.

John and I agreed that he would pick me up on the morning after next. We would drive to the processing house to collect the negatives and transparencies that I would be taking back with me to the UK. It was our intention to use the processing house facilities to work our way through these and to make our selections of the pictures that we both felt could be used in the Wrangler product merchandiser and at the point of sale.

This arrangement would allow me a whole day on my own to do whatever I wanted. My initial plan was to chill out and do absolutely nothing.

Next morning, after breakfast, I made my way to the rooftop pool. To my left, I could see the gridlock of work bound traffic heading towards the downtown area. On my right, the Hollywood sign glistened in the morning sunlight.

The temperature was 20°C. On the TV in my room, the weather forecaster predicted this would rise to 24°C by mid-afternoon. It was all very pleasant. A complete contrast to the discomfort of the high temperatures I had become accustomed to during our time in Las Vegas.

I am not a fan of sun-bathing. After several emersions in the pool and some time doing nothing on a sun lounger, I began to get bored. Looking at my watch, I found that it was approaching lunchtime.

My big decision of the day was how to fill the 7 hours until it was time for dinner!

Downtown Los Angeles was becoming shrouded with the sort of light smog that descends over it whenever the sun is shining. The Hollywood sign was beckoning. I had been to Los Angeles on several occasions but always on business. Despite having stayed in the Hollywood area before, I had never really visited all the tourist traps on Hollywood Boulevard.

This time, I determined to put that right!

After a very pleasant lunch, in a Mexican fast-food restaurant close to the hotel, I weighed up the options. I could hail a cab and travel to my destination in air-conditioned comfort, or I could walk in the afternoon sun in the general direction of the Hollywood sign.

Inexplicably, I choose the latter!

Nobody walks in Los Angeles unless they have no other choice. After 20 minutes, the Hollywood sign did not appear to be getting any closer. The area I was walking through was not as salubrious as the one I had left. I was beginning to attract some potentially unwanted attention.

Obviously, I was not a native of the city where the crime statistics, away from the West Hollywood glitz, were very high. Not wishing to become another stat on a crime sheet, I hailed the next cab that I saw and continued my journey, in comfort and safety, to my intended destination.

Once there, I visited all the usual tourist attractions, such as Grauman's Chinese Theatre (at the time named Mann's Chinese Theatre). I mingled with the crowds in the theatre's forecourt to view celebrity handprints, footprints, autographs, and messages left in the concrete by Hollywood stars both past and present.

I then wandered leisurely down the Hollywood Hall of Fame with its five-pointed terrazzo and brass stars embedded in the pavement. Each star immortalised the name of one of the great and good who had graced the film studios of "tinsel town." The walk covers 15 blocks of Hollywood Boulevard and along Vine Street. Many tourists cover the whole distance, walking slowly along peering intently at the pavement. Some even drop on their knees, to caress the "star" of a favourite film actor. This was not my scene, a couple of blocks proved enough for me "to get the idea."

After several hours, the lure of being a tourist had begun to fade. I flagged down a cab and returned to the relaxing poolside at my hotel, to catch the last of the sun before dinner in the restaurant.

Early next morning, John Rutter picked me up at the hotel and we drove to the offices of the processing house in downtown Los Angeles.

The Saturday morning traffic was heavy but nothing like as bad as it would have been during the week. We soon reached our destination, and our hosts provided us with an office, and all the equipment needed, to view the results of our labours in Las Vegas. They also provided endless coffee and refreshments, including lunchtime snacks.

Although the shoot may have been fraught with problems, thankfully, the results exceeded my expectations.

Despite some heated discussion, we were eventually able to agree on the black and white prints and colour transparencies that best provided the Wrangler range imagery that we had hired John to achieve.

Some of the images were "on the edge." It was my job to ensure that any shots that, in my opinion, "stepped over the line of decency," never saw the light of day. John was aware of my concerns. He pushed me hard to accept some shots that were very close to the edge and stepped back whenever I dug in my heels.

He won some of the arguments. I won most of the others. By the end of the session, we both made compromises whilst maintaining our individual creative integrity.

I left John with the technicians to do the fine tuning required and to work on the prints of the black and white shots we had selected. He arranged to bring round the prints, contact sheets and transparencies to the hotel early next morning so that I could pack them in my luggage for my flight back to the UK.

He did invite me to a party some of his friends had organised that evening. I politely declined. An early night was in order. Sunday was going to be a long day and I wanted to catch up on as much sleep as possible.

Immediately after breakfast, John arrived and handed over the packages. I thanked him for his hard work, shook his hand, gave him his cheque, and wished him well. We were never to work together again!

My flight back to Heathrow was scheduled to leave LA at 6.00pm and arrive in the UK at 10.30am the next morning. In 1990, airport security was not as tight as it is today. I had to check in no later than one hour before departure.

After a quick lunch, I checked out of the hotel and collected my hire car. At around 2.30pm, I was on my way, in the general direction of the airport. In the days before 'SAT NAV,' driving out of a city the size of LA, navigating the roads to the airport turnoff, and then finding the hire car drop-off point, was no easy feat.

At a little after 4.00pm, I was inside the terminal building and checking in my three large bags of luggage. This was achieved without incident, or excess baggage penalty. After negotiating immigration, I settled down in the departure lounge to wait for my flight to be called.

The journey from LA to London Heathrow took 10 hours and 30 minutes. It arrived in the UK on schedule. By the time I had collected my luggage, cleared immigration and customs, and transported my heavy bags to the bus for the long-term carpark, another hour had passed. Once in my car, there was the little matter of a three-hour drive back home. I had been away for nearly two weeks and was looking forward to the normality of family life.

Back in the office on the Monday morning, Lindah Kiddey reported that the Martin Hooper product shoot had gone very well.

Combining the results of both shoots, Design Associates, our London based creative design company, developed the product merchandiser for the 1991 Spring/Summer range. This was very well received by everyone. It was used by the salesforce and retailers during the range sell in shows that took place during August and September 1990. All the angst that I had experienced during the Las Vegas photographic shoot, seemed like a distant dream, or perhaps nightmare would be a more accurate description!

Three months later, I received a reminder of my time at the Las Vegas Hilton. A charge of $300 had been made against my corporate American Express card more than two months after I had been there. It stood out on my account statement. Someone, who had access to my card details had evidently used it at the hotel.

I had settled all my extras before leaving. The check-in desk at the Hilton had taken my card imprint when I had arrived at the hotel. Amex took it up with them and the money was refunded. I never found out exactly what had happened.

Looking at the merchandiser 27 years later, I was struck by how ahead of its time it was. The work of both photographers has stood the test of time. The pictures would not be out of place in a work portfolio of any of the current crop of fashion photographers.

Las Vegas was the last fashion shoot that I art directed for Wrangler. It was also a piece of work of which I am immensely proud.

In "my life after Wrangler," I worked with Martin Hooper again, and we are still in touch.

During my research, I was pleased to note that all the models who participated in the Las Vegas shoot had used the experience as a platform to bigger and better things in the fashion world.

Stylist, Tanya Gill forged an illustrious career in Los Angeles during which she worked with A-lister stars such as Kate Winslet, Hilary Swank, Jane Fonda, and Abbie Cornish. She also styled shoots for top fashion magazines in the USA and Europe. As a stylist and fashion designer, she created successful fashion shows for TV and the web and is well known for her "red carpet fashion commentaries."

Johnny Hernandez was still providing his expertise in hair and makeup and had built up an impressive portfolio of work for major fashion brands.

As far as I know, John Rutter continued to ply his trade in the USA as a photographer who operated "at the cutting edge."

PART SEVEN

THE FINAL WORD

Chapter Thirty-One

Life After Wrangler

For the first three months after I left Wrangler, I was too busy to give much thought to what was happening just a short distance down the road. Even though I was still receiving almost daily calls from my former colleagues, I confined the conversations to answering their queries and offering advice.

After this period, I arranged a pub lunch to thank them for all that they had contributed to the success of the marketing department whilst I was there, and to wish them well in the future. During the meal, I made it clear that all future queries would need to be addressed to the VF management team remaining. I was no longer on the payroll.

In my years as custodian of the Wrangler brand, I had developed several annoying traits.

Whenever I was on out and about with my family in the UK, I would be looking for the Wrangler product and making mental notes as to how it was being displayed instore. Even though I could identify most brands of jeans from the front, the most obvious branding was always on the back pocket. Checking my frontal observation with a careful glance of the encased bottom became a habit.

It almost got me into trouble on several occasions!

My family were often forced to watch programmes on television, that they would probably have preferred not to, because I knew a Wrangler advertisement, or one for a competitor, would be appearing in the commercial breaks.

Within months of leaving the company, nearly all these traits began to vanish. I was "becoming normal again." This must have been a great relief to my long-suffering wife and children!

That is probably the reason why, until I carried out my research for this book, I had little idea about what the Wrangler management team had finally decided to do about the advertising for 1991. It would appear, my recommendation to air the "Crosstown

Traffic" commercial had been acted upon. It had apparently won a bronze arrow at the 1991 television awards. The press and poster campaigns were given the go-ahead despite being initially rejected. My former colleagues had obviously backed down and the agency got their way.

Talking about the campaign many years later, Mark Denton of Simons Palmer was quoted as saying, "Levi's had the sexiest advertising at the time and the lion's share of the jeans market. The number two brand Pepe were a long way behind. And even further down the chart was Wrangler.

We did a lot of research with the target 15-25-year-olds and they slagged off Wrangler mercilessly. They hated the 'W' on the back pocket in particular. So rather than running away from 'W' we chose to make it the hero of the campaign.

Our line "Be more than just a number" not only encouraged the punters to be an individual and wear something other than Levi's but it also pitched the 'W' against the number 501.

That was our theory anyway.

But everyone knows 'it ain't what you do, it's the way that you do it'.

We knew that we couldn't compete with Levi's on their own turf, executionally or budget wise so we made our telly much grittier than theirs by setting it in a warts'n'all NYC and by picking a soundtrack that Levi's wouldn't have gone anywhere near, 'Crosstown Traffic' by Jimi Hendrix.

The follow-up commercial was shot in black and white and was set in LA with an all-black cast.

The accompanying poster campaign featured graphic interpretations of the letter 'W' just to get the youngsters thinking differently about the thing they said they hated about the product. Before very long Wrangler were the number two brand and the advertising was getting talked about. And then we parted company with the client (I can't remember why now)."

Clearly over time, some of Mark's recollections had become blurred. Pepe had never been ahead of Wrangler in respect of market share. The Wrangler brand was number two to Levi's when Simons Palmer took on the account. Levi's was the brand leader but not with a "lions share" and not "a long way ahead."

When I left VF, Wrangler was still the number two jeans brand. The same as it had been when Simons Palmer were appointed.

Simons Palmer Managing Director, Paul Simons, recalled the early days of Simons Palmer and my appointment of the agency, in these words, "Wrangler appointed Simons Palmer a year after the agency started giving us a high-profile client that provoked articles in the national press such as 'the jeans war', i.e., versus Levi, another early client for BBH.

I don't think it's a case of 'summers were better then.' There seemed to be plenty of clients attracted to a bunch of independent chancers trying to create something worth being talked about. Added to Wrangler were clients such as BT, Nike, PlayStation, amongst many others."

His comments have a certain resonance for me!

Wrangler took a risk that Simons Palmer would produce edgy advertising "worth being talked about." This was far from being our sole aim. We also wanted advertising that would change the buying habits of the non-Wrangler jeans wearers.

In my opinion, the agency succeeded with the former but not necessarily the latter. The truth of the matter was, that despite all the claims, the advertising did not increase sales of Wrangler jeans!

It would also appear, that the "Junk TV" television commercial, rejected during my tenure, was never made. Instead, a "rap commercial" was conceived in 1991 "over one long night in a New York hotel room" by Chris Palmer and Mark Denton in collaboration with top pop video, producer/director team Vaughan & Anthea. Called "DJ," it was shot in the USA using an all-black cast.

I assume that this commercial was aired in 1992. I was "a normal TV viewer" by this time. The advertising was not aimed at my demographic. As a result, I never saw it.

As I understand it, the commercial proved to be the last piece of work that Simons Palmer created for Wrangler. The relationship between client and agency went steadily down-hill, resulting in a parting of the ways.

Recriminations flowed thick and fast. In an article that appeared in the marketing trade press in 1993, Paul Simons claimed to have resigned the account claiming that the business was "guided by Americans who just don't understand our market." Mike Taylor, marketing director of Wrangler UK claimed, in the same article, there was a mutual disagreement over the direction that the company wanted to take the brand. "They got in first."

I suspect, Wrangler was seeking to develop a marketing communications strategy for the whole of Europe. The "gritty advertising," that Simons Palmer had gained a reputation for producing, would have proved "a step too far," for such a task.

In my years with the company, I was privileged to work with many first-class advertising, public relations, and sales promotional agencies. Some of the all-time creative greats worked on the Wrangler advertising account.

There had been many occasions when the Wrangler team had placed compete trust in recommendations from our agencies, despite our concerns! Behind closed doors, there had been many heated discussions and disagreements about company objectives and creative strategy. In the main, these were talked through, and a compromise was reached that enabled both parties to retain their integrity. Some creative and strategic differences could not be reconciled and resulted in a parting of the ways.

"The divorces" which occurred during my tenure, were, almost all harmonious. A mutual respect by all parties existed, even after the parting of the ways. As a result, I am still in touch with many of people I had worked with during that time.

During my research, I have found it extremely interesting to look back and recall events that took place in the distant past.

Because I had held on to a large portfolio of Wrangler "artefacts" from my time with the company, I have been able to cast a unique insight over the period of the so called "Jeans Wars" from the perspective of the "client."

The success, or otherwise, of creative communications, can be very subjective.

For a marketer, the achievement of goals has always been based on the delivery of measurable objectives. These principles have stayed with me since I started out in my advertising and marketing career, over 60 years ago.

I am proud of my record as custodian of the Wrangler brand, especially during the Blue Bell era.

The members of the Management Team brought together by Dick Webzell, still meet up from time to time. We enjoy good food and congenial company.

And yes, we sometimes recall events from the "good old days."

ROBIN DILLEY

After an early career in advertising agencies, Robin became Sales Promotion Manager in the Menswear Division at the CWS Ltd. He joined Wrangler Jeans UK in 1975, first as Head of Advertising and later Marketing Manager.

During 16 years with the company, communications campaigns, planned and developed under his guidance, not only achieved corporate objectives but also international acclaim with awards for advertising at festivals in New York and Cannes. They also won major awards in the UK for advertising, sales promotion, and in-store display.

In 1991 he left Wrangler to set up his own integrated marketing consultancy, Robin Dilley Associates.

Even though now well past retirement age, until very recently, he was still actively involved as Managing Director of his own cultural and heritage tourism business, Ambient Events Limited.

Printed in Great Britain
by Amazon